Sustainability in Accounting and Finance Education

BUSINESS INNOVATION STRATEGIES, GOVERNANCE AND SUSTAINABILITY

Series Editor Fadi Alkaraan – University of Gloucestershire, UK

The *Business Innovation Strategies, Governance and Sustainability* series is aligned with the United Nations Sustainable Development Goals (UNSDGs) and is rooted in a multidisciplinary perspective. It focuses on research streams from various paradigms, theoretical lenses and mixed method approaches to offer insights from both scholars and practitioners concerning understanding the current trends of business innovation strategies and corporate transformation towards governance and sustainability.

Given the immense scope of business innovation strategies, governance and sustainability and their relevance to environmental, social and governance (ESG) performance towards ecosystems, *Business Innovation Strategies, Governance and Sustainability* is a knowledge exchange hub for scholars, practitioners, policy-makers, students and other stakeholders. Books in the series incorporate the influence of technological innovation adoption, Industry 4.0 on green innovation strategies, green supply chain management, green manufacturing processes and green strategic investment decision-making.

Published Title in This Series

AI-Powered Business Innovation Strategies, Governance and Sustainability: Interdisciplinary Perspectives.
Edited by Fadi Alkaraan, Laura McQuade, and Elena Nichele

Forthcoming Title

Generative AI for Sustainable Finance: Innovation in Precision Economics, Governance, and ESG-Driven Stock Prediction.
Edited by Ali Ahmadian, Massimiliano Ferrara, Giampaolo Viglia, and Ashok Kumar Yadav

Sustainability in Accounting and Finance Education: Innovative Approaches Linking CSR, Digital Transformation, and Pedagogical Practice

EDITED BY

HALA ZAIDAN
The University of Jordan, Jordan

AND

KHALED HUSSAINEY
Bangor University, UK

emerald PUBLISHING

United Kingdom – North America – Japan – India – Malaysia – China

Emerald Publishing Limited
Emerald Publishing, Floor 5, Northspring, 21-23 Wellington Street, Leeds LS1 4DL

First edition 2026

Reprints and permissions service
Contact: www.copyright.com
Printed and bound by CPI Group (UK) Ltd, Croydon, CR0 4YY

British Library Cataloguing in Publication Data
A catalogue record for this book is available from the British Library

ISBN: 978-1-80686-394-5 (Print)
ISBN: 978-1-80686-393-8 (Online)
ISBN: 978-1-80686-395-2 (Epub)

Contents

Section 2: Tech and Innovation for Sustainable Accounting

Section 3: ESG, Governance and Performance

About the Editors

Dr. Hala Zaidan is an Assistant Professor of Accounting at the University of Jordan. Her research and teaching focus on corporate governance, sustainability and digital transformation in accounting.

Prof. Khaled Hussainey is a Professor of Accounting with extensive expertise in auditing, governance and sustainability. He has published widely and supervised numerous graduate research projects in the field.

About the Contributors

Mohammad Kamal Abuamsha, Associate Professor of Finance and Investment at Palestine Technical University – Kadoorie and Head of the Department of Banking and Finance.

Enas K. Abu Farha is an Assistant Professor of Accounting at the World Islamic Sciences and Education University, Jordan. Dr. Abu Farha is a dedicated academic with a PhD in Accounting, specializing in integration of artificial intelligence, managerial accounting, and accounting information systems, with extensive teaching experience at prominent institutions including the University of Jordan, Arab Open University, and Applied Science University, and World Islamic Sciences and Education University. Dr. Abu Farha is a certified academic practitioner – Academic Work Practice Certificate from the Ministry of Higher Education and Scientific Research in Jordan, and an active member of the Arab Academics and Scientists Union, playing a vital role in curriculum development, internal audit training, and the production of scholarly content tailored for modern management practices, contributed to advancing accounting education and research, focused on artificial intelligence and accounting information systems, with an emphasis on their role in driving organizational performance and decision-making reliability, with a number of peer-reviewed publications in top journals and academic conferences.

Lana K. Abu Farha, serves as the Director of the Financial Affairs Unit at the University of Jordan, Jordan. She is a seasoned financial professional with over two decades of progressive experience in financial management, budgeting, and institutional planning at the University of Jordan, holds a Master's degree in Accounting from the University of Jordan and is currently pursuing her PhD in Accounting at the World Islamic Sciences and Education University. Abu Farha Works as Director of the Financial Affairs Unit, leading strategic financial operations, regulatory compliance, digital transformation initiatives, as well as financial leadership roles, contributing to national committees in public sector funding and higher education finance. In addition to her administrative experience, she has also lectured in accounting and actively participates in institutional excellence, strategic planning, and digital transformation initiatives.

Zahra Adardour, PhD candidate at the National School of Commerce and Management (ENCG), Chouaib Doukkali University, El jadida, Morocco. She has embarked on a rigorous research journey aimed at unravelling the complexities of sustainable business practices. Through her multidisciplinary approach and adept use of analytical tools, she is deeply engaged in exploring the interplay between Environmental, Social and Governance (ESG) performance, board characteristics and risk-taking within corporate contexts.

Jaskiran Arora, Dean of Education Quality at BMU, brings over 17 years of industry and academic experience. Before BMU, she held senior positions in reputed institutions and corporate houses. She specialises in finance training for diverse audiences, covering topics like risk analysis, personal finance and mutual fund performance. A distinguished scholar, she holds a PhD, MBA in Finance, BCom, CFA (Level-I, USA) and a Postgraduate Certification from Lancaster University, UK. She has published extensively in finance and education, earning numerous awards for teaching, mentoring and research. Her key interests include investment valuation, financial reporting and microfinance.

Asuman Atik is an Associate Professor of Accounting at Marmara University. She has lectured on accounting at the undergraduate and graduate levels for more than 20 years. Her research areas are accounting education, non-financial reporting and tax accounting.

Nizar Baklouti is a Finance Researcher at the University of Sfax, Tunisia. He holds a joint PhD in Management Sciences from the University of Paris Nanterre and the University of Sfax. His research focuses on banking governance, financial distress and sustainable and green finance, with particular interest in Asian and European financial systems. His work has been published in several peer-reviewed journals, including the *Revue Française de Gestion*, the *Afro-Asian Journal of Finance and Accounting* and the *Journal of Economic Studies*. He has also contributed book chapters published by CRC Press and Taylor & Francis (Apple Academic Press) and has presented his research at various international conferences. Dr. Baklouti teaches corporate finance, financial engineering and risk analysis.

Adil Bami currently works at the Higher Institute of Business and Administration Studies (ISCAE) as a Full Professor in Management Science. He holds a PhD from the University of Paris 1 Panthéon-Sorbonne. He serves as the Head of the Accounting Expertise Programme. Dr. Adil conducts research on innovation, organisational innovation and governance.

Eya Belaid holds a Master's degree in Financial Engineering from FSEG Mahdia (University of Economics and Management of Mahdia). She is interested in FinTech and sustainability as a research area.

Prabal Chakraborty serves as an Associate Professor of Quantitative Analysis and Quality Management at Jagannath International Management School, Kalkaji, Delhi, India. With over 18 years of experience in educational management, he specialises in both quantitative and qualitative research methodologies. His academic focus includes research design, multidimensional research approaches and other methods.

Atar Derj, is an expert in Sustainability and ESG, who is currently pursuing a PhD in Management Sciences at the Higher Institute of Business and Administration Studies (ISCAE), Casablanca, Morocco. With a profound professional background in sustainability and ESG, her research is deeply focused on these areas, alongside interests in energy topics. Her expertise in sustainability and ESG is reflected in her scholarly pursuits, aiming to contribute significantly to these critical fields.

Hrishikesh Desai is an Associate Professor with tenure at Arkansas State University, where he is also the Director of the Master of Accountancy (MAcc) with Data Analytics Programme. His research explores accounting regulation, financial reporting, fraud examination and the integration of sustainability and emerging technologies, such as blockchain, artificial intelligence and machine learning, into accounting practice and education. His research has also been published in leading journals, and he has also authored numerous book chapters with leading publishers. For one of his crowdsourced papers related to accounting education and Generative AI, he also received the *Notable Contribution to Literature Award* from the Accounting Information Systems (AIS) section of the American Accounting Association (AAA). He has also been invited to deliver numerous educational presentations on emerging technologies by the Arkansas Society of Certified Public Accountants (ARCPA) and other learnt forums.

Deepika Dhingra is an Associate Professor at BML Munjal University with over 12 years of experience in finance education and research. She holds a PhD in Finance from the Faculty of Management Studies, Delhi University, and has previously taught at Bennett University and IILM Institute of Higher Education. With industry experience at Axis Bank, her research focuses on financial markets, volatility spillovers and FinTech. She has published in top journals, contributing significantly to finance education and sustainability.

Slimane Ed-Dafali is an Associate Professor of Management (HDR) at the National School of Commerce and Management (ENCG), Chouaib Doukkali University, Morocco, where he conducts teaching and research activities. His current research is focused on ESG, corporate governance, Fintech, sustainable entrepreneurship, entrepreneurial finance, corporate responsibility and corporate sustainability. He has published his research work in reputed refereed journals with strong ABDC and ABS rankings. He serves as the Head of the Research Team in Entrepreneurial Finance, Family Businesses and Responsible Finance (ER-FEEFFR). Dr. Ed-Dafali also serves as a referee for several international journals and has edited five books.

Hanan Hassan Gad Allah received her Master of Accounting from Mansoura University. She is a Lecturer in the Accounting Department, Faculty of Commerce, Damietta University. She has progressed academically from Teaching Assistant (1999–2004) to Assistant Lecturer (2004–2016) and currently serves as Lecturer since 2016. She has over 24 years of teaching experience in various accounting fields including financial accounting, cost accounting, managerial accounting, corporate accounting, banking accounting, governmental accounting, petroleum accounting, international accounting and computerised accounting applications. She holds the ICDL certificate and TOEFL and has completed the University Teacher Preparation Programme at Mansoura University, which focuses on modern pedagogical approaches and professional development for faculty members. Dr. Hanan has supervised several Master's and PhD theses in contemporary accounting topics and has published multiple research papers in financial accounting and taxation in recognised Egyptian academic journals. Her academic contributions reflect a commitment to advancing accounting education and research excellence.

Angela Ya Gao is the Faculty Admissions and Recruitment Lead and Course Director for the BSc Finance and Business at the University of Sussex Business School. She is a Lecturer in Accounting (Education and Scholarship). She holds a PhD in Corporate Governance from the University of Surrey and an MSc in Investment Management from the ICMA Centre, University of Reading. She is a member of CPA Australia (Certified Practising Accountant Australia) and a Senior Fellow of the Higher Education Academy (SFHEA). With 17 years' teaching experience in the United Kingdom and China, she has won multiple awards, including the 2024 Knowledge Exchange Grant for founding the Sustainability and AI Business Action Centre. She created a popular postgraduate core module, *Sustainable Business Finance*, and is passionate about researching how AI is transforming higher education. Prior to joining academia, Angela gained experience in the financial and environmental investment sectors.

Issal Haj-Salem completed her PhD in Accounting at the University of High Commercial Studies in Carthage (IHEC Carthage, Tunisia) in 2017. She is an Assistant Professor at the University of Economics and Management of Mahdia (FSEG Mahdia). Her principal research area is concerned with disclosure (voluntary disclosure, risk disclosure, content analysis), corporate governance and firm value. Her publications appear in *Journal of Accounting in Emerging Economies*, *International Journal of Disclosure and Governance*, *Journal of Risk and Financial Management*, *Journal of Financial Reporting and Accounting*, *International Journal of Business Governance and Ethics* and *IGI Global*. She is a reviewer for ranked journals: *Journal of Financial Reporting and Accounting*, *International Journal of Accounting, Auditing and Performance Evaluation*, *Journal of Applied Accounting Research*, and *International Journal of Emerging Markets*. She is a member of the Interdisciplinary Laboratory of University-Business Management (LIGUE, University of Manouba, Tunisia) and a member of the Tunisian Association of Accountants (ATC, Tunisia).

Maali Kachouri is an Assistant Professor at the Higher Institute of Finance and Taxation of Sousse. Their research interests include (e.g., corporate governance, sustainability, tax avoidance, CSR, financial reporting). She has published in internationally recognized journals, including the *Journal of Accounting in Emerging Economies, Journal of Financial Crime*, and *Recherches en Sciences de Gestion*. Maali Kachouri has actively participated in academic conferences, research seminars, and doctoral workshops.

Modimowabarwa Kanyane is the Executive Director: Research Development and Support at the University of Johannesburg. He is the former Executive Dean of the Faculty of Management, Commerce, and Law at the University of Venda and a former Research Director at the Human Sciences Research Council. Prof Kanyane is a governance expert with a strong local and international influence. His academic journey includes a doctoral degree in administration from the University of Pretoria and a certificate in international economic and financial negotiations from the International Institute of Public Administration in France. His local recognition is evident in the 2022 Star of Discovery global award, presented by the World Heritage Institute of Training and Research for the Asia and Pacific region, under the auspices of UNESCO. His contributions earned him a C-2 rating from NRF, a testament to his impact in the local government, ethics and governance. His peers cite his publications in high-impact journals, further solidifying his influence and recognition.

Usman Khalid has been involved in higher education since around 2013, mainly through teaching, mentoring colleagues and working on areas of quality assurance. Some of this work has been linked to curriculum design, although the scope was often shaped by partnership agreements. His mentoring style has been informed by the Professional Standards Framework 2023, while his contributions to assurance appear consistent with guidance from the QAA and the Office for Students. Khalid is recognised as a Senior Fellow of Advance HE and also holds professional titles such as Chartered Manager and Certified Management and Business Educator. His research interests focus on management, education and artificial intelligence, where he has raised doubts about how far AI can be trusted in policy. He has published on employability, though in practice these debates are still unsettled. Currently, he works at Elizabeth School of London, a Bath Spa University partner.

Randa A. Makled is an Assistant Professor of Statistics at Damietta University and holds a PhD in Statistics from Beijing University of Technology in China. Her expertise spans advanced statistical modelling, multivariate analysis, machine learning, econometrics, renewable energy, environmental degradation and urban sustainability. Her research integrates modern analytical approaches with real-world applications that support sustainable development and energy transition strategies. She has published in reputable international journals and contributed to studies using deep learning for renewable energy forecasting and decarbonisation pathways. With extensive experience teaching undergraduate and postgraduate students, she designs curricula, supervises research projects and provides academic and professional mentoring. In addition to her academic work, she serves in several leadership roles, including Executive Coordinator of the Department Council and Chair of the Academic Advising Committee. Dr. Makled has received multiple awards for scientific excellence, innovation and cultural engagement, reflecting her commitment to impactful, data-driven research in modern statistical and sustainability-oriented fields.

Asma Mechta is a PhD candidate at the University of Sopron, Hungary and a visiting PhD student at Bangor University, UK. She has disseminated her research through publications in international peer-reviewed journals and has presented at international conferences. Her current work focuses on the financial and sustainability consequences of technology and innovation.

Ranjeet Kumar Mishra is a postgraduate from Mumbai University and got his PhD from Department of Applied Economics and Commerce, Patna University. Currently, he is working as an Associate Professor, School of Commerce, Finance and Accountancy, CHRIST (Deemed to be University), Delhi NCR. His teaching areas are accountancy, taxation and business mathematics and statistics. His research interest is in the fields of corporate governance, working capital management, capital structure, corporate sustainability, determinants of firm performance and taxation. He has taught various national and international academic and professional courses like CA, CS, CIMA (UK), ACCA (UK), etc. He has around 20 years teaching experience. Before joining CHRIST, he has worked with many government and private institutions.

Vusani Moyo is an Associate Professor and Acting Deputy Dean for Research and Postgraduate Studies at the University of Venda, South Africa. He holds a PhD in Financial Management Sciences from the University of Pretoria (South Africa), an MSc in Finance from the University of Leicester (UK), an MBA in Finance from the University of Manchester (UK) and a BA (Hons) in Accounting and Finance (First Class) from the University of Derby (UK). Vusani is an ICAEW-qualified Chartered Accountant (FCA), Chartered Management Accountant (FCMA), Chartered Global Management Accountant (CGMA) and Chartered Certified Accountant (FCCA). His research focuses on African financial markets, capital structure, banking regulations, green finance and firm valuation. His work contributes to financial scholarship and policy, bridging academic insights with real-world applications.

Khakan Najaf is a faculty member at Canadian University Dubai, UAE. His work focuses on sustainability reporting, emerging markets and behavioural finance. He has published on CSR-related themes and continues to explore intersections of ethics and market response.

Rabia Najaf is a PhD holder affiliated with Sunway University, Malaysia. Her research focuses on corporate governance, financial performance and the socio-economic effects of CSR disclosures. She has published in peer-reviewed journals and presented her work at international conferences in the areas of corporate finance and sustainability.

Ayodeji Michael Obadire is a Senior Lecturer in Finance and Professional Accounting and serves as the Portfolio Manager for Research and Innovation at the Botswana Accountancy College, where he oversees research and innovation initiatives. He holds a PhD in Accounting and Finance from the University of Venda, South Africa, and a certificate in the Fundamentals of Statistics from Stanford University, USA. He is a qualified Chartered Accountant (ACA),

Chartered Management Accountant (CIMA), Chartered Global Management Accountant (CGMA) and Certified Public Accountant (CPA). His research interests encompass corporate finance, banking regulations, capital structure, green finance, firm valuation, corporate governance and ESG, contributing to advancements in financial management and sustainability.

Avijeet Paul is a young research enthusiast and a business graduate specialised in accounting, who has a zeal for doing dynamic research regardless of his field of study. He was awarded a gold medal for his excellent academic result (Master of Business Administration) in 2022 from his educational institution. He has been an author of two research articles on cost accounting and social phenomenon and his two chapters published in different publications. The author also participated in a national research conference of Bangladesh for a poster presentation. Apart from his interest in research, he is working as an Accountant in Alliance Française de Chittagong, which is a cultural wing of French Embassy in Bangladesh. He has a research interest in business dynamics, financial institutions, cost and forensic accounting.

Sumana Podder has been a Lecturer at Premier University Chittagong, Bangladesh, for the last 15 years, and right now she is pursuing 'Master of Management' at Crandall University, Moncton, New Brunswick, Canada. She has completed her BBA and MBA with a specialisation in accounting from Premier University, Chittagong, Bangladesh. She has five peer-reviewed articles published in international journals like *Asian Journal of Accounting Perspective*, *Asia Pacific Journal of Public Health* and *Journal of Global Communication*. She is a member of the Digital Transformation and Management (DT&M) Research Group of Crandall University. In September 2025, she presented a workshop paper from DT&M at the Atlantic School of Business Conference, 2025, held at St. Francis Xavier University, Nova Scotia, Canada. Sumana Podder has been awarded the 'Dean's Honour Roll' with Special Distinction from the Graduate School of Management at Crandall University, NB, Canada, for her academic excellence and for being among the top 1% of her cohort. She has participated in numerous trainings, workshops and research festivals and got recognition for her excellent performance. Her research interest covers environmental accounting, sustainability and corporate social responsibility.

Rakia Riguen is an Assistant Professor at the Faculty of Economics and Management of Sfax. Their research interests include (e.g., corporate governance, sustainability, tax avoidance, CSR, auditing). She has published several peer-reviewed articles on corporate governance and sustainability in international journals, including the *Journal of Accounting in Emerging Economies, Journal of Financial Crime, and Recherches en Sciences de Gestion*. Rakia Riguen is also actively involved in academic conferences and doctoral seminars, serving as a moderator and reviewer in various research events.

Ahmed I. Sakr holds a Bachelor of Accounting degree with a grade of 'Very Good' and is a Master's researcher in Financial Accounting at Damietta University. His thesis focuses on accounting for foreign exchange rate fluctuation exposure risk. He currently works as a Credit and Risk Researcher in the Central Bank Inquiries Department at the Central Bank of Egypt. His research interests centre on enhancing narrative accounting disclosure, developing the qualitative characteristics of accounting information and bridging the theoretical gap in the framework surrounding these characteristics. He has published four articles in different peer-reviewed scientific journals. His publications focus on promoting accounting disclosure for market risks and developing stress testing techniques using artificial intelligence to ensure the financial soundness of the banking sector.

Vrinda Santhosh holds a Bachelor of Business Administration in Finance and Accountancy from Christ (Deemed to be University), Delhi NCR. Her academic interests include financial management, corporate accounting and international reporting standards, with a strong inclination towards research in contemporary finance and ethical accounting practices. During her undergraduate studies, she actively engaged in academic inquiry and coursework that emphasised analytical rigour and practical application of financial principles. Her current focus lies in contributing to research that bridges theoretical frameworks with real-world financial systems. She is currently pursuing professional advancement through ACCA qualification and remains committed to academic and professional excellence in the field of finance and accountancy.

Sampadaa Saxena is an undergraduate student at Christ (Deemed to be University), Delhi NCR, India, with a keen academic interest in accountancy and finance. She is currently pursuing a degree in commerce, where she actively engages in coursework and projects that deepen her understanding of financial systems, accounting principles and economic frameworks. Her academic journey is marked by a consistent focus on analytical thinking and problem-solving, particularly within the domains of financial reporting and management accounting. Sampadaa has participated in seminars and student-led initiatives aimed at promoting financial literacy and is continually developing her skills through both academic and extracurricular engagements. She aspires to contribute to the evolving field of finance through further studies and research, with an emphasis on practical and policy-relevant applications.

Agnes Siklosi is an Associate Professor at the Budapest University of Economics and Business, Department of Accountancy, Hungary. Her research interests include financial reporting, sustainability disclosures and corporate governance. She has published in Hungarian and international journals and contributed to edited volumes on accounting and corporate responsibility. She teaches financial and sustainability accounting and actively connects academic research with professional practice.

Manisha Singh, Assistant Professor at VIT Bhopal University's Business School, holds a doctorate in Management from Maulana Azad National Institute of Technology, Bhopal, specialising in Human Resource Management. With 18 years of combined experience in industry and academia, her research focuses on the impact of Employer Brand on Employee Retention. Dr. Singh has numerous publications in esteemed international and national journals, along with contributions to book chapters with reputable publishers and in SCOPUS. Her research areas span organisational behaviour, human resource management and finance. She has presented research papers in various international and national conferences, seminars and has organised several short-term courses. Additionally, Dr. Singh serves as an external paper setter in multiple universities and holds design patents with grants from the Department for Promotion of Industry and Internal Trade, Government of India. She is actively involved as a reviewer of board of several journals.

Sonali Srivastava is currently working as an Assistant Professor (Senior Grade) at Jaypee Business School, JIIT, Noida. She holds a doctorate in Finance from Dayalbagh Educational Institute, Agra. She has an academic experience of more than 10 years with several reputed institutions, i.e. Symbiosis University, VIT Bhopal University, MNNIT Allahabad, IIM Ahmedabad, Ministry of Finance and Amity University. She has published a number of research papers in peer-reviewed international and national journals indexed in Scopus and WOS. She has also presented research papers in international and national conferences, seminars and conventions. Dr. Sonali has organised a number of conferences and short-term courses. She has authored books with reputed publishers. She has also published Indian and UK design patents with grants. She is a member of various professional bodies and a member of the Reviewer Board of various journals.

Sohana Sultana is a business graduate of accounting and was awarded the Chancellor's Gold Medal in 2022 for her outstanding academic result. Her research interest is mainly the business area, to be more specific, the dynamic uses and functions of business methods like cost and financial accounting, green finance, customer psychology and entrepreneurship. Her two articles and two book chapters were published in renowned publications. She has a diverse range of corporate experience, as she worked in different national and international organisations, and MNCs in Bangladesh. Currently she is working as a senior finance officer at 'Flydubai'. She is looking forward to doing more research on diversified fields of business.

Zsuzsanna Szeles is a Full Professor of Finance and Dean of the Alexander Lámfalussy Faculty of Economics at the University of Sopron, Hungary. Her research focuses on corporate reporting, sustainability accounting and financial management. She has published extensively in international journals and edited volumes and is active in professional and academic associations in accounting and finance.

Anojan Vickneswaran is a PhD student at the School of Business and Creative Industries, University of the Sunshine Coast, Australia, and a Senior Lecturer (currently on study leave) in Accounting at the Department of Accounting, University of Jaffna, Sri Lanka. He is a research-focused academic whose primary research interests include audit quality, internal auditing, financial reporting, taxation, public sector accounting and auditing and corporate governance. He has published several research papers in peer-reviewed and indexed international and national journals. In addition, he has authored five books on auditing, financial reporting and taxation and contributed two book chapters on integrated reporting and advancements in corporate reporting practices. His professional goal is to ensure that his research informs standard setters, policymakers and stakeholders, including management and auditors, to enhance the quality of audit, financial and non-financial reporting, thereby supporting business sustainability and contributing to the broader accounting, auditing and finance literature.

Preface

It is with great pleasure that we introduce this volume, *Sustainability in Accounting and Finance Education: Innovative Approaches Linking CSR, Digital Transformation, and Pedagogical Practice*. This book represents the collective efforts of scholars and practitioners who share a common vision: To reimagine accounting and finance education in ways that respond to the urgent challenges of sustainability, responsibility and digital transformation.

Accounting and finance have long been regarded as technical disciplines, grounded in numbers, measurement and reporting. Yet today, these fields are called upon to play a far greater role. Issues of climate change, ethical governance, corporate social responsibility (CSR) and digital disruption require educators to equip students not only with technical skills but also with the ability to lead responsibly and think critically about their impact on society and the environment.

The chapters in this book reflect both global and regional perspectives, drawing on contributions from Asia, Africa, the Middle East and Europe. The volume is organised into six thematic areas: curriculum and pedagogy, technology and innovation, ESG and governance, policy and inclusive development, finance and FinTech and sustainability-aware assurance. Collectively, these sections showcase innovative teaching strategies, case studies and conceptual insights that highlight how sustainability can be effectively embedded into accounting and finance education.

This volume is distinguished by the diversity of its contributors and the richness of its approaches. From gamification and behavioural change in teaching, to ESG performance and disclosure, to the skills needed by auditors in the digital era, the chapters reveal how sustainability is no longer peripheral but central to the future of the profession. By blending theory with practice, the book offers readers practical strategies as well as scholarly insights.

We extend our sincere gratitude to the authors, whose contributions make this volume possible, and to the institutions and colleagues who supported the project. We also thank our readers – academics, researchers, students and practitioners – for engaging with this work. It is our hope that this book will serve as both a resource and an inspiration, equipping the next generation of accountants and financial leaders to foster resilience, responsibility and sustainable growth.

Section 1

Curriculum and Pedagogy for Sustainability

Chapter 1

Sustainability Education in Accounting and Finance: Opportunities, Challenges and Strategies

Anojan Vickneswaran

University of the Sunshine Coast, Australia and University of Jaffna, Sri Lanka

Abstract

The growing demand and mandatory requirements for sustainability practices and reporting have increased stakeholders' attention to Sustainability Reporting (SR) globally. SR quality depends on the competence of the responsible party (firms/management) and the practitioner (auditors/assurers). Sustainability education in accounting and finance is more likely to increase the competence of accounting and finance professionals. This chapter explores the importance, opportunities, challenges and strategies of sustainability education in accounting and finance. Emerging interests, awareness, research and developments, regulatory arrangements and requirements, technological advancements, investments, interdisciplinary learning approach, professional development, lifelong learning, corporate social responsibility and ethical business practices and globalisation towards sustainability practices and reporting are key opportunities for sustainability education in accounting and finance. However, the lack of a standardised framework, the early stage of global sustainability-related standards, resource constraints, differences among economies, measurement and reporting difficulties and limited support for sustainable practices and reporting are challenges in this education. This chapter identified and discussed several challenges and opportunities in sustainability education in accounting and finance based on developments towards sustainability practices and reporting. It contributes to a better understanding of sustainability education in accounting and finance, opportunities, challenges and strategies. It provides insights into practical implications for

Sustainability in Accounting and Finance Education, 3–15

doi:10.1108/978-1-80686-393-820261001

stakeholders, especially policymakers, international bodies, academic and professional institutions and educators (academics). Due to the growing global interest and demand for SR, sustainability education in accounting and finance is more likely to be a top global agenda for relevant stakeholders such as policymakers, academic and professional institutions, educators and researchers over the next decade.

Keywords: Sustainability accounting and finance; sustainability reporting; sustainability education; sustainability assurance; sustainability education opportunities; sustainability education challenges

1. Introduction

The growing interest among stakeholders in sustainability has heightened regulatory and reporting requirements, especially for listed firms. This interest has grown since the introduction of the United Nations (UN) Sustainable Development Goals (SDGs) in 2015. Sustainability Reporting (SR) is crucial because firms are responsible for communicating about their sustainability practices, performance and position with internal and external stakeholders. In addition, it is considered a competitive advantage and contributes to firms' sustainability. Moreover, it is mandatory in some economies; for example, Climate-Related Financial Disclosure (CRFD) is required for over 1,300 of the largest registered companies and financial institutions in the United Kingdom, effective from 6 April 2022 (Gov.UK, 2021). Similarly, other developed nations, including the United States and Australia, pay much attention to SR, especially by announcing mandatory reporting requirements on non-financial reporting. For example, the Australian Sustainability Reporting Standards (ASRS) have been issued on CRFD, which is mandatory in Australia with effect from 1 January 2025 (Meg et al., 2025). Importantly, the International Sustainability Standards Board (ISSB) has issued two international SR standards, IFRS S1 and IFRS S2 (IFRS, 2023a, 2023b). Further, the International Auditing and Assurance Standard Board (IAASB) has issued a new global sustainability assurance standard called 'The International Standard on Sustainability Assurance 5000 (ISSA 5000): General Requirements for Sustainability Assurance Engagements designed to strengthen the global sustainability disclosure ecosystem' (IAASB, 2024).

These emerging interests and recent developments in sustainability and reporting are more likely to increase attention on sustainability education in accounting and finance professionals because they contribute significantly to the firms' sustainability practices, especially to SR. However, sustainable practices, sustainable reporting development and assurance standards are at an early stage. In addition, it can be seen that many different reporting and assurance frameworks and approaches have been adopted/used over the recent two decades, for example, Corporate Social Responsibility (CSR) Reporting, SR, Integrated Reporting (IR), Environmental, Social, and Governance (ESG) Reporting and CRFD. Furthermore, SR and assurance standards are not mandatory in many countries because they are at an early stage. Finally, many factors are associated with sustainable reporting and assurance. Exploring the opportunities and challenges of integrating sustainability education into accounting and finance is crucial for further development. A thorough examination of these factors is more likely to enhance the effectiveness of sustainability education, ultimately fostering a significant contribution to sustainability through improved pedagogical approaches in these disciplines. This chapter explores key challenges and opportunities in sustainability education in accounting and finance based on existing literature, with a focus on the following two important questions:

(1) What are the key opportunities in sustainability education in accounting and finance?
(2) What are the key challenges in sustainability education in accounting and finance?

The remaining sections of the chapter are structured as follows. The next section illustrates the importance of sustainability education in accounting and finance. Section three discusses opportunities for enhancing sustainability education in accounting and finance. The following section covers challenges in sustainability education in accounting and finance. The fifth section discusses strategies and educational approaches for sustainability education in accounting and finance. The final section is the chapter's conclusion.

2. Importance of Sustainability Education in Accounting and Finance

There is a conflict of interest between management and shareholders. It is more likely to increase agency problems (Jensen & Meckling, 1976). Agency problems may increase material misstatements in the financial statements. Shareholders are more concerned about financial reporting and audit quality due to agency problems. They rely on audited financial statements for economic decision-making. Due to the emerging interest and requirement for SR, shareholders' concerns about non-financial reporting (SR) and assurance have increased. Agency problems may increase material misstatements in the non-financial statements (for example, greenwashing) as well. On the other hand, quality SR is more likely to reduce information asymmetry and provide appropriate signals to the market. Corporate governance, especially institutional factors (for example, legal environment), is more likely to require more sustainability disclosure (for example, CRFD). SR is an internal and external communication like financial statements; therefore, firms should disclose sufficient and appropriate information to all shareholders (based on disclosure and stakeholder theories). The quality of SR primarily depends on the competence of responsible parties (SR preparers) and practitioners (assurers). Sustainability education in accounting and finance is more likely to increase the competence of responsible parties and practitioners. Therefore, sustainability education in accounting and finance is more likely to mitigate agency, information asymmetry and inaccurate signalling issues. It is more likely to increase disclosure and institutional compliance. Sustainability education in accounting and finance is rooted in several theories, including agency theory, information asymmetry theory, signalling theory, disclosure theory, stakeholder theory and institutional theory. Accounting, finance and audit literature underscore the importance of sustainability education in accounting and finance to increase the competence of responsible parties and practitioners regarding SR and assurance.

The role of accounting and finance professionals is crucial in SR. This is because they are responsible for the preparation and assurance of SR. Developments are going into sustainable reporting and assurance practices, especially the development of global standards on sustainability reporting (e.g., IFRS S1 and S2) and assurance (e.g., ISSA 5000). Sustainable reporting covers four crucial aspects: Economy, Environment, Social and Governance (EESG). The issue extends beyond numerical measures, making it difficult to define its scope. Therefore, sustainability reporting is called a reporting vehicle and value creation process (IIRC, 2013). SR is more likely to create a competitive advantage through the value-creation process. Accounting and finance professionals are experienced and competent regarding financial statement preparation and audits. Because these have been conducted for a long period, there are also many standards and generally accepted principles for the preparation and audit of financial statements. However, they have limited experience and competence in the preparation and assurance of sustainability reports than the preparation and audit of financial statements due to the early stage of SR and assurance practices. Further, only accounting firms provide financial statement audits because they are experts in accounting and finance. However, both accounting and non-accounting firms provide SR assurance services (Lu et al., 2023). Non-accounting firms have less experience in assurance services than accounting firms because they have newly entered into the assurance service market. Accounting firms are more likely to provide quality assurance on SR than non-accounting firms due to their long experience in assurance services, particularly financial statement audit. These aspects underscore the importance of sustainability education in accounting, finance and beyond.

Stakeholder pressures are crucial in corporate reporting. For example, a strong corporate governance and legal environment are more likely to demand high financial reporting and audit quality. Firms and auditors are more concerned about financial reporting and audit quality in strong corporate governance and legal environments due to the high litigation and reputation risks (Habib et al., 2014; Velte, 2023). Stakeholders especially regulators (for example, governments/government departments), standard setters (for example, the International Auditing and Assurance Standards Board), international agencies (for example, World Bank), international accounting bodies (for example, International Federation of Accountants) are more likely to encourage and demand SR (e.g., ‘ISSA 5000 is effective for assurance engagements on sustainability information reported for periods beginning on or after 15 December 2026, or reported as at a specific date on or after that date’). Regulators and stakeholders' pressure on sustainability practices and reporting underscores the importance of sustainability education in accounting and finance.

Finally, stakeholders use corporate reporting, including financial statements and sustainability reports, for various purposes. Due to the emerging interest in sustainability practices and reporting, they are more likely to demand more information and disclosures on financial and non-financial matters as a whole picture of the firms for better economic decision-making. The firms are responsible for informing stakeholders regarding sustainability practices. Sustainability education in accounting and finance is more likely to inform about sustainability practices and ensure the quality of SR.

3. Opportunities for Sustainability Education in Accounting and Finance

Several qualitative and quantitative factors determine sustainability education in accounting and finance. These factors are more likely to differ among economies worldwide. The following section discusses some key common opportunities in sustainability education in accounting and finance.

3.1 Awareness of Sustainability

Awareness of sustainability practices and reporting creates potential opportunities for sustainability education in accounting and finance. Today, many stakeholders have adequate awareness of the importance of sustainability practices and reporting. This awareness creates individual and corporate moral and ethical responsibility for sustainability practices and reporting. Sustainability-related awareness has increased among all stakeholders globally since the introduction of the UN's SDGs 17 in 2015. Importantly, the adverse consequences of climate change induce organisations towards sustainability and reporting. They have come to an understanding that without sustainability practices and reporting, any business is less likely to be sustained. This strong and deep awareness creates opportunities for sustainability education, especially in accounting and finance.

3.2 Regulatory Arrangements and Requirements

Globally, there are numerous arrangements on sustainability practices, including the UN's SDGs 17. These arrangements guide sustainability practices and increase compliance with sustainability practices. Sustainability practices, reporting and assurance standards are primarily developed and issued for large-scale businesses to guide their sustainability activities, reporting and assurance processes. For example, the International Sustainability Standards Board (ISSB) has been established by the International Financial Reporting Standards (IFRS) Foundation. ISSB has developed and issued two SR standards, IFRS S1 and S2. IFRS S1 is 'General Requirements for Disclosure of

Sustainability-related Financial Information', and IFRS S2 is 'Climate-related Disclosures' (IFRS, 2023a, 2023b). These two standards are effective for annual reporting periods beginning on or after 1 January 2024. In addition, recently, the IAASB has developed and issued ISSA 5000, 'the International Standard on Sustainability Assurance'. 'It is effective for assurance engagements on sustainability information reported for periods beginning on or after 15 December 2026' (ISSA, 5000). In addition, many countries have announced that CRFD is mandatory; for example, it is mandatory for large UK private companies and limited liability partnerships, effective 6 April 2022. These recent regulatory developments and requirements on sustainability practices and reporting underscore the need for sustainability education in accounting and finance.

3.3 Technology Innovation

Many technological advancements in the business environment include Enterprise Resource Planning (ERP), Data Analytics (DA), Blockchain, Artificial Intelligence (AI), Machine Learning (ML), Cloud Computing (CC), Cybersecurity, Digital Transformation and Robotic Process Automation. These technologies are interconnected with day-to-day business practices, sustainability practices and reporting. These technological advancements provide firms with a competitive advantage; moreover, it has become increasingly difficult for firms to sustain their operations without them. Most of these technologies are used by accounting and finance professionals; therefore, these technological advancements encourage sustainability education, including accounting and finance.

3.4 Investment in Sustainability

Globally, international agencies, regulatory bodies, including government and non-government organisations, large- and small-scale corporations, other businesses and individuals are more likely to invest in sustainability activities, including sustainability education. The role of accounting and finance professionals is crucial in sustainability practices and reporting. Therefore, they are more likely to invest in sustainability education in accounting and finance.

3.5 Revision of Academic Curriculum and Industry-Academia Collaboration

Universities, professional institutions and other educational institutions revise academic programmes, especially curricula, at regular intervals (e.g., every 5 years). Regular revisions provide opportunities to incorporate education towards sustainability accounting and finance in curricula. Further, academia and industry prefer collaboration to increase benefits to both parties. Academic and professional institutions provide opportunities to participate in curriculum development. Industries are more likely to finance several educational activities and programmes, including sustainability education, in line with the growing demand for sustainability practices and reporting.

3.6 Interdisciplinary Learning Approach

Globalisation and rapid changes in the environment, including the business environment, underscore the importance of an interdisciplinary learning approach. For example, doctors prefer to pursue master's degrees in business and finance because they manage/own hospitals. Sustainability covers several (financial and non-financial) aspects and activities of firms. It applies to all sectors, businesses and professions. They are interested in sustainability practices and reporting, especially the interdisciplinary learning approach. Furthermore, academic and professional institutions are more likely to offer interdisciplinary learning environments. These interests and engagements motivate sustainability education in accounting and finance.

3.7 Professional Development and Lifelong Learning

There are numerous changes in the internal and external business environment at regular intervals. Importantly, we can see the evolution in corporate reporting over the decades, from early corporate reporting to the latest. Financial statements were major elements of corporate reporting at the beginning. However, the latest corporate reporting covers not only financial statements but also non-financial statements. Further, we can see numerous new and revised reporting, accounting and auditing standards over the years. These evolutions, new standards and revisions in the existing standards underscore the importance of professional development and lifelong learning. Accounting and finance professionals have adopted professional development and lifelong learning concepts to ensure the quality of their practices and sustainability. Moreover, accounting and finance professionals and academic institutions are more likely to offer professional development and lifelong learning programmes. It aims to ensure the accounting and finance professionals' (members) professional development and lifelong learning in their profession, including new developments like SR and assurance. These professional development and lifelong learning concepts and programmes are more likely to encourage sustainability education in accounting and finance.

3.8 Research

Research findings significantly contribute to the existing literature and education. Accounting and finance research on new developments significantly proves theories, provides insightful findings and contributes to existing literature. Sustainability is an emerging interest where accounting and finance are closely connected with sustainability practices and reporting. Accounting and finance researchers' interests have increased in sustainability-related research over the last few decades, especially since the UN's SDGs 17 were introduced (e.g., Hahn & Kühnen, 2013; Kolk, 2003; Kuzey & Uyar, 2017; Orazalin & Mahmood, 2020; Siew, 2015). These growing research interests in sustainability practices and reporting and research findings are useful and underscore sustainability education in accounting and finance.

3.9 CSR and Ethical Business Practices

The firms' traditional focus is mainly on profitability. In the past, they prioritised profitability over sustainability practices and reporting, which has been identified as a key factor contributing to environmental challenges (e.g., climate change). In the present business environment, firms are responsible and accountable for CSR in addition to the primary objective of profit maximisation due to the demand for sustainability practices. Furthermore, firms are more likely to comply with ethical business practices due to regulatory requirements and moral obligations towards the community and environment. Firms' corporate responsibility and ethical practices motivate sustainability education in accounting and finance.

3.10 Globalisation

Today, business operates globally. Firms, especially large-scale firms, are more likely to comply with global practices and reporting, including sustainability. Corporate reporting's qualitative characteristics (e.g., comparability) underscore the importance of reporting harmonisation among firms in the globalised business environment. Sustainability practices and reporting are the globalised business practices; therefore, firms must adopt these practices and reporting in the globalised business environment and promote sustainability education in accounting and finance.

4. Challenges in Sustainability Education in Accounting and Finance

As discussed earlier, there are several opportunities in sustainability education in accounting and finance. However, there are also some challenges in sustainability education in accounting and finance. The following section discusses some key common opportunities in sustainability education in accounting and finance.

4.1 Standardised Framework and Global Standards

A few SR-related frameworks have been introduced and applied, including sustainability, CSR, integrated and ESG reporting. Still, there is no standardised global SR. Further, international SR and assurance standards are in the early stages of development. Only two reporting standards (IFRS S1 and S2) and one assurance standard (ISSA 5000) have been developed and issued on SR and assurance. The lack of globally standardised sustainability frameworks and the early development of international SR and assurance standards underscore the complexity of curriculum development for sustainability education in accounting and finance.

4.2 Resource Constraints/Limitations

Universities, professional institutions and other educational institutions have staff in well-established disciplines (developments) (e.g., financial reporting and auditing). These institutions are more likely to have limited expertise in sustainability accounting and finance because it is an emerging field. Existing accounting and finance teaching and research staff may show less interest in SR. Traditional accounting and finance educators mainly focus on financial reporting, making it challenging to shift towards sustainability-focused learning. Further, these institutions are more likely to have limited teaching resources, including textbooks, case studies and digital tools related to SR. Curriculum development on SR may demand more time and cost, including experts' fees. These institutions faced several difficulties and negative consequences during the COVID-19 pandemic and are now strategically moving forward during the post-pandemic era. They have limited resources, especially finances, due to the adverse COVID-19 consequences. Limited experts, resistance to change, teaching resources, time and finances are significant challenges for sustainability education in accounting and finance.

4.3 Differences Among Economies

Countries differ in many aspects, including income levels, legal environments and geographical locations. Sustainability positions and issues are more likely to differ among nations globally. For example, the sustainability issues faced by African countries differ from those encountered by European countries. Therefore, it is difficult to apply common sustainability practices and reporting standards uniformly across all nations. The common UN's 17 SDGs may be criticised due to the differences among economies. Still, there is no solid common SR framework and adequate standards. In addition, country-specific differences ought to be accommodated within SR frameworks and standards. These country-level differences towards sustainability and reporting are a key challenge in sustainability education. Therefore, common sustainability practices and reporting are less likely to be applicable among nations.

4.4 Measurement and Reporting Difficulties

Financial metrics cover only financial transactions and events; therefore, they are easy to measure. These are quantifiable. However, sustainability metrics are often qualitative, subjective and difficult to integrate into reporting frameworks. Measurement and reporting difficulties related to sustainability metrics are challenges in the curriculum development for sustainability education in accounting and finance.

4.5 Limited Supports

Technologies in accounting and finance are more likely to account for both financial and non-financial aspects of firms. SR should account for many aspects (the whole) of firms, including financial and non-financial activities. These are more likely to be beyond numbers and hard to quantify. Therefore, the available technologies in accounting and finance education are less useful for sustainability education in accounting and finance. Furthermore, awareness of sustainability practices and reporting is likely to differ among nations. Some stakeholders (countries) may perceive SR as less useful/important. They are less likely to motivate sustainability education. Further, some countries have limited collaboration between industries and academia, especially in developing nations. These are more likely to pose challenges for sustainability education, including accounting and finance.

4.6 Student Engagement

Students' engagement is key to the success of educational programmes. Sustainability practices and reporting are the latest developments and evolutions in accounting and finance. Further, accounting and finance students are more likely to view SR as secondary reporting. Students' perception and engagement with sustainability education may be a challenge.

5. Strategies and Educational Approaches

Based on the importance, opportunities and challenges of sustainability education in accounting and finance, this section suggests some strategies and educational approaches in sustainability education in accounting and finance.

5.1 Strategies

There are several opportunities and some challenges in sustainability education in accounting and finance. Strategies are crucial for capitalising on the opportunities and overcoming challenges in sustainability education in accounting and finance. Stakeholders have adequate awareness of sustainability practices and reporting. However, it is hard to ensure equal awareness among stakeholders globally. There is a high probability of country-level differences regarding sustainability awareness. Stakeholders, especially governments, international bodies and universities, should increase the general public and firms' awareness of sustainability, especially awareness related to issues in sustainability practices and reporting, the importance of significant contributions of accounting and finance professionals in sustainability practices and reporting, and the importance of sustainability education in accounting and finance. Ensuring and increasing awareness of sustainability practices and reporting is more likely to contribute to sustainability education in accounting and finance. There have been few reporting frameworks on sustainability over the last two decades, but no solid global framework. It is in the development process. Some international standards on SR and assurance have recently been issued. A solid SR framework and international standards on SR and assurance are more likely to ensure appropriate sustainability education in accounting and finance. There is no globally standardised sustainability education in accounting and finance; therefore, stakeholders ought to develop a standardised global sustainability education programme in accounting and finance to ensure quality and harmonisation of sustainability practices and reporting. The present digital transformation mainly concerns financial reporting and auditing; therefore, digital transformation towards SR will be useful for SR and education in the future. Sustainability-related issues differ among nations. Sustainability education in accounting and finance should account for these differences at the country or regional level for appropriate learning and practices. Collaborations among universities, professional institutions, governments, international bodies and industries are more likely to help and succeed in sustainability education in accounting and finance because they are responsible parties that ensure sustainability practices and the quality of SR.

5.2 Educational Approaches

Traditional teaching and learning approaches are less likely to be suitable in the modern teaching and learning environment due to the significant changes in the internal and external environment (ever-changing environment). These teaching and learning approaches are less suitable for sustainability education in accounting and finance because they differ from theoretical disciplines. Sustainability accounting and finance subjects are more practical-oriented subjects with strong theoretical foundations and guidance (standards and frameworks). These factors are likely to vary across economies globally. In the context of sustainability education in accounting and finance, both teachers and learners differ from those in purely theory-based disciplines. Teachers are more interested in providing both theoretical and practical knowledge and experience related to sustainability practices and reporting in the business environment. Similarly, students are more interested in acquiring both theoretical and practical knowledge and experience related to sustainability practices and reporting in the business environment. Therefore, sustainability education in accounting and finance approaches is more likely to differ from traditional approaches. Integrated teaching and learning approaches, industrial visits, team learning, case studies, internships, project studies, action research, experimental studies, research projects, active learning, practical learning environments, problem-based learning and simulation-based learning (Cho & Costa, 2024; Leal Filho et al., 2018; Mburayi & Wall, 2018; Sharma et al., 2021; Sharma & Stewart, 2022) towards sustainability practices and reporting are more likely to contribute to quality sustainability education in accounting and finance.

6. Conclusion

Accounting and finance professionals contribute significantly to sustainability practices and reporting. Stakeholders rely on accounting and finance professionals for sustainability practices and reporting. Sustainability education is crucial in accounting and finance. It is more likely to increase the quality of sustainability practices and reporting. There are many qualitative and quantitative opportunities and challenges in sustainability education in accounting and finance globally. Stakeholders, especially policymakers, international bodies, academic and professional institutions, educators and researchers, are responsible for developing appropriate policies and programmes to overcome these challenges and meet the global demand. The demand for sustainability practices and reporting has increased. It is more likely to increase in the future due to the announcements of mandatory sustainability practices and reporting. Sustainability education in accounting and finance is more likely to become a top priority for policymakers, academic and professional institutions, educators and researchers worldwide over the next decade.

References

Cho, C. H., & Costa, E. (2024). Sustainability accounting education: Challenges and outlook. *International Journal of Sustainability in Higher Education*, *25*(7), 1412–1425.

GOV.UK. (2021, October 29). *UK to enshrine mandatory climate disclosures for largest companies in law*. GOV.UK. https://www.gov.uk/government/news/uk-to-enshrine-mandatory-climate-disclosures-for-largest-companies-in-law

Habib, A., Jiang, H., Bhuiyan, M. B. U., & Islam, A. (2014). Litigation risk, financial reporting and auditing: A survey of the literature. *Research in Accounting Regulation*, *26*(2), 145–163. https://doi.org/10.1016/j.racreg.2014.09.005

Hahn, R., & Kühnen, M. (2013). Determinants of sustainability reporting: A review of results, trends, theory, and opportunities in an expanding field of research. *Journal of Cleaner Production*, *59*, 5–21.

IAASB. (2024). *Understanding International Standard on Sustainability Assurance 5000*. IAASB. https://www.iaasb.org/focus-areas/understanding-international-standard-sustainability-assurance-5000

IFRS. (2023a). *IFRS S1 general requirements for disclosure of sustainability-related financial information*. https://www.ifrs.org/issued-standards/ifrs-sustainability-standards-navigator/ifrs-s1-general-requirements/

IFRS. (2023b). *IFRS S2 climate-related disclosures*. https://www.ifrs.org/issued-standards/ifrs-sustainability-standards-navigator/ifrs-s2-climate-related-disclosures/

International Integrated Reporting Council (IIRC). (2013). *The international <IR> framework*. IFRS Foundation. https://integratedreporting.ifrs.org/wp-content/uploads/2013/12/13-12-08-THE-INTERNATIONAL-IR-FRAMEWORK-2-1.pdf-Search

Jensen, M. C., & Meckling, W. H. (1976). Theory of the firm: Managerial behavior, agency costs, and ownership structure. *Journal of Financial Economics*, *3*(4), 305–360. https://doi.org/10.1016/0304-405X(76)90026-X

Kolk, A. (2003). Trends in sustainability reporting by the Fortune Global 250. *Business Strategy and the Environment*, *12*(5), 279–291.

Kuzey, C., & Uyar, A. (2017). Determinants of sustainability reporting and its impact on firm value: Evidence from the emerging market of Turkey. *Journal of Cleaner Production*, *143*, 27–39.

Leal Filho, W., Raath, S., Lazzarini, B., Vargas, V. R., de Souza, L., Anholon, R., Quelhas, O.L.G., Haddad, R., Klavins, M., & Orlovic, V. L. (2018). The role of transformation in learning and education for sustainability. *Journal of Cleaner Production*, *199*, 286–295.

Lu, M., Simnett, R., & Zhou, S. (2023). Using the same provider for financial statement audit and assurance of extended external reports: Choices and consequences. *Auditing: A Journal of Practice and Theory*, *42*(1), 125–154. https://doi.org/10.2308/AJPT-19-080

Mburayi, L., & Wall, T. (2018). Sustainability in the professional accounting and finance curriculum: An exploration. *Higher Education, Skills and Work-based Learning*, *8*(3), 291–311.

Meg, F., Megan, W., & Glenn, B. (2025). Mandatory climate-related financial disclosures updates. Ey.com. https://www.ey.com/en_au/insights/sustainability/sustainability-disclosure-hub/mandatory-climate-related-financial-disclosures-updates

Orazalin, N., & Mahmood, M. (2020). Determinants of GRI-based sustainability reporting: Evidence from an emerging economy. *Journal of Accounting in Emerging Economies*, *10*(1), 140–164.

Sharma, S., Goyal, D. P., & Singh, A. (2021). Systematic review on sustainable entrepreneurship education (SEE): A framework and analysis. *World Journal of Entrepreneurship, Management and Sustainable Development*, *17*(3), 372–395.

Sharma, U., & Stewart, B. (2022). Enhancing sustainability education in the accounting curriculum: An effective learning strategy. *Pacific Accounting Review*, *34*(4), 614–633.

Siew, R. Y. (2015). A review of corporate sustainability reporting tools (SRTs). *Journal of Environmental Management*, *164*, 180–195.

Velte, P. (2023). The link between corporate governance and corporate financial misconduct. A review of archival studies and implications for future research. *Management Review Quarterly*, *73*(1), 353–411. https://doi.org/10.1007/s11301-021-00244-7

Chapter 2

The Future of Accounting and Finance Education in the Era of Sustainability and Digitalisation

Usman Khalid

Elizabeth School of London, UK

Abstract

Accounting and finance education is undergoing significant change, shaped by the demand for sustainable practices and the rapid expansion of digital technologies. Recent frameworks such as IFRS S1 and S2, the EU Corporate Sustainability Reporting Directive and India's Business Responsibility and Sustainability Reporting (BRSR) indicate that knowledge of environmental, social and governance (ESG) issues is no longer optional but central to graduate competencies (IFRS Foundation, 2024). Alongside this, digital tools including artificial intelligence, blockchain and data analytics are increasingly embedded in professional practice, requiring students to develop both financial expertise and digital fluency.

Universities are responding, though with varied success. In the United Kingdom and parts of Europe, sustainability is now embedded in core modules, whereas colleagues in China and India report slower progress due to faculty training needs and limited infrastructure. Pedagogical innovations such as flipped classrooms and simulations have produced mixed outcomes: students may engage with interactive tasks but still face difficulties applying concepts in traditional assessments.

Faculty development remains inconsistent, and digitalisation introduces its own paradox. Technologies such as blockchain can facilitate sustainability reporting yet consume significant energy, raising questions about whether tools used to teach sustainability align with environmental goals (IEA, 2023). Despite these tensions, the direction of travel is clear. Accounting and finance education is being redefined by regulation, digitalisation and global pressures, with the challenge lying in preparing

Sustainability in Accounting and Finance Education, 17–39

Published under exclusive licence by Emerald Publishing Limited
doi:10.1108/978-1-80686-393-820261002

graduates who can combine technical competence with ethical reasoning and a broad international outlook.

Keywords: Sustainability; digitalisation; accounting education; finance education; environmental, social and governance (ESG); FinTech; artificial intelligence (AI); blockchain; curriculum innovation; Corporate Social Responsibility (CSR)

1. Introduction

1.1 Context: Sustainability and Digitalisation in the Global Financial Sector

Accounting and finance education is undergoing significant change, influenced by two intersecting forces: the rise of sustainability and the rapid acceleration of digitalisation. Regulators have introduced ambitious frameworks such as the International Sustainability Standards Board's IFRS S1 and S2, applicable to reporting periods beginning in 2024. These frameworks may suggest that graduates need more than a passing familiarity with sustainability; they are expected to demonstrate competence in environmental, social and governance (ESG) disclosures (IFRS Foundation, 2024). At the same time, digital technologies including artificial intelligence (AI), blockchain and big data analytics (DA) appear to be reshaping professional practice, creating demand for graduates who can blend financial expertise with technological adaptability (Appelbaum et al., 2022).

These changes are not limited to corporate boardrooms or large audit firms. They extend directly into the classroom, placing pressure on higher education to prepare students for a professional environment where ESG reporting and digital finance are increasingly routine. Scholarship in sustainability accounting has long argued that accounting education should support accountability to society at large, not just to shareholders (Bebbington & Unerman, 2018; Gray, 2010). This perspective implies that embedding sustainability into accounting curricula is not simply a technical exercise but also an ethical responsibility.

Digitalisation adds layers of complexity. Automated systems may promise efficiency and transparency, yet risks remain. Issues such as data privacy, algorithmic bias and the energy demands of advanced computing (IEA, 2023) remind us that technological progress is rarely cost-free. For educators, the challenge lies in balancing optimism with critical scrutiny of ethical and environmental implications. This twin shift may modernise curricula and enhance employability, but aligning outcomes with shifting regulatory and societal expectations appears uncertain.

1.2 Purpose and Scope of the Chapter

This chapter explores how sustainability and digitalisation appear to be converging to reshape accounting and finance education. Regulatory frameworks such as the EU's Corporate Sustainability Reporting Directive (CSRD), the

United Kingdom's climate disclosure requirements and India's Business Responsibility and Sustainability Reporting (BRSR) suggest that ESG literacy is becoming a core graduate expectation (European Commission, 2023; FCA, 2022; SEBI, 2021). At the same time, digital tools including FinTech, blockchain auditing and AI-driven analysis are altering professional skillsets, highlighting new demands for curriculum reform and pedagogical adaptation.

The scope is intentionally global, drawing examples from the United Kingdom, EU, the United States, China, India and Türkiye. This perspective reflects the interconnected character of financial markets and higher education systems. It also recognises that sustainability and digitalisation are uneven processes. Some jurisdictions act as regulatory leaders, setting ambitious standards, while others are still building basic frameworks or technological infrastructure. Identifying these differences provides a comparative lens that is valuable both for students trying to understand the profession they are entering and for practitioners reflecting on international diversity.

The chapter is designed for multiple audiences. Undergraduate students may be introduced here to sustainability accounting concepts for the first time. Postgraduates will engage with more complex debates about regulation and digital transformation. Practitioners engaged in continuing education will find material relevant to professional adaptation. Lecturers seeking to refresh course materials can also draw on the examples and learning points included throughout.

1.3 Structure of the Chapter

The chapter is structured into six sections. Section 2 considers how sustainability principles are being embedded into accounting and finance education, with particular attention to ESG regulation, curriculum design and pedagogy. Section 3 examines the impact of digital transformation, focusing on AI, blockchain and big data analytics and their influence on both the industry and higher education curricula. Section 4 discusses teaching strategies such as flipped classrooms, gamification and simulation-based learning that may help bridge the gap between industry expectations and academic practice. Section 5 turns to challenges and future directions, including regulatory fragmentation, the environmental costs of digital tools and skills shortages that are especially pronounced in emerging markets. Section 6 concludes with reflections on how the convergence of sustainability and digitalisation can prepare graduates who are not only technically competent but also socially responsible and globally competitive.

2. Integrating Sustainability in Accounting and Finance Education

2.1 The Rise of ESG in Corporate Reporting and Regulation

The increasing prominence of ESG reporting reflects a wider shift in how corporate accountability is defined. What began as voluntary sustainability disclosures or corporate social responsibility (CSR) statements has, over the past decade, become a set of binding reporting requirements in many jurisdictions. Regulators now expect companies to produce information that is not only consistent but also comparable across borders. This development inevitably shapes accounting and finance education, as universities and professional bodies must prepare graduates to interpret, apply and, at times, question ESG frameworks.

At the international level, the creation of the International Sustainability Standards Board (ISSB) and its release of IFRS S1 and S2 marks an attempt to harmonise sustainability reporting. These standards, effective from 2024, may be seen as establishing a baseline for disclosures with a particular emphasis on climate risk (IFRS Foundation, 2024). For educators, the implication is clear. Modules once narrowly centred on financial reporting now need to incorporate sustainability accounting, requiring students to engage not only with disclosure mechanics but also with the wider implications for investor confidence and stakeholder trust.

National and regional approaches vary. In the United Kingdom, the Financial Conduct Authority (FCA) requires listed firms to report in line with the Task Force on Climate-related Financial Disclosures (TCFD), making knowledge of scenario analysis and carbon metrics an expectation for future professionals (FCA, 2022). The European Union's CSRD expands disclosure obligations to thousands of companies, with digital tagging requirements through the European Sustainability Reporting Standards (European Commission, 2023). The scale of this initiative suggests that curricula must train students to handle both narrative sustainability commentary and quantitative indicators.

In the United States, the Securities and Exchange Commission (SEC) adopted climate disclosure rules in 2024, though implementation has been delayed following legal disputes (SEC, 2024). Subsequently, in 2025, the SEC formally withdrew these rules, highlighting the political vulnerability of sustainability regulation even in major economies. Even so, leading business schools have introduced ESG courses to maintain global competitiveness (Christensen et al., 2021). India's Securities and Exchange Board (SEBI) has gone further by mandating BRSR the top 1,000 listed companies by market capitalisation, for listed companies, embedding ESG within governance systems and creating demand for graduates capable of conducting sustainability assurance (SEBI, 2021). In China, green finance has become central to the 14th Five-Year Plan, while Türkiye has moved towards alignment with EU standards through its own sustainability reporting framework (OECD, 2023).

The implications for teaching are significant. As Bebbington and Unerman (2018) suggest, sustainability accounting education should extend beyond compliance training and instead prompt students to reflect on how accounting might contribute to wider social challenges. Critical engagement is essential, particularly given uneven global adoption, the financial burden of compliance for smaller firms and the ever-present risk of greenwashing. By combining technical instruction in ESG frameworks with space for questioning their limitations, universities can help graduates to develop both professional competence and the capacity to shape a financial sector that aspires to be more sustainable.

2.2 Embedding Sustainability and CSR into Curricula

The integration of sustainability and CSR into accounting and finance programmes has accelerated in response to evolving regulatory frameworks and shifting societal expectations. Topics that were once positioned as optional electives are increasingly embedded within undergraduate, postgraduate and professional courses. This development reflects a growing recognition that future accountants and finance specialists will encounter ESG disclosures, ethical dilemmas and sustainability-focused investment choices alongside traditional financial reporting.

Universities have begun to adapt curricula accordingly. In the United Kingdom and across Europe, business schools now offer modules in areas such as sustainability accounting, climate finance and social impact measurement (Adams, 2021). In the United States, some leading institutions have gone further by embedding sustainability case studies directly into core financial accounting modules, reducing the risk that ESG issues are treated as peripheral knowledge (Christensen et al., 2021). This shift arguably signals a move from CSR as a voluntary corporate initiative towards sustainability as a defining expectation of professional preparation.

Cross-disciplinary teaching strengthens this trajectory. Sustainability does not fit neatly within the boundaries of accounting and requires insights from law, environmental science, economics and ethics. Increasingly, courses are delivered in collaboration with policy or environmental departments, giving students opportunities to analyse issues such as carbon accounting or biodiversity loss from multiple perspectives (Bebbington & Unerman, 2018). Such approaches may better equip graduates to interpret financial decisions within a broader societal and ecological context.

Professional bodies and accreditation standards have reinforced these changes. The United Nations Principles for Responsible Management Education (PRME) encourage business schools to integrate sustainability across both teaching and research, while the Association to Advance Collegiate Schools of Business (AACSB) now includes ethics, responsibility and sustainability in its accreditation requirements (AACSB, 2020; UN PRME, 2024). These frameworks appear to signal that embedding ESG is no longer optional if institutions wish to retain credibility and international recognition.

The impact on students is noteworthy. Graduates of programmes that integrate sustainability often demonstrate greater ethical reasoning, critical awareness and sensitivity to stakeholder interests. They acquire technical knowledge of reporting frameworks such as IFRS S1 and S2 or the EU's CSRD, while also learning to question their limitations, including inconsistent global adoption and the possibility of greenwashing.

Embedding sustainability and CSR is not only an addition to technical material. It may be reshaping accounting and finance education, preparing graduates to address global challenges while maintaining attention to financial accuracy and accountability.

2.3 Pedagogical Approaches: Case Studies, Sustainable Development Goals (SDGs) and Interdisciplinary Teaching

How sustainability is actually taught in accounting and finance appears almost as important as what is taught. Traditional lectures, usually anchored in technical standards, still matter for building foundations, but in practice, they often fall short of preparing students for the wider and less tidy challenges linked to sustainability. Scholars have argued that approaches that encourage critical reflection, practical application and cross-disciplinary dialogue may offer stronger preparation, though this is easier said than done in busy classrooms.

Case-based activities are frequently used. For example, when students analyse a corporate sustainability report or debate a controversy over ESG claims, they see how frameworks work outside the textbook. Looking at disclosures under the EU CSRD allows learners to test comparability and credibility (European Commission, 2023). Even so, some find the level of detail overwhelming, and scepticism can drift into disengagement rather than deeper insight.

The UN's SDGs are also used to frame learning. Mapping a company's reporting against SDG 13 or SDG 10 can highlight connections between finance and global issues (UN, 2015). However, as Bebbington and Unerman (2018) point out, many disclosures risk being more symbolic than substantive. Students sometimes grow frustrated when they feel the numbers do not really prove genuine progress.

Experiential learning appears promising but is not without its difficulties. Tasks such as preparing integrated reports for hypothetical firms or working with dashboards that model supply chain risks can improve data literacy and give a taste of professional practice (Adams, 2021). However, technical issues, patchy access to software and time pressures often limit their impact.

Cross-disciplinary teaching has gained traction, too. Sessions run with law or policy colleagues expose students to carbon accounting and human rights debates. Gray (2010) suggested long ago that accounting should be seen as part of broader systems of accountability rather than only as a technical craft, and such collaboration illustrates both the potential and the limits of financial reasoning.

Taken together, these approaches show promise. Yet their effectiveness varies, and much depends on staff training, resources and the willingness of students to engage with messy, sometimes uncomfortable realities.

2.4 Preparing Graduates for Sustainability-Focused Roles

The demand for graduates with sustainability expertise is steadily rising across accounting and finance. Employers increasingly expect new entrants to demonstrate knowledge that goes well beyond conventional financial reporting. The Big Four audit firms, for instance, are expanding their climate and sustainability practices, creating opportunities for staff who can interpret ESG disclosures, provide assurance on sustainability data and advise clients on regulatory compliance (KPMG, 2023). Specialist consultancies and investment houses are also recruiting ESG analysts capable of integrating sustainability factors into valuation models or risk assessments (PwC, 2022). Such expectations suggest that sustainability competence is no longer a niche asset but is becoming a mainstream requirement.

Meeting this demand requires graduates to acquire a mix of technical and transferable skills. On the technical side, literacy in frameworks such as IFRS S1 and S2 or the EU's CSRD is increasingly important. Students must learn to analyse non-financial datasets, carbon measures and supply chain disclosures (IFRS Foundation, 2024; European Commission, 2023). Equally significant are transferable skills: critical thinking, ethical reasoning and the ability to communicate sustainability insights to a wide range of stakeholders. Gray (2010) argued that accounting education should move beyond compliance to encourage graduates to interrogate the social and environmental implications of financial decisions.

Data literacy appears especially pressing. ESG reporting relies heavily on large and complex datasets that demand confidence with digital tools and analytics. Employers are beginning to value graduates who can interpret sustainability dashboards, assess the reliability of ESG ratings and detect risks such as inconsistent disclosures or greenwashing (World Economic Forum, 2023). This points to the convergence of sustainability with digitalisation, underscoring the case for interdisciplinary approaches in higher education.

Curricula are gradually adjusting to reflect these career trajectories. Business schools are embedding ESG-focused modules, establishing internships within sustainability teams and designing projects that replicate real-world reporting challenges. Professional bodies and accreditation initiatives, including the United Nations Principles for Responsible Management Education (PRME), reinforce the expectation that courses should combine technical competence with ethical awareness (UN PRME, 2024). Aligning curricula with these employer needs may not guarantee immediate success for all graduates, but it positions them to contribute meaningfully to the shaping of sustainable finance on a global scale.

3. Leveraging Digital Transformation for Enhanced Learning

3.1 Digital Transformation in the Finance Industry: AI, Blockchain and DA

Digital transformation is reshaping financial services at a remarkable speed. AI, blockchain and DA have shifted from being experimental projects to becoming mainstream tools in banking, audit and investment management. These technologies promise efficiency, accuracy and transparency, yet they also introduce new risks and uncertainties that education in accounting and finance can no longer ignore.

3.1.1 Artificial Intelligence

AI now underpins fraud detection, credit scoring, algorithmic trading and elements of audit automation. Financial institutions report that AI systems process data at scales far beyond human capacity, enabling quicker and more accurate risk assessments (Bank of England and FCA, 2022). Machine learning (ML), for instance, has become central to anti-money laundering checks, identifying suspicious transaction patterns that auditors might overlook. Still, AI is hardly a straightforward solution. Concerns about algorithmic bias, opaque decision-making and model fragility remain unresolved (IOSCO, 2025). For universities, this dual nature suggests a need to teach both the capabilities of AI and its limitations, particularly in relation to explainability and ethical governance.

3.1.2 Blockchain and Distributed Ledger Technology

Blockchain is increasingly used to enhance the transparency and security of transactions. J.P. Morgan and HSBC, among others, have trialled blockchain platforms for cross-border payments and tokenised assets, with the aim of reducing settlement delays and transaction costs (BIS, 2023). Other pilots have explored applications in supply chain finance and digital identity verification. Yet significant challenges persist. Public blockchains consume large amounts of energy, while permissioned systems raise questions of interoperability and governance. Regulators caution that adoption without safeguards risks undermining cybersecurity, financial stability and investor protection (FSB, 2022). Students, then, need both technical understanding of blockchain and critical tools to assess its feasibility and risks.

3.1.3 Data Analytics

The rise of big data has altered how firms make financial decisions. Predictive analytics is now used to forecast market movements, optimise portfolios and assess creditworthiness. FinTech platforms rely on real-time consumer data to personalise services (World Economic Forum, 2023). Yet over-reliance on complex models brings vulnerabilities. Privacy concerns, weak data quality and security breaches can destabilise firms as well as markets. The European Central Bank (2024) has warned that poorly governed analytics systems may undermine both accuracy and accountability. Teaching, in this context, should emphasise data literacy, critical interpretation and familiarity with regulatory frameworks such as the EU's General Data Protection Regulation (GDPR).

3.1.4 Opportunities and Risks

Taken together, AI, blockchain and DA appear to offer considerable benefits: efficiency, lower costs, improved risk management and stronger transparency. Yet they also generate systemic risks, including concentrated control by a few technology providers, exposure to cyberattacks and environmental pressures from energy-intensive computing (IEA, 2023). These tensions matter for education. Graduates must not only master technical applications but also develop awareness of their broader implications for ethics, sustainability and regulation.

Digital transformation is not only reshaping the industry; it is also reshaping the expectations of what accounting and finance graduates need to know. By examining how these technologies alter practice, educators can see why curricula and pedagogy must adapt in response.

3.2 Implications for Accounting and Finance Curricula

Digital transformation in the financial sector has clear implications for accounting and finance education. Universities and professional training providers are under growing pressure to produce graduates who can operate confidently in technology-driven workplaces. This requires curricula that move beyond traditional staples such as financial reporting, taxation and auditing and instead incorporate material on financial technologies, digital risk and data-informed decision-making.

3.2.1 Reshaping Course Content

Integrating digitalisation means students must grasp both the practical use of emerging tools and their wider significance. Increasingly, modules now include the fundamentals of blockchain for recording transactions, the application of AI in audit testing and the use of predictive analytics in financial planning (Appelbaum et al., 2022). These elements are not treated as optional extras but are embedded within core subjects. For instance, audit courses may introduce AI-based sampling and anomaly detection, while management accounting classes experiment with interactive dashboards. Such integration appears more effective than teaching digital tools in isolation, since it situates technology within professional practice.

3.2.2 FinTech and AI Audit Modules

Dedicated FinTech modules are becoming common, particularly at the postgraduate level. These often cover digital payments, cryptocurrencies and robo-advisory services, encouraging students to weigh both opportunities and regulatory risks. AI audit courses serve a similar purpose. They illustrate how ML can support fraud detection and efficiency but also prompt discussion of bias, accountability and the difficulty of validating opaque models (IOSCO,

2025). Embedding these debates supports the formation of graduates with hybrid finance-technology skillsets.

3.2.3 Data Science Integration

The growing reliance on big data has increased demand for accountants who are data literate. Business schools now expose students to programming basics, statistical modelling and analytics platforms (World Economic Forum, 2023). While few are expected to become expert coders, familiarity with Python, R, or SQL enables effective collaboration with data specialists. More important is the ability to interpret outputs critically: students are encouraged to question data quality, ethical use and the implications for business decisions (European Central Bank, 2024).

3.2.4 Accreditation and Professional Expectations

External expectations reinforce these curricular shifts. The Association to Advance Collegiate Schools of Business (AACSB) highlights digital literacy as part of its standards for curriculum quality (AACSB, 2020). Professional bodies such as the Association of Chartered Certified Accountants (ACCA) and the Chartered Institute of Management Accountants (CIMA) have also embedded digital finance skills in their qualification frameworks. The message is clear: universities that neglect digital transformation risk losing credibility and relevance in global education markets.

Adapting curricula in this way prepares students for workplaces where AI, blockchain and DA are routine. Yet challenges remain. Faculty may need retraining, teaching resources must be updated, and unequal access to technology can reinforce existing divides. Balancing technical competence with critical awareness will be essential if graduates are to thrive in digitally transformed financial professions.

3.3 Digital Tools in Education: Simulations, Dashboards and Blended Learning

The adoption of digital tools in accounting and finance education has gathered pace, shaped both by changes in the industry and by the wider demand for interactive learning. Instead of relying solely on lectures, educators are increasingly turning to simulations, dashboards and blended formats to help students build practical and critical skills in financial reporting and sustainability. These approaches mirror professional practice, where digital technologies underpin ESG analysis, risk modelling and investment strategies.

3.3.1 Simulations

Simulations allow students to experience decision-making under conditions that resemble real life. A classroom exercise, for instance, might require students to prepare an integrated sustainability report or carry out a blockchain-based transaction. Scenarios often include incomplete or uncertain data, pushing learners to develop problem-solving and ethical reasoning skills (Adams, 2021). Such experiential learning appears particularly effective with postgraduate or professional learners, as it encourages active participation and aligns with employers' calls for graduates who can apply theory to practice.

3.3.2 Dashboards

Visualisation tools such as Tableau or Power BI are now common in teaching. Students use them to create sustainability scorecards or analyse financial and ESG data side by side. Interactive dashboards can increase engagement by letting students test 'what if' scenarios, for example, modelling the impact of carbon pricing or supply chain disruption (European Central Bank, 2024). Yet, the clarity of visuals may be deceptive. Educators must remind students that outputs depend on assumptions built into the models and that attractive charts do not guarantee reliable evidence.

3.3.3 AI-Powered Case Studies

Generative AI is starting to support scenario-based assignments where students examine ESG disclosures, identify anomalies in financial statements or spot signs of greenwashing. Evidence suggests that these tools can build confidence in analytical work but may also lead to over-reliance if reflective activities are neglected (World Economic Forum, 2023). Effective integration, therefore, requires careful framing around responsible and ethical use.

3.3.4 Blended Learning

Blended approaches combine digital tools with in-person teaching, offering both flexibility and inclusivity. Online platforms make it possible for students in different regions to collaborate on simulations or joint dashboard projects, extending learning beyond a single classroom. Yet inequalities persist. Not every student has access to powerful devices or stable connections, and institutions that overlook this risk reinforcing divides (UNESCO, 2022). Investment in infrastructure and provision of alternatives remain necessary.

When integrated thoughtfully, digital tools can make accounting and finance education more applied and globally relevant. At the same time, they raise enduring pedagogical questions about inclusivity, critical engagement and the potential dangers of over-reliance on technology.

3.4 Reskilling and Lifelong Learning for Finance Professionals

Digitalisation and sustainability are altering the skills demanded in finance at a speed that outpaces traditional education cycles. For accountants, auditors and finance managers already in practice, continuing professional development (CPD) has become essential rather than optional. Professional bodies such as ACCA and CIMA now highlight digital finance, ESG assurance and DA within their CPD frameworks, reflecting employer interest in graduates and professionals who can navigate hybrid roles (ACCA, 2023). Online platforms add flexibility by offering courses on blockchain applications, AI-supported auditing and climate risk modelling. Such accessibility is particularly valuable for mid-career professionals attempting to balance ongoing employment with further study.

Universities are expanding their role in this landscape. Executive education programmes increasingly focus on digital finance and sustainability, offering short courses on integrated reporting, ESG data management or digital assurance. These courses allow participants to gain targeted skills without pursuing full degree programmes. In many instances, delivery is shaped in collaboration with the industry. Partnerships between business schools and the Big Four, for example, have produced modules on AI in auditing and strategies for sustainable finance (KPMG, 2023).

Collaboration extends beyond course design. Professionals often mentor students on ESG projects, while academics may advise firms on embedding sustainability within reporting practices. Such exchanges appear mutually beneficial: universities maintain curricula that reflect industry developments, and firms gain access to academic expertise (World Economic Forum, 2023).

Yet challenges remain. Access to reskilling opportunities is uneven, particularly in emerging markets where digital divides are more visible. There is also the risk that lifelong learning becomes narrowly focused on compliance rather than broader accountability. As Gray (2010) reminds us, accounting education should encourage professionals to reflect on ethical and societal consequences, not just regulatory requirements.

4. Innovative Teaching Strategies

4.1 Active Learning Approaches: Flipped Classrooms and Problem-Based Learning (PBL)

Active learning has become increasingly central to contemporary accounting and finance education. Traditional lectures often position students as passive recipients of information, whereas active approaches invite them to engage critically through dialogue, collaboration and applied problem-solving. Research in higher education suggests that these methods improve performance, motivation and long-term retention (Freeman et al., 2014; Prince, 2004). Within the context of sustainability and digitalisation, active learning appears especially valuable because it exposes students to complex, uncertain and interdisciplinary problems that more closely resemble professional practice.

4.1.1 Flipped Classrooms

Among active learning models, the flipped classroom is perhaps the most widely adopted. Here, students engage with lecture material or readings before class, leaving in-person sessions for interaction. In accounting and finance, this often involves short pre-recorded lectures on subjects such as blockchain applications or sustainability reporting. Class time can then be used for analysing case studies, interpreting ESG data or debating regulatory issues. Evidence indicates that flipped classrooms can improve engagement, particularly for students who struggle with abstract concepts when delivered in purely didactic formats (Gilboy et al., 2015).

For sustainability and digitalisation, the model offers opportunities for applied exploration. Students might review IFRS sustainability disclosure guidance independently, then critique a company's climate-risk report in groups. This not only develops technical literacy but also prompts reflection on whether disclosures address stakeholder concerns or simply meet minimum compliance.

4.1.2 Problem-Based Learning

PBL is another approach that places students at the centre of the learning process. In finance, tasks may include assessing the ESG implications of an investment portfolio or designing an audit plan for a firm introducing AI tools. What makes PBL relevant is that sustainability and digitalisation rarely present neat answers. Students are required to research independently, negotiate perspectives in teams and justify conclusions with evidence (Savery, 2015).

One example is an assignment in which students act as consultants advising a multinational on integrating the UN SDGs into reporting systems. Such exercises demand technical analysis while also requiring ethical reasoning and stakeholder awareness, reflecting employer expectations for graduates with hybrid skillsets.

4.1.3 Benefits and Challenges

Both flipped classrooms and PBL encourage deeper learning, collaboration and adaptability, qualities essential in tackling sustainability and digitalisation challenges. Yet they also require more preparation from students and substantial redesign by faculty. Equitable access to pre-class resources and adequate scaffolding for learners unfamiliar with self-directed approaches remain important considerations (Akçayır & Akçayır, 2018).

Even with these challenges, evidence suggests that active learning cultivates graduates better prepared for the uncertain, data-driven and ethically complex environments of modern finance.

4.2 Gamification and Experiential Learning in Accounting and Finance

Gamification has become increasingly prominent in accounting and finance education, often promoted as a way to make participation less passive, while experiential learning is more about involving students directly in tasks that resemble what they might do in practice. Although they look different, both strategies aim to turn abstract or technical ideas into something more concrete and, hopefully, transferable.

The most visible examples are usually game-style quizzes. Students earn points or badges for answering questions on reporting standards or sustainability rules. Some studies indicate that this can help with motivation in subjects that are sometimes regarded as dry or technical (Dichev & Dicheva, 2017). In practice, though, in practice, some learners concentrate on winning rather than learning, which may undermine the deeper outcomes. Careful planning is therefore needed, though that is not always easy in large or mixed groups.

Leaderboards and digital certificates push this further. While competition may be energising for some, repeated low rankings can be demoralising. Badges or micro-credentials can serve as proof of competence, for example in blockchain simulations or ESG reporting, and employers may view them as positive signals (Huang & Hew, 2018). Yet, the credibility of these tokens is uneven and depends on whether they are tied to standards that professionals actually trust.

Experiential learning is often linked with business simulations. Students might be asked to run a virtual company or build an investment portfolio, taking into account both financial and ESG measures. Such activities seem valuable in highlighting the tension between short-term profit and long-term responsibility. Still, they remain simplified models, and no simulation can capture the full complexity of volatile markets (Apostolou et al., 2013).

Overall, gamification and experiential methods do seem promising, but they are far from a perfect solution. Their success may rest on how well teachers balance enthusiasm for new tools with inclusivity and realism, avoiding the risk that competition or technology overshadows learning itself.

4.3 Simulation-Based Teaching: ESG, FinTech and Digital Finance Labs

Simulation-based teaching links classroom learning with professional practice by replicating industry environments. It gives students the chance to apply theory in realistic contexts, developing both technical competence and critical judgement. In areas shaped by sustainability and digitalisation, simulations appear especially useful because they expose learners to problems where solutions are uncertain and often interdisciplinary.

4.3.1 ESG Simulations

Sustainability reporting simulations allow students to prepare or critique disclosures using frameworks such as IFRS S1 and S2 or the EU's CSRD. A typical exercise might involve analysing a company's carbon metrics, governance practices and stakeholder narratives before drafting a mock integrated report. Studies indicate that such simulations not only deepen understanding of reporting complexity but also foster ethical reasoning and scepticism about practices like greenwashing (Christensen et al., 2021). These skills align closely with roles in assurance and consulting, where employers value graduates able to scrutinise sustainability claims.

4.3.2 Blockchain and FinTech Labs

Some universities now run blockchain labs where students record sample transactions, tokenise assets or explore how smart contracts function. These activities echo experiments undertaken by major banks and FinTech firms, offering learners first-hand familiarity with the infrastructure of digital finance (BIS, 2023). While few graduates will require deep technical expertise, awareness of blockchain concepts is increasingly attractive in audit, compliance and broader financial services.

4.3.3 Digital Audit Labs

AI-enabled audit simulations replicate tasks such as risk assessment, anomaly detection and sampling. They allow students to experiment with digital audit tools while also considering risks around bias, explainability and data governance (IOSCO, 2025). Incorporating such labs into curricula supports technical competence but also highlights ethical and regulatory responsibilities attached to technology-driven assurance.

4.3.4 Employability Implications

Employers consistently signal a preference for graduates who can demonstrate applied skills and adapt to emerging technologies. Simulation-based teaching provides tangible evidence of such abilities, helping bridge the divide between academic study and workplace expectations (World Economic Forum, 2023). Still, adoption requires investment in software, training and infrastructure and, without careful planning, may risk widening digital inequalities.

4.4 Assessment Innovation: Digital Projects, Peer Review and Scenario-Based Testing

Assessment remains central in shaping how and what students learn. Traditional exams and essays often test memory or individual performance, yet they do not always capture the blend of skills demanded in contemporary finance roles. As sustainability and digitalisation transform the workplace, universities appear increasingly drawn to assessment formats that mirror professional practice.

4.4.1 Digital Projects

Digital assessments invite students to apply technology directly to finance and sustainability challenges. A project might involve building an ESG dashboard, evaluating the effectiveness of a blockchain-based reporting system or using analytics software to interpret non-financial data. Such activities resemble the tasks graduates are likely to face in audit, consultancy or investment contexts. Evidence suggests that digital projects enhance technical competence and problem-solving while motivating students through their practical relevance (Apostolou et al., 2013). Yet these benefits assume equal access to technology, which is not always the case in under-resourced settings.

4.4.2 Peer Review

Peer assessment has become a common tool for developing collaboration and evaluative judgement. In group projects, students may review each other's sustainability reports or FinTech case studies, offering structured feedback against set criteria. This echoes professional practices such as audit reviews or peer checks within consultancy teams. Research indicates that peer review can encourage deeper learning and accountability, though risks of bias and superficial comments remain (Topping, 2018). Including reflective components, where students explain and justify their evaluations, appears to strengthen fairness and learning outcomes.

4.4.3 Scenario-Based Testing

Scenario-based assessments place students in decision-making situations that feel closer to professional reality. One case might simulate an audit team assessing a company's climate disclosures under IFRS S1, while another asks a financial analyst to weigh the risks of adopting AI-driven trading systems. These assessments cut across technical, ethical and regulatory dimensions, requiring students to exercise judgement under uncertainty (Boud & Soler, 2016). Such formats are particularly relevant to sustainability and FinTech, where standards continue to evolve and consensus is often lacking.

By combining digital projects, peer review and scenario-based testing, assessment becomes more authentic and aligned with employer expectations. Yet effective implementation depends on clear rubrics, staff preparation and reliable infrastructure to ensure fairness as well as rigour.

5. Challenges and Future Directions

5.1 Operational and Regulatory Challenges: Energy Use, AI Governance and Assurance

The spread of digital technologies across finance brings with it operational and regulatory questions that higher education cannot ignore. Three areas stand out in particular: the energy costs of new systems, the governance of AI and the credibility of sustainability disclosures.

Technologies that are often described as efficient, such as blockchain or AI, also come with heavy energy demands. The International Energy Agency (2023) estimates that data centres and AI workloads could double electricity consumption by 2030. Public blockchains like Bitcoin are widely criticised for their energy use, while training complex AI models is also resource intensive. For finance professionals who are expected to contribute to net-zero targets, this contradiction is not easy to resolve. Students, therefore, need opportunities to weigh both potential benefits and environmental costs, even if this balance is difficult to judge in practice.

The use of AI in finance, from fraud detection to ESG analysis, creates further uncertainty. IOSCO (2025) warns of risks, including bias, opacity and the dominance of a few large firms. The EU's AI Act, which entered into force in 2024 lists financial services as a high-risk area. Teaching cannot simply be about technical tools. Learners should also explore governance frameworks and ethical concerns, so they learn to question AI rather than treat it as neutral.

Finally, mandatory ESG standards such as IFRS S1 and S2 have created a demand for assurance. The Financial Stability Board (2022) and IFRS Foundation (2024) stress the need for independent verification, but assurance is messy work, relying on forward-looking indicators and patchy datasets. Introducing students to such limitations may prepare them better for professional practice.

Digitalisation in finance is both an opportunity and a risk. Effective curricula seem to be those that equip graduates to handle ambition with a sense of accountability.

5.2 Skills and Infrastructure Gaps: Faculty Development and Emerging Markets

Rapid regulatory and technological shifts have stretched the distance between what employers want and what many universities still deliver. The question of staff expertise is central. A number of lecturers were trained in more traditional forms of accounting and can feel unprepared when asked to introduce sustainability frameworks or digital tools such as AI-based auditing. Adams (2021) suggests that embedding sustainability goes beyond compliance training and needs interdisciplinary thinking, but in practice this is difficult to achieve without structured support. Otherwise, the risk is that teaching lags behind what is now happening in professional practice.

There are encouraging signs. In parts of the United Kingdom and the EU, universities have started to run workshops on ESG reporting and digital finance, sometimes supported by firms like Deloitte or KPMG who provide guest lectures and materials. Even so, sustaining these initiatives is not straightforward. Workloads are already heavy, incentives remain patchy and not every academic is equally motivated to adopt new methods. The danger is that improvements stay piecemeal rather than systemic.

Infrastructure adds further obstacles. Good teaching of digital finance requires access to reliable networks, software licences and large datasets. Wealthier institutions can afford blockchain labs or ESG dashboards, while many universities in emerging economies face budget limits and patchy connections. UNESCO (2022) has warned that such digital divides reinforce global inequalities, which leaves some graduates less competitive.

Evidence from India and Türkiye shows modest progress in embedding sustainability and FinTech, but with uneven access to training and technology (OECD, 2023). European and US institutions may lead in piloting digital finance labs, though even their expertise varies. The World Economic Forum (2023) has pointed out that lifelong learning applies to educators as well as students.

Closing these gaps probably requires long-term cooperation between universities, industry and governments. Faculty development and fairer access to infrastructure are not easy goals, but they appear necessary if higher education is to prepare students for the realities of sustainability and digital change.

5.3 Balancing Digitalisation With Sustainability Goals

Digitalisation is often promoted as a force for efficiency and transparency in finance. Tools such as AI, blockchain and advanced analytics can reduce human error, accelerate decision-making and enhance the quality of ESG reporting. Yet the same technologies also raise uncomfortable sustainability questions, particularly in relation to energy consumption, carbon emissions and electronic waste.

The International Energy Agency (2023) cautions that demand from data centres and AI workloads could double global electricity use by 2030. Public blockchains illustrate the dilemma: while valued for decentralisation and transparency, they remain notoriously energy-intensive. At the same time, digital technologies have become indispensable for sustainability reporting under frameworks such as IFRS S1 and S2, which require firms to manage and disclose vast volumes of ESG data (IFRS Foundation, 2024). The result is a paradox: digital tools are needed to demonstrate sustainability, yet their own footprint may undermine environmental goals.

From an educational perspective, this tension needs to be made explicit. Students should be encouraged to consider both benefits and trade-offs. A blockchain simulation, for example, might demonstrate gains in efficiency but should be paired with a discussion of energy demands and emerging low-carbon alternatives. Similarly, AI audit labs can showcase improvements in fraud detection while also prompting reflection on issues of bias, opacity and excessive resource use.

As Gray (2010) suggested, accounting ought to be understood within wider systems of accountability. This principle extends to evaluating the environmental consequences of the technologies that underpin disclosure. Embedding such debates into curricula may not resolve the contradictions, but it equips future finance professionals to recognise them and make more balanced, sustainable choices.

5.4 Future Pathways: Embedding ESG and Digital Skills into Global Finance Education

The convergence of sustainability and digitalisation is reshaping finance education in ways that appear both inevitable and uneven. Future pathways are likely to depend on how effectively universities, professional bodies and regulators coordinate to embed ESG literacy and digital competence as core, rather than optional, elements of learning.

Universities carry the first responsibility. Programmes that place sustainability at the margins risk leaving graduates underprepared. Instead, ESG concepts should be embedded in financial reporting, auditing and corporate finance modules, ensuring all students acquire baseline literacy. A similar logic applies to digital skills. Familiarity with DA, blockchain applications and AI-driven auditing should be treated as mainstream content, not specialist electives (World Economic Forum, 2023).

Professional bodies and accreditation agencies also shape priorities. The IFRS Foundation's sustainability standards (2024) already provide a baseline for global ESG reporting. Accreditation organisations such as AACSB (2020) and professional institutes like ACCA (2023) can reinforce consistency by requiring evidence of integration across curricula. Yet the degree to which such requirements translate into practice will depend on institutional resources and incentives.

Industry collaboration offers another pathway. Employers can contribute case studies, guest lectures and projects addressing real challenges, from climate finance strategies to AI-enabled risk assessment. These initiatives help ensure that classroom teaching reflects the evolving realities of professional practice.

Looking forward, finance education may need to embrace a global model of lifelong learning. ESG and digital competencies will not remain static, and graduates must be prepared to update their skills continuously if they are to shape financial systems that are both sustainable and accountable.

6. Conclusion

This chapter has looked at how sustainability and digitalisation are gradually reshaping accounting and finance education. New frameworks such as IFRS S1 and S2, the EU CSRD and SEBI's BRSR suggest that ESG knowledge is becoming more than optional, though not every institution is fully prepared. At the same time, AI, blockchain and DA are changing practice in ways that students must face. Universities may struggle with uneven resources, yet digital competence now seems as necessary as traditional technical skills.

Section 2 examined how sustainability education is shifting from optional electives to a core feature of curriculum design, supported by interdisciplinary teaching and accreditation standards such as PRME and AACSB. Section 3 explored the effects of digital transformation, highlighting how AI, blockchain and DA are influencing both course content and teaching practice. Section 4 discussed active learning, gamification, simulations and new forms of assessment as ways of creating more applied and professionally relevant learning. Section 5 turned to operational and regulatory challenges, including the energy demands of digital tools, questions of AI governance and faculty and infrastructure gaps, before setting out possible pathways for alignment.

Taken together, these sections suggest that sustainability and digitalisation are not peripheral concerns. They are now central drivers of reform in curriculum design, accreditation and graduate employability.

The chapter makes three contributions. First, it takes a global perspective, drawing on examples from both advanced and emerging economies to underline differences as well as shared challenges. Second, it links industry practice with pedagogy, showing how digital tools and sustainability standards can be embedded through simulations, case projects and authentic assessments. Third, it identifies the skillsets most in demand: competence in ESG reporting, data literacy, and ethical reasoning.

By engaging with sustainability scholarship (Bebbington & Unerman, 2018; Gray, 2010) alongside regulatory and technological developments, the chapter aims to bridge theory and practice, ensuring education remains tied not only to professional needs but also to broader societal expectations of accountability and transparency.

The challenge for educators will be to integrate sustainability and digitalisation rather than treating them separately. Future graduates will need to interpret ESG disclosures through digital dashboards, assess AI-based audit tools with a critical eye and weigh technological efficiency against environmental costs. Embedding these capabilities within curricula, reinforced by professional bodies and industry partnerships, appears essential.

Ultimately, the future of accounting and finance education lies in producing graduates who are technically capable, ethically aware and globally attuned. With sustainability and digitalisation as guiding principles, institutions can prepare students not only to adapt to change but to lead it, shaping financial systems that are transparent, inclusive and accountable.

References

AACSB (Association to Advance Collegiate Schools of Business). (2020). *2020 business accreditation standards: Frequently asked questions*. AACSB. https://www.aacsb.edu/accreditation/standards. Accessed on September 7, 2025.

Adams, C. A. (2021). Sustainability accounting and reporting education: Preparing students for a rapidly changing world. *Sustainability Accounting, Management and Policy Journal*, *12*(5), 889–907.

Akçayır, G., & Akçayır, M. (2018). The flipped classroom: A review of its advantages and challenges. *Computers & Education*, *126*, 334–345. https://doi.org/10.1016/j.compedu.2018.07.021

Apostolou, B., Dorminey, J., Hassell, J. M., & Rebele, J. E. (2013). Accounting education literature review (2010–2012). *Journal of Accounting Education*, *31*(2), 107–161. https://doi.org/10.1016/j.jaccedu.2013.03.001

Appelbaum, D., Kogan, A., & Vasarhelyi, M. A. (2022). Big data and artificial intelligence in accounting: Opportunities and challenges for future curricula. *Journal of Emerging Technologies in Accounting*, *19*(1), 1–15.

Association of Chartered Certified Accountants (ACCA). (2023). *Professional accountants—The future: Careers in a disrupted world*. ACCA. https://www.accaglobal.com/uk/en/professional-insights/technology/accountants-future.html. Accessed on September 7, 2025.

Bank of England and Financial Conduct Authority (FCA). (2022). *Artificial intelligence public–private forum: Final report*. Bank of England/FCA. https://www.bankofengland.co.uk/research/artificial-intelligence-public-private-forum. Accessed on September 7, 2025.

Bank for International Settlements (BIS). (2023). *Project mBridge: Connecting economies through cross-border wholesale central bank digital currencies*. BIS. Available at: https://www.bis.org/publ/othp67.htm. Accessed on September 7, 2025.

Bebbington, J., & Unerman, J. (2018). Achieving the United Nations Sustainable Development Goals: An enabling role for accounting research. *Accounting, Auditing & Accountability Journal*, *31*(1), 2–24. https://doi.org/10.1108/AAAJ-05-2017-2929

Boud, D., & Soler, R. (2016). Sustainable assessment revisited. *Assessment & Evaluation in Higher Education*, *41*(3), 400–413. https://doi.org/10.1080/02602938.2015.1018133

Christensen, H. B., Hail, L., & Leuz, C. (2021). Mandatory CSR and sustainability reporting around the world: A research synthesis. *Review of Accounting Studies*, *26*(3), 1176–1248. https://doi.org/10.1007/s11142-021-09609-5

Dichev, C., & Dicheva, D. (2017). Gamifying education: What is known, what is believed and what remains uncertain. *International Journal of Educational Technology in Higher Education*, *14*(1), 9–36. https://doi.org/10.1186/s41239-017-0042-5

European Central Bank (ECB). (2024). *Financial stability review: Special feature on artificial intelligence and data analytics in finance*. ECB. https://www.ecb.europa.eu/pub/financial-stability. Accessed on September 7, 2025.

European Commission. (2023). *Corporate Sustainability Reporting Directive (CSRD)*. European Commission. https://finance.ec.europa.eu/capital-markets-union-and-financial-markets/company-reporting-and-auditing/company-reporting/corporate-sustainability-reporting_en. Accessed on September 7, 2025.

Financial Conduct Authority (FCA). (2022). *Sustainability disclosure requirements and investment labels*. FCA. https://www.fca.org.uk/publications/policy-statements/ps22-3-sustainability-disclosure-requirements-investment-labels. Accessed on September 7, 2025.

Financial Stability Board (FSB). (2022). *Assessment of risks to financial stability from crypto-assets and decentralised finance*. FSB. https://www.fsb.org. Accessed on September 7, 2025.

Freeman, S., Eddy, S. L., McDonough, M., Smith, M. K., Okoroafor, N., Jordt, H., & Wenderoth, M. P. (2014). Active learning increases student performance in science, engineering, and mathematics. *Proceedings of the National Academy of Sciences*, *111*(23), 8410–8415. https://doi.org/10.1073/pnas.1319030111

Gilboy, M. B., Heinerichs, S., & Pazzaglia, G. (2015). Enhancing student engagement using the flipped classroom. *Journal of Nutrition Education and Behavior*, *47*(1), 109–114. https://doi.org/10.1016/j.jneb.2014.08.008

Gray, R. (2010). Is accounting for sustainability actually accounting for sustainability… and how would we know? An exploration of narratives of organisations and the planet. *Accounting, Organizations and Society*, *35*(1), 47–62. https://doi.org/10.1016/j.aos.2009.04.006

Huang, B., & Hew, K. F. (2018). Implementing gamification in education: A systematic review of empirical studies. *Educational Technology Research & Development*, *66*(3), 691–710.

International Financial Reporting Standards (IFRS) Foundation. (2024). *IFRS Sustainability Disclosure Standards (IFRS S1 and IFRS S2)*. IFRS Foundation/ISSB. https://www.ifrs.org/issued-standards/ifrs-sustainability-standards. Accessed on September 7, 2025.

International Organization of Securities Commissions (IOSCO). (2025). *Consultation report on the use of artificial intelligence in securities markets*. IOSCO. https://www.iosco.org. Accessed on September 7, 2025.

International Energy Agency (IEA). (2023). *Electricity 2023: Data centres and AI demand outlook*. IEA. https://www.iea.org. Accessed on September 7, 2025.

KPMG. (2023). *KPMG announces global investment in sustainability and climate reporting services*. KPMG International. https://home.kpmg/xx/en/home/news.html. Accessed on September 7, 2025.

Organisation for Economic Co-operation and Development (OECD). (2023). *OECD business and finance outlook 2023: Sustainability and resilience*. OECD Publishing.

Prince, M. (2004). Does active learning work? A review of the research. *Journal of Engineering Education*, *93*(3), 223–231. https://doi.org/10.1002/j.2168-9830.2004.tb00809.x

PwC. (2022). *ESG: The growth opportunity of the century*. PricewaterhouseCoopers. https://www.pwc.com/gx/en/services/esg.html. Accessed on September 7, 2025.

Savery, J. R. (2015). Overview of problem-based learning: Definitions and distinctions. *Interdisciplinary Journal of Problem-Based Learning*, *1*(1), 9–20. https://doi.org/10.7771/1541-5015.1002

Securities and Exchange Board of India (SEBI). (2021). *Business responsibility and sustainability reporting by listed entities*. Circular SEBI/HO/CFD/CFD-SEC2/P/CIR/2021/562. SEBI. https://www.sebi.gov.in/legal/circulars/jul-2021/business-responsibility-and-sustainability-reporting-by-listed-entities_50750.html. Accessed on September 7, 2025.

Securities and Exchange Commission (SEC). (2024). *SEC adopts rules to enhance and standardize climate-related disclosures for investors*. https://www.sec.gov/news/press-release/2024-32. Accessed on September 7, 2025.

Topping, K. J. (2018). Peer assessment: Learning by judging and discussing the work of other learners. *Interdisciplinary Education and Psychology*, *2*(1), 1–17. https://doi.org/10.31532/InterdiscipEducPsychol.1.1.007

UNESCO. (2022). *Global education monitoring report: Technology in education.* UNESCO. https://www.unesco.org/reports/global-education-monitoring-report. Accessed on September 7, 2025.

United Nations Principles for Responsible Management Education (UN PRME). (2024). *PRME initiative: Advancing responsible management education.* United Nations. https://www.unprme.org. Accessed on September 7, 2025.

United Nations (UN). (2015). *Transforming our world: The 2030 Agenda for sustainable development.* United Nations. https://sdgs.un.org/2030agenda. Accessed on September 7, 2025.

World Economic Forum (WEF). (2023). *Future of jobs report 2023.* WEF. https://www.weforum.org/publications/future-of-jobs-report-2023. Accessed on September 7, 2025.

Chapter 3

Redefining Accounting and Finance Education: Sustainability Imperatives and Digital Disruption

Deepika Dhingra[a], *Jaskiran Arora*[a] *and Prabal Chakraborty*[b]

[a]BML Munjal University, India
[b]Lingaya's Vidyapeeth, India

Abstract

To tackle the combination of digitalisation and sustainability, accounting and finance education would need a radical change in the future. In this chapter, it is argued that there should be a new educational paradigm of equipping students with the traditional technical skills as well as a very deep understanding of sustainability principles, such as the environmental, social and governance (ESG) factors, climate risk and the circular economy. Moreover, it shows how the finance of the 21st century incorporates blockchain and artificial intelligence, and data analytics (even including ethical deliberation on the use of these technologies), and how it trains such skills as critical thinking, problem-solving and 21st-century skills. Integration of these elements provides the opportunity for future professionals to leverage accounting and finance education to manage the difficulties of a more sustainable and internet-connected world and to make a more accountable and solidified future. In particular, this chapter will take a closer look at case studies on real-world sustainability issues that provide pedagogical approaches, experiential approaches through simulations and internships with information companies that promote social responsibility, integration of technology-based tools and platforms to enhance learning and engagement. More importantly, it will examine how the role of professional accounting bodies and regulators will evolve in the future to dictate the profession's future and ensure that all elements of financial decisions are based on ethical considerations.

Sustainability in Accounting and Finance Education, 41–61

doi:10.1108/978-1-80686-393-820261003

Keywords: Sustainable accounting; digital finance; financial technology; ethical accounting; accounting innovation; finance digitalisation

1. Introduction

The digital transformation is a significant era of technological integration of the physical and digital processes into distributed systems, which is restructuring the organisational and societal structures. This transformation influences nearly every aspect of life, from how societies function to how businesses operate and how economies generate value. Accounting, long considered a cornerstone of economic systems, is not immune to this change. As Jasim and Raewf (1) assert, 'the usage of information technology has been in progress for more than 140 years to streamline accounting processes for the accountant', underscoring how deeply technology has been intertwined with the discipline over time.

The central aim of accounting education (AE) is to equip future professionals with the knowledge and skills needed to contribute meaningfully to both organisations and society (Barac, 2009; IFAC, 2003; Wilkin, 2022). In this rapidly changing environment, educators in the field of accounting are tasked with producing new practical knowledge to address the evolving demands of the 'real world' (Bakre, 2006; Lubbe, 2014; Paisey & Paisey, 2017; Sarfraz et al., 2022). Since accounting educators must continually update and adapt their roles and responsibilities to stay relevant and effective, it is essential to enhance security measures in the several ways. These include updating their understanding of the proliferation and evolution of regulatory standards, incorporating advanced teaching methodologies that complement traditional pedagogies, effectively disseminating knowledge to a diverse student body across cultural backgrounds, engaging in research that advances their discipline and aligning curricula with the expectations of professional accounting bodies (de Villiers & Dumay, 2014; Duff et al., 2020; Evans et al., 2010; James, 2008; Mulder & van Oordt, 2016; O'Connell et al., 2015; Samkin & Stainbank, 2016; Sollosy & McInerney, 2022; Wright & Chalmers, 2010). However, these tasks bring to the fore the need for continuous updating of the curriculum in line with the dynamic nature of the workplace requirements (Hassall et al., 2005) and supported by the insights of accounting practitioners who live in these changes (Rebele, 2002; Sarfraz et al., 2022).

Despite an increasing pace of digitalisation, there is little early evidence of the long-term impacts that digitalisation will have on the accounting profession. On a large scale, decision-making processes will be significantly automated by the emergence of Big Data, blockchain technology (distributed ledgers) and cloud-based analytical platforms based on artificial intelligence (AI) [2–5]. These tools facilitate the rationality and efficiency of the decision-making and, at the same time, raise concerns regarding the quality of the information produced [6]. In addition, the large volume and complexity of the data offer new layers of uncertainty and risk in the financial decision-making process [7]. We can therefore look ahead, and the future of accounting and finance education is to actively adapt to these digital and sustainability-motivated changes now with agility and innovation to be relevant. This chapter investigates how AE can adapt to the demands of digital transformation and sustainability imperatives to produce a workforce not just technologically astute but equally ethically grounded and socially responsible.

1.1 COVID-19 Pandemic and Considerations on Necessary Educational Change

In December 2019, the COVID-19 outbreak began in Wuhan, China, prompting global restrictions on human contact. During this crisis, AI played a key role in pandemic management (Ciotti et al., 2022; Sarfraz et al., 2022), and digital tools like videoconferencing rapidly advanced. However, sectors such as higher education experienced negative side effects (Aldahray, 2022; Sollosy & McInerney, 2022). Post-pandemic, expectations for the future of business and AE remain mixed due to the impacts of digitalisation (Aldahray, 2022; Petrolo et al., 2023; Sollosy & McInerney, 2022; Tharapos & Marriott, 2020). These circumstances highlighted the need for rethinking accounting and business management education (Apostolou et al., 2020; Hosseini et al., 2021; Mantai & Calma, 2022; Samkin & Schneider, 2014a, 2014b). Additionally, factors like rapid technological advancements, AI, global capital markets and growing sustainability standards are shaping AE (Sollosy & McInerney, 2022). Educators are thus urged to anticipate trends, adapt curricula and equip students with relevant skills for the evolving job market.

1.2 Objectives and Significance of the Chapter

This chapter is an attempt to delve into and critically engage with the changing landscape of accounting and finance education in the face of the increasing influence of sustainability and digitalisation. It endeavours to explore the impact of global focus on sustainable development on curriculum design and teaching methods, and professional competences needed in this field. The chapter also examines the transforming effects of digital technologies such as AI, blockchain and big data analytics on the skills that future accounting and finance professionals will need. The fact that it is underpinned by the need for ESG principles to be included in educational frameworks to meet stakeholder requirements and adhere to emerging regulatory standards of compliance is underscored. Moreover, the chapter identifies the obstacles and feasible solutions that educators and institutions face as they aim for harmonisation of academic teaching with the industrial requirements and introduces alternative strategies to bridge the gap between theoretical knowledge and practical practice in a digitally evolved and sustainability-concerned expert environment.

2. Methodology

2.1 Research Design

The research design used in this study adopts a qualitative approach, and the method takes a descriptive and exploratory approach to finding out the impact of sustainability and digitalisation on accounting and finance education. Thus, the aim is to have a synthesis by combining scholarly literature and professional insights to explore the emerging trends, curriculum innovations and future implications (Creswell & Poth, 2018).

2.2 Data Collection Method

A systematic literature review was done on subjects that were published between the years 2018 and 2024 on both academic and professional sources, which helped in collecting data. Included in the retrieved relevant documents are those from databases such as Scopus, Web of Science, JSTOR and Google Scholar. In addition, the review included peer-reviewed journal articles, reports from the OECD, IFAC, and ACCA, policy papers, educational frameworks, and white papers. The keywords used included 'sustainability in accounting education', 'digitalisation in the finance curriculum', 'AI in accounting education' and 'future of the accounting profession'. However, this broad way provided enough insight to determine key gaps in the existing literature (Boell & Cecez-Kecmanovic, 2015).

2.3 Data Analysis

The results were synthesised using the thematic analysis method. The following categories were grouped into recurring themes under the category of core ideas.

Curriculum Transformation: Integration of ESG, ethics and sustainability.

Technological Integration: Inclusion of AI, blockchain and data analytics.

Sustainability Alignment: Educational responses to global sustainability standards and institutional missions.

Based on constructivist learning theory, where real-world problems were to be used as a basis for learning (Piaget, 1976a, 1976b) and institutional theory, where academic institutions were to be understood as a response to external societal and technological influences (DiMaggio & Powell, 1983), the analysis was developed. This is limited to English language publications, though, so any perspective from non-English speaking regions might be excluded. In addition, the findings largely relate to the realities of current practices and challenges experienced among higher education institutions in developed countries for the reason because access to and relevant literature are available. No human participants were involved because the research is based only on secondary data. In the course of the study, ethical standards of conduct were set as accurate citation, responsible reporting and complete compliance with academic integrity regulations (APA, 2020).

3. Conceptual Framework

The two predominant forces that are leading to the transformation of accounting and finance education are digital technologies and the emphasis placed on sustainability. These dynamics are ushering in new paradigms for future professionals to be learnt and are prompting a shift from a traditional theory-based instruction to a more whole of focused and forward-looking kind of educational model.

Tools like AI, big data analytics, blockchain and cloud computing leverage digital transformation, which automates routine processes and helps make better financial decisions. Furthermore, sustainability imperatives require institutions to embed environment, social, and governance (ESG) elements, green finance and ethical accountability in the curriculum. Together, these drivers demand reimagining accounting and finance education to train professionals who not only possess technical skills but also have the human compass to act responsibly in society.

These changes are seen in several areas. Digital competencies and ESG frameworks now need to be included in curricula, whereas pedagogical approaches move towards experiential, interactive and hybrid models. Such developments are intended to instil critical thinking, data literacy, ethical reasoning and problem-solving skills deemed necessary in the current financial ecosystem. However, this has been hindered by several challenges. Outdated curricula, a lack of technological infrastructure, insufficient training of faculty and dereliction of quality academic outputs from the industry demand are a few of the reflections of these parameters.

All of these obstacles represent good opportunities for the shift. To improve student engagement and global employment, as well as closer integration between academia, industry and regulatory bodies, advanced digital tools and the concepts of sustainable finance can be used. There exist hybrid learning models of digital platforms combined with traditional classroom methods that provide flexibility and inclusiveness, as well as updated curricula, aligned to the current world trends that are relevant and competitive.

This educational shift is based on conceptual foundations of constructivist and transformative learning theories, emphasis on experiential knowledge building and critical reflection. On top of this, stakeholder theory emphasises the value of bringing educational goals congruent with the needs of employers, regulators and society in general. To do this successfully, organisations need to adapt to an integrated teaching approach and continuous curriculum renewal, in addition to enabling lifelong learning pathways that drive ongoing skill development and adaptability.

Ultimately, the intended result of this transformation is graduates who are ready for the industry with a blend of complete technical and analytical skills, along with ethical judgement and a good, sustainable mind to succeed in the evolving global economy. The Need for Transformation in Accounting and Finance Education.

Traditional accounting relies on manual processes using physical spreadsheets, journals and ledgers. While some professionals remain comfortable with these methods, they are increasingly inefficient, time-consuming and incompatible with modern financial demands. Manual data entry, limited automation and onsite-only access hinder cost tracking, real-time reporting, collaboration and overall operational efficiency. Moreover, traditional systems pose security and storage risks due to localised data handling and a lack of digital backups.

These limitations highlight the urgent need for transformation. As the industry shifts towards digital and sustainable accounting solutions, the traditional model is gradually being phased out. Digital accounting offers automation, integration, secure cloud-based storage, real-time insights and enhanced compliance capabilities, making it essential for businesses aiming to remain competitive, efficient and future-ready. Transitioning to digital systems is no longer optional but a necessary step towards streamlined, secure and strategic financial management.

4. Transforming AE for a Digital and Sustainable Future

4.1 The Emergence of Sustainability and Digitalisation as Key Drivers of Change

Changes in accounting and auditing processes have been a result of the digital uprising. The Internet of Things (IoT), cyber-physical systems and Internet of Systems technology are being experienced and used by organisations to enable auditors and accountants to store, process, analyse and provide reports from data efficiently and speedily (Lohapan, 2021). Improving the service quality isn't the only thing the use of analytics tools and robotics contributes to. Furthermore, AI and cognitive technology further help in decision-making through automating particular tasks and providing historical offerings of the practices of scenarios (Lohapan, 2021; Manita et al., 2020) in compliance with sustainability reporting and accounting from the external stakeholders of the businesses. Therefore, organisational managers are forced towards emerging sustainable accounting practice, which must be based on these principles (Susilowati et al., 2023; Tran Trung & Huu Nguyen, 2023; Yadiati et al., 2024).

The main benefits of digital transformation in accounting and finance are to increase efficiency by saving considerably in terms of time and money. In other words, it allows one to get timely insights that can be used for improvement in data handling and also to improve the level of accuracy of the decision overall. Other than that, digital systems are easy to scale due to which the organisations can grow easily.

4.2 The Demand for New Skill Sets in AE

- Practical implications

Accounting and business educators need to consider digital technology's impact on this profession, categorise what must attain digital skills accountants must attain and discuss with stakeholders to make these skills part of courses. Subsequently, they should report the problems they encounter while teaching digital technologies. This transformative opportunity also needs engagement with the professional bodies to determine the professional curriculum.

- Accounting education: The role and evolution

The objective of AE is to produce skilled professionals to make positive contributions to their organisations and society (Barac, 2009; IFAC, 2003; Wilkin, 2022). Academics in the field of accounting work to create new knowledge to solve critical problems and satisfy the needs of clients (Bakre, 2006; Lubbe, 2014; Paisey & Paisey, 2017; Sarfraz et al., 2022).

The new curriculum of accounting and financial education involves more than just implementing state-of-the-art technologies like, cloud computing, and but also aligning the technology with the goals of the company, improving operational effectiveness, safeguarding data and optimising accounting and financial functions.

- Strategic Vision and Digital Literacy

To lead the digital transformation process, educators and industry leaders need to have a clear understanding of technologies like AI, machine learning (ML) and data analytics to align technology and education with the goals of the industry. The curriculum must educate and promote expertise in corporate financial planning, corporate digital transformation, financial modelling and forecasting to make informed decisions. To ensure the work is compliant, educators should be educated on accounting standards and regulatory frameworks. This will not only improve the efficiency of students and institutions but also industry operations.

- Reskilling and Upskilling for Evolving Needs

To stay competitive in the accelerating environment, it is crucial to arrange programmes for reskilling and upskilling. The training in financial risk management, corporate accounting, fraud detection and corporate quantitative finance is vital in the interpretation of complex data. These skills empower professionals to adapt to transformation and make smart accounting and financial decisions based on data.

Training programmes in evolving technologies like Robotic Process Automation (RPA) and AI in financial analysis will reduce human error, automate repetitive work, expedite accounting workflows and financial reporting, and allow professionals to pay more attention to strategic activities.

- 'Blended-learning' and learner-centric approach: a new possibility in AE:

The blended learning design approach in AE seems to be a new possibility to achieve the ultimate objectives and scope, making it an experiential event. 'Blended learning' refers to considering all activities or techniques and adding them to conventional methods, even synchronous or asynchronous supplemental ones (e.g., vodcasts, podcasts, quizzes, lectures and voice-over-PowerPoint). That's how merging their different strengths integrates face-to-face learning with online learning activities.

'Blended learning' international trends are becoming crucial in open and distance learning for education institutes of any level to stay in a competitive and contested market. The research done in recent times has established that this method promotes student-centred learning, bridges the gap between students and educators and increases flexibility.

5. Integrating Sustainability in Accounting and Finance Education

The United Nations (UN) declared the period 2005–2014 as the Decade of Education for Sustainable Development (DESD), emphasizing the integration of sustainability principles into all levels of education. Integration of 'the principles and practices of sustainable development into all aspects of learning and education', whereas sustainability education was earlier considered primarily a part of higher education.

Due to the continuous demand for accountants to have the competencies and knowledge to contribute to sustainable business practices, educators also have a responsibility to upgrade accounting curricula. Advanced knowledge of sustainable AE in curricula at all levels will ensure sufficient coverage and alignment to keep pace with developments worldwide.

However, the role of accounting is getting bigger in sustainable business (Khan et al., 2019). Accountants need to be more active (Botes et al., 2014; Collins et al., 2011).

5.1 Understanding ESG in AE

ESG factors are increasingly vital in evaluating organisational performance and risk. While traditionally seen as non-financial, ESG criteria now directly impact investment decisions, regulatory compliance and corporate reputation. For AE, this necessitates a shift from technical training alone to embedding ESG frameworks into the curriculum.

The growing emphasis on sustainability has also transformed expectations from accounting education, requiring institutions to integrate environmental stewardship, ethical decision-making, and stakeholder accountability into curricula. Previous studies highlight that sustainability education strengthens ethical reasoning, interdisciplinary thinking, and professional competencies while preparing graduates to address climate-related risks, circular economy principles, and responsible corporate practices (Alcott, 2005; Ascani et al., 2021; Botes et al., 2014; Calder & Clugston, 2005; Collins et al., 2011; Energy Innovation:

Policy and Technology LLC, 2021; Freedman, 2019; Gray et al., 1994; Khan, 2013; Kahn et al., 2019).

Accounting students must be trained to interpret ESG disclosures, assess sustainability-related risks and ensure transparent, ethical reporting. Educators should integrate ESG case studies and data analysis exercises that simulate real-world challenges in ethical investing, carbon accounting and social impact reporting. This alignment prepares future professionals to navigate evolving regulatory standards and stakeholder expectations.

5.2 Three Core Principles of ESG

Nowadays, business leaders are increasingly focused on ESG as a functional approach to doing business. Every feature of ESG plays a crucial role in increasing an organisation's focus on ethical and sustainable practices. The following are the common ESG criteria used by organisations and investors (see Fig. 3.1).

5.3 Climate Finance, Risks and Accounting/Climate Risk and the Role of Accounting

For the stability of the global economy in 2030, climate change is listed as a top concern among environmental issues. Environmental and climate issues have gained substantial attention worldwide in the last few decades. Academics, policymakers, regulators and central banks have started questioning how climate change affects financial stability. Climate-related risks are anticipated to impose

Fig. 3.1. The Three Key Factors Behind ESG Initiatives Are Environmental, Social and Governance. *Source:* Author's own illustration, 2025.

costs that are so large they are difficult to measure but are likely to be in the trillions of dollars worldwide.

Below are the steps stakeholders can take to bring those tools to address the crises of climate change. Comprehensive implementation of existing requirements of accounting and related disclosure to showcase the financial impacts of the climate crisis and the transition to a low-carbon economy.

I. Updating disclosures, through guidance and staff accounting bulletin, to spread best practices.
II. Leveraging the audit to build a bridge between corporate financial reporting and climate-related risks.

5.4 The Circular Economy: Implications for Accounting Curriculum

The circular economy means resource use is sustainable with recycling, reuse and waste reduction in place, not the traditional linear economic model. This presents new responsibilities for accountants to cost allocate, measure performance and sustainability report related to extended product lifecycles.

On the other hand, in AE, this could mean integrating the principles of life-cycle costing, sustainability metrics and integrated reporting in the coursework. Students should investigate how financial decisions can be linked to environmental priorities, for instance, return on sustainability investments or reporting on circular business models. It is a preparation for graduates who can provide support to organisations committed to sustainable growth and innovation.

6. Digital Tools and Platforms: Enhancing Learning and Practice

The world of accounting is being completely changed by AI, blockchain and data analytics. These technologies are transforming management accounting by automating routine tasks, improving accuracy and enabling real-time decision-making (Quattrone, 2016). Yet, their integration in the education arena would be limited only to the technical application, and not the strategic use. Instructors can leverage digital platforms and simulations to teach financial modelling, fraud detection and automated auditing. Immersive technologies like Virtual Reality (VR) and Augmented Reality (AR) provide engaging, scenario-based learning environments. By fostering digital fluency alongside ethical and analytical thinking, educators can better prepare students for a dynamic and tech-driven profession.

6.1 Benefits of Sustainability Education

Sustainability education prepares students for the 'challenges and opportunities they are likely to face' in the future (Rangarajan & Joshi) by giving them exposure to ethical and moral considerations (Mangion) and increasing their ethical reasoning (Gray et al., 1994). The real-life situations improve students' experience (Gray et al., 1994), and they develop inter-disciplinary skills (Saravanamuthu). Further, students can develop more information-based 'knowledge, skills, abilities, values and dispositions' (Shephard & Furnari, p. 1578), which creates broader career opportunities in related areas of sustainability and climate change.

7. Digitalisation and Technological Advancements in Finance Education

Technology has become a significant part of the financial industry; technology has entirely renovated the functionality of finance, including how transactions are carried out, encompassing data quality, advanced analytics, automated systems and continuous accounting.

The industry comprises an extensive range of digital platforms and products with cutting-edge technologies such as big data analytics, blockchain and AI. These technologies are empowering finance teams to be more efficient.

Let's explore more about the crucial role of technology in the financial industry and its comprehensive impact on the financial landscape.

7.1 Blockchain, AI and Data Analytics: Their Role in Modern Finance

Recent scholarship indicates that digital transformation is fundamentally reshaping accounting and finance by integrating artificial intelligence, big data analytics, cloud computing, and intelligent automation into financial reporting, auditing, and managerial decision-making. These technologies improve operational efficiency, facilitate real-time analysis, enhance the quality of financial information, and enable more strategic decision-making while simultaneously requiring accountants to acquire new digital competencies and analytical capabilities (Bromwich & Scapens, 2016; Damerji & Salimi, 2021; Granlund, 2011; Guandalini, 2022; Korhonen et al., 2020; Moll & Yigitbasioglu, 2019; Richins et al., 2017).

The financial industry has experienced a major technological transformation that was radically re-invented by AI in recent years, now providing novel solutions to a data-intensive and ever more sophisticated marketplace.

As financial markets become more complex and the data keeps growing at an exponential rate, the need for innovative solutions that can support better decision-making, operational efficiency and customer experience has become more critical. AI technologies like ML, natural language processing (NLP) and big data analytics have become enablers of these changes, helping financial institutions adapt to the fast-changing environment and stay relevant (Cao & Cao, 2022; Goodell et al., 2021).

7.2 Digital Tools and Platforms for Enhanced Learning

Digital learning tools are increasingly revolutionising the modern education system as to how students can learn and how teachers deliver instruction. In times of advancing digitalisation, they offer an extensive range of benefits and opportunities for students. These tools allow students to access a wealth of resources, collaborate remotely and learn at their own pace. Due to adaptive technology, these platforms enhance the experience and improve engagement.

Beyond engagement, platforms such as Google Classroom and Microsoft Teams enable seamless communication between students and teachers, supporting remote learning and ensuring educational continuity in times of disruption. However, challenges such as unequal access to technology must be addressed to ensure inclusivity.

- Types of digital learning tools

There are different types of digital learning tools customised for different learning needs and styles. Here are some examples: Platforms and websites for interactive education: These educational platforms and websites offer extensive learning materials. They provide accessibility to various courses, interactive learning games, exercises and flexibility in the learning environment. Software and apps for learning: These software and apps are installed on mobiles or computers. They offer interactive quizzes, exercises and learning games that make the learning process entertaining. Online lectures and video tutorials: These tools let students connect with faculty and experts by watching content and classroom videos, and offer flexibility to explore knowledge at their convenience, time and place. Digital textbooks and E-books: These are electronic versions of books that can be read on tablets, e-readers or computers. It provides interactive elements for enhanced learning, like audio/video files and interactive exercises. Gamified learning tools: These tools make the learning experience more entertaining and engaging by using video games. The use of reward points, stages and contests can track their progress.

7.3 The Use of Simulations and Experiential Learning Methodologies

Innovative pedagogies are required for ESD that motivate students to engage, ensure effective learning outcomes and develop their attitudes towards sustainability.

In the realm of finance and AE, emphasis is increasing on equipping students with the necessary knowledge, skills and tools required to foster sustainable development. This 'global character' of new age education is reflected in the practice of teaching sustainable development, educational policy and discourse.

Traditional teaching methods are not adequate to support the learning styles of diverse students. Accompanying traditional teaching methods with simulation-based experiential learning has displayed positive results in bridging the gap between theoretical knowledge and practical application.

7.4 21st Century Skills for Future Accounting Professionals

To succeed in a tech-driven, sustainability-conscious financial environment, accounting professionals must master a blend of 21st-century skills, including critical thinking, ethical reasoning and digital literacy. As emerging technologies automate routine tasks, human value increasingly lies in problem-solving, strategic decision-making and the ability to interpret complex, data-driven insights responsibly.

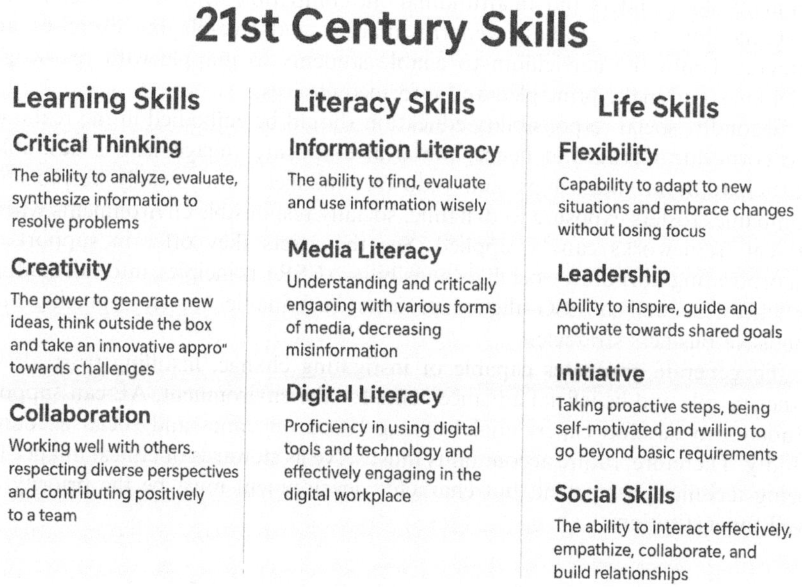

Fig. 3.2. Three Main Categories of 21st Century Skills: Learning Skills, Literacy Skills, Life Skills. *Source:* Author's own compilation based on World Economic Forum (2016a, 2016b), and UNESCO (2017).

Educational programmes must prioritise these competencies through blended and experiential learning models, such as simulations, case-based scenarios and digital platforms, preparing students to adapt to continuous change and ethical complexity in the accounting profession.

In addition to developing critical thinking and digital competencies, AE must also nurture a strong ethical foundation and social responsibility mindset to prepare students for the broader impact of financial decisions (see Fig. 3.2).

8. Ethical and Social Dimensions of Accounting Practice

In the era of sustainability and digital transformation, ethical and social responsibilities have become a cornerstone of modern accounting practice. As the profession evolves, the expectation for accountants to act with integrity, transparency and accountability has intensified. Ethical decision-making is no longer confined to compliance with regulations; it encompasses a broader understanding of moral reasoning, societal impact and long-term value creation.

Students today need to be socially sensitive and ethically conscious; hence, it becomes essential for education to develop with such parameters. It involves skills in ethical reasoning, understanding the consequences of financial decisions on many stakeholders and an attitudinal one compatible with public interest and sustainability. Case studies, scenario analysis and role-playing exercises are integrated into the curriculum to enable students to grapple with real-world dilemmas and make principled and informed choices.

Secondly, social responsibility education should be embodied in the realm of the corporate world, and hence, practical corporate engagement is desirable. Participation in internships and industry linkages with socially responsible companies fosters exposure to dynamic, socially responsible environments where ethical frameworks can be applied. See the assets they offer in support of incorporating corporate social responsibility (CSR) principles into accounting practices, as well as ESG-aligned projects, sustainable finance reporting and inclusive business strategies.

To generate graduates capable of instigating change, instilling trust about other people and beneficial advancements for the environment, AE can support students to develop experiential learning based on ethics and social accountability. Therefore, future accountants must serve as stewards of ethical finance by being technical competent, but character development must be the priority as well for institutions.

9. Role of Professional Accounting Bodies and Regulators

The provision of accounting regulatory bodies serves various crucial functions aimed at ensuring the reliability and integrity of financial reporting and the accounting profession. These institutions ensure transparent, consistent and accurate reporting of financial information by creating and sustaining standards. Their role is to safeguard the interests of stakeholders and investors by providing reliable financial information and instilling faith in financial markets. They do examinations, education and ethical requirements, licensing and regulation. For instances of violations, these bodies also penalise to maintain discipline through investigations. They also convey the interest of the public by lobbying for the profession, overseeing the integrity of the audit and researching to maintain financial integrity.

9.1 The Evolving Expectations for Accounting Professionals

Global mobility and continuous professional development contribute to improved service quality and greater consistency in accounting practices across jurisdictions. The increasing global mobility of accounting professionals enhances knowledge transfer, international collaboration, and the adoption of best practices. These are some benefits of accountancy professionals' skills that help them to work all over the world.

This evolution process is a challenge and an opportunity for the accountants to evolve into a more strategic role, helping businesses more out of success. The key to thriving in this dynamic environment is to accept change, continuous learning and adoptable new technologies and methodologies. Those who view these changes are not threats, but opportunities, and redefine their role, are the ones of the future.

9.2 Regulatory Frameworks That Support Sustainable and Ethical Financial Practices

Any interest in sustainable finance should be understood from the perspective that it is altering the very fabric of the financial system by embedding ESG principles into investment decisions, long-term value creation and economic resilience. Climate risk, along with social and governance factors, is now becoming more about regulatory evolution. To remain competitive and attract sustainable investments, businesses must invest in ESG capabilities, engage stakeholders and respond to these changes.

Specifically, sustainable finance draws a connection between the financial performance and the societal and environmental well-being, however, challenges persist such as the inconsistent, non-standardised ESG metrics and the change of regulations. Building a sustainable financial ecosystem requires strong collaboration between businesses, investors and regulators. Adopting regulatory best practices in a proactive manner can improve reputation and play into wider sustainability initiatives.

9.3 Future Trends in Professional Accreditation and Standards

There are several regulatory changes expected in 2025 that will reshape the sustainable finance framework, with the European Union (EU) set to refine the landscape and bring in new regulations to improve credibility and transparency in the green bond market. Furthermore, the Task Force on Nature-related Financial Disclosures (TNFD) released its final report in 2024, highlighting financial reporting related to biodiversity and nature. These changes underline the increasing recognition of ESG aspects in financial decision-making, with new expected regulations to drive sustainability and innovation in 2025. Its impact will go beyond investors and influence the larger social and economic environment comprehensively.

- Global trends and regional variations

The method of sustainable finance regulations differs significantly across regions, based on:

Varied priorities and regulatory viewpoints: EU: The EU leads in regulations on sustainable finance with the Sustainable Finance Disclosure Regulation, Taxonomy Regulation and the forthcoming Corporate Sustainability Reporting Directive Corporate Sustainability Reporting Directive. The structure encourages sustainable investment, in line with the EU's Green Deal. The initiative has an objective of climate neutrality by 2050 in the United States. The United States is embracing sustainable finance regulations gradually, with the climate disclosure rules. Standards are less strict than the EU, emphasising voluntary reporting and solutions driven by the market. The country's biggest climate investment is the Inflation Reduction Act (IRA), which targets reductions in emissions by 1 billion tons by 2030.

Asia: Asia is moving forward in sustainable finance, with China and Japan following diverse approaches (U.S. Department of Energy, 2023). The financial services agency of Japan has presented ESG investment outlines, while China is working to develop a green taxonomy and standardisation of green bonds. To categorise sustainable economic events, ASEAN has executed the ASEAN Taxonomy for Sustainable Finance.

10. Academic Innovations for Future-Ready Education

Developments in information technology have changed the entire education in the business function as well as altered the role of accounting professionals. After knowing the importance of information and technology, several professional associations and employers have frequently called for emerging technologies in the future of AE practice, as they found, especially during the era of the COVID-19 pandemic, that its implementation is gravely limited.

The pandemic emphasised planning for changes in the future that will comprise business, accounting and management studies at both an educational and professional level (Mantai & Calma, 2022; Samkin & Schneider, 2014a, 2014b).

With the quick development in technology and growing complexities in business operations, the methods of traditional accounting are being tested. The observations are pushing the incorporation of Business Intelligence tools into AE to ensure transformation.

10.1 Experiential and Case-Based Learning (CBL) Approaches

CBL is an active approach that allows students to use their theoretical knowledge in real scenarios to solve problems and make decisions. It encourages experiential learning by motivating students for teamwork and stressing practical application. Teachers promote discussions, motivate students to raise questions, understand dilemmas and find solutions in collaboration. It improves critical thinking by finding gaps in learning. In short, CBL bridges the gap between theoretical and practical knowledge and prepares students for challenges in the real world.

10.2 Integrating Sustainability and Digitalisation in Curriculum Design

The accounting digitalisation of sustainability is in line with Industry 4.0, supported by innovative automation and data-driven processes. Businesses are positively working on adopting sustainable practices by integrating economic, social and environmental aspects while evaluating performance. This is redefining the role of accounting in risk management, reporting and policy design to further enhance accountability and transparency in sustainable economic development.

However, there are some assumptions as well. The most predominant one is associated with the capacity of digitalised sustainable accounting to enhance decision-making and protection of the environment. There are some apprehensions connected to the integration of sustainable digitalisation with two correlated subfields: (i) accounting information systems and (ii) sustainable accounting. Moreover, today's accountants are also apprehensive regarding this digital transformation in accounting due to a lack of digital proficiency, and this may further harm the legitimacy of accountants.

Researchers and decision-makers diagnose that digitalisation can be a solution for environmental protection; still, it could also exacerbate the problem in case of misuse of new technology. But if properly used, it has the potential to contribute to achieving sustainability goals.

11. Conclusion and Future Directions

In this new era of the turbulent business environment and rapidly advancing technology, students and practitioners should focus on honing both technical and non-technical skills. Accounting institutions must have a curriculum in line with market requirements. We are already observing trends that the new generation is influencing AE by their inclination towards advanced technology. There is a need to adopt new curricula, innovative methods of teaching and better learning results to prepare students to face the demands of the evolving job market (see Fig. 3.3).

11.1 Challenges and Opportunities in Implementing the New Educational Paradigm

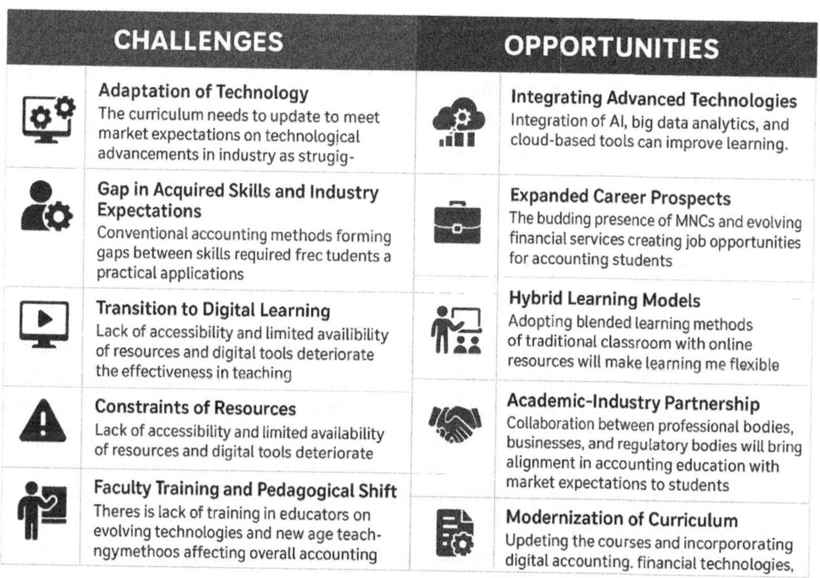

Fig. 3.3. Challenges and Opportunities in Implementing the New Educational Paradigm. *Source:* Author's own conceptual Model, 2025.

11.2 Future Research and Policy Implications

In AE, future research should focus on enhancing professional knowledge, technical skills and ethics; also, the deficiencies in current teaching and training methods must be addressed. Policymakers must modify the curricula to update the role of an accountant by including new-age courses like ML, big data analytics, advanced statistical methods and forensic accounting. A relative assessment of global AE underlines disproportions in curriculum, process of certification and accountant-to-population ratios. Policies should be made and implemented for uniformity in academic durations, professional certification exams, practical training, employability and performance. Advanced technology and global best practices in AE will help produce skilled and capable professionals.

References

Alcott, B. (2005). Jevons' paradox. *Ecological Economics*. https://doi.org/10.1016/j.ecolecon.2005.03.020

Aldahray, A. (2022). The impact of digital transformation on higher education post-COVID-19. *Journal of Educational Technology & Society*, *25*(3), 45–60.

American Psychological Association. (2020). *Publication manual of the American Psychological Association* (7th ed.). American Psychological Association. https://doi.org/10.1037/0000165-000

Apostolou, B., Hassell, J. M., Rebele, J. E., & Watson, S. F. (2020). Accounting education literature review (2017–2019). *Journal of Accounting Education*, *50*, 100655.

Ascani, C., Balland, P. A., Morrison, A., & Rigby, D. (2021). Smart specialization policies and new venture creation: An empirical analysis of European regions. *Regional Studies*, *55*(5), 924–939.

Bakre, O. M. (2006). The problem with accounting education in developing economies: The case of Nigeria. *Accounting Forum*, *30*(2), 150–170.

Barac, K. (2009). South African training officers' perceptions of the knowledge and skills requirements of entry-level trainee accountants. *Meditari Accountancy Research*, *17*(2), 19–46.

Boell, S. K., & Cecez-Kecmanovic, D. (2015). On being 'systematic' in literature reviews. *Journal of Information Technology*, *30*(2), 161–173. https://doi.org/10.1057/jit.2014.26

Botes, V., Low, M., & Chapman, J. (2014). Is accounting education sufficiently developing students' professional skills? *Accounting Education*, *23*(6), 562–589.

Bromwich, M., & Scapens, R. W. (2016). Management accounting research: 25 years on. *Management Accounting Research*, *31*, 1–9. https://doi.org/10.1016/j.mar.2016.03.002

Calder, W., & Clugston, R. (2005). Education for a sustainable future. *Journal of Sustainability Education*, *1*(1), 1–6.

Cao, L., & Cao, L. (2022). AI in finance: Challenges, techniques, and opportunities. *ACM Computing Surveys*. https://doi.org/10.1145/3502289

Ciotti, M., Ciccozzi, M., Terrinoni, A., Jiang, W.-C., Wang, C.-B., & Bernardini, S. (2022). The COVID-19 pandemic: Viral variants and vaccine efficacy. *Critical Reviews in Clinical Laboratory Sciences*, *59*(1), 1–19.

Collins, E., Lawrence, S., Roper, J., & Haar, J. (2011). Sustainability practices of New Zealand businesses. *Business Strategy and the Environment*, *20*(6), 456–470.

Creswell, J. W., & Poth, C. N. (2018). *Qualitative inquiry and research design: Choosing among five approaches* (4th ed.). Sage.

Damerji, H., & Salimi, A. (2021). The mediating effect of use perceptions on technology readiness and adoption of artificial intelligence in accounting. *Accounting Education*, *30*, 107–130. https://doi.org/10.1080/09639284.2021.1872035

de Villiers, C., & Dumay, J. (2014). Integrated reporting: Insights, gaps and an agenda for future research. *Accounting, Auditing & Accountability Journal*, *27*(7), 1042–1067. https://doi.org/10.1108/AAAJ-06-2014-1736

DiMaggio, P. J., & Powell, W. W. (1983). The iron cage revisited: Institutional isomorphism and collective rationality in organizational fields. *American Sociological Review*, *48*(2), 147–160.

Duff, A., Fawcett, R., & McCreadie, C. (2020). Developing accounting graduates for the future: Professional skills and curriculum innovation. *Accounting Education*, *29*(6), 593–615.

Energy Innovation: Policy and Technology LLC. (2021). *The costs of delay*. Energy Innovation: Policy and Technology LLC.

Evans, E., Burritt, R., & Guthrie, J. (2010). *Accounting education at a crossroad in 2010*. Institute of Chartered Accountants in Australia.

Freedman, A. (2019, August 19). Climate change could cost the U.S. up to 10.5 percent of its GDP by 2100, a study finds. *Washington Post*.

Goodell, J. W., Satish, K., Lim, M. W., & Pattnaik, D. (2021). Artificial intelligence and machine learning in finance: Identifying foundations, themes, and research clusters from bibliometric analysis. *Journal of Behavioral and Experimental Finance*. https://doi.org/10.1016/j.jbef.2021.100577

Granlund, M. (2011). Extending AIS research to management accounting and control issues: A research note. *International Journal of Accounting Information Systems*. https://doi.org/10.1016/j.accinf.2010.11.001

Gray, R., Bebbington, J., & McPhail, K. (1994). Teaching ethics and the ethics of accounting teaching: Educating for immorality and a possible case for social and environmental accounting education. *Accounting Education*, *3*(1), 51–75.

Guandalini, I. (2022). Sustainability through digital transformation: A systematic literature review for research guidance. *Journal of Business Research*.

Hassall, T., Joyce, J., Arquero Montaño, J. L., & Donoso Anes, J. A. (2005). Priorities for the development of vocational skills in management accountants: A European perspective. *Accounting Forum*, *29*(4), 379–394.

Hosseini, M., Dehghan, F., & Hashemi, M. (2021). Digitalization in accounting education: Challenges and future perspectives. *Accounting Education*, *30*(2), 175–192.

International Federation of Accountants (IFAC). (2003). *International education standards for professional accountants and aspiring professional accountants*. IFAC.

James, K. (2008). A critical theory and postmodernist approach to the teaching of accounting ethics. *Critical Perspectives on Accounting*, *19*(5), 643–676.

Jasim, Y. A., & Raewf, M. B. (2020). Information technology's impact on the accounting system. *Cihan University Journal of Humanities and Social Sciences*, *4*(1), 50–57. https://doi.org/10.24086/cuejhss.v4n1y2020.pp50-57

Kahn, M. E., Mohaddes, K., Ng, R. N., Pesaran, M. H., Raissi, M., & Yang, J. C. (2019). *Long-term macroeconomic effects of climate change: A cross-country analysis*. National Bureau of Economic Research.

Khan, M. T. (2013). Mapping sustainability in management education: A conceptual framework. *Journal of Business Ethics*, *115*(4), 567–577.

Korhonen, T., Selos, E., Laine, T., & Suomala, P. (2020). Exploring the programmability of management accounting work for increasing automation: An interventionist case study. *Accounting, Auditing & Accountability Journal*, *34*(2), 253–280. https://doi.org/10.1108/AAAJ-12-2016-2809

Lohapan, N. (2021). The impact of emerging technologies on accounting and auditing practices. *International Journal of Accounting Information Systems*, *41*, 100575.

Lubbe, I. (2014). Educating professionals to meet the expectations of the accounting profession. *Meditari Accountancy Research*, *22*(1), 26–46.

Manita, R., Elommal, N., Baudier, P., & Hikkerova, L. (2020). The digital transformation of external audit and its impact on corporate governance. *Technological Forecasting and Social Change*, *150*, 119751. https://doi.org/10.1016/j.techfore.2019.119751

Mantai, L., & Calma, A. (2022). Preparing graduates for uncertain futures: Higher education responses after COVID-19. *Higher Education Research & Development*, *41*(7), 2233–2248.

Moll, J., & Yigitbasioglu, O. (2019). The role of Internet-related technologies in shaping the work of accountants: New directions for accounting research. *The British Accounting Review*, *51*, 100833. https://doi.org/10.1016/j.bar.2019.04.002

Mulder, C., & van Oordt, T. (2016). Educating accountants for the future. *Meditari Accountancy Research*, *24*(4), 523–543.

O'Connell, B., Carnegie, G., Carter, A., de Lange, P., Hancock, P., Helliar, C., Watty, K., & Stoner, G. (2015). *Shaping the future of accounting in business education in Australia*. CPA Australia.

Paisey, C., & Paisey, N. J. (2017). Student learning in accounting education: Global issues and future directions. *Accounting Education*, *26*(4), 337–339.

Petrolo, R., Battisti, E., & Caputo, F. (2023). Digital transformation in accounting education: Emerging trends and future directions. *Accounting Education*, *32*(5), 523–545.

Piaget, J. (1976a). *The grasp of consciousness: Action and concept in the young child*. Harvard University Press.

Piaget, J. (1976b). Piaget's theory. In B. Inhelder & H. H. Chipman (Eds.), *Piaget and his school* (pp. 11–23). Springer.

Quattrone, P. (2016). Management accounting goes digital: Will the move make it wiser? *Management Accounting Research*, *31*, 118–122.

Rebele, J. E. (2002). Accounting education's uncertain environments: Descriptions and implications for accounting programmes and accounting education research. *Accounting Education*, *11*(1), 3–25.

Richins, G., Stapleton, A., Stratopoulos, T., & Wong, C. (2017). Big data analytics: Opportunity or threat for the accounting profession? *Journal of Information Systems*, *31*(3), 63–79. https://doi.org/10.2308/isys-51805

Samkin, G., & Schneider, A. (2014a). Sustainability, ethics and accounting education. *Accounting Education*, *23*(3), 245–262.

Samkin, G., & Schneider, A. (2014b). Sustainability, ethics and accounting education. *Accounting Education*, *23*(6), 495–497.

Samkin, G., & Stainbank, L. (2016). Teaching and learning in accounting education. *Accounting Education*, *25*(6), 535–538.

Sarfraz, M., Mohsin, M., Naseem, S., & Khan, M. (2022). Digital transformation in accounting education: Challenges and opportunities. *Sustainability*, *14*, 13521.

Sollosy, M., & McInerney, C. (2022). The future of accounting education in a post-pandemic world. *Accounting Education*, *31*(5), 465–482.

Susilowati, D., Yulianto, A., & Sari, N. (2023). Sustainability accounting education in the era of digital transformation. *Sustainability*, *15*, 10987.

Tharapos, M., & Marriott, N. (2020). Accounting education and COVID-19: Challenges and opportunities. *Accounting Research Journal*, *33*(6/7), 669–675.

Tran Trung, T., & Huu Nguyen, T. (2023). Digital transformation and sustainability in accounting education. *Journal of Accounting Education*, *64*, 100872.

UNESCO. (2017). *Education for Sustainable Development Goals: Learning objectives*. UNESCO.

U.S. Department of Energy. (2023). *Inflation reduction act: Delivering clean energy and reducing emissions*. https://www.energy.gov/edf/inflation-reduction-act-2022

Wilkin, C. L. (2022). Accounting education in the digital era: Preparing graduates for the future profession. *Journal of Accounting Education*, *58*, 100769.

World Economic Forum. (2016a). *The future of jobs: Employment, skills and workforce strategy for the Fourth Industrial Revolution*. World Economic Forum.

World Economic Forum. (2016b). *New vision for education: Fostering social and emotional learning through technology*. World Economic Forum.

Wright, S., & Chalmers, K. (2010). The future of accounting education: Challenges and opportunities. *Accounting Education*, *19*(6), 535–546.

Yadiati, W., Mulyani, S., & Nuswantara, D. A. (2024). Digital sustainability and accounting education: Preparing future accountants for ESG reporting. *Journal of Cleaner Production*, *434*, 140119.

Chapter 4

Environmental Accounting and Its Focus in Business Education in Bangladesh: A Review

Sumana Podder[a], *Avijeet Paul*[b] *and Sohana Sultana*[b]

[a]Crandall University, Canada and Premier University, Bangladesh
[b]Premier University, Bangladesh

Abstract

Environmental Accounting (EA) represents a specialised branch of accounting that integrates the assessment of environmental costs and benefits into financial and managerial reporting frameworks. This discipline encompasses the systematic collection, recording, classification, extraction and summarisation of information pertinent to the natural environment. In recent years, EA has emerged as a dynamic and increasingly significant field within the global academic and business communities. In Bangladesh, business academicians have been showing their interest in the discourse of environment-related information, as an emerging and dynamic field, through scholarly publications, particularly in the form of e-articles. This paper examines the current nature of e-articles on EA and their contribution to higher business education in Bangladesh. Many e-resources on EA contributed by the academicians of different higher education in Bangladesh are reviewed, which are available on the internet. The reviewed e-articles indicate that businesses are increasingly attentive to environmental considerations, which exert a material impact on their financial statements. Specifically, EA is conceptualised as a vital tool for environmental management, enabling businesses to integrate ecological considerations into strategic decision-making processes. The scholarly contributions highlight the role of EA in promoting transparency and accountability in corporate environmental performance, thereby aligning financial reporting with sustainability objectives. Moreover, the e-articles underscore the growing importance of EA in shaping business education curricula. By addressing

Sustainability in Accounting and Finance Education, 63–80

Published under exclusive licence by Emerald Publishing Limited
doi:10.1108/978-1-80686-393-820261004

topics such as environmental cost accounting, sustainability reporting and the integration of environmental metrics into financial analysis, these publications provide valuable resources for educators and students.

Keywords: Environmental accounting; e-article; higher education; environmental policies; Bangladesh

1. Introduction

For modifying national accounts, the concepts of environmental accounting (EA) have been able to gain popularity, and several proposals have been taken to include a consideration of resource depletion and environmental deterioration (Serafy, 1997). Moreover, different literature has coined several names such as 'Green Accounting', 'Resource Accounting' and 'Integrated Economic and Environmental Accounting' (Rahman, 1998). Therefore, the concept is based on properly assessing a country's income and wealth. Hence, the economic sectors have to account for all the activities and their impact on resource depletion and degradation (Nations & Fund, 2003). Furthermore, there are various meanings for the term 'Environmental Accounting' (Boyd, 1998). Thus, EA is regarded as incorporating principles of environmental management, conservation, reporting practices and cost/benefit analysis of the environment (Raju, 2018). In many developing countries, such as Bangladesh, it can be observed that there is a poor environmental system. Moreover, authorities should also take steps to identify whether the companies are continuously demonstrating environmental policies by using their environmental management techniques and strategies (Rahman et al., 2021). Khalid et al. (2012) investigated many organisations that emphasised to costs reduction rather than environmental conservation and environmental cost are not being identified and remain unrecognised. The first journey of EA started in Norway and after the 1990s, environmental degradation has expanded the uses of EA rapidly (Sarkar & Ahmed, 2020). Through EA, a business can see the impact of ecological and sustainable practices in every aspect of their supply chain which can facilitate the business expansion also. Moreover, the economic impact of shareholder's decisions can be made by the accountant's report and it will help in proactive decision-making which congregates environmental regulations simultaneously.

EA serves a critical function in quantifying the costs associated with an organisation's adherence to environmental regulations, representing one of its most prominent applications. Within this domain, environmental accountants are tasked with overseeing activities such as the licensing of clean technologies and the trading or sale of pollution permits. Additionally, they play a pivotal role in identifying potential new sources of income, such as the monetisation of waste materials, thereby contributing to the financial sustainability of the organisation. A central aspect of EA within corporate financial accounting involves the systematic recording, analysis and reporting of the financial and ecological consequences arising from a firm's current or prospective activities. Environmental accountants also support the implementation of the organisation's environmental management system by providing data-driven insights. To achieve this, robust systems, methodologies and processes are essential for the accurate documentation, evaluation and dissemination of environmental information. Such frameworks are indispensable for ensuring efficient and effective management, positioning EA as a cornerstone of strategic decision-making in corporate sustainability. When a company faces any negative environmental incident or disaster, it can overcome this with the help of disclosing the environmental information in its annual report or any other way. Moreover, environmental disclosure provided by a company may also assist them in the long run (Das et al., 2008).

Nonetheless, there is a commonly used explanation of EA which is identifying, measuring and allocating the environmental cost and then integrating these environmental costs into business decisions. In another definition, it is a combination of differentiated conventional accounting and ecological accounting which also includes the environment in consideration (Hussain et al., 2016). Therefore, it will communicate the information to the company's stakeholders. Thus, indirect costs and benefits of a product or activity are also included in the practice of EA. For instance, a firm considers the environmental effects on health and the economy when making business decisions. Business management information systems and environmental and financial accounting systems are the sources of collecting the EA data. It also involves recording or disclosing environmental liabilities and reporting on environmental stewardship. This has also incorporated the measures of environmental well-being in the national accounts. For improving environmental performance, inventory and controlling costs, fewer pollutant technologies and non-polluting products are the reason for using this managerial tool (EA). It has been observed that accountants are not committed and attached while dealing with corporate environmental and social accounting issues in most developing countries. Therefore, this attribute of the accountants has led to some cultural and national factors for example there is an unawareness, no state regulation and national accounting bodies are not taking any initiative (Islam & Dellaportas, 2011). There are some factors considered by EA that involve all costs of products and environmental costs of an economic entity. Hence, the assumptions of implementing EA are distinct environmental costs, provisions for risks and afferent costs, specific information in explanatory notes (financial report's annotation), etc. Biodiversity-related product costs, human health and aesthetic values can be effectively determined by EA. While carrying out environment-related policies, social and EA largely depends on the attributes of how the company perceives the environment-related issues (Ardillah, 2021). In another definition of EA, it is considered an arrangement that provides information on the declining natural fundamentals of the organisation's object of activities and the actions taken to evade this decline. In response to the business houses' activities that exert stress over environmental makeup, EA has emerged in the last two decades. In Norway, during the 1970s, EA was first put up. Since then, disclosure of environment-related information in the corporate financial report began and expanded sharply in the 1990s (Kokubu et al., 2002). There are fewer studies regarding environmental reporting based on developing countries, most of the studies have focused on developed countries (Belal, 2000). Moreover, there is less environment-related information and data available at the organisational level as many organisations do not find it necessary to evaluate their environmental performance. Organisations often emphasise more on financial accounting because, they believe that, EA will not benefit them in the future just like financial accounting (Zulkifli, 2011). We still have limited knowledge of EA as there is a dearth of empirical studies in developing countries. In the present research, the authors emphasised e-articles rather than printed articles because nowadays, many business students at the tertiary level find it easy to access these e-resources. In this regard, the present paper attempts to create an opportunity by reviewing the present nature of e-articles on EA and their academic contributions to higher business education in Bangladesh.

2. Purposes of the Study

This study focuses on examining the present nature of e-articles on EA and their academic contributions to higher business education in Bangladesh. The prime objectives of the study are demonstrated here:

i. To understand the concept and need of EA in Bangladesh as an emerging and dynamic field.
ii. To review the contributions of EA in Bangladesh through the present research.
iii. To assess the learning of EA in higher business studies through SWOT analysis.

3. Methodology of the Study

E-resources or secondary data are the main basis of this review paper. This paper is based on relevant literature on the topic collected from different journals. A systematic literature search was carried out through different online database sources or academic search engines. For instance, Google Scholar, ResearchGate, Scopus, Science Direct, etc. used to review the selected papers on EA. Literature related to EA, EA disclosure and EA practices in Bangladesh were the focus. Literature was searched by the authors using some key terms, like 'Environmental Accounting', 'Environmental Accounting in Bangladesh' and 'Applications of Environmental Accounting' to find the e-resources in the search engines.

Some specific criteria were established by the authors for the literature to be eligible for review. Articles on the same topic were excluded and only peer-reviewed English journals were selected for this review paper. During the selection tenure of e-articles, any type of editorial, dissertation, master's or PhD thesis or blogs were excluded. The selected e-articles covered the period between 1995 to 2020. This review paper finds the EA and the focus of EA in business education from the existing literature. As a result, the authors have decided to review the existing papers on EA strategically. Four phases (P-1: Design, P-2: conduct; P-3: Data Abstraction & Analysis; P-4: Structuring and Writing the Review) guidelines of Snyder (2019) were followed to fulfil the quality of this review paper.

Thirteen e-resources (academic articles) on EA are taken for this study, which is contributed by the business academicians of different higher education in Bangladesh. The articles are selected based on their subject matter or content related to EA (summarised in Table 4.1). All the reviewed articles are available on the internet or different websites published in different reputed journals of the country. The author emphasised the e-articles rather than the printed articles because nowadays, many students at the tertiary level get easy access to these e-resources. The collected articles are reviewed manually. Important information related to EA (without the below listed selected articles) was noted in a separate note sheet for additional reference purposes. To achieve all specific objectives, the qualitative approach is used in this article as a methodology for both analysis and presentation purposes.

Table 4.1. Selected E-articles on Environmental Accounting in Bangladesh.

Theme & Author
Application of environmental accounting in Bangladesh (Rahman, 1998)
Environmental reporting in developing countries (Belal, 2000)
Corporate environmental reporting practices in Bangladesh (Rahman & Muttakin, 2005)
Environmental disclosure – a Bangladesh perspective (Shil & Iqbal, 2005)
Environmental accounting and reporting in fossil fuel sector (Bose, 2006)
Corporate environmental reporting on the internet in Bangladesh (Dutta & Bose, 2008)
Accounting for ecology and reporting in developing Countries (Roy & Jewel, 2009)
Environmental accounting and its applicability in Bangladesh (Ali et al., 2010)
Environmental accounting and reporting practices (Ahmad, 2012)
Environmental accounting in financial reporting standard (Biswas & Rahaman, 2011)
Present status of corporate environmental accounting (CEA) (Chowdhury & Hamid, 2013)
Environmental accounting and reporting practices of listed banking companies in Bangladesh (Masud et al., 2017)
Prospects of environmental accounting practices of selected manufacturing enterprises in Bangladesh (Hossain, 2019)

4. The Necessity of EA

EA serves as a critical tool for quantifying the financial implications of a nation or organisation's interactions with the environment. It generates essential data that supports decision-making processes for a diverse range of internal and external stakeholders. Hence, the prime aims of EA are expenses and revenues with environmental protection and also taking necessary precautions for the financial level environment. In recent years, Bangladesh has been facing environmental issues like land degradation, substandard waste management, biodiversity loss, coastal erosion, poor processing of chemical wastage, etc. Accountability of business entities can be created through Environmental Accounting and Reporting (EAR) and by making environment protection-related corporate decisions (Masud et al., 2017).

In the last 10 years recognising the necessity of the environment, there is a need for appropriate environmental management has developed. Moreover, in both developed and developing countries environmental problems should be addressed with high importance and social awareness also has to be made (Bracci & Maran, 2013). By addressing environmental issues, companies can reduce overall costs and improve the efficiency and image of the company. However, traditional accounting still does not highlight this area (Hossain, 2019). Achieving sustainable development is one of the aims of EA. A favourable relationship with the community can be built with the help of EA. Nowadays, to save the earth, effective and efficient environmental conservation activities are necessary. To promote environmental preservation, organisations can implement conservation initiatives through the framework of EA. This discipline significantly contributes to effective business management by providing a structured approach to the quantitative assessment of environmental conservation efforts, serving as a valuable tool for achieving and sustaining robust managerial practices. Furthermore, EA enables companies and non-profit organisations to accurately identify, measure and evaluate data related to investments and costs associated with environmental conservation activities. By employing appropriate EA methodologies and generating comprehensive conservation reports, business entities can systematically analyse these data to inform strategic decision-making. Moreover, a company can improve the efficiency of its business activities with the help of deep insight into the potential benefits of environmental investments and costs. EA works as a catalyst for the sustainable development of the company. Besides these, it is a required tool to analyse the costs and benefits generated by the company's environmental activities. EA helps develop the control mechanism and implement the practices and policies related to environmental pollution. Research related to alternative solutions like the recycling process as per the EA undoubtedly helps select the production materials and minimise the production cost. Every business entity has some social and environmental responsibility regarding its business activities. EA has been used widely to present the social and environmental responsibility of the company as an environmental cost. Cost management is a vital concern for any organisation and it is essential for organisations to identify and allocate the different cost associated with the business (Sultana et al., 2023). On the other hand, environmental-related costs distinguish a company's financial position from the general companies that do not have any environmental-related costs. Environmental costs reflect financial statements and an effective information system as well as the business activities on the scale of reducing the natural elements. The control of pollution and the costs of waste management are included in EA. Furthermore, costs of surveillance activities are associated with environmental concerns and also repair or prevent any environmental damage is included as environmental expenses. Classification of environmental costs can be as follows: costs for the environmental control due to business activities, management activity's costs for environmental awareness, social activity costs for improving social structure, environmental development and damage recovery costs.

Environmental cost can be calculated by the following formula (Sultana, 2017):

Protection costs of the environment (Emission treatment and prevention of pollution)
+ Wasted material costs
+ Wasted capital and labour costs
= Corporate Environmental Costs (Total)

Environmental management or the activities related to pollution control is a vital issue in the current scenario. Nowadays, environmental management is a significant portion of companies and other organisations that are proactively engaging with environmental management issues. EA is a part of management strategies to specify a company's initiative for dealing with environmental issues. Through EA, they can carry out internal environmental conservation-related activities.

The concern for the environment is a much-discussed matter in the first world countries as well as in the third-world countries. Being a third-world country, Bangladesh faces environmental catastrophes, such as massive air pollution in Dhaka, the worst condition of river Buriganga, arsenic in the underground water, Magurchara disaster (Ahmad, 2012). Roy and Jewel (2009) also opined that environmental degradation had reached such an alarming level in the river water, leading to a hazard and threat, especially for the public health, economic growth and ecosystem of surrounding areas.

Ali et al. (2010) explained how the industrial and corporate sector severely spoils the environment of Bangladesh. It is mentionable that most industries (especially textiles, pharmaceuticals, chemicals, tannery, etc.) do not follow required waste management guidelines, which ultimately hampers biodiversity. Only a small number of manufacturing companies in the industrial zone have their waste management plant, though the number is insignificant in Bangladesh. In 1995, with the necessary assistance from the United Nations Development Programme

(UNDP), the National Environment Management Action Plan was enacted and to check and improve the pollution and environmental conditions, the Government of Bangladesh passed the 'Bangladesh Environmental Conservation Act', 1995, which can force the companies for collecting environmental clearance certificate, especially in the industrial zone, to disclose environmental cost information (Ahmad, 2012; Roy & Jewel, 2009). The Ministry of Environment and Forests has also working on different environmental issues in Bangladesh since 1989. To reduce the environmental damages and protect the environment there are several laws (see Table 4.2) exist in Bangladesh. Corporate EA disclosure has no mandatory or specific treatment in Bangladesh on the other hand, many developed or developing countries in the world are practising corporate EA and reporting (Pramanik et al., 2007; Sarkar & Ahmed, 2020; Sultana, 2017).

Giant companies in Asia consider the different environmental issues in accounting and have developed items associated with EA to justify their

Table 4.2. Some Important Legal Frameworks Associated With Environmental Accounting and Reporting (EAR) in Bangladesh.

Legal Framework of EAR in Bangladesh (Masud et al., 2017; Roy & Jewel, 2009)
Ministry of Environment and Forests
Forest Department
Department of Environment
Planning Commission
National Environment Policy, 1992
Companies Act, 1994
National Environmental Management Action Plan, 1995
Environmental Conversion Act, 1995
Environmental Conversion Rules, 1997
Bankruptcy Act, 1997
Ozone Depleting Substances Rules, 2004
Environmental Court Act, 2010
Climate Change Trust Act, 2010
Credit Risk Management Industry Best Practices by Bangladesh Bank in 2010
Environmental Risk Management Guidelines, 2011
Bangladesh Biodiversity Act, 2012
Tax Ordinances
IFIC guidelines
IASC guidelines
FASB guidelines
BFRS guidelines

applicability to companies' reporting in Bangladesh (Roy & Jewel, 2009). Prominent companies such as Hyundai (Korea), Mabuchi Group (Japan) and TATA (India) frequently reported the pollution control equipment and facilities, solid waste disposal, CO_2 emission and hazardous substances reduction information, company policies for environmental factors, environment-friendly products development and consider forestation is an important aspect of environmental issues in accounting (Roy & Jewel, 2009).

5. Educational Dimension of EA

Today's world is thriving for a sustainable society with environmental protection. Environmental studies are essential to ensure environmental action and advocacy and they also enhance the environmental awareness, literacy and citizenship among the people. In response to the growing concern of sustainability, social and environmental governance and business activities to address climate change, EA is highly involved in higher education all over the world (Shakkour et al., 2018). However, in Bangladesh, EA studies are yet to develop but here we discussed the methods across the universities and business schools in brief which includes curriculum structure, pedagogical approaches, student engagement and efforts of organisation.

5.1 Curriculum Structure

In higher education in Bangladesh, the institutions offer courses under which related topics or chapters focusing on Sustainable Accounting, EA, EA Management or Environmental liability are taught. There are topics related to EA, such as environmental costs and liabilities, carbon accounting and emission reporting, life cycle assessment, environment management accounting, green finance, regulatory compliance, effluent treatment plant (ETP) and environmental, social and governance (ESG) disclosure framework which are covered under different courses at the university level. In this paper, we have gathered data from different secondary sources and could not find any information where any distinct courses relating to EA are being taught in Bachelors and Masters programs (Business School). However, as one of the prominent private universities in Chittagong, Bangladesh, Premier University used to provide a three-credit course for the Master of Business Administration (Accounting major) from the year 2019–2021, under the title 'Social and Environmental Accounting', where the students got to know about the core concepts of social and EA, corporate EA, environmental management accounting and proactive corporate EA. Even though that course helped students to develop their ability to evaluate the approaches of different firms to social and EA, that course was removed from the curricula. However, the authors believe that the structure should be organised in such a way that, the learners can easily understand the concept and policies to ensure a sustainable environment. The students should be able to explain social and EA both theoretically and practically after the successful completion of the course. The designed EA curriculum must aware the students about current trends and future directions for social and EA in national and global circumstances.

5.2 Pedagogical Approach in EA

Though there is no individual course relating to EA at the undergraduate and the graduate level, the universities signify teaching the technical aspects to identify and measure the environmental cost and it also focuses on sustainability, responsibility and business impact on the environment through other courses. The most common method in classrooms in Bangladesh is case study or project work where the students get to know more about sustainability reporting practices, environmental audits or costing of pollution. Institutions also try to engage students with local firms and Non-governmental Organisations (NGOs) and assist in identifying environmental impact or facilitating environmental reporting (Uzorka et al., 2024). Apart from that, different courses are combined to provide insights about EA such as concepts of accounting, law regarding business and environment, core environmental science, environmental management and environmental economics. Nonetheless, universities are also trying to implement data analytics tools and software that include environmental sustainability and governance modules. However, it is important to become familiar with real-world EA problems and challenges by encouraging the students to figure out the problems, analyse the issue and develop strategic solutions for sustainable decision-making. The institution can play a vital role in promoting sustainable development by integrating ESG values in the education curriculum (Alenezi & Alanazi, 2024). Therefore, universities can focus on integrating AI tools to assess sustainability metrics.

5.3 Student Involvement

The authors believe that one of the convenient ways of teaching EA is project-based learning where the students will be engaged in environmental audits or sustainability reports either in real firms or hypothetical firms. Bramwell-Lalor et al. (2020) conducted a study on project-based learning for environmental sustainability action, where they opine that project-based learning creates a large dimension of sustainability competencies through a teaching-learning strategy. Clubs and competitions are also a great process to engage students more intensively in EA as student groups can organise environmental sustainability competitions within the departments or outside the university. Students can also arrange waste management projects at university and they can implement them to other organisations later on. Universities are now focusing on sustainability research or internships for the students to get hands-on experience.

5.4 Organisational Initiatives

Many universities can implement sustainability centres where events related to sustainable EA can be organised to foster multidisciplinary research. By collaborating with other organisations that maintain environmental sustainability students can get involved with activities of sustainable EA. (Sundarasen et al., 2024). Educational institutions can also collaborate with organisations that practice EA to offer more realistic education to the students. Moreover, establishing a lab in the university can be helpful which will measure energy and waste of the campus and report the findings.

6. Contribution of EA in Bangladesh

The environmental problems have become global, and as a result, at several levels, interpretation of EA is necessary, such as organisational, regional and national. The role of EA is instrumental in disclosing environmental factors irrespective of industrial types and nature of operations, commercial or non-commercial activities at every level, whether micro, meso or macro. On the United Nations Environment Programme (UNEP) initiative, a working group on EA was formed in 1983. Accounting at the national level, physical and monetary accounts of environmental assets, the environmental depletion and degradation costs are included in EA. Through the application of EA, organisations can accurately determine the true costs associated with their products and operational processes. This approach facilitates improved business decision-making and supports sustained profitability across the entire life cycle of products or services. However, environmental pollution and climate change, predominantly driven by industrialised nations, disproportionately burden developing countries such as Bangladesh with adverse consequences. This issue has been extensively explored by Bangladeshi business academicians in various electronic journals, highlighting the inequities and challenges faced by the nation.

It is observed that few comprehensive studies highlight the EA practices and their adequacy in the context of Bangladesh. Available studies are based on environmental disclosure practices (Hossain, 2019). In the area of EA in Bangladesh, Rahman (1998) published an article on EA practices in Bangladesh. The main aim of his study is to examine the use of EA to consolidate environmental consideration into economic policymaking with special emphasis on checking the policy issues in a different setting based on environmental data. A study conducted by Belal (2000) on environmental reporting in developing countries. The study found that the maximum number of environmental reporting studies has emphasised developed countries, and on the other hand, there are a handful number of studies regarding developing countries. The study also illustrated that selected companies disclose only a limited number of environmental issues in their annual reports. Rahman and Muttakin (2005) disclosed that the practice of environmental accounting reporting (EAR) is done voluntarily by a few listed corporate companies in Bangladesh. The disclosure level of environmental issues was limited to descriptive information and quantification was also poor. EAR-related problems are also mentioned and put forward some suggestions to remove the same problems in the corporate sector. Shil and Iqbal (2005) conducted another study on environmental disclosure, which is also remarkable. According to the study, the practices of EAR have not been a broad concept in the related companies. In Bangladesh, disclosure of environmental issues is still at a primary stage, as mentioned in the study. Bose (2006) examined a study on EAR in the fossil fuel sector, and this study expressed that Petrobangla takes a significant environment-friendly initiative to provide green energy in the economy. Bose (2006) and Shil and Iqbal (2005) also indicated that industrial activities are viewed increasingly today as accountable for their social and environmental impact. It is common to believe that environmental impacts are significant in industrial sectors, so for sustainable development, economic valuation, accounting and reporting are carrying a huge weight.

Dutta and Bose (2008) showed that web-based environmental reporting is still at the foundation level in Bangladesh as the disclosure practice of environmental issues on corporate websites is not significant. This paper can add new knowledge to EA (Hossain, 2019). Roy and Jewel (2009) mentioned that initiatives such as EA and reporting of business houses could indirectly play a great role in checking pollution resulting from industrial effluents. The study has deliberately investigated the current law for EA and the implications of the preparation of annual reports by the industrial and corporate houses. The business houses disclose an insufficient amount of environmental information voluntarily as a part of their publicity and little implication has been found. Ali et al. (2010) pointed out the EA nature in Bangladesh and the presentation procedure of the effect of company activities on the environment. They mentioned that in Bangladesh, the practice for environmental costs treatment and benefits in the financial statements of several companies' annual reports has not yet been developed. The authors recommended that the business companies of Bangladesh have to pay attention to the disclosure of costs and benefits related to the environment in their annual reports. In the Bangladeshi banking sector, environmental-related information like 'Green Banking' and 'Renewable Energy' is expressed mostly in the annual report but disclosed the least waste management or environmental recognition (Masud et al., 2017). The stakeholders of banks can get environmental information in various sections like the table of contents or index, a message from the company's chairman or director, footnote, notes and explanation section in the annual report but the study of Masud et al. (2017) showed that a significant portion of banks disclosed environment-related information through a separate section in the annual reports. Regarding the issue of the significance of EA in reporting practice, Ahmad (2012) stated that in the annual reports on expenditure on environmental energy, disclosures in the form of expenditure on energy, waste management costs and safety-related and environment protection costs were not remarkably presented. Though some major problems involved in EAR have been identified mentioned that the EAR practice is not satisfactory, in the real sense, the EAR term is poor. A paper published by Biswas and Rahaman (2011) checked whether the financial reporting standards of Bangladesh could be used for monitoring environmental degradation. In that paper, contemporary EA-related literature was examined and attempts to explore an obligatory reporting mechanism in EA. Both authors contributed to the strengths and weaknesses of Bangladesh's relevant financial reporting standards. Insufficient global reporting initiative guidelines and the private sector's self-regulation to monitor environmental disclosure were found in this study. The paper also proposed a separate statement of assets and liabilities related to the environment in this regard. Chowdhury and Hamid (2013) aimed to describe the current scenario of EA in the Bangladeshi corporate sector. The authors highlight that managers have the potential to shape environmental performance, underscoring the significant need for EA practices. However, in practice, the implementation of such practices remains limited. The study identifies a broad spectrum of obstacles that hinder the widespread adoption of corporate EA.

7. Learning Assessment of EA in Higher Business Studies

The interpretations of the above e-resources and other EA readings show that there are many strengths of this discourse in Bangladesh and mentionable weaknesses. In addition, various opportunities and threats are found and observed in this emerging field of EA. The SWOT analysis *(Strengths, Weaknesses, Opportunities, and Threats)* of EA at the tertiary business education level in Bangladesh is demonstrated here:

7.1 Strengths (S)

- EA has special dynamics and is also a modern field.
- Many universities (both public and private) have curricular in this field.
- Students have a good interest in this prospective field.
- The necessity of learning EA is increasing.
- The employment opportunity for business graduates has increased.
- Many universities have developed a link with industry to understand the real situation.
- Recently the government of Bangladesh has been emphasising the issue of the environment to different stakeholders, especially in the commercial and industrial sectors.
- The level of technology for exploring environmental deterioration has been improved and become handy.
- Both government and private sectors have increased their fund for the environmental sector.
- The human resource or capacity in EA is significant.

7.2 Weaknesses (W)

- Only a few academicians, particularly in the field of accountancy, have an interest in this field.
- As EA requires much integration, it costs time and money.
- Student requires fundamental knowledge of environmental pollution and harmful waste.
- Most of the curricular in this field are theoretical rather than empirical.
- Only a limited scope for field checking or orientation.

- Many universities have no link with industry as their (university) authorities do not recognise the importance of EA.
- There is a serious lack of information gap between the public and private sectors related to the environment.
- To recycle and take value from waste or prevent pollution old modelled technologies are used.
- Academicians often lack proper knowledge of environmental aspects and how they are connected to what is reflected in EA.

7.3 Opportunities (O)

- There is a high scope of training for amateur personnel in EA.
- The present global situation of EA, such as syllabus, teaching tools and techniques, can be applied to tertiary business education in Bangladesh.
- The EA prospects in the academic arena of Bangladesh are very bright because the government has recognised the 3R *(Reduce, Re-use and Recycle)* concept.
- High-tech equipment is increasing in different sectors of the environment in Bangladesh, especially in commerce and industry, which ultimately helps in the diverse field of EA.
- The possibilities of interaction between the public and private sectors in Bangladesh, including the educational sector, will increase in the future.
- There is a great scope for awareness building among the business students on EA.

7.4 Threats (T)

- The tertiary level education has a serious lack of funding which constraints the progress of the research in EA.
- The industry owners have a common tendency to skip the environmental information or components as a whole, which seriously disrupts the relationship between business students of EA and industrialists.
- The environment-related corresponding legislations for the industries are very reluctant.
- The government budget for introducing EA in the academic curricular of business education and implementing the syllabus for the betterment of the students is very little.
- The benefits that come from EA are not obtained immediately.

EA is not a well-recognised sub-discipline in the mother subject of accountancy in Bangladesh. In addition, it is not a much practised issue in the industrial setting of Bangladesh, where various environmental components are considered for assessment in financial terms. Shil and Iqbal (2005) classified the different contexts of EA practices into two classes at macroeconomic and microeconomic levels and termed as EA umbrella (see Appendix A). They opined that costs associated with natural resources (renewable or non-renewable resources) and the flow of goods and services of an economy are used in the national resources accounting and national income accounting respectively at the macroeconomic level. On the other hand, EA is used in financial accounting to disclose the environmental liabilities and costs and for internal decision-making purposes, such as material use and environmental operation costs, it is used in managerial accounting at the microeconomic level (Shil & Iqbal, 2005). Business academicians in Bangladeshi higher education institutions frequently engage in research by analysing corporate annual reports to assess the disclosure of financial information related to environmental issues. Despite the increasing global emphasis on EA, driven by its ecological, social and economic importance, Bangladeshi scholars in this domain have yet to fully achieve their research objectives. The quantification of environmental liabilities and costs remains challenging due to limited engagement from industrial stakeholders and the high costs associated with technologies required to measure environmental impacts. In this case, an ETP or hazardous waste management plant can be an example. All the causes mentioned above are hindering the progress of EA in Bangladesh among business academicians. However, proper and easy-going guidelines are needed to measure the environmental-related danger. To recapitulate, it can be said that a well-prepared financial statement on environmental liabilities, cost and good auditing can enlarge the opportunity of the new accounting system in the area of EA in Bangladesh among the academicians of higher business education. All the environmental or natural assets and environmental liabilities (both current and potential) should be considered in the financial statement to disclose the environmental issues.

8. Conclusion

The environment is a growing concern in the contemporary world. Every individual and business entity is really worried about the safety of the global environment. It is now a very common phenomenon that sustainable development is an ineffective attempt without proper accountability of natural resources (Rahman, 1998). There is a high necessity to develop EA education as an alternative approach to knowing the environment-related issues in higher business education in Bangladesh. Therefore, initiatives should be taken by the industry level (industrialists) business concerns and academicians for sustainable environmental conservation. EA information should be clear and specific as part of financial reporting. All related business authorities or social organisations should play an indispensable role in this connection. Finally, in EA, more research or comprehensive studies by business academicians are encouraged to make the world more liveable.

The availability of e-resources in EA is not very high among the academicians of Bangladesh. EA practice or EA concept-related resources is not much experienced like the concept of management accounting or cost accounting and other fields of accounting. Only a few academicians have contributed to this issue. The authors used secondary data only, and it would be better if the authors managed some primary data in this regard.

References

Ahmad, A. (2012). Environmental accounting and reporting practices: Significance and issues: A case from Bangladeshi companies. *Global Journal of Management and Business Research, 12*(14).

Alenezi, M., & Alanazi, F. (2024). Integrating environmental social and governance values into higher education curriculum. *International Journal of Evaluation and Research in Education, 13*(5), 3493–3503.

Ali, M. M., Rashid, M. M., & Islam, M. A. (2010). Environmental accounting and its applicability in Bangladesh. *ASA University Review, 4*(1), 23–37.

Ardillah, K. (2021, November). Environmental Accounting and reporting: Case study of Accounting education in Indonesia's universities that includes in qs World University Rankings. In *Proceedings of the 1st International Conference on Social Science, Humanities, Education and Society Development, ICONS 2020* (Vol. 30). 30 November, Tegal, Indonesia. Humanities, Education and Society Development.

Belal, A. R. (2000). Environmental reporting in developing countries: Empirical evidence from Bangladesh. *Eco-Management and Auditing: The Journal of Corporate Environmental Management*, 7(3), 114–121. https://doi.org/10.1002/1099-0925(200009)7:3<114::AID-EMA131>3.0.CO;2-E

Biswas, M. I., & Rahaman, M. M. (2011). Bangladesh financial reporting standard (BFRS) and environmental accounting: A case study of listed manufacturing companies in Bangladesh. *Journal of Business and Technology (Dhaka), VI*(02), 1–20. https://doi.org/10.3329/jbt.v6i2.14514

Bose, S. (2006). Environmental accounting and reporting in fossil fuel sector: A study on Bangladesh oil, gas and mineral corporation (Petrobangla). *Cost and Management, 34*(2), 53–67. https://mpra.ub.uni-muenchen.de/id/eprint/7995

Boyd, J. (1998). *The benefits of improved environmental accounting: An economic framework to identify priorities*. Discussion Paper. Resources for the Future.

Bracci, E., & Maran, L. (2013). Environmental management and regulation: Pitfalls of environmental accounting? *Management of Environmental Quality: An International Journal, 24*(4), 538–554.

Bramwell-Lalor, S., Kelly, K., Ferguson, T., Gentles, C. H., & Roofe, C. (2020). Project-based learning for environmental sustainability action. *Southern African journal of environmental education, 36*.

Chowdhury, M. A. A., & Hamid, M. K. (2013). Present status of corporate environmental accounting (CEA) in Bangladesh: A study based on some selected textile companies. *Research Journal of Finance and Accounting, 4*(17), 122–129.

Das, N., Sen, M., & Pattanayak, J. K. (2008). Assessment of students' perception towards developing a course in environmental accounting. *International Journal of Accounting and Information Management, 16*(2), 122–139.

Dutta, P., & Bose, S. (2008). Corporate environmental reporting on the internet in Bangladesh: An explanatory study. *International Review of Business Research Papers*, *4*(3), 138–150.

Hossain, M. M. (2019). Prospects of environmental accounting practices of selected manufacturing enterprises in Bangladesh. *Impact: International Journal of River Basin Management*, *7*(2), 39–54.

Hussain, M. D., Halim, M. S. B. A., & Bhuiyan, A. B. (2016). Environmental accounting and sustainable development: An empirical review. *International Journal of business and Technopreneurship*, *6*(2), 335–350.

Islam, M., & Dellaportas, S. (2011). Perceptions of corporate social and environmental accounting and reporting practices from accountants in Bangladesh. *Social Responsibility Journal*, *7*(4), 649–664.

Khalid, F. M., Lord, B. R., & Dixon, K. (2012). Environmental management accounting implementation in environmentally sensitive industries in Malaysia. Presented at *6th NZ Management Accounting Conference*, Palmerston North, 22-23, November 2012. https://ir.canterbury.ac.nz/server/api/core/bitstreams/ab6c86c6-39dc-49c3-ae69-0048bb8e59fe/content

Kokubu, A., Onishi, Y., Shinabe, T., & Nigashida, A. (2002). *An examination of corporate disclosure on environmental report publication and its quality in Japanese companies*. Kobe University.

Masud, M. A. K., Bae, S. M., & Kim, J. D. (2017). Analysis of environmental accounting and reporting practices of listed banking companies in Bangladesh. *Sustainability*, *9*(10). https://doi.org/10.3390/su9101717

Nations, U., & Fund, I. (2003). *Integrated environmental and economic accounting*. Studies in Methods-Handbook of National Accounting.

Pramanik, A. K., Shil, N. C., & Das, B. (2007). Environmental accounting and reporting with special reference to India. *The Journal of the Institute of Cost and Management Accountants of Bangladesh*, *35*(6), 16–28.

Rahman, A. (1998). Application of environmental accounting in Bangladesh. *Journal of International Affairs*, *4*(1).

Rahman, M., & Muttakin, M. (2005). Corporate environmental reporting practices in Bangladesh – A study of some selected companies. *Cost and Management*, *33* (4), 13–21.

Rahman, M. M., Rahman, M. S., & Deb, B. C. (2021). Competitive cost advantage: An application of environmental accounting and management approach with reference to Bangladesh. *Cost and Management*, *49*(3), 47–59.

Raju, K. (2018). Green accounting practices. *Indian Journal of Accounting (IJA)*, *50* (1), 59–68. https://indianaccounting.org/downloads/009 Dr. K.Kanaka Raju.pdf

Roy, M. L., & Jewel, M. H. (2009). Accounting for ecology and reporting in developing countries – A Bangladesh perspective. *Daffodil International University Journal of Business and Economics*, *4*(1 & 2), 107–119.

Sarkar, S. H., & Ahmed, R. (2020). Corporate environmental accounting disclosure in Bangladesh. *International Journal of Applied Business and Economic Research*, *18*(1), 39–53.

Serafy, S. El. (1997). Green accounting and economic policy. *Ecological Economics*, *21*(3), 217–229. https://doi.org/10.1016/S0921-8009(96)00107-3

Shakkour, A., Alaodat, H., Alqisi, E., & Alghazawi, A. (2018). The role of environmental accounting in sustainable development empirical study. *Journal of Applied Finance and Banking*, *8*(1), 71–87.

Shil, N. C., & Iqbal, M. (2005). Environmental disclosure- a Bangladesh perspective. *Cost and Management*, *33*(4), 85–93. https://mpra.ub.uni-muenchen.de/id/eprint/7707

Snyder, H. (2019). Literature review as a research methodology: An overview and guidelines. *Journal of Business Research*, *104*, 333–339.

Sultana, R. (2017). "Application of environmental accounting reporting practices and problems regarding the presentation of it in Bangladesh" (A case study on fossil-fuel sector). *European Scientific Journal*, *13*(2), 348–361. https://doi.org/10.19044/esj.2016.v13n2p348

Sultana, S., Paul, A., & Podder, S. (2023). Analysing cost accounting standards, practices and implementations: A study on some selective manufacturing companies of Bangladesh. *Asian Journal of Accounting Perspectives*, 75–96.

Sundarasen, S., Rajagopalan, U., & Alsmady, A. A. (2024). Environmental accounting and sustainability: A meta-synthesis. *Sustainability*, *16*(21), 9341.

Uzorka, A., Akiyode, O., & Isa, S. M. (2024). Strategies for engaging students in sustainability initiatives and fostering a sense of ownership and responsibility towards sustainable development. *Discover Sustainability*, *5*(1), 320.

Zulkifli, N. (2011). Social and environmental accounting education and sustainability: Educators' perspective. *Journal of Social Sciences*, *7*(1), 76–89.

Appendix A

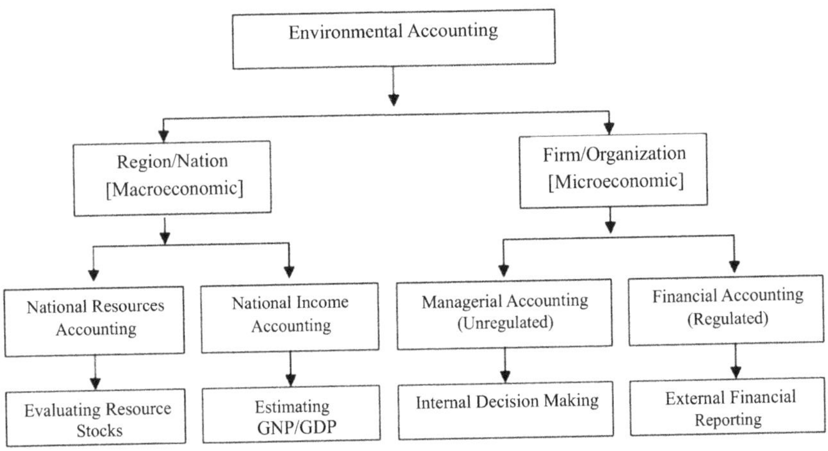

Environmental Accounting Umbrella (Shil & Iqbal, 2005)

Chapter 5

Integrating Modern Slavery Into Accounting Education

Asuman Atik

Marmara University, Türkiye

Abstract

The growing importance and widespread adoption of non-financial reporting have led accountants to take on new responsibilities. They must improve their abilities, knowledge and wisdom to collect, analyse and present non-financial information. The modern slavery report is the latest non-financial report and is becoming widespread due to the Modern Slavery Act of the United Kingdom (2015) and Australia (2018). The responsibilities of accountants in the preparation of modern slavery reports also give them essential roles in eradicating modern slavery. These recent developments underscore the need to incorporate modern slavery topics into accounting education. The main objective of this chapter is to discuss the importance and challenges of integrating modern slavery topics into the accounting curriculum. The discussions are based on the author's teaching experiences and insights from research conducted with accounting students.

Keywords: Modern slavery; accounting education; accounting; SDGs; modern slavery reports

1. Introduction

Environmental accounting and social externalities appeared in accounting books in the early 1970s. As investors and other stakeholders became more interested in sustainability issues, demand for non-financial reporting continued to grow. Over the past few decades, the number of articles on sustainability reporting, integrated reports and corporate social responsibility (CSR) has steadily increased in the accounting literature.

Sustainability in Accounting and Finance Education, 81–94

Published under exclusive licence by Emerald Publishing Limited
doi:10.1108/978-1-80686-393-820261005

The United Nations (UN) focused on the Sustainable Development Goals (SDGs) to build a better future for all and aimed to achieve them by 2030. Goal 8.7 includes issues related to modern slavery and 'calls on all to take immediate and effective measures to eradicate forced labor, end modern slavery and human trafficking and secure the prohibition and elimination of all forms of child labor' (United Nations, 2015). Parallel to the SDGs, many countries began taking action against modern slavery and passed laws (Burritt & Christ, 2023; Guix & Lotfi, 2025).

Companies that meet the laws' criteria must prepare modern slavery reports, but many others also choose to do so voluntarily. The European Union's (EU's) non-financial reporting directives might accelerate the global spread of mandatory modern slavery reporting. These developments make integrating modern slavery topics into accounting education crucial to better preparing accounting students for their careers.

This study aims to discuss how to integrate modern slavery into accounting curricula and the challenges that accompany this integration. These discussions are based on the author's teaching experiences in undergraduate and doctoral accounting courses, as well as on the results of a survey designed to explore accounting students' views on integrating modern slavery into accounting education.

The following part explains the methodology. The third part summarises the related literature. The paper continues with the parts explaining 'modern slavery', 'the role of accountants in eradicating it' and 'integrating modern slavery into accounting education'. The last part presents the concluding remarks.

2. Methodology

To achieve the study's objectives, a literature review was conducted first, using the keywords "modern slavery" and 'accounting education'. The review identified only one article on integrating modern slavery into accounting curricula, by Gheorghiu (2019). Since modern slavery is under social sustainability, the literature search was broadened to encompass studies on integrating 'sustainability', 'social sustainability', 'justice' and 'human rights' into accounting education.

The author assigned articles from the modern slavery accounting research literature to students in the doctoral course Empirical Research in Accounting in the fall semesters of 2021 and 2022. Before the students read the articles, the author requested them to share their personal experiences about modern slavery. The author observed the students' awareness and interest in modern slavery topics before, after and in the following weeks, following discussions of the assigned articles.

In the spring semester of 2022, the author lectured on modern slavery from an accounting perspective in one session of an undergraduate-level accounting course. She also surveyed 84 undergraduate business administration students about modern slavery in that special session. The survey aimed to determine who students hold responsible for ending modern slavery, which types of modern slavery they believe exist in Türkiye and their views on the necessity and usefulness of integrating modern slavery issues into accounting courses. Table 5.1 summarises the research process.

3. Literature Review

Gheorghiu (2019) criticises traditional teaching methods, stating that they create followers rather than leaders and stresses the importance of an affirmative connection between practice and critical thinking. Focusing on modern slavery allows students to reflect critically and enhances their awareness of its potential implications (Gheorghiu, 2019).

The deans and administrators of top business schools are promoting the inclusion of sustainability, ethics and social responsibility in functional business courses, such as accounting, to offer a comprehensive view of the economy, politics and society (Sisaye, 2013).

Al-Hazaima et al. (2021) analysed the views of various parties, including accounting educators, accounting students and government representatives. They concluded that all parties agree on the importance and necessity of integrating sustainability into the accounting curriculum in Jordanian universities. After an extensive literature review, Cho and Costa (2024) express the importance of sustainability accounting education in transforming future accountants. Incorporating the SDGs and sustainability accounting education into the curriculum equips future accountants and professionals with the knowledge and expertise to achieve these goals and create a more sustainable world. Integrating topics about human social and environmental behaviours can potentially transform society. Education in sustainability accounting can help shift a society from capitalism towards a more democratic and inclusive framework (Cho & Costa, 2024). Professional accounting bodies are also supporting sustainability

Table 5.1. Summary of the Research

Course	Semester	Number of Students	Method of Integrating Modern Slavery into the Course	Data Collection
8020 Empirical research in accounting	Fall 2021	4	Assignment of case study articles	Discussion and observation
8020 Empirical research in accounting	Fall 2022	3	Assignment of case study articles	Discussion and observation
3042 Managerial accounting	Spring 2022	84	Lecture (one session)	Survey and discussion

accounting education (Al-Hazaima et al., 2021; Cho & Costa, 2024; Sharma & Stewart, 2022).

Sharma and Stewart (2022) say that accounting course lecturers at Delta Business School prefer integrating sustainability topics into their syllabi rather than offering them as separate courses, because this approach may help students recognise sustainability as an essential aspect of accounting. However, the lack of coordination among course contents leads students to perceive significant repetition, and in some cases, sustainability topics are not covered in depth. The participants in Al-Hazamia et al.'s (2021, p. 384) survey also strongly agreed on the importance of 'including sustainability accounting topics in existing accounting courses and lectures'.

According to Cho and Costa (2024), there is an urgent need for more technical courses in sustainability accounting and management. These courses should not only cover theories, concepts, frameworks, standards and principles, but also practical exercises and quantitative case studies involving cost calculations and assessments. This approach will enable students to apply these techniques and skills more effectively, enhancing their competitiveness in the sustainability job market. They also highlight the importance of the new pedagogies that consider the psychological dimension of education. They propose a transformative approach where the teacher is seen as a facilitator rather than an expert or content provider.

Björnberg et al. (2015) explored how social sustainability can be integrated into the curriculum and found that offering sustainability training for instructors and using role-play as an educational tool are essential for successfully incorporating social sustainability into teaching. Similarly, Sharma and Stewart (2022) recommended role-playing activities in which students assume the roles of managers, shareholders or other stakeholders concerned about a hypothetical company's sustainability policies.

Case studies in accounting education serve as a valuable tool for fostering critical thinking (Kimmel, 1995). Case-based teaching helps students meet learning objectives in knowledge and professional skills related to sustainable development (Prado et al., 2020). Tran and Herzig (2023) explored how a blended case-based learning approach can enhance students' learning towards accounting for sustainability. Alawattage and Wickramasinghe (2024) explored why current management accounting teaching limits consideration of social and ecological justice and how these values can be integrated into the Strategic Management Accounting (SMA) curriculum.

4. Modern Slavery – From History to the Present

Throughout human history, slavery has constituted one of the most pervasive institutions from ancient times to the present day. It has manifested in various forms; the buying and selling of individuals, as well as the inheritance of human beings, represent the most critical aspects of slavery. Greece and Rome were the first societies where slavery emerged. It evolved independently in America, Africa and Asia (Bradley & Cartledge, 2011).

Although slavery is technically regarded as a crime under international law, it persists as a viable and profitable management practice for businesses. It continues to be viewed as a logical consequence of structuring the political economic system and its historical roots in colonial enterprises (Banerjee, 2020). Although there is no generally accepted definition of modern slavery, Mende (2019) determines three important parts of it: (1) 'the control of a person over another', (2) 'an involuntary aspect in their relation', and (3) 'the element of exploitation' (p. 233).

According to the latest report of the International Labour Organisation, Walk Free and the International Organisation for Migration (2022), 'modern slavery is comprised of two principal components – forced labor and forced marriage. Both refer to situations of exploitation that a person cannot refuse or cannot leave because of threats, violence, deception, abuse of power, or other forms of coercion' (p. 2). In this report, it is mentioned that due to crises worldwide, such as wars, COVID-19 and environmental issues, the estimated risk of modern slavery has increased sharply. People who have faced worsening conditions regarding education, poverty and violence were forced to migrate, and they are now in situations of greater vulnerability. This report also mentions that 'there are 50 million people in situations of modern slavery on any given day, either forced to work against their will or in a marriage that they were forced into (p. 1)'. These numbers are truly tragic and indicate that modern slavery is much more widespread and worse than we can imagine.

Some authors included working under unsafe conditions, working extremely long hours and unfair wages in the definition of modern slavery. For example, Caruana et al. (2021) included the act of forcing individuals to work under poor conditions through threats and coercion, and Lashley (2018, p. 6) employed the term 'neo-slavery' to describe scenarios where workers are formally free yet 'face restricted chances to oppose exploitation due to poverty and consistent unemployment'.

In recent years, Türkiye has been experiencing a massive influx of migrants from Syria, Afghanistan and neighbouring countries. The Ministry of Internal Affairs announced that Türkiye hosts 4,6 million refugees (BBC News Türkçe, 2023). A massive number of refugees, high inflation rates and high unemployment rates create a suitable environment for modern slavery in Türkiye. Especially on social media, there is news and tweets about brutal working conditions, extremely low wages (especially for the refugees without work permission) and slavery-like practices of employers.

As mentioned previously, the survey questionnaire included questions to gauge participants' opinions on the existence of modern slavery. Table 5.2 summarises respondents' views on modern slavery in Türkiye. Eighty-four students participated in the survey, and all of the participants think that modern slavery exists in Türkiye. The respondents could mark more than one item provided in the questionnaire. All items got high scores. Two students filled in the 'other (specify)' part and wrote that working for minimum wage is also an example of modern slavery.

5. The Role of Accountants in Eradicating Modern Slavery

The literature highlights how individuals often hesitate to assume responsibility in fighting modern slavery. Stevenson (2022) notes that when witnesses share responsibility, they usually expect others to take action. In particular, government and legal authorities are viewed as the main parties responsible for eradicating modern slavery (Ishaya et al., 2024; Smith & Johns, 2020).

On the other hand, researchers from various study areas strive to develop strategies and methods to eradicate modern slavery. Some researchers assign responsibility to big multinational companies, especially for abolishing slavery in their supply chains, while others focus on consumer responsibilities and on demand and supply conditions. Consumers, who want to buy more products at cheaper prices, and companies, that try to cut prices and consequently costs, are like the gears of a wheel in causing modern slavery. Internal management controls and external audits from stakeholders (e.g., governments, civil society

Table 5.2. The Respondents' Views About the Existence of Modern Slavery in Türkiye

	Yes	No
Do you think there is modern slavery in Türkiye?	84	0
If you answer yes, which of the following do you think exists in Türkiye? (You can mark more than one.)		
Making workers work long hours.	79	
Paying workers less than minimum wage.	79	
Making immigrants who don't have work permits work for very low wages and without insurance.	79	
Making workers work under bad conditions.	78	
Making workers work without taking safety measures.	77	
Employing child labour.	70	
Sex slavery.	65	
Buying and selling people for their organs.	56	
Confiscating foreign home workers' passports and forcing them to do housework.	50	
Other (specify): Two respondents mentioned 'working for minimum wage'.		

organisations, communities and trade unions) can help businesses end modern slavery in their supply chains (Burritt & Christ, 2023).

Accounting research is one field that focuses on the role of accounting and accountants in the fight against modern slavery. Sharma and Stewart (2022, p. 631) state that accountants' roles are shifting 'from being concerned only with the stewardship of financial capital to becoming custodians, guardians and agents of the wider public interest, including environmental and social concerns'. Accounting is crucial in the public interest by enabling economic activities, driving development and improving decision-making for accountable and effective public and private leaders (Othman & Ameer, 2024).

The reporting and auditing functions of accounting have also been stressed following the recent modern slavery legislation. Modern slavery reports that provide information about the country, industry, culture and the acceptance of modern slavery as a common business practice inform stakeholders about the risks associated with modern slavery in the supply chain (Christ & Burritt, 2020). Direct observation of modern slavery is often impossible or extremely difficult. In response, Christ and Burritt (2020) propose three types of supply chain audits: internal operations assurance, supplier audits and independent assurance. Accountants generally conduct these audits.

Enterprises seeking to establish business relationships with other organisations should review these reports before deciding whether to proceed with such engagements. This practice diminishes business opportunities for companies that exhibit a heightened risk of modern slavery within their operational frameworks. Consequently, the financial resources allocated to them are decreased, potentially leading to the end of their operations.

The survey questionnaire included a question asking students who they perceived as responsible for ending modern slavery. The respondents believe that state administrators are primarily responsible for eradicating it. Only nine respondents think that accounting professionals are responsible for preventing modern slavery. Table 5.3 summarises respondents' views on the responsible parties for eliminating modern slavery in Türkiye.

Table 5.3. The Respondents' Views Regarding the Accountable Parties to Eradicate Modern Slavery in Türkiye

Whose Responsibility is Preventing Slavery? (You Can Mark More Than One)	
State administrators	81
Government agencies	69
Society	50
Private companies	36
Accounting professionals	9

6. Integrating Modern Slavery Into Accounting Curriculum

6.1 Teaching Experiences and the Results of the Final Section of the Survey

I assigned the studies of Siddiqui et al. (2020) and Flynn and Walker (2021) to doctoral students. Siddiqui et al. (2020) explained the Rana Plaza Case, which describes thousands of people who were working like slaves in an old building and lost their lives when the building collapsed. Flynn and Walker (2021) conducted a content analysis of modern slavery reports and examined how firms respond to modern slavery risks in their supply chains.

Before studying and discussing these papers, I tried to understand the students' awareness of modern slavery. They were unaware of the recent developments. I asked about slavery-like situations around them; they didn't answer. Only one student mentioned construction workers working in extremely hot weather. She said this is the fate of the workers. After studying the articles, she changed her mind and no longer accepted this situation as fate. Instead, she wanted to learn how to change it.

Increased awareness about modern slavery has changed all students' understanding of the issue. During the latter part of the semester, they mentioned their increased interest in slavery-like events and news on conventional and social media. At the end of the semester, I asked the students which articles and subjects affected them the most; all pointed to the Rana Plaza Case and modern slavery, as these subjects are life-and-death matters.

In the undergraduate-level course, I lectured on modern slavery. It was a one-session lecture that covered slavery in history, the Modern Slavery legislation, the format and contents of Modern Slavery Reports, and how these recent developments may impact the accounting profession and the roles of accountants and auditors. I benefited from the article by Siddiqui et al. (2020) when preparing the lecture materials, as it explains the victims' situations very well, thereby increasing students' empathy. It also includes the victories of stakeholders who persuaded government agencies and garment companies to take action against modern slavery, increasing the students' optimism. I also lectured about whistle-blowing, companies' hotlines and the state's hotline.

At the end of this session, the students completed the final section of the survey, and 54 of 84 answered 'agree' or 'strongly agree' to the statement 'I believe that modern slavery subjects should be integrated into accounting courses'. Additionally, 62 of 84 respondents agreed or strongly agreed with the statement 'I believe that integrating modern slavery subjects into accounting courses is useful'. Table 5.4 summarises the views of respondents about the necessity and usefulness of integrating modern slavery into accounting education.

The discussions following the survey and the feedback from the students have also revealed fruitful insights. Some of them mentioned that they couldn't connect accounting and modern slavery. Since they have focused on preparing and auditing financial reports, they found it challenging to classify modern slavery reports as the outcome of accounting information. One student who interned at

Table 5.4. The Respondents' Views Regarding the Necessity and Usefulness of Integrating Modern Slavery Into Accounting Education

I Believe That Modern Slavery Subjects Should Be Integrated Into Accounting Courses				
Strongly Disagree	*Disagree*	*Neither Agree nor Disagree*	*Agree*	*Strongly Agree*
6 (7.1%)	11 (13.1%)	13 (15.5%)	33 (39.3%)	21 (25%)
I Believe That Integrating Modern Slavery Subjects Into Accounting Courses is Useful				
Strongly Disagree	*Disagree*	*Neither Agree nor Disagree*	*Agree*	*Strongly Agree*
4 (4.8%)	9 (10.7%)	9 (10.7%)	29 (34.5%)	33 (39.3%)

an audit firm commented that auditors and interns work long hours and feel like slaves at audit firms. He posed a reasonable question: 'They can't save themselves, will they be able to save others?'

Another concern of students was about whistle-blowing. They don't trust companies' and even the state's promises regarding the confidentiality of hotline calls. As a result, some students mentioned that they would hesitate to call a hotline, even when necessary.

More students believe integrating modern slavery into accounting is more useful than necessary. This means they are interested in taking such a course but do not want it to be compulsory. After the survey, discussions clarified why students did not agree on the necessity and usefulness of integrating modern slavery into accounting education at higher percentages. A one-session intensive course did not help some of them clarify the relationship between modern slavery and accounting.

6.2 Suggestions Drawn From My Teaching Experience

At the undergraduate level, integrating and harmonising modern slavery topics with accounting subjects helps students (1) better understand the relevance of modern slavery to accounting and (2) better prepare them for their future jobs. Additionally, accounting textbooks have just started to include sustainability topics, but modern slavery has not yet been included in these resources. An accounting academic who wants to teach a one-term course on modern slavery and accounting may have difficulty finding adequate resources. Therefore, at the first stage, it is a good strategy for a lecturer to integrate modern slavery into the current syllabus of any accounting course, rather than lecturing on it as a stand-alone course.

Especially after the UK Modern Slavery Act and the Australian Modern Slavery Act, mandatory reporting of modern slavery has raised the necessity of including modern slavery reports in the accounting curriculum. Lecturers should teach *Modern Slavery Reports*. Because mandatory reporting is required only from big corporations, companies that plan to make voluntary reporting may prefer to continue to use the Global Reporting Initiative (GRI) standards. Teaching GRI standards may be beneficial. Burritt and Christ (2023) examine the GRI standards' compatibility with SDGs and the aim of eradicating modern slavery. They conclude that the GRI sustainability reporting standards do not address modern slavery directly, but rather provide standards on some components, such as child labour.

Cost and Managerial Accounting courses should include modern slavery, especially when teaching standard costing, incremental analysis (decisions on make or buy and eliminating a segment), labour and purchasing budgets and performance evaluation. Setting very high cost standards and budgets related to labour and making managerial decisions without considering the factors affecting workers' legal rights and human rights may create slavery-like situations. When teaching purchasing budget, purchasing from suppliers free from modern slavery should be emphasised. Sustainable balanced scorecards should include modern slavery items.

Auditing courses should include sessions on 'auditing for modern slavery', and students should learn to discover slavery-like situations. The case of Mr. Gielgud, who was wilfully blind to slavery (Walker, 2023), is a very interesting case study for class discussion.

As mentioned in the literature review, *case studies* are very important and useful tools for teaching modern slavery, especially when teaching industries that are more prone to slavery, such as, garment (Begum & Solaiman, 2016; Siddiqui et al., 2020), construction (Alzoubi et al., 2023), mining (Bansal et al., 2023), tourism (Guix & Lotfi, 2025), domestic workers (Diab, 2022), global supply chains (Ishaya et al., 2024), information technology (Jones & Comfort, 2023) and fashion industry (Lusty & Richards, 2024).

Lecturers of *Accounting Theory* should link voluntary modern slavery reporting to legitimacy and institutional theories. In his valuable book, Deegan (2014) establishes the connection between these theories and sustainability.

Critical thinking skills of accounting students should be improved; they should be able to evaluate modern slavery situations from different perspectives before taking action. The possibility of harming themselves alongside the modern slaves should not be forgotten. Students who learn about modern slavery may feel stressed and under pressure because of the difficulty of the topic itself. Gheorghiu (2019, p. 8) mentions reflexive practices that can be very useful in teaching modern slavery and that 'emerge using guided experiential learning, dialogue, and discussion, not teaching'. On the other hand, 'this method of learning can be achieved by releasing upsetting emotions and leaving students feeling vulnerable'.

6.3 The Challenges Accounting Instructors May Face

Teaching modern slavery is very challenging due to its complex nature. Each modern slavery case has unique characteristics and generally includes illegal activities, crimes and criminals. The steps taken to help victims may worsen the situation or cause harm to the helper as well. Providing effective guidance to students to evaluate situations from various perspectives and think critically is difficult, especially given the limited teaching materials and resources.

Moreover, understanding modern slavery alone is insufficient for prevention. Students may become perplexed and anxious when considering the possibility of encountering a case of modern slavery in reality. They often ask, 'If I encounter such a case, what actions should I take? What can be done?' If the instructor fails to deliver satisfactory responses, students might lose interest and motivation for the course.

Lastly, lecturers need to develop their teaching materials, which can be complicated and time-consuming.

7. Conclusion

As human beings' cognitive and emotional development and the acceptance of global ethical standards advance, steps are being taken to prevent slavery. The general trend is always to seek out who, other than ourselves, can be instrumental in ending it. However, we must take responsibility and consider what we can do, as individuals, citizens, parents, consumers, instructors, students and accountants, to eradicate it.

Accountants have historically played important roles related to slavery; for example, they documented slaves as assets and expenses. Today, their roles have evolved. Their new responsibilities include external reporting on modern slavery, internal management accounting to raise awareness and aid in planning to mitigate modern slavery risks, and audit and assurance (Christ et al., 2023).

These new responsibilities call on accounting educators to take action and integrate modern slavery topics into their curricula. Modern slavery continues to have substance because it has many roots, such as regional clustering, legitimacy, labour intensity, poverty, education, awareness, traditions, religious beliefs and governance (Crane, 2013). Multiple fights should be started to weaken it. Education is one of the most important arenas.

This study aims to guide accounting lecturers and make some suggestions. The author shares the knowledge gained from experiences lecturing on modern slavery topics to undergraduate and doctoral students. The survey insights have also been presented. Students think that modern slavery is widespread in Türkiye, and the government and state authorities have the most significant responsibility to eradicate it. Most of them agree on the necessity and usefulness of accounting courses covering modern slavery.

This study also highlights the significant and urgent need for teaching materials and research on curriculum planning regarding integrating modern slavery into accounting education.

References

Alawattage, C., & Wickramasinghe, D. (2024, September 18). Teaching strategic management accounting with sustainability. *Accounting Education*. https://doi.org/10.1080/09639284.2024.2404923

Al-Hazaima, H., Low, M., & Sharma, U. (2021). Perceptions of salient stakeholders on the integration of sustainability education into the accounting curriculum: A Jordanian study. *Meditari Accountancy Research*, *29*(2), 371–402. https://doi.org/10.1108/MEDAR-02-2020-0708

Alzoubi, Y., Locatelli, G., & Sainati, T. (2023, October 29). The ugly side of construction: Modern slavery in the 2022 FIFA World Cup program. *Construction Management & Economics*. https://doi.org/10.1080/01446193.2023.2269434

Banerjee, B. (2020). Modern slavery is an enabling condition of global neoliberal capitalism: Commentary on modern slavery in business. *Business and Society*, *60*(2), 415–419.

Bansal, V., Wallach, J., Lira Brandão, J., Lord, S., Taha, N., Akoglu, T., Kiss, L., & Zimmerman, C. (2023). An intervention-focused review of modern slave labor in Brazil's mining sector. *World Development*, *171*, 106362. https://doi.org/10.1016/j.worlddev.2023.106362

BBC News Türkçe. (2023, November 9). https://www.bbc.com/turkce/articles/c1e29v09d3eo. Accessed on December 9, 2023.

Begum, A., & Solaiman, S. M. (2016). Rana disaster: How far can we proceed with CSR? *Journal of Financial Crime*, *23*(4), 748–768.

Björnberg, E. K., Skogh, I.-B., & Strömberg, E. (2015). Integrating social sustainability in engineering education at the KTH Royal Institute of Technology. *International Journal of Sustainability in Higher Education*, *16*(5), 639–649. https://doi.org/10.1108/IJSHE-01-2014-0010

Bradley, K. & Cartledge, P. (Eds.). (2011). *The Cambridge World History of Slavery. Volume 1. The Ancient Mediterranean World*. Cambridge University Press.

Burritt, R. L., & Christ, K. L. (2023). Modern slavery and the Global Reporting Initiative – A bridge too far? *Business Strategy and Development*, *6*(3), 296–309.

Caruana, R., Crane, A., Gold, S., & G. Lebaron, G. (2021). Modern slavery in business: The sad and sorry state of a non-field. *Business & Society*, *60*(2), 251–287.

Cho, C. H., & Costa, E. (2024). Sustainability accounting education: Challenges and outlook. *International Journal of Sustainability in Higher Education*, *25*(7), 1412–1425. https://doi.org/10.1108/IJSHE-02-2024-0152

Christ, K., & Burritt, R. (2020). *Modern slavery compass: A new tool to point business in the right direction*. CPA Australia.

Christ, K. L., Burritt, R. L., & Islam, M. A. (2023). Modern slavery and the accounting profession. *The British Accounting Review*, *55*(3). https://doi.org/10.1016/j.bar.2023.101174

Crane, A. (2013). Modern slavery as a management practice: Exploring the conditions and capabilities for human exploitation. *Advances in Magnetic Resonance*, *38*, 49–69. https://doi.org/10.5465/amr.2011.0145

Deegan, C. (2014). *Financial accounting theory*. McGraw-Hill Education.

Diab, A. (2022). Modern slavery, accountability and technology: Evidence from a West Asian Contex. *Journal of Accounting in Emerging Economies*, *12*(5), 908–933.

Flynn, A., & Walker, H. (2021). Corporate responses to modern slavery risks: An institutional theory perspective. *European Business Review*, *33*(2), 295–315.

Gheorghiu, L. (2019). Reflexive practices: Making business schools more 'critical' by teaching modern slavery. Practical workshop. In *The Asian Conference on Education Official Conference Proceedings*. Aston University.

Guix, M., & Lotfi, M. (2025). Doing the right thing? The hotel industry's management of, and reporting on, modern slavery. *Tourism Management*, *107*, 105084. https://doi.org/10.1016/j.tourman.2024.105084

International Labour Organization, Walk Free and the International Organization for Migration. (2022, September). *Global estimates of modern slavery forced labour and forced marriage executive summary*. https://www.ilo.org/sites/default/files/wcmsp5/groups/public/%40ed_norm/%40ipec/documents/publication/wcms_854795.pdf. Accessed on April 4, 2025.

Ishaya, B. J., Paraskevadakis, D., Bury, A., & Bryde, D. (2024). A systematic literature review of modern slavery through benchmarking global supply chain. *Benchmarking: An International Journal*, *31*(2), 558–589. https://doi.org/10.1108/BIJ-09-2022-0554

Jones, P., & Comfort, D. (2023). A review of the leading information technology companies' modern slavery statements. *Athens journal of business & economics*, *9*(1), 59–72.

Kimmel, P. (1995). A framework for incorporating critical thinking into accounting education. *Journal of Accounting Education*, *13*(3), 299–318.

Lashley, C. (2018). Slavery, neo-slavery and business ethics. *Research in Hospitality Management*, *8*(1), 5–10. https://doi.org/10.1080/22243534.2018.1501175

Lusty, N., & Richards, H. (2024). Modern slavery legislation and the limits of ethical fashion. *Cultural Studies*, *38*(2), 322–347. https://doi.org/10.1080/09502386.2022.2103165

Mende, J. (2019). The concept of modern slavery: Definition, critique, and the human rights frame. *Human Rights Review*, *20*, 229–248. https://doi.org/10.1007/s12142-018-0538-y

Othman, R., & Ameer, R. (2024). Rethinking accounting education for a sustainable future: Charting a course for sustainable development goals 2030. *Meditari Accountancy Research*, *32*(5), 1809–1836.

Prado, A. M., Arce, R., Lopez, L. E., García, J., & Pearson, A. A. (2020). Simulations versus case studies: Effectively teaching the premises of sustainable development in the classroom. *Journal of Business Ethics*, *161*(2), 303–327.

Sharma, U., & Stewart, B. (2022). Enhancing sustainability education in the accounting curriculum: An effective learning strategy. *Pacific Accounting Review*, *34*(4), 614–633. https://doi.org/10.1108/PAR-02-2021-0029

Siddiqui, J., McPhail, K., & Rahman, S. S. (2020). Private governance responsibilisation in global supply chains: The case of Rana Plaza. *Accounting, Auditing and Accountability Journal*, *33*(7), 1569–1594.

Sisaye, S. (2013). The development of sustainable practices in complex organizations: Implications and potentials for integration into the accounting curriculum. *World Journal of Entrepreneurship, Management and Sustainable Development*, *9*(4), 223–245. https://doi.org/10.1108/WJEMSD-01-2013-0010

Smith, A., & Johns, J. (2020). Historicizing modern slavery: Free-grown sugar as an ethics-driven market category in nineteenth-century Britain. *Journal of Business Ethics*, *166*, 271–292.

Stevenson, M. (2022). Hidden in plain sight: The bystander effect and the mobilisation of modern slavery whistleblowing. *Supply Chain Management: An International Journal*, *27*(1), 128–139. https://doi.org/10.1108/SCM-08-2020-0373

Tran, T. T., & Herzig, C. (2023). Blended case-based learning in a sustainability accounting course: An analysis of student perspectives. *Journal of Accounting Education*, *63*, 100842. https://doi.org/10.1016/j.jaccedu.2023.100842

United Nations. (2015). *The SDGs in action*. United Nations.

Walker, S. P. (2023). The blindfold witness? An Accountant's response to slavery and atrocity in the Devil's paradise. *The British Accounting Review*, *55*, 101068.

Chapter 6

Behavioural Change in Sustainable Accounting Education: A Gamification-Based Approach

Hrishikesh Desai

Arkansas State University, USA

Abstract

The integration of sustainability into accounting education is important for preparing future professionals to address global challenges, yet promoting enduring behavioural change in students and professionals remains elusive. This study develops a novel analytical framework to investigate how gamification, which is grounded in behavioural economics and network theory, can drive sustained adoption of sustainable practices. The model developed in this study quantifies student engagement through a utility function that includes intrinsic motivation, extrinsic incentives, social influence, effort and introduces a network-based system to simulate peer interactions. A reward system and fatigue function are also included to capture diminishing returns and temporal declines in engagement. Numerical experiments across small world, scale free and random networks reveal distinct engagement dynamics. Small world topologies optimise engagement diffusion due to efficient peer influence, while scale free networks risk polarisation if hubs (influential learners) disengage. Threshold effects, modelled via sigmoid activation, demonstrate that minor interventions (e.g., lowering effort barriers) can trigger nonlinear behavioural shifts. Fatigue-induced declines highlight the necessity of periodic reinforcements. Key practical insights for accounting educators include structuring classrooms as small world networks, incentivising early adopters, front loading rewards and rotating gamification elements to combat fatigue. The study bridges gaps in domain-specific gamification research and provides a validated, computational approach to sustainability education.

Sustainability in Accounting and Finance Education, 95–107

doi:10.1108/978-1-80686-393-820261006

Keywords: Gamification; sustainability education; network theory; behavioural economics; accounting pedagogy; learning fatigue

1. Introduction and Theory

The integration of sustainability in accounting education has been considered indispensable for preparing future business leaders (Othman & Ameer, 2024). However, promoting behavioural change among students and shifting them from passive learners to active adopters of sustainable practices, remains a challenge. Gamification and behavioural incentives have emerged as effective tools to promote engagement and adoption of sustainable practices (Lim et al., 2025; Mulcahy et al., 2021; Shahzad et al., 2023), but existing frameworks often overlook the role of social networks and long-term motivation in educational contexts. This study addresses these gaps by developing an analytical model that integrates behavioural economics, network theory and game theory to systematically analyse how reward systems and peer interactions drive sustainable behaviour adoption. Numerical experiments validate the framework and provide important insights for optimising gamification strategies in sustainability-focused accounting education.

Gamification strategies, including leaderboards, badges and point systems, have shown promise in increasing student engagement (Bouchrika et al., 2021; da Rocha Seixas et al., 2016; Rivera & Garden, 2021). They use extrinsic rewards to stimulate short-term behavioural changes, often aligning with principles of operant conditioning and self-determination theory (Hammerschall, 2019; Lewis et al., 2016). However, while the broader educational literature highlights the efficacy of gamification, its application to sustainability-focused accounting education remains underexplored (Silva et al., 2021). This gap is important, as sustainability education demands not only transient engagement but also enduring behavioural shifts towards ethical decision-making and resource-conscious practices, a challenge compounded by the abstract nature of sustainability concepts in accounting curricula.

Most gamification studies focus on general educational outcomes (e.g., course completion rates, quiz scores) rather than domain-specific behavioural changes (Sanchez et al., 2020). In accounting education, where sustainability intersects with technical skill development, the lack of tailored frameworks limits the translation of engagement into actionable sustainable practices (Othman & Ameer, 2024).

While social influence is recognised as a driver of behaviour, few models incorporate network-based interactions to explain how peer norms and competitive dynamics propagate student engagement. Traditional approaches treat students as isolated agents and overlook the role of classroom networks in increasing or stifling sustainable behaviours (Moolenaar, 2012; Wang et al., 2024). Extant research also emphasises initial engagement spikes from rewards, but fails to address sustained motivation. The diminishing returns of extrinsic incentives and the onset of learning fatigue is important to long-term behavioural adoption and rarely modelled quantitatively (Lewis et al., 2016; Mulcahy et al., 2021).

To address these gaps, this study synthesises insights from behavioural economics, network theory and gamification design into a unified analytical framework. The analytical model reveals that sustained engagement in sustainability education hinges on balancing intrinsic motivation, peer influence and adaptive reward systems. Numerical experiments demonstrate that small world networks, characterised by clustered local groups and sparse global connections, optimise engagement diffusion and achieve stable equilibria, even amid fatigue-induced declines. Threshold effects, modelled via sigmoid activation, highlight how minor interventions (e.g., lowering effort barriers) can trigger nonlinear behavioural shifts in learners, while scale free networks risk polarisation if key influencers disengage. For educators, these findings translate to actionable strategies: structuring classrooms as small world networks, front loading rewards to capitalise on early engagement spikes and introducing periodic reinforcements to counteract diminishing motivation. Thus, by aligning gamification design with network dynamics and behavioural thresholds, this framework equips educators to transform transient participation in sustainability education into enduring sustainable practices.

2. Analytical Model

2.1 Student Motivation for Sustainable Practices

In this section, I present a formalised theoretical model that quantifies student engagement, motivation and behavioural change in response to gamification elements. The model is structured around three core components, namely, the behavioural utility function, the gamification reward system and the social dynamics of competition. These elements collectively provide a mathematical foundation to examine how students respond to gamification strategies in sustainability education.

To assess the effectiveness of gamification strategies, I define a behavioural utility function U, which represents the overall motivation of a student to engage in sustainable accounting practices. The function is constructed as follows:

$$U = \alpha M + \beta I + \gamma S - \delta E$$

Where, M denotes intrinsic motivation that captures personal satisfaction, curiosity and interest in sustainability topics; I represents extrinsic incentives, which include tangible and intangible rewards such as gamification points, leaderboard rankings and achievement badges; S captures social influence, and includes peer norms, competition and collaborative learning; and E denotes the effort required to engage in sustainable accounting practices, including cognitive load, time commitment and perceived complexity of tasks.

The intrinsic motivation component is quite important as self-determined learners are known to exhibit greater long-term engagement (Hammerschall, 2019). Extrinsic incentive elements drive short-term engagement but may have diminishing effects over time (Lewis et al., 2016). The social factor accounts for the impact of classroom interactions and external pressures on student behaviour (Xu et al., 2023). The presence of effort E as a negative factor in the model accounts for the cognitive and time-based trade-offs students make when participating in sustainability-related activities. α, β, γ, and δ are weight parameters that determine the relative importance of each factor, which would be calibrated through empirical validation. In summary, the behavioural utility function provides a foundation for analysing how different students respond to gamification, which is then used to determine the optimisation of engagement strategies based on intrinsic and extrinsic motivators.

2.2 Gamification Reward System

Gamification elements such as leaderboards, badges and point systems act as external stimuli that influence students' decision-making. To formally represent the reward system, I model rewards as a time-dependent function as follows:

$$R(t) = R_0 \ln(1 + k \cdot t)$$

Where, R_0 is the base reward (students receive an initial level of reinforcement when they start engaging in sustainable practices); k is a scaling parameter that controls the rate of reward accumulation over time, which can be adjusted to prevent diminishing returns and maintain student engagement; and t represents time that could correspond to learning progress, number of completed tasks or sustained engagement.

This logarithmic reward function models the concept of diminishing marginal returns, which is frequently observed in behavioural reinforcement settings. Initially, students experience a significant increase in motivation as they receive rewards, but over time, the incremental benefit of additional rewards decreases. This function maintains a high engagement in the early stages but requires additional incentives, such as new challenges or social reinforcements, to sustain long-term participation.

The reward system also interacts with the behavioural utility function through the extrinsic incentives term I, which allows for tests of how different reward structures influence student engagement. By varying k and R_0, educators can tailor gamification strategies to maintain optimal motivation levels.

At the beginning of time ($t = 0$), no reward is given initially, which requires students to engage in the task to start accumulating rewards. Thus,

$$R(0) = R_0 \ln(1 + k \cdot 0) = R_0 \ln(1) = 0$$

For small values of t (early stages of engagement), the function increases rapidly since ln (x) grows quickly for small x. This provides strong early reinforcement and motivates students to engage with sustainability-related tasks. For large values of t (long-term engagement), the function grows slowly because the logarithm increases at a decreasing rate. Thus, additional effort yields smaller increases in rewards, which prevents students from becoming overly reliant on gamified rewards for motivation.

2.3 Social Influence and Competition

Beyond individual incentives, the model includes the role of social influence and competition, which recognise that students do not operate in isolation but within a networked learning environment. To incorporate these dynamics, I use a network-based game-theoretic approach, where students are represented as nodes in a social graph. The behavioural state of each student evolves based on their interactions with peers as follows:

$$x_i(t+1) = f\left(x_i(t), \sum_{j \in N_i} w_{ij} x_j(t)\right)$$

where, $x_i(t)$ represents the engagement level of student i at time t; N_i is the set of neighbours that influence student i, which could be defined based on seating arrangements (physical classrooms), group assignments (team projects) or digital interactions (online discussions); and w_{ij} denotes the influence weight between students i and j (measures the strength of peer interactions). This equation is rooted in network theory and social reinforcement, where a student's level of engagement at the next time step $t + 1$ depends on both their prior engagement and the weighted influence of their peers. The w_{ij} measures how much student j's engagement affects student i. Higher values indicate stronger influence (e.g., close friends, influential classmates), while lower values indicate weaker influence. $\sum_{j \in N_i} w_{ij} x_j(t)$ represents the total peer influence on student i. If many high-engagement students surround a given student, the summed value is high, which would encourage that student to also engage in sustainability practices. The function $f(\cdot)$ governs how behavioural engagement updates from $x_i(t)$ to $x_i(t+1)$. It is modelled using sigmoid activation functions to capture thresholds for behavioural shifts so that once a critical mass of students adopts sustainability practices, others follow. A sigmoid activation function is used here to model behaviour shifts in social networks. It takes the form:

$$f(x) = \frac{1}{1 + e^{-\lambda(x-\theta)}}$$

where λ (steepness parameter) controls how quickly the transition occurs from low to high engagement; and θ (threshold parameter) represents the peer influence needed for student i to significantly increase their engagement. If peer influence is low, i.e., $\sum_{j \in N_i} w_{ij} x_j(t)$ is small, the sigmoid function outputs a small value, which indicates little change in engagement. If peer influence is high (i.e., many engaged peers), the function shifts rapidly towards higher engagement. Also, below a certain threshold of engaged peers (θ), a student remains disengaged. But once that threshold is exceeded, engagement rapidly increases.

The formulation of this equation reflects the social reinforcement effect, where students are more likely to adopt sustainable behaviours if they observe peers engaging in them (Abrahamse & Steg, 2013; Wang et al., 2024). The network structure of the classroom, whether random, small-world or scale free, affects the speed and extent of behavioural adoption. In random networks, connections between students are formed at random, i.e., each student has approximately the same probability of being connected to any other student. Information spreads evenly but slowly, as there are no highly influential nodes (students with many connections). In these structures, engagement can be fragmented, and adoption may take longer since influence is distributed randomly (Yuan et al., 2019).

Small-world networks have a high degree of local clustering (students are connected to their immediate peers) with a few long-range connections (students connected to peers from other groups). These networks exhibit the 'six degrees of separation' phenomenon, where most nodes can be reached from any other node through a small number of steps (Samoylenko et al., 2023). This structure optimises information diffusion and collaborative learning because local clusters quickly influence each other, while long-range connections bridge distant groups leading to rapid spread across the entire network. Engagement spreads faster than in random networks because of the balance between local influence and global reach.

In a scale free network, most students have few connections, but a few students serve as highly connected hubs (influential students). This network follows a power-law distribution, and thus, influencers or opinion leaders (such as highly motivated students) play a key role in information dissemination (Broido & Clauset, 2019). Once key hubs adopt sustainable practices, they would quickly influence many others. However, if these hubs remain disengaged, adoption would stagnate despite a large network. These structures are not as common (Broido & Clauset, 2019).

In summary, the network structure in a classroom profoundly impacts the speed and extent of behavioural adoption in sustainability education (Moolenaar, 2012). Based on the prior discussion, small-world networks provide an ideal balance of efficient information diffusion, peer influence and collaborative learning. This makes them a preferred structure for promoting sustainability through gamified accounting education. However, my model supports varying network topologies to test different educational environments.

2.4 Learning Fatigue and Engagement Retention

To further refine the model, I include a learning fatigue function that accounts for diminishing enthusiasm over time. Students may initially respond positively to gamification, but without proper reinforcement, engagement may decline. This is modelled as follows:

$$F(t) = \frac{1}{1 + e^{-\lambda(t - t_0)}}$$

where, $F(t)$ represents the fatigue factor that reduces engagement over time; λ controls the steepness of fatigue onset; and t_0 represents the time threshold after which engagement starts to decline (i.e., the time threshold when fatigue starts to become noticeable). The fatigue factor ranges between 0 and 1, where $F(t) \approx 0$ indicates no fatigue (high engagement), and $F(t) \approx 1$ indicates high fatigue (low engagement). A high λ indicates fatigue sets in quickly and sharply, while a low λ indicates fatigue develops slowly and gradually. Before t_0, fatigue remains low; after t_0, fatigue rises significantly.

Thus, by including fatigue, the model can test strategies such as periodic reinforcement (e.g., introducing new game elements) to sustain student engagement over an extended period. Also, by manipulating λ and t_0, educators can design adaptive gamification strategies that maintain high engagement in sustainability education so that students remain motivated despite prolonged exposure to challenging material.

2.5 Equilibrium Analysis

To analyse the long-term stability of student engagement in sustainability practices under gamified learning environments, I derive equilibrium conditions for the analytical model. Equilibrium occurs when engagement levels across the network stabilise, i.e., $x_i(t+1) = x_i(t) = x_i^* \ \forall i$. This section formalises the equilibrium states, evaluates their existence and stability and discusses implications for educational design.

Thus, at equilibrium, engagement no longer changes over time. This is represented as follows:

$$x_i^* = f\left(x_i^*, \sum_{j \in N_i} w_{ij} x_j^*\right)$$

This implicit equation defines the equilibrium engagement level x_i^* for each student, dependent on their intrinsic engagement and peer influence, i.e., students settle into a state where their intrinsic motivation and peer influence balance the effort required to engage in sustainable practices.

For simplicity, let's assume a homogeneous classroom where all students share identical parameters (α, β, γ, and δ) and symmetric influence weights ($w_{ij} = w$). Let x^* denote the uniform equilibrium engagement. The equilibrium condition simplifies to:

$$x^* = \frac{1}{1 + e^{-\lambda(x^* + \mathrm{wkx}^* - \theta)}}$$

where k is the average degree (number of peers) in the network. Now, let $\phi = \lambda((1 + \mathrm{wk})x^* - \theta)$. The term x^* appears on both sides of the equation, which indicates a feedback loop. A student's engagement (x^*) depends on their own prior engagement and the engagement of their peers. Higher engagement today (x^*) amplifies future engagement through peer influence (wkx^*), which creates a virtuous cycle. This finding is quite intuitive in that early success in gamification (e.g., initial rewards or peer adoption) can trigger long-term engagement by utilising this feedback.

The sigmoid function introduces a nonlinear threshold effect. When $x^*+\text{wkx}^*>\theta$, engagement rapidly increases towards 1 (high engagement). When $x^*+\text{wkx}^*<\theta$, engagement collapses towards 0 (low engagement). Small changes in parameters (e.g., lowering θ or increasing peer influence wk) can push the system past critical thresholds and cause abrupt shifts in engagement. The term wkx* quantifies peer influence, where k is the average number of peers (network density), and w is the strength of peer influence. In dense networks ($k \gg 1$), even weak peer influence (w) can dominate equilibrium outcomes, while sparse networks ($k \ll 1$) require stronger intrinsic motivation (x^*) to sustain engagement. Thus, small-world networks (high k) seem optimal for spreading engagement due to efficient peer influence.

Further, lowering θ (e.g., simplifying tasks or reducing effort) makes it easier to surpass the critical threshold for engagement. Higher λ sharpens the transition between low and high engagement, which creates 'all-or-nothing' adoption. While not explicit in this equation, rewards $R(t)$ and fatigue $F(t)$ indirectly shape x^* by modulating θ and λ over time. Incorporating fatigue $F(t)$ and rewards $R(t)$, long-term equilibrium requires steady-state conditions as follows:

$$\lim_{t\to\infty} R(t) = R_0 \ln(1+\text{kt}) \approx R_0 \ln(\text{kt}), \lim_{t\to\infty} F(t) = 1.$$

As $t \to \infty$, fatigue dominates ($F(t) \to 1$), which reduces engagement unless periodic reinforcement (e.g., new rewards) resets t_0. Equilibrium engagement thus depends on balancing reward accumulation and fatigue mitigation.

Moreover, the transcendental nature of the equation suggests that multiple equilibria (e.g., $x^* \approx 0$ or $x^* \approx 1$) are possible depending on initial conditions. A high engagement equilibrium is sustainable if early adoption triggers sufficient peer influence, while a low engagement equilibrium is likely if initial participation fails to reach critical mass. Thus, interventions by educators must ensure early wins to steer the system towards high-engagement equilibria.

In summary, sustained engagement in sustainability education emerges from a balance of individual motivation, peer influence and gamification design. The equilibrium condition shows that (a) peer networks are force multipliers for engagement, (b) thresholds must be calibrated to classroom dynamics, (c) periodic reinforcements are needed to counteract fatigue and (d) nonlinear feedback creates tipping points, and thus, small interventions can drive large scale behavioural shifts. This highlights the importance of network-aware gamification: tailoring rewards, effort thresholds and social interactions to leverage peer effects and stabilise engagement. In small world networks, high clustering and short path lengths enable rapid convergence to equilibria with moderate x^*, as peer influence propagates efficiently. In scale free networks, engagement concentrates around hubs. If hubs stabilise at high x^*, peripheral students follow, which creates polarised equilibria. In random networks, sparse connections lead to fragmented equilibria, where engagement varies widely across subgroups.

Now, solving for x^*,

$$x^* = \frac{1}{1+e^{-\phi}} \Rightarrow \phi = \ln\left(\frac{x^*}{1-x^*}\right)$$

Then, substituting ϕ,

$$\lambda((1 + wk)x^* - \theta) = \ln\left(\frac{x^*}{1 - x^*}\right)$$

This transcendental equation admits solutions only for specific parameter ranges. Thus, I use numerical methods are required to solve for x^*.

3. Numerical Experiment

To validate the analytical model, following Knox (2020), I design a numerical experiment simulating engagement dynamics under three network topologies, small world, scale free and random, to evaluate how peer influence, rewards and fatigue shape long-term engagement.

The simulation involved 100 students over 50 time steps, with parameters calibrated to reflect realistic educational environments. Initial engagement levels were set uniformly between 0.1 and 0.3 to represent modest baseline motivation. The three distinct network topologies were generated to test their impact on engagement propagation. The small-world network was constructed using the Watts-Strogatz model with four neighbours per node and a 10% rewiring probability to balance local clustering and global connectivity (Channarond, 2015). The scale free network employed the Barabási-Albert model to simulate hubs (highly connected students) and peripheral nodes, while the random network used the Erdős-Rényi model with a 5% connection probability to mimic sparse, unstructured interactions (Channarond, 2015).

At each time step, engagement levels were updated using a sigmoid activation function to model threshold-driven behavioural shifts. Peer influence was calculated as a weighted sum of neighbours' engagement, with a uniform influence weight $w = 0.1$. Fatigue was introduced as a time-dependent factor and modelled by a sigmoid function that reduced engagement after a threshold $t_0 = 20$ to simulate diminishing enthusiasm. Concurrently, a logarithmic reward function, $R(t) = R_0 \ln(1 + k_{\text{reward}} t)$, was applied to incentivise engagement, with rewards accumulating rapidly in early stages and plateauing over time. Engagement values were clipped to the range [0, 1] to ensure biological plausibility. The simulation iterated across all networks to capture engagement trajectories and equilibrium states.

Fig. 6.1 presents the results, which reveal stark differences in engagement patterns across network topologies. In small-world networks, engagement surged rapidly and reached an average of $\overline{x} \approx 0.7$ within 10 time steps, driven by efficient peer influence propagation through clustered local groups and long-range connections. Post-fatigue onset ($t_0 = 20$), engagement stabilised near $\overline{x} \approx 0.65$ and demonstrated resilience due to the network's robust information diffusion. In contrast, scale free networks exhibited polarisation. Hubs maintained high engagement ($\overline{x} > 0.6$), while peripheral students stagnated near $\overline{x} \approx 0.6$. This bifurcation highlights the dependency on influential nodes. Fatigue caused a 15%

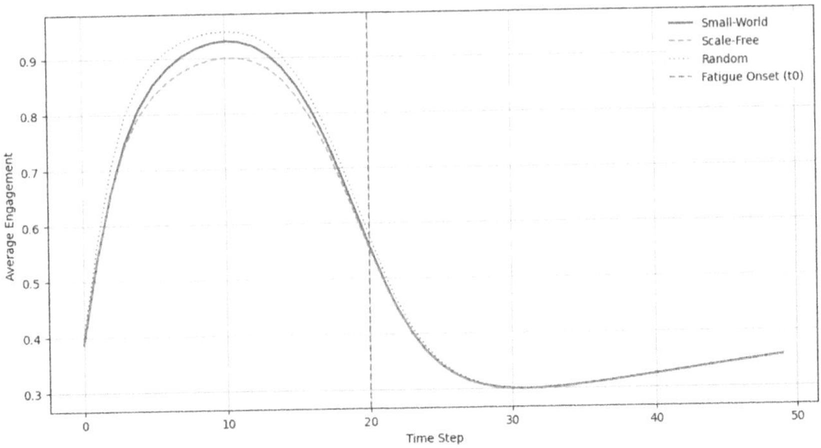

Fig. 6.1. Engagement Dynamics Under Different Network Topologies.

decline in average engagement post t_0, which suggests vulnerabilities in hub centric structures.

Random networks displayed slow, linear growth in engagement, reaching $\overline{x}\approx 0.5$ by $t = 50$, with high variance suggesting fragmented peer influence. Fatigue exacerbated disparities and reduced engagement by 10%, which indicates the need for structured interventions. Across all topologies, fatigue universally diminished engagement, though small-world networks showed the least decline (5%), attributable to their balanced connectivity. The logarithmic reward structure initially boosted engagement but proved insufficient to counter long-term fatigue without periodic reinforcement.

In summary, the simulation validated the analytical model's equilibrium predictions. Small world steady-state engagement ($\overline{x} \approx 0.65$) aligned closely with the theoretical equilibrium suggested from the model. Threshold effects, central to the sigmoid function, were empirically observed. For example, engagement in small-world and scale-free networks exhibited nonlinear tipping points, transitioning rapidly once peer influence surpassed critical thresholds. These findings once again highlight the importance of network-aware gamification design. Small world structures, with their optimal balance of local and global connectivity, emerge as superior environments for sustaining engagement. Educators should prioritise strategies that utilise peer networks, periodically refresh rewards to counteract fatigue and target influential students in scale free settings to prevent polarisation.

4. Conclusion, Practical Implications and Future Research Agenda

This study developed a novel analytical framework to investigate how gamification and network dynamics drive behavioural shifts in sustainability-focused accounting education. Key findings include:

- Small-world networks, with their balance of local clustering and global connectivity, optimise engagement diffusion and resilience to fatigue. They achieve steady-state engagement levels that align with theoretical predictions.
- The results revealed nonlinear tipping points, where engagement rapidly escalates once peer influence surpasses critical thresholds. Small interventions, such as lowering effort barriers or targeting influential students, can trigger large-scale behavioural shifts.
- The logarithmic reward system initially boosts engagement but diminishes in efficacy over time. Fatigue-induced declines after a certain period of time highlight the need for periodic reinforcements to sustain motivation.
- Scale free networks risk engagement polarisation, where reliance on hubs creates vulnerabilities if key influencers disengage.

Following from these results, accounting educators need to design classroom interactions to balance local teamwork and global connectivity. For example, they may consider organising small study pods with periodic inter-group activities or use online platforms to connect students across project teams. Accounting educators should also target early adopters, i.e., identify and incentivise influential students to act as sustainability champions. They should also consider lowering initial effort barriers to simplify introductory tasks to help students cross the engagement threshold quickly. They should also introduce new challenges or rewards midway through courses (e.g., bonus points for mid-term sustainability projects) and rotate gamification elements (e.g., switch from leaderboards to team-based achievements). They should also front load rewards by offering larger incentives early to boost initial participation. They may also need to shift to intrinsic/social rewards by gradually replacing points/badges with peer recognition or real-world impact showcases (e.g., 'Your sustainable audit saved X tons of CO_2').

Accounting educators should also monitor influencers, i.e., regularly check in with highly connected students to maintain their motivation. They may also try to decentralise influence by assigning rotating leadership roles to prevent over-reliance on a few students. Scaffolding tasks, i.e., breaking complex sustainability tasks into smaller, gamified steps, could also help. They may also consider using simulations or case studies to reduce cognitive load while maintaining rigour.

Thus, by integrating behavioural economics, network theory and dynamical systems, my model provides educators with practical insights to design gamified strategies that translate transient engagement into lasting sustainability practices.

While the proposed analytical model advances the understanding of gamification in sustainability education, several limitations need to be acknowledged. The model assumes uniform parameters (e.g., identical intrinsic motivation weights) and symmetric peer influence across students. Real-world classrooms exhibit heterogeneity in learning styles, cultural backgrounds and motivation levels, which the model does not fully capture. The analysis focuses on idealised small world, scale free and random networks. Real social networks in educational settings often exhibit hybrid or evolving structures, which may alter engagement dynamics.

The logarithmic reward and fatigue functions, while mathematically tractable, oversimplify the nonlinear and context-dependent nature of human motivation. For example, rewards in practice may follow non-logarithmic patterns, and fatigue could be influenced by external stressors. Empirical validation with real-world classroom datasets is necessary to confirm the model's predictive accuracy, particularly in diverse institutional contexts. The model also isolates classroom interactions but does not account for external influences (e.g., family, societal norms or workplace pressures) that may affect student engagement with sustainability practices.

To address the limitations and expand upon this work, future research should prioritise conducting longitudinal studies in real classrooms to test the model's predictions using observational and experimental data. Future researchers may also investigate how cultural differences in competitiveness, collaboration and sustainability attitudes modulate gamification efficacy.

Note: During the preparation of this work, the author used Anthropic's Claude AI in order to perform spelling and grammar checks and debug Python code. After using this tool/service, the author reviewed and edited the content as needed and takes full responsibility for the content of the publication.

References

Abrahamse, W., & Steg, L. (2013). Social influence approaches to encourage resource conservation: A meta-analysis. *Global Environmental Change*, *23*(6), 1773–1785. https://doi.org/10.1016/j.gloenvcha.2013.07.029

Bouchrika, I., Harrati, N., Wanick, V., & Wills, G. (2021). Exploring the impact of gamification on student engagement and involvement with e-learning systems. *Interactive Learning Environments*, *29*(8), 1244–1257. https://doi.org/10.1080/10494820.2019.1623267

Broido, A. D., & Clauset, A. (2019). Scale-free networks are rare. *Nature Communications*, *10*(1), 1017. https://doi.org/10.1038/s41467-019-08746-5

Channarond, A. (2015). Random graph models: An overview of modeling approaches. *Journal de la Société Française de Statistique*, *156*(3), 56–94.

da Rocha Seixas, L., Gomes, A. S., & de Melo Filho, I. J. (2016). Effectiveness of gamification in the engagement of students. *Computers in Human Behavior*, *58*, 48–63. https://doi.org/10.1016/j.chb.2015.11.021

Hammerschall, U. (2019, April). A gamification framework for long-term engagement in education based on self determination theory and the transtheoretical model of change. In *2019 IEEE Global Engineering Education Conference (EDUCON)* (pp. 95–101). IEEE. https://doi.org/10.1109/EDUCON.2019.8725251

Knox, B. D. (2020). Semantic processing theory could help explain the effectiveness of creativity incentives: A numerical experiment. *Journal of Management Accounting Research, 32*(3), 155–178. https://doi.org/10.2308/jmar-18-051

Lewis, Z. H., Swartz, M. C., & Lyons, E. J. (2016). What's the point?: A review of reward systems implemented in gamification interventions. *Games for Health Journal*, *5*(2), 93–99. https://doi.org/10.1089/g4h.2015.0078

Lim, W. M., Das, M., Sharma, W., Verma, A., & Kumra, R. (2025). Gamification for sustainable consumption: A state-of-the-art overview and future agenda. *Business Strategy and the Environment*, *34*(1), 1510–1549. https://doi.org/10.1002/bse.4021

Moolenaar, N. M. (2012). A social network perspective on teacher collaboration in schools: Theory, methodology, and applications. *American Journal of Education*, *119*(1), 7–39. https://doi.org/10.1086/667715

Mulcahy, R. F., McAndrew, R., Russell-Bennett, R., & Iacobucci, D. (2021). "Game on!" Pushing consumer buttons to change sustainable behavior: A gamification field study. *European Journal of Marketing*, *55*(10), 2593–2619.

Othman, R., & Ameer, R. (2024). Rethinking accounting education for a sustainable future: Charting a course for sustainable development goals 2030. *Meditari Accountancy Research*. https://doi.org/10.1108/MEDAR-05-2023-2009

Rivera, E. S., & Garden, C. L. P. (2021). Gamification for student engagement: A framework. *Journal of Further and Higher Education*, *45*(7), 999–1012. https://doi.org/10.1080/0309877X.2021.1875201

Samoylenko, I., Aleja, D., Primo, E., Alfaro-Bittner, K., Vasilyeva, E., Kovalenko, K., Musatov, D., Raigorodskii, A.M., Criado, R., Romance, M., Papo, D., Perc, M., Barzel, B., & Boccaletti, S. (2023). Why are there six degrees of separation in a social network? *Physical Review X*, *13*(2), 021032. https://doi.org/10.1103/PhysRevX.13.021032

Sanchez, D. R., Langer, M., & Kaur, R. (2020). Gamification in the classroom: Examining the impact of gamified quizzes on student learning. *Computers & Education*, *144*, 103666. https://doi.org/10.1016/j.compedu.2019.103666

Shahzad, M. F., Xu, S., Rehman, O. U., & Javed, I. (2023). Impact of gamification on green consumption behavior integrating technological awareness, motivation, enjoyment and virtual CSR. *Scientific Reports*, *13*(1), 21751. https://doi.org/10.1038/s41598-023-48835-6

Silva, R., Rodrigues, R., & Leal, C. (2021). Games based learning in accounting education–which dimensions are the most relevant? *Accounting Education*, *30*(2), 159–187. https://doi.org/10.1080/09639284.2021.1891107

Wang, M., Zhu, Y., Liu, S., Zhang, Y., & Dai, X. (2024). Can social learning promote farmers' green breeding behavior? Regulatory effect based on environmental regulation. *Sustainability*, *16*(13), 5519. https://doi.org/10.3390/su16135519

Xu, L., Zhang, J., Ding, Y., Zheng, J., Sun, G., Zhang, W., & Philbin, S. P. (2023). Understanding the role of peer pressure on engineering students' learning behavior: A TPB perspective. *Frontiers in Public Health*, *10*, 1069384. https://doi.org/10.3389/fpubh.2022.1069384

Yuan, E., Feng, M., & Liu, X. (2019). The R/evolution of civic engagement: An exploratory network analysis of the Facebook groups of occupy Chicago. *Information, Communication & Society*, *22*(2), 267–285. https://doi.org/10.1080/1369118X.2017.1371786

Section 2

Tech and Innovation for Sustainable Accounting

Chapter 7

Technology-Driven Innovations in Social Accounting for Sustainable Business Growth

Sonali Srivastava[a] *and Manisha Singh*[b]

[a]Jaypee Institute of Information Technology, India
[b]VIT Bhopal University, India

Abstract

The chapter explores how technology has been instrumental in the development of social accounting (SA) practices and in the promotion of sustainable business growth. It strives to establish how such seemingly digital innovations as blockchain, artificial intelligence (AI), big data analytics and green technologies are increasing the possibilities for organisations to report on and manage their social and environmental concerns. Beyond conventional frameworks, there seems to be a shift occurring into event-driven and stakeholder-focused accounting models that use real-time data and multimedia applications to represent better an organisation's social impact. Looking from the perspective of the Indian business environment, the chapter attempts to offer paid context on SA while simultaneously providing some insights transferable to the developing economies. It goes on to provide a critical assessment of the problems and potentials arising out of engaging technology in social accountability frameworks while putting emphasis on the need for reporting methods that are inclusive, transparent and adaptable. The discussion also traverses regulatory frameworks, stakeholder interaction and emerging trends in this line of study. This chapter argues for the positioning of technology within SA so as to affect some corporate transparency and environmental responsibility; thereby, it engenders stakeholder trust and strategic positioning. This integration is thus necessarily pursued by whichever company that would like to sustain itself in a global market increasingly aware of sustainability aspects. Hence, the SA domain might create pathways for value addition through SA

Sustainability in Accounting and Finance Education, 111–126

Published under exclusive licence by Emerald Publishing Limited
doi:10.1108/978-1-80686-393-820261007

technologies that enhance long-term value creation for society and shareholders alike.

Keywords: Sustainable business; social accounting; big data; green projects; blockchain; machine learning; green technology

1. Introduction to Social Accounting

Social accounting (SA) is a method used to assess and evaluate the impact of an organisation on society and its stakeholders. It is an evolving process in helping an organisation respond to internal and external stakeholders, constrained beyond shareholding (Chatzivgeri et al., 2018). SA has several steps such as setting context and objectives, identifying inputs, activities, impacts and outcomes, measuring inputs, outputs and outcomes, verifying the propriety of the measurement values and methods, aggregating the data, interpreting the results and finally reporting. Based on the information collected during the SA process, the organisation can produce a narrative that details how it has accounted for its impact and the resulting decisions that have been made. Based on the preceding narrative and the systemic results, an action plan can be devised containing targets for improvement, responsibilities for action and action plans (Mio et al., 2022; Pollok et al., 2021).

Helpful comparisons can be made with the conventional accounting process to illustrate how SA differs. Essentially, while financial accounting is designed to report on the performance of a business, SA is designed to assess the organisation as a business, an organisation with inputs, activities and outputs to be accounted for or evaluated (Ahmad & Ahmad, 2024) (Schaltegger et al., 2022). SA can cover all stakeholders and impacts on society, whereas conventional accounting is mostly concerned with shareholder value and profits. Conventional financial accounting relies heavily on quantitative data, while SA is based on qualitative data. While both accounting processes have a chain of linked steps, SA is far less defined than accounting, creating confusion about terminology and processes. Analysis or assessment design across organisations can vary widely (Paterson et al., 2021) (Kuruppu et al., 2022).

The acceptance of SA processes and narratives can be far lower than that of financial reports. The turnaround time to complete a SA process is typically greater than for a financial accounting process. Social accountability assessment demands skill sets that current conventional accountants lack, and SA presents several inherent challenges in data (Markham et al., 2021).

This chapter uses literature-based and concept-driven approaches to investigate how new technologies are reshaping SA with regard to the long-term objectives of sustainable business expansion. Rather than presenting new information, it rather follows and feeds from a rich body of existing literature and research – from academic research and industry reports down to practical exemplar emerging tools such as blockchain, artificial intelligence (AI) and big data, and attempting to establish the link between their growing influence on corporate accountability. In order to align such ideas with reality, this chapter introduces SysEngage – a working model for tech-enabled corporate social responsibility (CSR). Although it has not been yet tested in primary research, SysEngage rests on design science foundations and secondary data to steer companies earnestly in innovating their sustainability initiatives.

2. Emerging Technologies in Accounting

The advent of emerging technologies has spawned an instance level of improvement in productivity, service delivery and business landscape in general. The accounting profession is no exception to the seismic changes that result from technological innovations. Recent technological advancements such as AI, Robotic Process Automation (RPA), Blockchain Technology, Big Data Analytics and Cloud Computing have contributed to significant changes in the way accountants work. Technological advancement is transforming the accounting profession to the extent that many accounting tasks traditionally performed by human beings are now completed by computers and accounting software (Schut, 2023) (Leitner-Hanetseder et al., 2021).

Emerging technologies as applied technologies, and the effects of these technologies on the accounting profession defined as accounting applications are now applicable, and this specific review focuses on the public accounting profession, therefore a more refined categorisation is appropriate. Accounting applications of all types of emerging technologies are included with the exception of accounting education, and applicability refers to the use of associated technologies, tools or products being available for psychologists to study their impact on the public accounting profession but emphasises applications currently available and widely used (Baiod & Hussain, 2024; Wang, 2022).

2.1 Blockchain Technology

Blockchain technology is a promising approach to overcome the challenges of credibility and traceability of SA. It has been designed to serve as a decentralised, secure, cryptographic and distributed ledger of transactions between different parties that do not need to trust each other. It consists of a chain of blocks where each block stores different pieces of information and a specific number of transactions are registered (Zhang et al., 2023). The decentralised nature of blockchain implies that the blockchains are maintained on a peer basis, with each peer storing a complete copy of the blockchain. As a result, tampering with information in the blockchain is extremely difficult because one would have to alter a large number of copies of the same information maintained by other peers in different locations. Moreover, the nature of the blockchain makes it impossible to restore previous transactions. Each information record is encrypted cryptographically and saved in the block ledger in a special data format, causing it to be more secure against tampering (Mukherjee & Pradhan, 2021).

Blockchain can increase goodwill through social legitimacy, efficiency, exposure, incentives and motivations by creating a threshold trail of information that cannot be corrupted; the link of transactions of the activities of the firm, their probabilities and relationships. Towards the other stakeholders at large, these benefits can mitigate the agency issues between state-owned/worker cooperatives firms that hold stakes in the organisation, the firms' employees, its providers and agents of credit risk. Within this group, legitimate actions happen to be recorded, and capabilities accrue to examine decisions/potential opportunities that affect the other stakeholders at large (Chaudhuri et al., 2023; Sheikh, 2024).

Blockchain is often described as a game-changer for transparency and trust – and when it comes to SA, that description holds up. It provides a secure, decentralised way to record data, helping ensure that social impact reports and sustainability claims are not just talk, but verifiable. Picture it as a digital ledger where every entry is locked in and visible to all, making it far harder to manipulate facts or hide mistakes. This has huge potential for CSR reporting, donation tracking or measuring community impact. But like any promising technology, blockchain has its challenges – especially when rolled out in developing countries.

First, there's the issue of infrastructure. Reliable internet, electricity and suitable hardware in theory are the minimum requirements to run a blockchain system; yet, most rural or remote areas do not have any of these basics. It comes replete with a technical language-full of cryptography, smart contracts, decentralisation – something that can leave laymen practically dizzy. Many social impact practitioners simply are not versed in these areas, and so adoption is slow on the uptake. In many zones of the planet, there's still much confusion about whether these chains are even legal and, if so, how they are regulated. Without legal clarity, understandably, organisations remain cautious, especially when dealing with sensitive social data.

Even from an environmental perspective, criticisms may rise against blockchain. These systems, through a Proof-of-Work, seek enormous energy consumption, thus clashing with sustainability values. Newer, greener blockchain models exist, but they're still gaining traction. That said, there are hopeful examples. Kenya's experiment with blockchain for land records aimed to cut corruption and make ownership more transparent. It was a bold step, though not without setbacks – like resistance from local officials and the headache of digitising old paper records. Elsewhere, nonprofits in Latin America are using blockchain to follow the path of donations, giving donors confidence that their money is making a real impact. Blockchain has real potential – but only when the groundwork is in place. That means investing in infrastructure, education and legal support. And most importantly, it means collaboration – between governments, tech experts, Non-governmental Organisations (NGOs) and the communities they serve.

2.2 Artificial Intelligence

AI has the potential to assay knowledge work in limitless dimensions. Most menial tasks are contract and out performed by simple, convex, algorithm-based automation to sophisticated AIs that sift reams of information. Deep learning image and network annotators rival humans in several applications. Cognitive robots suggest actions and decisions that can equal or exceed the expertise of specialists. Unsupervised language models generate human-like texts. Supervised predictors forecast outcomes that affect millions of lives. Brought together in a 'knowledge' economy, AIs could absorb and act on all knowledge from blueprints to living documents and news (Dattathrani & De', 2023; Pasquinelli & Joler, 2021). Human capital devoted to devising action could collapse vastly. Storm or tidal levels of profit and obligation would ensue. Humans must conjoin, collide and compete with machines to find purpose in cognition-augmented work and ensure that all flourish. Empirical estimates of generally inconceivable global impacts are needed to assess prospects both after disruptive adoption and when machine cognition ameliorates sociality and nudges an enduring 'knowledge' economy (Mitra et al., 2023).

Strategic intelligence (SI) is a precursor of human and AI that resolves the current cognitive impasse. SI is the ability to manage the many competing variants of knowledge, for machine and human, and decides scope and means for conversion to action. It exposes and analyses key attributes of deep change as inputs and consumed evidence transform search and change. It proposes a computational framework for modelling and simulating step-changes from smart to intelligent systems. The first-generation consumer new economy took years to pervade global network (Flavián & Casaló, 2021; Martin & Freeland, 2021). Transformational foresight and simulation can augment understanding of competing strategies. Through black-swan testing, analyst agents might tell the story of the next decades in incremental advents, reversals, competition and conspiracy. Hands are grasping at a massively complex, unknowable future. Co-evolving emergences offer radically new attributes unprecedented in human history, glimpses of desires and beliefs in a conjoined agency/technology choice (Napier, 2019).

AI is changing the game when it comes to how we collect, analyse and use data – and SA is no exception. With its ability to process huge amounts of information, spot patterns and even predict trends, AI has the potential to transform how organisations understand their social and environmental impact. It can help companies go beyond numbers and deliver real-time, meaningful insights into how their actions affect people and the planet. But for all its promise, putting AI into practice – especially in developing countries – is far from straightforward.

One of the biggest obstacles is a lack of digital infrastructure. Without stable Internet speeds, dependable electricity supplies and access to basic computing equipment, one cannot rely on the provision of these essential services in many parts of South Asia or sub-Saharan Africa. Small and medium-sized enterprises are truly the backbone of the economy in these regions, but they come up against many issues, such as smaller budgets and lack of technical know-how in implementing AI systems. Another major roadblock is in the data itself. For AI algorithms to do their job well, they require quality data, but in many setups reliable social and environmental data is not readily available due to uneven platform development or just inaccuracies. To pile on, there is also bad data governance: hence, the worries about privacy, ethical use and bias, whenever data fails to reflect the realities confronted by marginalised communities. A very real human barrier exists in that many organisations are hesitant to embrace AI systems for fear of loss of jobs, mistrust in decisions of automated systems or just plain ignorance about what AI can really do.

Adding to the reluctance is the absence of any formal standards or guidelines on AI implementation in non-financial reporting, thus increasing the uncertainty. Consider how Tata Consultancy Services (TCS) in India implemented an AI-powered platform to monitor and evaluate the impacts of its rural education initiatives. Although the technology helped them make decisions in a much smarter and faster way, the process was not without challenges. Training of local personnel, assuring data collection was legitimate and forging trust in the system took time. This calls for a balanced and inclusive approach. Governments, nonprofits and private companies must work together to invest in digital literacy, open-data platforms and ethical frameworks that reflect local values and needs. With the right support, AI can become not just a tool for efficiency, but a force for transparency, fairness and sustainable development.

2.3 Big Data Analytics

Big data allows you to tap into a wealth of social insights that influence behaviour such as preferences, needs, resources and stressors. It offers the opportunity to map the presence of any of those social insights across space, over time and against other variables, providing a powerful lens of understanding that can be used to tackle development challenges. The potential of big data has not yet been realised by many of those interested in its applications for social good – nonprofits, governments and others with a social mission (Nathan et al., 2022; Smith & Pinter-Wollman, 2021). Though these organisations produce and access vast amounts of social data every day, big data practices are only emerging informally. Pockets of forward-thinking social organisations are innovating new methods for analysing the huge array of social data they have, and across sectors, there is rising awareness of the potential that big data offers to fuel significant positive change in people's lives. However, on the whole, use of big data for social good remains limited. From an analytics vantage, social organisations appear to be laggards in using heterogenous, unstructured, real-time data that is external to their own operations – and in combining these to glean key insights. However, with the advent of technology across the country, there is increasing interest in harnessing it to drive social change at scale. Activity and explorations of big data in the sector have increased remarkably in the last couple of years (Chaudhry, 2022).

Big data is everywhere these days – and when used right, it can be a powerful ally in understanding and improving social impact. In SA, big data helps organisations tap into a wide range of information – from social media posts and mobile phone usage to environmental sensors and satellite images. The result? A more immediate, detailed picture of how business activities affect people, communities and the planet. For one, the data just isn't always there – or if it is, it's scattered, outdated or stored in handwritten logs. Rural NGOs, for example, might collect excellent data on education or health outcomes, but if it's all in notebooks or Excel files that aren't shared, it's hard to do much with it. That's a major roadblock for organisations trying to understand or prove their social impact.

Another issue is ethics and trust. Just because data is available doesn't mean it should be used. People need to know how their information is being collected and why. Communities could feel uneasy, or even exploited if they discover that their data has been accessed without their consent in countries with poor data protection laws.

And though these big data analysis tools continue to evolve and get cheaper, they still require human intervention. Having data is only the start; you also need someone that can pose the right questions, analyse the numbers and make actionable insights. It's a scarce capability within most organisations today. Nevertheless, the success stories identify the potential. The Global Pulse of the United Nations (UN) has cooperated with the governments of Uganda and Indonesia to use big data – from the source of mobile phone signals, to social media and satellite images – for monitoring public health and development trends. With examples such as these, it is clear that, with the right partnerships, big data can work even in challenging environments.

In SA, it is the basic things that nations must do first if they really want big data to do some good: improved infrastructure, greater training and better frameworks for ethical use. Equally importantly, local communities should be an integral part of the process, not just sources for data. Big data is not just a buzzword if used with respect, regard and collaboration. It becomes a vital tool for accountability, inclusion and sustainable change.

3. Sustainability in Business Practices

The contemporary business landscape is characterised by the rapid growth of firms seeking to capture market value through profit generation. However, the lack of alignment between business practices and public expectations, especially in light of sustainability concerns, has led to an increasing demand for corporate accountability from stakeholders. As a result, businesses are displaying growing concerns regarding these issues, especially if their social accountability and sustainability efforts expire unmet (Arogyaswamy, 2019). The expectation from firms to incorporate a socially responsible and sustainable dimension into their businesses is becoming a prerequisite for survival.

Sustainability in the business context refers to the practices, processes and business decisions that foster business growth while still accommodating environmental, social and economic considerations. Sustainability, therefore, calls for a simultaneous trade-off between short- and long-term business values and the concern for present generations and future ones. Above all, by harmonising the growing climate and distrust in the economy with the need for sports growth, sustainable sporting endeavours create a shared presence for all social actors (Jindal, 2025; Wolniak et al., 2023). Sustainability, when considered an appropriately parsed dimension, invariably leads to a greater knowledge of social accountability through grammars of action and socially embedding accountability context.

Recognising the growing expectation and concern for sustainability, effective and technology-driven measures are needed to optimise the realisation of these efforts. By ensuring harmony between social benefit and self-interest, and embracing underlying deliberative measures that optimise the social currency of accountability, firms can track the degree of social accountability aspects systematically while simultaneously enhancing, sharing and projectable concern for sustainable growth (Kannan & Gambetta, 2025; Tran-Dang et al., 2025). Thus, sustainability-driven approaches combined with innovative technology can significantly boost organisational monitoring of firms' social capital and sustainability measures, allowing for a more balanced and meritocratic competition prevailing among expectations, concerns and disciplinary negotiations in the evolving context of public practices.

4. Integrating SA With Sustainability Goals

Prior to pursuing this objective, there needs to be a clear understanding of the relationship between SA and sustainability. Sustainability needs to be explained in the context of SA and a few examples highlighted. As discussed previously, SA has been described as which encompasses a broader range of considerations in the accounting process. However, a broader framework raises questions about how to operationalise that framework (Tsiligiris & Bowyer, 2021). If organisations are to genuinely measure themselves against sustainability standards, organisations need to know what standards are and how they can be met. Sustainability is a highly contested concept that is invariably interpreted in different ways by actors both in the corporate sector and in society. Social accounting/sustainability reporting initiatives can encourage the managerial capture of sustainable development in organisations, because reporting companies can choose their preferred initiative and, equally importantly, the extent of disclosure thereof (Ragainis, 2018). Commonly used definitions of sustainability include the venerable, albeit vague and frequently contested, definition of sustainable development. This definition states that sustainability is development that meets the needs of the present without compromising the ability of future generations to meet their own needs. A more specific definition of sustainability is based on the concept of civil commons. This encompasses cooperative constructs that protect access to life goods (Onyango et al., 2018). Clean air, clean water, healthy food, education, health care and equivalent earnings, and human rights are examples of life goods. The term life goods is used to exclude destructive goods, including pollution, the disintegration or privatisation of social webs, and excessive inequality. An organisation is considered more sustainable the greater is its capacity to address the quantity and quality of life goods it provides with respect to the planet and people. In other words, the greater is the inclusivity of an organisation's sphere of influence with respect to environmental, social and economic life goods (i.e., extent) and the better is the ability of the enterprise to furnish them (i.e., performance).

5. Challenges in Implementing SA

Though the combination of qualitative and quantitative techniques can address the limitations of each of the approaches, it is not without its difficulties (Chatzivgeri et al., 2018). An organisation's risk profile is defined by the environment in which it operates, and this risk profile will determine the type of sustainability information collected and reported (Zvezdov, 2013). In the face of stakeholder globalisation and global capital flows it is the investor who drives the information agenda. Traditional sustainability accounting and reporting practices do not adequately accommodate this new information agenda, resulting in information asymmetries that undermine the credibility of sustainability information and possibly of sustainability initiatives themselves. Therefore, it may be that instead of determining the environmental and social impacts of corporate activities, how to standardise access to this information will drive the new turn in social and environmental accounting. More open, less controlled forms of SA may become dominant as greater access to sustainability information is demanded by stakeholders. Deliberative tendencies, and actions that result from a commitment to sustainability, would become less controllable and of a different generative nature (Akhavan & Zvezdov, 2021; Martínez-Peláez et al., 2023).

6. Regulatory Framework for SA in India

There have been increasing pressures on Indian corporations to be associated with SA practices. These pressures are both voluntary and mandatory. Societal need has been a core motivating factor to take up SA practices in the early days but with a recent regulatory intervention by the government have left participation in SA to the newer SA systems. Growing awareness and a surge in faith on corporations to exercise their ownership on resources carefully became the core voluntary factors driving SA incorporates (Singh & Verma, 2014). Many corporates have been taking up historical marginal, strategic initiatives in measuring, managing and disclosing their societal responsibilities. These voluntary efforts encouraged SA researchers and practitioners to capture and aggregate practices of SA and calculate indices. However, it is always important to strike a balance between mandatory and optional regulatory requirements and their monitoring. The Indian Government, realising the fiscal shortages in welfare investments, required new solutions to its welfare financing problems. Hence, it started using various ways with taxation, rationalising tax structures and tax deductions on various economic endeavours. (Larasati et al., 2023; Taneja et al., 2022).

For the Government, it remains a question of the mode of sharing the social costs associated with various financial policies. The major corporations in India hold a significant amount of cash reserves. Still, it is believed that apart from a few exceptions, firms rarely make a comprehensive approach for a consolidated and larger allocation in welfare investments, thereby putting the SA requirements on them. The main incentive behind these measures was to spread reliance on philanthropic funding, which could widen the resource pool of local public sector institutions at minimal fiscal cost. Efforts were undertaken to invest and disclose at predetermined standards by the government (Elliott et al., 2025; Pauly & Burns, 2024). Recognition and motivation policies were used, especially in the early years of implementation of the mandatory measure, to more voluntarily appropriate practices. However, inflationary pressures and a growing perception that these requirements impose adverse financial and operational consequences have led to significant non-compliance with the early monitoring regime over the years. Compliance drift has been turned into a blatant omission in still many operations and units, especially in its philanthropic or SA side. Hence the Government intends to move into an audit and penalty.

7. Stakeholder Engagement and Communication

Based on the literature on Intermediary Stakeholder Theory (IST) and supported by empirical evidence from face-to-face interviews with departments within six large companies, this chapter contributes to the theoretical foundation of both the role of intermediary stakeholders in sustainability decision-making processes and their influence on corporate sustainability performances (Arvidsson, 2018). The study reveals that within companies the influence of non-member intermediary stakeholders on the decision-making processes on sustainability corporate governance is relatively large while the influence on the decisions regarding corporate sustainability performance is minor. This is in contrast to the views of member intermediary stakeholders.

Theories on the influence of different stakeholders on corporate sustainability governance and performances rely exclusively upon the category of primary versus secondary stakeholders. A theoretical extension of stakeholder influence theories by focusing on the intermediary category of stakeholders is developed here through the theoretical frameworks of IST and Stakeholder Strategy Theory (SST). The foundations of these novel conceptions are developed based on two different insights on stakeholder influence which combine to better understand how intermediary stakeholders influence corporate sustainability decisions (Góes et al., 2023; Martos-Pedrero et al., 2023).

8. Future Trends in SA

SA research is worthwhile when it is both local and global. Local studies uncover cultural richness, probe the role of social and cultural values in information production and ensure any changes accord with local values. Global studies aim towards knowledge-sharing and shared knowledge-building. Local studies reveal diverse potentials, while a globalised market ensures interconnectedness, technology transfers and capacity sharing (Chatzivgeri et al., 2018).

It is also vital to analyse human-made SA systems across diverse landscapes of governance of different types, with multiple systems of governance assuredly governing social issues equally differently. SA systems need to reflect intrinsic governance provisions, with careful consideration of the SA assemblage: SA conceptualisation and use must take heed of diverse facets of social existence. Cognisance of such factors makes the architecture of SA systems fit for purpose. There is space for research on conceptualising SA, assemblages of SA technologies threaded with governance logics, a coherence-informed collapse of SA systems and non-relational governance logics spurring multiple and divergent SA systems (Leventon et al., 2021; Palmer et al., 2022).

9. Measuring the Impact of Technology on SA

The objective of the study is to examine how technology is augmenting CSR and offer a process for multinationals to implement social good initiatives through AI and machine learning (ML) platforms. A design science approach was adopted to develop and evaluate SysEngage, a tech-enabled CSR process. The sustainability of firms is inherently linked with the sustainability of societies. Multinational enterprises (MNEs) are increasingly launching CSR initiatives in the countries they operate in to give back to the society that allows them to do business (Napier, 2019). In particular, impactful CSR has been termed as a way to improve employee attraction and retention, enhance firm reputation and brand image, mitigate risk and avert scandal, as well as reduce the liability to foreignness in order to establish a strategic competitive advantage. However, few MNEs have been able to create an impact that goes beyond simple grant giving. MNEs have Accountability, Sustainability and Transparency (AST) related challenges that arise from their global nature, multi-businesses and affecting communities. Furthermore, a donation focus within CSR does not create any social or business sustainability and firms lack the key performance indicators to accurately forecast or measure impact. Firms need to instead adopt a differentiated giving model that creates shared value in order to translate reputation into competitive advantage. When technology is linked with CSR, MNEs are able to adapt to the different social, political and economic country specific contexts and overcome CSR challenges. Technology empowered CSR is the infusion of AI and ML into social engagement and impact creation, some believe this shift will nominally be less impactful than past least-philosophy dropped innovations. Others, however, take the opposing viewpoint, asserting that the magnitude and variety of social initiatives at MNEs will be far greater, impacting more lives to a greater degree. Technology and on-line accessibility could also render social ills more visible in societies where MNEs operate (Gulati et al., 2025; Mahajan, 2025; Selvaraj, 2024). Technology enabled CSR leads to more engagement touchpoints and hence better social initiatives as they are more attuned to social needs.

10. Best Practices for Sustainable Business Growth

An emerging discourse on Societal Resilience can better comprehend this challenge and enhance understanding of grand challenges as inter-related and wicked problems needing transformational systems-based global solutions. To identify the best practices in Indian companies for sustainable business growth and develop a conceptual framework as best practice models, focus group interviews were undertaken with academic professionals and industry representatives in the field of CSR, corporate finance, financial accounting and accounts management, to identify the best practices being followed by firms (Bulchand-Gidumal et al., 2024; Morley et al., 2022). Further, the Indian financial regulators were consulted to find out the existing measures of disclosure of the above best requested practices by firms. It was suggested that firms should voluntarily submit such disclosures, which could be checked by the regulators on a sample basis. A self-disclosed index may also be recommended by the regulators for firms to disclose their practices and measures. The future of sustainability depends on the education, stewardship and passion of future business leaders. An increase in demand for climate business leaders is expected and participation in climate change efforts no longer excludes business action. Efforts should be made to fix the cost to advance and rectify decarbonisation technology (Raja & Muthuswamy, 2023; Schwepker & Dimitriou, 2021).

11. Conclusion

This chapter has explored how SA is being transformed by emerging technologies in the journey towards sustainable business growth. By reviewing a wide range of literature and practical insights, we've shown how tools like blockchain, AI, big data analytics and green technologies are moving accounting practices beyond traditional financial reporting. Instead of focusing only on numbers, today's systems are becoming more real-time, interactive and inclusive – capturing a company's social and environmental impact alongside its economic performance. A key takeaway is the powerful role technology plays in making social accountability more transparent and measurable. If applied adequately, digital infrastructure can assist companies in tracking their sustainability efforts with more precision and in conveying these to their relevant stakeholders in a more meaningful manner. The framework of SysEngage that was forwarded in this chapter gives a glimpse of how technology, when apt, can nurture consciously responsive CSR strategies. These tools don't merely enrich data: the very existence of these tools allows for meaningful stakeholder engagement, trust and intelligent choices.

Practitioners must see this as an opportunity to embrace a new mindset that goes beyond right tools. Companies need to invest in digital infrastructure and build teams blending the best technology with sustainability expertise, and weave excitement for accountability into daily decisions. In a world where sustainability weighs heavily on conscience, these steps can further compliance, facilitate reporting and enhance the goodwill of a company.

The next chapter can witness the putting into practice of models such as SysEngage across real-world commercial settings in several industries, and in various regions. Further on, it would be worthwhile to understand the challenges that companies face, especially those in developing countries, when adopting these technologies. For instance, infrastructure constraints, policy voids or an awareness gap are all issues worthy of consideration. Exploring to what extent the rules or regulations, culture and organisational readiness influence adoption could see us coming up with better-warranted solutions. Thus, the application of technology to SA is no longer an option, quite the opposite. With businesses facing increasingly big demands for transparency and responsibility, technology-enabled approaches present a viable, worthwhile way forward. Taking this seriously essentially positions the company to stay ahead while fulfilling stakeholder expectations and giving back to the cause of society and the environment. The chapter, therefore, foregrounds improving adaptive thinking and innovativeness in the walk towards building a more responsible and future-ready business practice.

References

Ahmad, A. Y. B., & Ahmad, B. (2024). Firm determinants that influence implementation of accounting technologies in business organizations. *WSEAS Transactions on Business and Economics*, *21*, 1–11.

Akhavan, R. M., & Zvezdov, D. (2021). Addressing sustainability information needs along supply chains. *Sustainability Accounting, Management and Policy Journal*, *12*(4), 643–666.

Arogyaswamy, B. (2019). Business strategies for sustainability-motivated innovation: A conceptual framework. *Journal of Management for Global Sustainability*, *7*(1), 3.

Arvidsson, S. (2018). How are stakeholder relations communicated in sustainability reports? A longitudinal and cross-country focus. *Medienjournal-Zeitschrift für Medien-und Kommunkiationsforschung*, *42*(1), 51–70.

Baiod, W., & Hussain, M. M. (2024). The impact and adoption of emerging technologies on accounting: Perceptions of Canadian companies. *International Journal of Accounting and Information Management*, *32*(4), 557–592.

Bulchand-Gidumal, J., William Secin, E., O'Connor, P., & Buhalis, D. (2024). Artificial intelligence's impact on hospitality and tourism marketing: Exploring key themes and addressing challenges. *Current Issues in Tourism*, *27*(14), 2345–2362.

Chatzivgeri, E., Paterson, A., Eliwa, Y., Jackson, W., Chatzivgeri, E., Paterson, A., Eliwa, Y., & Jackson, W. (2018). Tomorrow's accounting and society's future. https://hdl.handle.net/2134/28401

Chaudhry, S. (2022). *The assault on civil society: Explaining state crackdown on NGOs*. International Organization.

Chaudhuri, A., Bhatia, M. S., Kayikci, Y., Fernandes, K. J., & Fosso-Wamba, S. (2023). Improving social sustainability and reducing supply chain risks through blockchain implementation: Role of outcome and behavioural mechanisms. *Annals of Operations Research*, 1–33.

Dattathrani, S., & De', R. (2023). The concept of agency in the era of artificial intelligence: Dimensions and degrees. *Information Systems Frontiers*, https://doi.org/10.1007/s10796-022-10336-8

Elliott, J. T., Houngbonon, G. V., Ivaldi, M., & Scott, P. T. (2025). Market structure, investment, and technical efficiencies in mobile telecommunications. *Journal of Political Economy*, *133*(5), 1401–1459.

Flavián, C., & Casaló, L. V. (2021). Artificial intelligence in services: Current trends, benefits and challenges. *Service Industries Journal*. https://doi.org/10.1080/02642069.2021.1989177

Góes, H. A. D. A., Fatima, G., Santos Jhunior, R. D. O., & Boaventura, J. M. G. (2023). Managing for stakeholders towards corporate environmental sustainability. *Corporate Social Responsibility and Environmental Management*, *30*(4), 1561–1572.

Gulati, P., Komal, K., & Mahajan, A. (2025). AI-Driven environmental protection through Corporate Social Responsibility (CSR) activities: A global perspective. In *Convergence of AI, education, and business for sustainability* (pp. 233–260). IGI Global Scientific Publishing.

Jindal, P. (2025). Economic, social, and environmental aspects of sustainable development-direct and indirect effects on business practices. In *Greening our economy for a sustainable future*. Elsevier.

Kannan, S., & Gambetta, N. (2025). Technology-driven sustainability in small and medium-sized enterprises: A systematic literature review. *Journal of Small Business Strategy*. *35*(1), 129–157.

Kuruppu, S. C., Dissanayake, D., & de Villiers, C. (2022). How can NGO accountability practices be improved with technologies such as blockchain and triple-entry accounting? *Accounting, Auditing and Accountability Journal*, *35*(7), 1714–1742.

Larasati, Z. W., Yuda, T. K., & Syafa'at, A. R. (2023). Digital welfare state and problem arising: An exploration and future research agenda. *International Journal of Sociology & Social Policy*, *43*(5/6), 537–549.

Leitner-Hanetseder, S., Lehner, O. M., Eisl, C., & Forstenlechner, C. (2021). A profession in transition: Actors, tasks and roles in AI-based accounting. *Journal of Applied Accounting Research*, *22*(3), 539–556.

Leventon, J., Duşe, I. A., & Horcea-Milcu, A. I. (2021). Leveraging biodiversity action from plural values: Transformations of governance systems. *Frontiers in Ecology and Evolution*, 9.

Mahajan, A. (2025). Protection through corporate social responsibility. *Convergence of AI, Education, and Business for Sustainability*, 233.

Markham, R., Hunt, M., Woollard, R., Oelke, N., Snadden, D., Strasser, R., Betkus, G., & Graham, S. (2021). Addressing rural and Indigenous health inequities in Canada through socially accountable health partnerships. *BMJ Open*, *11*(11).

Martin, A. S., & Freeland, S. (2021). The advent of artificial intelligence in space activities: New legal challenges. *Space Policy*. https://doi.org/10.1016/j.spacepol.2020.101408

Martínez-Peláez, R., Ochoa-Brust, A., Rivera, S., Félix, V. G., Ostos, R., Brito, H., Félix, R. A., & Mena, L. J. (2023). Role of digital transformation for achieving sustainability: Mediated role of stakeholders, key capabilities, and technology. *Sustainability*, *15*(14).

Martos-Pedrero, A., Jiménez-Castillo, D., Ferrón-Vílchez, V., & Cortés-García, F. J. (2023). Corporate social responsibility and export performance under stakeholder view: The mediation of innovation and the moderation of the legal form. *Corporate Social Responsibility and Environmental Management*, *30*(1), 248–266.

Mio, C., Costantini, A., & Panfilo, S. (2022). Performance measurement tools for sustainable business: A systematic literature review on the sustainability balanced scorecard use. *Corporate Social Responsibility and Environmental Management*, *29*(2), 367–384.

Mitra, T., Kapoor, R., & Gupta, N. (2023). Studying key antecedents of disruptive technology adoption in the digital supply chain: An Indian perspective. *International Journal of Emerging Markets*, *18*(10), 4669–4689.

Morley, J., Murphy, L., Mishra, A., Joshi, I., & Karpathakis, K. (2022). Governing data and artificial intelligence for health care: Developing an international understanding. *JMIR formative research*, *6*(1).

Mukherjee, P., & Pradhan, C. (2021). Blockchain 1.0 to blockchain 4.0—The evolutionary transformation of blockchain technology. In *Blockchain technology: Applications and challenges* (pp. 29–49). Springer International Publishing.

Napier, E. (2019). *Technology enabled social responsibility projects and an empirical test of CSRu27s impact on firm performance*. https://scholarworks.gsu.edu/items/d34a0d6b-b62c-4dac-b43d-4125cae0a209

Nathan, R., Monk, C. T., Arlinghaus, R., Adam, T., Alós, J., Assaf, M., Baktoft, H., Beardsworth, C. E., Bertram, M. G., Bijleveld, A. I., & Brodin, T. (2022). Big-data approaches lead to an increased understanding of the ecology of animal movement. *Science*, *375*(6582).

Onyango, S., Wanyoike Muchina, S., & Irura Ng'ang'a, S. (2018). Accounting education: The role of universities in imparting sustainability accounting knowledge to the stakeholders through industry linkages. *Accounting Research Journal*, *2*(1), 1–12.

Palmer, C. G., Fry, A., Libala, N., Ralekhetla, M., Mtati, N., Weaver, M., Mtintsilana, Z., & Scherman, P. A. (2022). Engaging society and building participatory governance in a rural landscape restoration context. *Anthropocene*, *37*.

Pasquinelli, M., & Joler, V. (2021). The Nooscope manifested: AI as instrument of knowledge extractivism. *AI and society*. *36*(4), 1263–1280.

Paterson, A. S., Jackson, W. J., & Haslam, J. (2021). Critical reflections of accounting and social impact (Part II). *Critical Perspectives on Accounting*, *80*, 102342.

Pauly, M. V., & Burns, L. R. (2024). Equity investment in physician practices: What's all this brouhaha? *Journal of Health Politics, Policy and Law*, *49*(4), 631–664.

Pollok, L., Spierling, S., Endres, H. J., & Grote, U. (2021). Social life cycle assessments: A review on past development, advances and methodological challenges. *Sustainability*, *13*(18), 10286.

Ragainis, A. (2018). *Social accounting and the obstacles to implementation for Ontario's co-operatives*. http://hdl.handle.net/10315/34743

Raja Santhi, A., & Muthuswamy, P. (2023). Industry 5.0 or industry 4.0 S? Introduction to industry 4.0 and a peek into the prospective industry 5.0 technologies. *International Journal on Interactive Design and Manufacturing*, *17*(2), 947–979.

Schaltegger, S., Christ, K. L., Wenzig, J., & Burritt, R. L. (2022). Corporate sustainability management accounting and multi-level links for sustainability – A systematic review. *International Journal of Management Reviews*, *24*(4), 480–500.

Schut, L. G. (2023). *Investigating the impact of technological advancements on the job of a management accountant: Identifying capabilities required for the future*. https://essay.utwente.nl/fileshare/file/97208/Schut_MA_BMS.pdf

Schwepker, Jr., C. H., & Dimitriou, C. K. (2021). Using ethical leadership to reduce job stress and improve performance quality in the hospitality industry. *International Journal of Hospitality Management*, *94*.

Selvaraj, J. T. (2024). *Aligning AI systems with corporate sustainability and CSR strategies: Providing actionable insights and guidelines for enhanced integration*. https://urn.fi/URN:NBN:fi-fe2024081464821

Sheikh, F. (2024). *Challenging accounting fraud and the corporate psychopath accountant through blockchain technology*. https://salford-repository.worktribe.com/output/3077055/challenging-accounting-fraud-and-the-corporate-psychopath-accountant-through-blockchain-technology

Singh, A., & Verma, P. (2014). From philanthropy to mandatory CSR: A journey towards mandatory corporate social responsibility in India. *International Journal of Business and Management Invention*, *3*(8), 72–78. https://www.ijbmi.org/papers/Vol(3)8/H038072078.pdf

Smith, J. E., & Pinter-Wollman, N. (2021). Observing the unwatchable: Integrating automated sensing, naturalistic observations and animal social network analysis in the age of big data. *Journal of Animal Ecology*, *90*(1), 62–75.

Taneja, S., Kaur, S., & Özen, E. (2022). Using green finance to promote global growth in a sustainable way. *International Journal of Green Economics*, *16*(3), 246–257.

Tran-Dang, H., Kim, J. W., Lee, J. M., & Kim, D. S. (2025). Shaping the future of logistics: Data-driven technology approaches and strategic management. *IETE Technical Review*, *42*(1), 44–79.

Tsiligiris, V., & Bowyer, D. (2021). Exploring the impact of 4IR on skills and personal qualities for future accountants: A proposed conceptual framework for university accounting education. *Accounting Education*, *30*(6), 621–649.

Wang, T. (2022). The impact of emerging technologies on accounting curriculum and the accounting profession. *Pacific Accounting Review*, *34*(4), 526–535.

Wolniak, R., Gajdzik, B., & Grebski, W. (2023). Environmental sustainability in business. Scientific Papers of Silesian University of Technology. *Organization and Management Series*, *175*, 611–630. https://doi.org/10.29119/1641-3466.2023.175.39

Zhang, X., Sheng, Y., & Liu, Z. (2023). Using expertise as an intermediary: Unleashing the power of blockchain technology to drive future sustainable management using hidden champions. *Heliyon*. https://doi.org/10.1016/j.heliyon.2023.e23807

Zvezdov, D. (2013). Rolling out corporate sustainability accounting: A set of challenges. *Journal of Environmental Sustainability*, *2*(2), 3.

Chapter 8

Effective AI Practices and the Reliability of Accounting Profits: A Strategy for Enhancing Financial Performance and Achieving Institutional Excellence

Enas K. Abu Farha[a] *and Lana K. Abu Farha*[b]

[a]The World Islamic Sciences and Education University, Jordan
[b]The University of Jordan, Jordan

Abstract

This chapter explores the relationships and connections between the reliability of financial performance and adoption of artificial intelligence (AI) techniques. It analyses how different AI techniques influence the reliability of organisational profits and sustainable performance.

Recent literature has demonstrated that technology improvements alongside AI experts can generate positive outcomes and results. These relationships receive significant fairness from relative factors that combine regulatory strength and organisational complexity.

Keywords: Financial performance; organisational performance; artificial intelligence; expert systems; machine learning and robotics

1. Introduction

With the rushing leap of digital transformation, Information and Communication Technology (ICT) has become a fundamental driver of both economic and social development. Nowadays, countries often evaluate their growth and advancement by the extent to which they integrate modern technologies such as cloud computing, cloud accounting and artificial intelligence (AI). Due to the extraordinary capabilities of these techniques within communication and data

Sustainability in Accounting and Finance Education, 127–141

Published under exclusive licence by Emerald Publishing Limited
doi:10.1108/978-1-80686-393-820261008

accessibility, they significantly reshape organisational operations, deeply influence organisational performance, accounting information practices and financial systems. As a result, a structural shift in the economy and its broader macroeconomic has been established.

The growing pressure to accomplish sustainability has become imperative for organisations to reassess their accounting tools and financial reporting systems, in order to ensure their reliability and consistency with environmental, social and governance (ESG) objectives. The accounting sector is undergoing a fundamental transformation due to the adoption of AI technologies, which are used in a wide range of activities, such as analysing complex financial data, generating accurate reports, and help decision-makers in assessing financial and non-financial performance more quickly and accurately (Areiqat & Jaber, 2025).

However, transformation requires strong governance framework to ensure that technologies are not used only as operational tools, but rather as strategic tools that enhance reliability, transparency and accountability to support long-term sustainable growth. Reliable accounting earnings help build trust among stakeholders and achieve a balance between profitability and compliance with ESG principles (Lee et al., 2024).

A deeper understanding of the relationship between reliable accounting and sustainable ESG objectives requires an analytical model that integrates technical, financial and governance dimensions to assess the impact of AI practices on sustainable financial performance. Therefore, this chapter aims to explore how AI practices, if implemented within an effective governance environment, can enhance the reliability of accounting earnings, while contributing to achieving ESG objectives and enhancing sustainable corporate performance.

2. Financial Performance

Economic environment is a Known for its dynamic, ever-evolving space and continuous decision-making. These decisions are characterised by their heavy dependence on data and information extracted from financial reports analysis. Managers and decision-makers need to produce effective decisions, and thus must rely on trustworthy and accurate data that can serve as a foundation for achieving the organisation's various goals and objectives – of which financial performance is arguably the most critical.

2.1 The Concept of Financial Performance

Financial performance is an organisation's ability to utilise its assets to generate current and future revenues and profits, which reflected in cash flows from its primary operating activities. Financial performance serves as one of the most significant indicators for comparing performance among companies within the same industry; also financial performance is a key element for evaluating entire sectors, considered as a benchmark for an entity's overall financial health for both short and long term (Abner & Ferrer, 2018).

Financial performance is considered a comprehensive process to evaluate the overall outcomes of an organisation's operations in financial terms, assessing its ability to achieve short- and long-term objectives and goals. The process involves determining the efficiency of using resources, aligning those resources with actual results and evaluating the relevance of the stated strategic goals. Ultimately, financial performance reflects the entity's overall success in overcoming difficulties and achieving sustainable financial growth.

2.2 Evaluation of Financial Performance

Given the vital role of financial performance, a huge emphasis must take place on its assessment through financial analysis. Financial analysis is a process that involves the examination of available financial statements and reports, key performance indicators and relevant data collected through applying various mathematical and statistical methods.

The goal of financial analysis is to extract meaningful indicators that reveal and show up the relationships among financial statement components, enabling a comprehensive evaluation of the organisation's economic and managerial position. This process also simplifies identifying any existed deviations, their primary causes and suggesting appropriate policies for making effective decisions (Awad & Awad, 2021).

2.3 Financial Performance Indicators

Financial analysis may take multiple forms and ways, and must be supported by reliable and suitable indicators and dimensions. Among the most widely used and academically recognised techniques are financial ratios. The following indicators are the most used among organisations, making them easily comparable (Gibson, 2012):

- *Return on Assets (ROA):*

An indicator that measures a company's profitability relative to its total assets, reflecting how efficiently the firm uses its assets to generate profit. It is calculated by dividing net income by total assets, typically expressed as a percentage to allow for comparisons across companies of different sizes.

- *Return on Equity (ROE):*

An indicator that assesses the firm's ability to generate profits from shareholders' equity. It indicates how efficiently management is using the shareholders' capital and is calculated as the ratio of net income to shareholders' equity.

- *Earnings per Share (EPS):*

An indicator that represents the monetary value of earnings allocated to each outstanding share of common stock. EPS is considered a fundamental metric, that investors relies upon, to evaluate company's profitability and its effectiveness in utilising shareholders' equity. EPS is calculated by dividing net income, after deducting preferred dividends, by the weighted average number of outstanding common shares.

Accounting fields experienced a qualitative leap caused by the recent technological advancements. Traditional accounting operations and processes have been automated, starting from routine bookkeeping to complex auditing and data analysis procedures and transactions (Al-Hashem et al., 2022).

This digital transformation leads to significant changes. These changes can be summarised as follows:

- cost reductions;
- time savings;
- enhanced accuracy and quality;
- gaining competitive advantages;
- improving the reliability of financial reporting;
- optimising the use of human resources.

3. Artificial Intelligence

The origins of AI trace back to the 1950s, emerging from foundational work in mathematics, computing, psychology, linguistics and engineering. Over decades, AI has progressed into a distinct, interdisciplinary domain that leverages advances in these fields through continuous research and technological innovation. Today, AI represents a specialised area within computer science and information technology (IT), aimed at developing systems and software capable of simulating human cognitive processes (Alalwan, 2022). These capabilities allow for AI applications across diverse sectors, facilitating knowledge acquisition and decision-making traditionally associated with human intelligence.

3.1 AI Definition

The Financial Stability Board (FSB, 2017) defines AI as a complex integration of algorithms, computational systems and theoretical models designed to perform tasks that require cognitive abilities, such as visual perception, speech recognition and text interpretation. AI systems progressively improve by identifying patterns in data, enhancing their learning and decision-making capabilities (Puthukulam et al., 2021).

In accounting, AI tools aid managerial decision-making by optimising operational efficiency, accuracy and cost-effectiveness, thus revolutionising the profession (Kulkarni & Bansal, 2024). For the accounting purposes, AI can be viewed as an advanced methodology in the accounting and finance sectors that assist in both operational and administrative tasks, through intelligent systems capable of data analysis and situational learning, often yielding predictive insights with capabilities comparable to or exceeding human intelligence.

AI's analytical prowess in processing vast datasets facilitates enhanced problem-solving, alternative evaluation and evidence-based decision-making. In banking, AI has transformed traditional practices by fostering digital services that are both precise and efficient, enabling customer-tailored, smart banking models that offer competitive advantages. Within financial services, AI's predictive capacities and robust data analysis capabilities have been shown to reduce operational costs and increase profitability (Akpanobong & Essien, 2022). AI offers numerous advantages in the accounting field, which can be summarised as follows:

- The ability to represent information and knowledge, to build knowledge base that provides relevant data for problem-solving.
- The ability to deal with incomplete or unavailable information and to effectively address any deficiencies.
- The potential to learn from past experiences and avoid any previously committed errors.
- The ability to derive solutions to raised problems through logical analysis of situations and conduct relevant comparison with prior cases stored in the knowledge database.
- The use of an optimistic experimental approach to solve unfamiliar problems, relying on trial-and-error rather than fixed rules, sequential steps or traditional methods.

3.2 Core AI Technologies

AI introduces technologies that transform decision-making and automation across sectors. Key technologies used in organisations, especially in accounting departments include the following.

3.2.1 Expert Systems

Expert Systems are among the oldest and most established AI techniques; these systems appeared since early periods and continued to evolve with enhanced features and performance that influence users over time. Expert Systems referred to knowledge engineering, that is used in practical applications, particularly in accounting and auditing, due to their significant role in supporting decision-making and reducing subjective judgement. This process positively impacts the quality, speediness and accuracy of decisions, while at the same time minimising related costs, making Expert Systems a powerful tool that challenges human expertise (Rifai, 2022).

Expert Systems depend on computer programs designed to simulate expert level thinking and decision-making. Systems operate through a set of logical steps to solve accounting problems, for example, based on domain specific data and knowledge that are stored in their accounting databases, by incorporating memory structures to remember learnt experiences and then employ reasoning engines to interpret and make conclusions, such as human experts (Gupta & Nagpal, 2020).

Expert System can be defined as technology that analyses and matches methods used to perform tasks, using software programs, which consist mainly of a knowledge base, an inference engine, an explanation facility and a user interface. Given that when expert systems face problems, they translate human responses and knowledge into a set of rules and structures, storing them for future use in similar contexts, making them highly applicable in organisational accounting settings (Hassanein, 2023).

Expert Systems origin goes to the 1980s, when designed to replicate human expertise through converting experience and knowledge into a structured set of rules. These systems can process problems autonomously by simulating human reasoning in order to reach to the optimal end (Abdelhalim, 2022; Gwanmeh et al., 2023).

In accounting domain, Expert Systems function as a technological assistant in decision-making by offering tailored support. Addressing specific financial problems becomes more easy and feasible using expert systems, especially in expertise-intensive areas. This has made Expert Systems a preferred investment for modern organisations to analyse, detect and solve any financial aspects that need human interactions (Abusalma, 2021).

In accounting and financial areas, a well-structured Expert System should include the following core components (Al-Jaber, 2020; Qasaymeh, 2021):

- *Knowledge Base:*

Contains domain-specific accounting and financial knowledge and expert-derived experiences. This knowledge is extracted, codified and stored for future accounting and financial references and use.

- *Working Memory:*

Stores accounting and financial facts, conclusions and context-specific information acquired from previous experiences, sensor data and available accounting and financial databases.

- *Inference Engine:*

Processes the information from the accounting and financial knowledge base and working memory to generate new insights and solve new accounting and financial problems.

- *User Interface:*

Provides a simple and accessible interface through which accounting and financial end-users interact with the system using natural language and intuitive formats.

- *Explanation Facility:*

Offers justifications and explanations for the accounting and financial conclusions drawn, enhancing the system's transparency and trustworthiness and maximising organisations' profits.

The operational model of Expert Systems involves extracting knowledge from accounting and financial experts, storing it in the accounting and financial knowledge base, and analysing queries through the working memory and inference engine. The system returns financial results with clear explanations through the user interface, mirroring the expert behaviour in a relevant manner.

Although literature and scholars may differ in the terminology and frameworks' designs about expert systems, the core principles underlying these systems are mostly consistent.

This reliability ensures practical effectiveness within the organisational settings. Accordingly, expert systems offer a range of valuable benefits, including (Rifai, 2022):

- efficient knowledge storage, recovery and reprocess;
- supporting rational, unbiased decision-making;
- preserving expert knowledge from loss or damage;
- immediate problem-solving capability;
- enhancing decision accuracy and cost-effectiveness.

Accordingly, we can summarise that expert systems can be viewed as a fundamental element of AI techniques in accounting and financial performance. Their high adaption across economic sectors made them especially relevant among the current rapidly evolving business environment.

3.2.2 Automated Machine Learning (Auto ML)

Auto ML represents an advanced branch of AI that integrates different areas from computer science, engineering and statistics within one integrated framework (Leo et al., 2019).

Auto ML technology relies heavily on algorithms, that are capable of learning and adapting to dynamic environments, either with minimal human supervision or entirely autonomously, and thus enable them to make independent decisions through iterative learning processes (Gwanmeh et al., 2023).

On the other hand, Qutb (2023) defines Auto ML as a sophisticated and adaptive learning platform, designed to organise and classify accounting and financial data, in a way that allows systems to specify patterns and make knowledgeable decisions with minimal human interaction.

Auto ML automates repetitive processes by generating workflows and algorithms that identify unique features in each operation, cluster similar cases and refine models through ongoing feedback.

In the accounting field, Auto ML can be categorised into the following types (Al-Jaber, 2020; Siddiqi, 2023):

- *Reinforcement Learning:*
  Goal-driven accounting and financial learning using observation, adaptation and trial-and-error techniques to improve performance over time.
- *Unsupervised Learning:*
  Algorithm-driven accounting and financial discovery and classification in the absence of labelled data using clustering methods.
- *Supervised Learning:*
  Relies on labelled accounting and financial input provided by humans to train the system using classification and regression techniques.
- *Semi-Supervised Learning:*
  Combines small labelled accounting and financial datasets with large volumes of unlabelled data using sampling and pattern recognition.
- *Deep Learning:*
  Involves repetitive task performance with incremental improvements to optimise accounting and financial outcomes over time.

Auto ML has seen widespread application, particularly in technology and financial sectors. Self-learning and decision-making capabilities have made it an attractive option for organisations aiming to automate recurring processes and analyse large financial data volumes efficiently (Kaminskyi et al., 2021).

Auto ML excels in handling complex tasks with minimal time, effort and risk. The potential to improve customer interaction, reduce operational costs and support strategic growth, make it a valuable investment for data-driven enterprises.

3.2.3 Robotics

Robotics is a prominent field of AI. The Robot Institute of America (1979) defined a robot as a programmable machine capable of performing tasks and manipulating materials with precision, designed to interact with its surroundings much like humans (Abdelhalim, 2022).

Robotics merges AI with IT, computer science and engineering to produce machines that perform human-like tasks. These systems use sensors to collect environmental data, process it and respond accordingly (Siddiqi, 2023).

Robots interpret inputs such as speech or movement and respond optimally, often engaging in conversations with users to complete tasks or provide services (Umamaheswari et al., 2023). Rifai (2022) describes robots as mechanical machines operating under direct or indirect human control through computer programming. Robot components include sensors, power units, control systems and actuators that function cohesively.

Robotics has found broad applications, especially in accounting and auditing, due to its ability to reduce repetitive tasks, lower costs and improve decision-making through timely and accurate data provision. Known as robotic process automation (RPA), these systems replicate human interaction with digital systems to automate routine tasks, enhancing productivity and reliability (Hassanein, 2023).

A widely used application is chatbot – software designed to simulate human conversation using natural language processing (NLP), to analyse inputs and deliver responses that mirror human interaction, which are intensively used among banks (Al-Abdallat, 2020).

Robots technique can perform accounting operations in a rapid, accurate and consistent way, without any human debilitation or error existence. This makes Robotics highly valuable in accounting, as they perform continuous operation in a cost effective manner and user-friendly interfaces (Sayiwal, 2020).

4. AI in Accounting

AI techniques play an essential role in enhancing organisational performance and restructuring operational processes within the organisations. Nowadays, organisations are extensively employing AI techniques, like machine learning (ML) and robotics, to simplify transactions, reduce costs and save required time for executing tasks.

This rapid advancement significantly improved organisational capabilities, particularly in the accounting areas, through accurate analysis of customers' behaviour and predicting future preferences and needs. These insights build a strong foundation for sustainable, strategic decision-making process, opening the way to improve service quality, higher customer satisfaction and strong financial performance.

AI applications also offer organisations a distinguished competitive advantage, that contributes in achieving sustainable growth, by optimising efficiency and reducing direct human involvement (Feuerriegel et al., 2022).

These techniques are often characterised by:

- capacity to process complex transactions and big data, in an accurate speedy way;
- reducing the load on human resources, and minimising systemic errors;
- advancing financial evaluation methods;
- increasing the precision of fraud detection and reducing opportunities for manipulation.

This, in turn, promotes financial stability and accelerates the adoption of these transformative techniques among various sectors.

4.1 AI as a Compound for Financial Innovation and Performance Enhancement

AI has emerged as the central nervous system of economic and organisational development in the 21st century. It represents the peak of contemporary technological advancement and employs a deep influence on the strategic directions of individuals, institutions and governments worldwide.

The main reason behind AI's significance is its high degree of flexibility and applicability across diverse sectors, and especially in accounting and economic areas, which makes it as a core player of the innovation process, and a main driver of competitive advantages.

Accounting and finance have undergone a notable shift towards the integration of AI-based tools, which aims to achieve the following goals and objectives:

- improving service quality;
- enhancing operational efficiency;
- boosting financial performance.

AI techniques paved the way for more innovative accounting systems, by automating repetitive tasks, reducing operational costs and freeing human capital to be able to focus on strategic activities that maximises the value. This revolution can be linked directly to better customer satisfaction, improved institutional performance on multiple levels and optimising financial profitability (Taybi & Moulay, 2023).

Given the above facts, numerous countries launched national strategies to develop and adopt AI techniques. For example, in Jordan, the Ministry of Digital Economy and Entrepreneurship introduced 2020 national AI policy – a regulatory and ethical framework for AI use (Jordan Strategy Forum, 2024). This policy emphasises human resources growth, infrastructure regeneration and improved governance (Ministry of Digital Economy and Entrepreneurship, 2020). On the other hand, the Central Bank of Jordan merged AI into its broader fintech vision, in order to support the goals of Jordan's Economic Modernization Vision 2033 through the application of big data, blockchain and predictive analytics (Central Bank of Jordan, 2023).

Thus, organisations may deploy AI in different domains, such as biometric security, intelligent chatbots and automated risk analysis, which enhances accounting operations models, reduces fraud detection and builds strong customer relations (Almustafa et al., 2023). These outcomes can be obtained through different techniques, for instance, systems based on iris recognition and fingerprint verification; AI-powered feedback tools can enrich customer experiences and improve operational transparency. Therefore, it enables real time analysis, the development of predictive models, stronger compliance frameworks and more accurate financial forecasting (Al-Abdallat, 2020).

Integrating AI into accounting systems is no longer optional; it has become a strategic necessity. Given today's highly competitive and rapidly evolving financial environment, organisations that delay AI adoption, suffer the risk of falling behind. AI is not merely a technical tool, it is a fundamental substance for more reliable strategic decisions and sustainable financial performance. Moreover, AI is reshaping the role of accounting from a function centred on routine data processing to one deeply rooted in intelligent analysis, empowering financial leadership to play a more dynamic role in value creation process.

5. AI, Accounting Earnings and Corporate Sustainability

Given the digital transformation, it has become very important to examine the relationship between the adoption of AI techniques and the reliability of financial reporting and accounting information systems, especially regarding achieving ESG sustainability goals.

The integration of AI techniques within accounting systems and its operations obviously enhances accuracy and reliability of earnings, which has been clearly indicated through recent literature. These advancements announce for new possibilities beyond what traditional ways could offer, which supports more reliable decision-making process, sustainable performance and financial transparency (Lee et al., 2024).

However, this adoption raises legitimate questions about whether AI outputs are reliable, neutral, transparent and subject to adequate institutional oversight.

A causal sequence model includes four main levels:

(1) adopting AI within a good governance framework;
(2) improving corporate ESG performance;
(3) enhancing the reliability of accounting earnings;
(4) and building stakeholder trust and promoting sustainable growth.

This model developed based on a systematic literature review (SLR) covering many peer-reviewed studies, and using advanced analytical tools such as Preferred Reporting Items for Systematic Reviews and Meta-Analyses (PRISMA) and VOSviewer, as well as analytical frameworks (Areiqat & Jaber, 2025). The model demonstrates that the relationship between AI and sustainability goes beyond enhancing operational efficiency or accelerating data processing. It also supports the reliability and quality of accounting information system itself, directly impacting investment decisions, governance compliance and business continuity (Abusalma, 2023).

AI-powered predictive analytics, enable organisations to accurately assess their environmental and social performance, thereby gaining the trust of financiers and investors, and improving ESG reporting. This integration reduces reputational and compliance risks, which are among the key factors in financial sustainability decisions (Murikah et al., 2024).

However, many risks and challenges surrounding this relationship may be addressed as follows:

(1) Algorithmic bias, where some intelligent models exhibit biases based on distorted or incomplete historical data, potentially replicating patterns of discrimination or misunderstanding in accounting analyses or ESG assessments (Murikah et al., 2024).
(2) Many AI models suffer from a lack of transparency, often referred to as "black box" models, where it is difficult for the end user, whether an auditor or financial analyst, to explain how specific results were reached. This complicates auditing and ethical decision-making (Areiqat & Jaber, 2025).
(3) The risk of overreliance on AI, as the high efficiency and automation provided by these systems could weaken human review and diminish professional evaluation skills, as demonstrated by a 2024 Stanford SFI study on the impact of automation on the accounting profession.
(4) Also, the computing-intensive models (such as Large Language Models and Generative Pre-trained Transformers) consume massive amounts of electricity and produce a significant carbon footprint, which could undermine sustainability claims unless accompanied by green strategies such as the use of renewable energy and an environmental impact assessment of the technical systems themselves (Murikah et al., 2024).

Based on the above, a digital governance framework is important to ensure that the use of AI in accounting information system and financial reporting, is managed within transparent, auditable standards that are consistent with ethical sustainability principles. Integrating such models into accounting and professional education will enhance the readiness of future talent to handle big digital data and deliver highly reliable reports that serve the goals of sustainable growth and social trust.

6. Conclusion

AI has been showed as a key driver in enhancing organisational efficiency and improving financial performance. In today's dynamic business environment, organisations must increasingly rely on intelligent technologies that align with digital transformation and contribute to the quality of accounting information and decision-making processes.

This chapter explored the key role that AI plays in determining earnings and outcomes by analysing concepts, indicators, evaluations and practical techniques within accounting and Accounting Information Systems contexts. Techniques like expert systems, ML and robotics have proved their effectiveness in supporting all kinds of activities, through automating processes, analysing big data and optimising resource utilisation. The key strengths of these techniques lies in the ability to handle incomplete information, analyse past experiences, and merge and expand learning capabilities. These capabilities contribute to more accurate forecasting and much reliable financial decision-making.

On the other hand, the real effect of AI on financial performance extends beyond the technology itself. It is heavily liked and affected by many factors, including the level of digital maturity within organisations, the availability of appropriate technological infrastructure and the willingness of human resources to interact with these techniques.

Consequently, any integration of AI into accounting information systems can't be considered as a temporary trend, rather, it should be handled as a long term strategic decision. The main goal of this adoption is to enhance financial performance, achieve sustainable competitive advantage and shift the way from traditional towards intelligence.

References

Abdelhalim, A. M. M. (2022). Artificial intelligence in managerial accounting and its impact on accounting performance and decision support: An analytical study. *Journal of Financial and Commercial Research*, *23*(2), 465–521.

Abner, R., & Ferrer, R. (2018). Impact of real earnings management on financial performance and firm value: Evidence from the Philippines. *Institute for Global Business Research Conference Proceedings*, *1*(2).

Abusalma, A. (2021). The effect of implementing artificial intelligence on job performance in commercial banks of Jordan. *Management Science Letters*, *11*(7), 2061–2070.

Abusalma, W. (2023). The role of E-accounting disclosure as a mediating variable in the relationship between AI technologies and the quality of accounting information: An empirical study on companies listed on the Egyptian Stock Exchange. *Journal of Advanced Studies in Finance and Accounting*, *6*(1), 20–47.

Akpanobong, U. E., & Essien, N. P. (2022). Artificial intelligence adoption for financial services optimizations and innovation by commercial banks in Nigeria. *International Journal of Advancement in Education, Management, Science and Technology*, *5*(1), 5–15.

Al-Abdallat, A. (2020). Applications of artificial intelligence and their impact on achieving competitive advantage: A study on Jordanian banks. *Mu'tah Journal for Research and Studies*, *35*(5), 78–122.

Alalwan, J. (2022). Roles and challenges of AI-based cybersecurity: A case study. *Jordan Journal of Business Administration*, *18*(3), 437–456.

AL-Hashem, A., Al-Laham, M., & Almasri, A. (2022). E-personalization and E-customization model for enhancing E-customer satisfaction in the case of Covid-19: Empirical evidence from banking sector in Jordan. *Jordan Journal of Business Administration*, *18*(2), 263–276.

Al-Jaber, G. (2020). *The impact of artificial intelligence on the efficiency of accounting systems in Jordanian banks*. Unpublished Master's Thesis. Middle East University. http://search.mandumah.com/Record/1056763

Almustafa, A., Ramli, A., Bin Jalil, A., & Alawneh, M. (2023). The impact of artificial intelligence systems on enhancing the quality of banking services in

Jordanian Islamic banks. *International Journal of Specialized Islamic Studies*, *8*(2), 79–90.

Areiqat, A. Y., & Jaber, H. A. N. (2025). AI and sustainable accounting: Balancing innovation and responsibility. *Journal of Management World*, *2025*(3), 10–16.

Awad, M., & Awad, M. (2021). Indicators and ratios for evaluating financial performance. *Journal of Economic Analysis and Foresight*, *2*(1), 350–371.

Central Bank of Jordan. (2023). *Jordan's financial technology vision*. https://www.cbj.gov.jo

Feuerriegel, S., Shrestha, Y. R., von Krogh, G., & Zhang, C. (2022). Bringing artificial intelligence to business management. *Nature Machine Intelligence*, *4*(7), 611–613.

FSB. (2017). *Artificial intelligence and machine learning in financial services*. https://www.fsb.org/wp-content/uploads/P011117.pdf

Gibson, C. H. (2012). *Financial reporting and analysis* (13th ed.). Cengage Learning.

Gupta, I., & Nagpal, G. (2020). *Artificial intelligence and expert systems*. Mercury Learning and Information.

Gwanmeh, A., Ramli, A., Bin Jalil, A., & Alawneh, M. (2023). The impact of artificial intelligence systems on enhancing the quality of banking services in Jordanian Islamic banks. *International Journal of Specialized Islamic Studies*, *8*(2), 79–90.

Hassanein, W. (2023). The role of E-accounting disclosure as a mediating variable in the relationship between artificial intelligence technologies and the quality of accounting information: An empirical study on companies listed on the Egyptian Stock Exchange. *Journal of Advanced Studies in Finance and Accounting*, *6*(1), 20–47.

Jordan Strategy Forum. (2024). *Jordan's position on the government AI readiness index*. https://www.jsf.org

Kaminskyi, A., Nehrey, M., & Zomchak, L. (2021). Machine learning methods application for consumer banking. In *SHS Web of Conferences* (Vol. 107, p. 12001). EDP Sciences.

Kulkarni, N. D., & Bansal, S. (2024). The impact of artificial intelligence in banking and finance sector – A review. *International Research Journal of Modernization in Engineering Technology and Science*, *6*(1), 4036–4043.

Lee, S. U., Perera, H., Liu, Y., Xia, B., Lu, Q., Zhu, L., Cairns, J., & Nottage, M. (2024). Integrating ESG and AI: A comprehensive responsible AI assessment framework. *AI and Ethics*, *5*(5), 5121–5148.

Leo, M., Sharma, S., & Maddulety, K. (2019). Machine learning in banking risk management: A literature review. *Risks*, *7*(1), 29–53.

Ministry of Digital Economy and Entrepreneurship. (2020). *Jordan artificial intelligence policy 2020*. http://ai_final_english_version.pdf(modee.gov.jo)/. Accessed on April 18, 2022.

Murikah, W., Nthenge, J. K., & Musyoka, F. M. (2024). Bias and ethics of AI systems applied in auditing: A systematic review. *Scientific African*, *25*, e02281.

Puthukulam, G., Ravikumar, A., Sharma, R. V. K., & Meesaala, K. M. (2021). Auditors' perception on the impact of artificial intelligence on professional skepticism and judgment in Oman. *Universal Journal of Accounting and Finance*, *9*(5), 1184–1190.

Qasaymeh, G. (2021). *The impact of artificial intelligence on the characteristics of accounting information: The moderating role of accounting system efficiency in Jordanian commercial banks*. Unpublished Doctoral Dissertation. World Islamic Sciences and Education University.

Qutb, J. A. (2023). Research on AI tools and their application areas in academic research writing. *Journal of Arts, Literature, Humanities and Social Sciences*, (98), 443–469.

Rifai, M. (2022). An analytical study for evaluating the role of artificial intelligence techniques in improving the electronic accounting disclosure process. *Journal of Administrative, Financial and Quantitative Research*, *2*(2), 82–96.

Sayiwal, S. (2020). Chatbots in banking industry: A case study. *Journal of Emerging Technologies and Innovative Research*, *7*(6), 1498–1502.

Siddiqi, K. B. (2023). Investing in AI technologies to develop information retrieval: An applied study for building a search engine using IBM Watson discovery. *Scientific Journal of Libraries, Documentation, and Information*, *5*(16), 99–122.

Taybi, I., & Moulay, A. (2023). The impact of artificial intelligence on the performance of commercial banks: A case study of banks in El Bayadh and Tiaret provinces. *Economic Studies*, *23*(1), 33–48.

Umamaheswari, S., Valarmathi, A., & Lakshmi, M. (2023). Role of artificial intelligence in the banking sector. *Journal of Survey in Fisheries Sciences*, *10*(4S), 2841–2849.

Chapter 9

A Proposed Index for Cybersecurity Risk Disclosure and Its Impact on Faithful Representation of Accounting Information

Ahmed I. Sakr, Hanan Hassan Gad Allah and Randa A. Makled

Damietta University, Egypt

Abstract

This study addresses the critical gap in standardised frameworks for cybersecurity risk disclosure a voluntary practice that often results in ambiguous or incomplete reports, leaving financial stakeholders with insufficient information. To bridge this gap, we propose a novel 54-item Cybersecurity Disclosure Index – that distinguishes between incident/risk disclosure – and examine its impact on faithful representation (FR), measured through discretionary accruals. Using data from a set of major telecommunications and fintech companies operating in Egypt between 2020 and 2024, we provide empirical evidence that increased Cyber Risk Disclosure is significantly associated with lower discretionary accruals, suggesting enhanced FR. In contrast, cybersecurity Governance Disclosure shows a positive association with discretionary accruals, indicating that more extensive disclosures may introduce complexity and create opportunities for earnings management. The analysis employs Panel Least Squares (PLS) regression with firm and year fixed effects to address unobserved heterogeneity. The results from the Modified Jones model and a Kothari robustness check confirm the reliability of these findings. The R-squared values of 0.8936 and 0.8935 in the models indicate strong explanatory power, with significant implications for both corporate governance and financial reporting practices. Overall, the proposed Cybersecurity Disclosure Index offers a standardised and transparent framework that advances the field of cybersecurity risk disclosure and contributes significantly to improving both corporate governance and financial reporting practices.

Sustainability in Accounting and Finance Education, 143–164

doi:10.1108/978-1-80686-393-820261009

Keywords: Accounting disclosure; cybersecurity risks; cybersecurity management; qualitative characteristics of information; faithful representation

1. Introduction

Digital transformation has become one of the most critical factors for ensuring corporate sustainability. This has led companies to rely heavily on automation and digital solutions for storage and task management. Consequently, this reliance has significantly increased these companies' exposure to cybersecurity risks that critically threaten corporate assets and client data (Gao et al., 2020). This necessitates the establishment and development of cybersecurity management to protect corporate digital assets and electronic systems from cyber risks, which may originate from threats either inside or outside the company (Mazumder &Hossain, 2023). In addition to meeting stakeholders' needs for information related to cyber risks, their resulting impacts and the preventive and protective measures taken against them (Amin, 2024).

The need for investors and stakeholders regarding cybersecurity risk disclosure lies in clear provisions for disclosing cyber threats and risks, affected assets, remediation costs and protection measures. This is in addition to clear items outlining the responsibilities of cybersecurity management in protecting the company's digital environment from cybersecurity risks (Chen et al., 2023). No specific international accounting standard has yet been issued that mandates and interprets the process of cybersecurity risk disclosure. However, due to stakeholders' need for cybersecurity risk disclosure, several businesses and professional bodies have developed cyber risk disclosure and management frameworks (SEC, 2011 – CPA Canada, 2017 – NCA_KSA, 2018; AICPA, 2017 - ESCC Egypt, 2014). Additionally, many researchers have proposed indicators to standardise cybersecurity risk reporting (Basiouny et al., 2024; Cheng et al., 2022; Li et al., 2018).

These contributions were important in assisting companies with cybersecurity risk disclosure. However, they consisted of overlapping and non-granular items, which management could potentially exploit to prepare disclosures using complex language. This complexity hinders stakeholders' ability to understand the items or distinguish between those related to remediation tasks and those concerning protection tasks, ultimately leading to a lack of faithful representation (FR) of this information. Amidst efforts to classify and unify these items to develop a comprehensive cybersecurity risk disclosure index that distinguishes between the disclosure of actual cyber risks and management's tasks in achieving cybersecurity to ensure the FR of these disclosures, the following research question can be proposed:

- Can a proposed index for cybersecurity risk disclosure be constructed, and its impact on the FR of information be measured?

2. Literature Review

Cybersecurity management has become a primary objective for all countries and companies, due to the trillions of dollars in losses caused by cyber risks to the global economy. Beyond direct financial damages, these risks weaken investor confidence in affected firms and diminish trust across entire industries (Lavion, 2018). This section discusses studies that have examined the direct and indirect relationships between the research variables, aiming to develop a proposed index for cybersecurity risk disclosure and measure its impact on the FR of financial information.

2.1 Cybersecurity Risk Disclosure

Cybersecurity is a collection of technical procedures and operational activities that safeguard an organisation's digital assets by addressing risks and fighting assaults targeting electronically processed information across linked network systems (CSA, 2017) From Kävrestad et al. (2025). Academics argue that cybersecurity is an organisations' due diligence to protect its Digital assets, which encompass its IT infrastructures against cyberattacks, phishing and unauthorised access via strategies, tools and processes (Morshed & Khrais, 2025).

Different scholars have characterised cybersecurity risk. The Committee on National Security Systems (CNSS, 2015) defines it as an organisation's exposure to technology risks from events or conditions that may harm it. The International Telecommunication Union (ITU, 2018) further notes that such threats include computer network-enabled crimes.

Based on these viewpoints, this research defines cybersecurity risks as operational and technological flaws that compromise corporate IT security. Risks aim to compromise, steal or damage digital assets and customer data. External breaches and internal threats from workers or other organisational insiders might cause them.

According to studies by Li et al. (2018), Singh (2025), and Smaili et al. (2023), cybersecurity threats fall into four categories:

- Security breaches: Use network or electronic security flaws to obtain unwanted access and disclose sensitive data.
- Digital fraud: Using phishing or other bogus emails to steal private information.
- Infecting organisational systems with malware to lose data and impair key operations and services.
- Insider Threats: Employee or internal stakeholder cyberattacks to steal secret data or compromise crucial resources.

This categorisation emphasises the complexity of cybersecurity threats and the necessity for strong frameworks to minimise external and internal vulnerabilities.

Narrative disclosure is optional accounting disclosure outside of financial statements. Through narrative reporting, it explains and interprets internal or external events impacting the organisation to Investors and Stakeholders (Smaili et al., 2023). The company's future performance may be assessed using risks, analytics and general business information. No laws or accounting rules require narrative accounting disclosures. Researchers define narrative cybersecurity risk disclosure as: Corporations voluntarily reveal in narrative reports their cyber security policies, plans and technology, as well as any cyber events they have faced. This includes detailing the system repair, company costs and remediation actions.

Regarding the factors to consider when disclosing cybersecurity risks, the study by Morshed and Khrais (2025) and Schaffner et al. (2023), established that certain core and enhanced disclosure processes must be considered in this procedure, as follows:

- *Core Disclosure Processes:*

These include several key factors, most notably alignment with strategic objectives, risk appetite, along with detailed information about protection frameworks, processes and mitigation strategies, as well as disclosures regarding the nature of cyber incidents and their direct impacts.

- *Enhanced Disclosure Processes:*

These involve providing reports on both opportunities and threats, along with detailed information on adopted cyber scenarios including Duration of disruption, Incurred costs and Organisational response measures.

- *Additional Disclosure Considerations:*

When disclosing cybersecurity risks, companies must address:

(1) The organisation's capability to manage cyber risks
(2) The likelihood of cyber threats and which assets could be affected.
(3) Policies and plans followed for cybersecurity risk management.

2.2 Faithful Representation of Financial Information

In order to understand FR, we must first understand the qualitative qualities of meaningful financial information. These traits impact main Users' financial report decision-usefulness, according to Abdel-khalik (2019). Accounting information is useful when it possesses the following characteristics: relevance, faithful representation, understandability, verifiability, comparability and timeliness.

Financial reports must accurately reflect an entity's economic activities and transactions within a reporting period to be faithfully represented. According to Neel and Irfan (2024), financial statements must provide all required information to help users comprehend reported occurrences. The conceptual framework for financial reporting suggests three key qualities to develop this idea:

(1) Completeness – Financial reporting must provide all essential information about a transaction or occurrence to help users comprehend its effects. Thus, completeness ensures a complete financial picture.
(2) Neutrality – FR demands impartial financial knowledge. Preparers must avoid selective disclosure that Favours one stakeholder group over another to ensure impartiality and serve all users.
(3) Free from Material Error – Financial reports should not include major errors or omissions in economic observation or accounting. While exact accuracy is seldom feasible owing to estimations and expert judgements.

2.3 The Impact of Cybersecurity Risk Disclosure on Faithful Representation

The level of cybersecurity disclosure significantly impacts the FR of information, as cyber risks affect a company's assets, financial and operational performance, market value and reputational risks (Ramirez et al, 2022). This makes the disclosure of these risks a critical concern for stakeholders and a key requirement, comparable to mandatory financial disclosures.

Prominent cyber incidents have caused severe losses for companies, exposing them to risks of failure and litigation by stakeholders, as seen in cases such as Equifax, Target and Sony. These cyber incidents cost the global economy approximately one trillion dollars by the end of 2020 (Cheng et al., 2022). Additionally, they threaten the integrity of companies' financial data, leading to inaccuracies and unreliability in financial information. This, in turn, results in the preparation of distorted financial reports that negatively impact audit processes and the performance of financial analysts who rely on such information for their investment analyses (Basiouny et al., 2024).

The disclosure of actual cyber incidents and how companies handle and respond to them provides investors and stakeholders with a more complete and truthful picture of potential financial and operational risks, thereby enhancing the credibility of accounting information (Foya & Garikayi, 2021). It also helps reduce information asymmetry, mitigate agency problems and lower associated costs (Al Amosh & Khatib, 2025). Moreover, higher levels of cybersecurity risk disclosure led to reduced earnings management practices, which improves the quality and reliability of financial statements and underscores the credibility and completeness of information related to cybersecurity risks (Basiouny et al., 2024).

Adequate and detailed disclosure of management's efforts in cybersecurity, asset protection and customer data safeguarding enhances the reliability and quality of financial reports (Foya & Garikayi, 2021). It also meets stakeholders' expectations regarding their need for such information, yielding financial benefits and contributing to improved corporate profitability and financial performance (Al Amosh & Khatib, 2025). Furthermore, effective cybersecurity management helps maintain investor confidence in the company and its accounting information, while maximising the firm's market value (Basiouny et al., 2024).

Given the importance of cybersecurity risk disclosure and its impact on the reliability and truthfulness of accounting information, coupled with the findings of Chen (2020) that cybersecurity and related risk disclosure is an ethical imperative that enhances the quality and authenticity of information provided to users and stakeholders and that non-disclosure weakens already vulnerable organisations, as indicated by Amani et al.'s (2025) study, which reviewed literature related to cybersecurity risk and incident disclosures from 2020 to 2024 found that most companies suffer from deficiencies in the quality of cybersecurity disclosure. This is largely because financial report preparers tend to draft these disclosures in standardised, complex and unreadable language due to fears of negative repercussions from such disclosures and caution regarding litigation risks.

The research gap identified in this study pertains to the absence of a standardised framework for cybersecurity risk disclosure and its voluntary nature, which may lead financial statement preparers to either disclose such items in a complex and unreadable manner that is difficult for non-specialist stakeholders to comprehend or avoid disclosure altogether due to fears of potential harm or litigation risks to the company. This necessitates the proposal of an accounting index for cybersecurity risk disclosure that clearly distinguishes between actual cybersecurity risks and cybersecurity management responsibilities. The index should be designed in a transparent manner that addresses all stakeholder requirements for cybersecurity-related information, ensuring the completeness, accuracy and freedom from material error of these disclosures, while adhering to the principle of adequate disclosure that does not undermine the company's interests.

3. A Proposed Index for the Disclosure of Cyber-Related Implications (Security – Risks)

3.1 Reference Framework

The disclosure of cybersecurity risks in financial reports enhances the quality and transparency of financial information (Basiouny et al., 2024). This, in turn, increases the confidence of financial information users when making investment decisions, as cybersecurity risk disclosure represents a strategic initiative that improves corporate communication with stakeholders (Li et al., 2018). With the fulfilment of cybersecurity disclosure requirements and the resulting information quality assurance, such information must faithfully represent cybersecurity-related events, maintain complete neutrality without bias towards any party and be free from material misstatements in the disclosure process.

3.2 Index Construction Methodology

The index construction methodology draws upon two primary sources:

- leading international regulatory frameworks, including cybersecurity disclosure guidelines from the U.S. SEC (2018), Saudi NCA's governance framework, CPA Canada's risk reporting standards, AICPA's SOC criteria and Egypt's Supreme Cybersecurity Council regulations.
- and academic frameworks from prior research such as Chen et al. (2023), Li et al. (2018), and Morshed and Khrais (2025) on cybersecurity disclosure.

3.3 Details of the Proposed Indicator

To improve the disclosure process of cybersecurity risks and ensure the completeness and clarity of the disclosed information in financial reports, the researchers propose dividing the indicator into two sub-indicators, as follows:

3.3.1 The First Sub-indicator

This concerns the disclosure of actual cybersecurity risks the company has encountered. Its items included detailed disclosure about the type of cyber risk, its causes, the assets affected by it and the costs incurred to confront the risk and repair its damages. We proposed the first sub-indicator concerning the disclosure of actual cybersecurity risks in financial reports. This sub-indicator contains five main items, with each item comprising several elements, totalling 21 elements, as shown in Table 9.1.

3.3.2 The Second Sub-indicator

It focuses on disclosing the company's cybersecurity management responsibilities. Its items included detailed disclosure about cybersecurity management information, cybersecurity governance, management of cyber assets, financial expenditures to enhance cybersecurity, as well as disclosure of the roles and attestations of internal and external audit in financial reports.

The researchers also proposed the second sub-indicator concerning the disclosure of cybersecurity management in secondary reports. This sub-indicator contains six main items in Table 9.2, with each item comprising several elements totalling 33 elements.

3.4 Cybersecurity Disclosure Index Analysis

The proposed Cybersecurity Disclosure Index is divided into two sub-indicators: cybersecurity risk disclosure and cybersecurity management disclosure. The index measures the quality of cybersecurity disclosures in terms of both

Table 9.1. Items and Elements of the Proposed Cybersecurity Risk Disclosure Indicator.

Item	Sub-indicators
Risks faced by the company	Data Destruction Attacks
	System Breach Attacks
	Phishing Attacks
	Website Defacement and Breach Attacks
Source of the Cyber Risk	Fraudulent Methods from Within the Company
	Incorrect Practices and Managerial Lapses
	External Fraudulent Methods
Risk-impacted assets	Fixed or technological Assets
	Security and Safety Risks
	Customer Data Leakage
	Technology Infrastructure Risks
Risk-related costs	Reputational Damage Costs
	Customer Trust Loss Costs
	System Repair Costs
	Service Recovery Costs
Repair and safety procedures	Assessment of Damage Scope
	Isolation of Affected Assets
	Damage Assessment and Quantification
	Notifying Affected Parties
	Repair Operations and System Restoration
	Enhancing Cyber security

Source: Proposed by the researchers.

Table 9.2. Items and Elements of the Proposed Cybersecurity Management Disclosure Indicator.

Item	Sub-indicators
Key management information	Organisational structure and task allocation
	Cybersecurity management plans and objectives
	Supervisory and tracking protocols
	Board oversight of security management operations

Table 9.2. *(Continued)*

Item	Sub-indicators
Governance of cybersecurity practices	The implemented cybersecurity framework
	The specific mandate of working committees
	Board engagement in business activities
	Cyber risk management
	Submission of management activities for audit
	Workforce and client cybersecurity protection
	Continuous audit of budgets, programmes and assigned duties
	Compliance with local laws and regulations
Cybersecurity safeguarding	Cybersecurity asset management
	Cybersecurity protection
	Backup management
	Protection of websites, email and digital platforms
	Protection testing, encryption and penetration
	Unauthorised system access controls
	Designing a cybersecurity oversight framework
Cybersecurity support costs	Cybersecurity upgrades costs
	Cyber insurance premiums
	Costs of purchasing and developing Security software.
	Employee training course costs
	External expert/developer service fees
Internal Audit Responsibilities	Critical cyber risk threat assessment report
	Effectiveness Report of Cyber Risk Mitigation Procedures.
	Governance mechanism efficacy report
	Cyber risk management process effectiveness report
	Assessment of cyber risk management practices
Evaluation and auditing tasks/functions	Compliance assessment with cyber security requirements
	Effectiveness evaluation of cybersecurity policy implementation

(Continued)

Table 9.2. *(Continued)*

Item	Sub-indicators
	Systems, applications and devices vulnerability analysis
	Cybersecurity enhancement recommendation

Source: Proposed by the Researchers.

risk-related and governance aspects. Below, we report the detailed statistics for each sub-indicator and their components.

3.4.1 Cybersecurity Risk Disclosure Sub-indicator

The cybersecurity risk disclosure sub-indicator comprises five key items, with the following results (see Table 9.3).

The total alpha for the cybersecurity risk disclosure sub-indicator is 0.814, indicating strong internal consistency. The items show moderate to high mean values, reflecting a fairly comprehensive approach to disclosing cybersecurity risks across the firms. This is consistent with the studies of Amin (2024) and Chen et al. (2023).

3.4.2 Cybersecurity Management Disclosure Sub-indicator

The cybersecurity management disclosure sub-indicator consists of six items, with the following statistics (see Table 9.4).

The total alpha for the cybersecurity management disclosure sub-indicator is 0.793, demonstrating robust internal consistency. These items reveal that firms are generally providing substantial details on cybersecurity management practices, with relatively high mean values across all components. This is consistent

Table 9.3. Descriptive Statistics for Cybersecurity Risk Disclosure Sub-indicator.

Item	Alpha	Mean	Std. Dev.
Risks Faced by the Company	0.794	2.62	0.607
Source of the Cyber Risk	0.867	2.61	0.686
Risk-impacted Assets	0.766	2.66	0.615
Risk-related Costs	0.827	2.68	0.618
Repair and Safety Procedures	0.851	2.64	0.652

Table 9.4. Descriptive Statistics for Cybersecurity Management Disclosure Sub-indicator.

Item	Alpha	Mean	Std. Dev.
Key Management Information	0.827	2.63	0.655
Governance of Cybersecurity Practices	0.782	2.63	0.665
Cybersecurity Safeguarding	0.829	2.63	0.667
Cybersecurity Support Costs	0.772	2.61	0.694
Internal Audit Responsibilities	0.750	2.68	0.609
Evaluation and Auditing Tasks	0.842	2.68	0.620

with the studies of Daoud and Serag (2022), Basiouny et al. (2024) and Li et al. (2018).

3.4.3 Overall Cybersecurity Disclosure Index

The overall Cybersecurity Disclosure Index (CDR), which combines both cybersecurity risk disclosure and cybersecurity management disclosure, yields a total alpha of 0.801, indicating excellent reliability across the full index. This comprehensive index provides a clear, standardised measure of cybersecurity disclosure quality.

3.4.4 Item-Level Correlations and Internal Consistency

The items within both sub-indicators exhibit high Pearson correlations, ranging from 0.930 to 0.996, all of which are statistically significant at the 0.01 level (two-tailed). This suggests a high degree of internal consistency, with each item contributing meaningfully to the overall sub-indicator and the Cybersecurity Disclosure Index as a whole.

4. Methodology

This chapter uses descriptive-analytical methods to answer the research topic. After identifying and characterising the important cybersecurity risk factors that should be included in financial reports, the researchers create a recommended index to promote financial information accuracy. The researchers reviewed books, academic references, earlier studies and Internet resources and publications by professional organisations and regulatory authorities that establish cybersecurity risk disclosure requirements to write this chapter. After that, a panel of accounting academics reviewed the proposed index to ensure its elements supported faithful representation. This structured method combines theoretical research with practical validation to develop a solid financial reporting cybersecurity risk disclosure framework.

4.1 Research Hypotheses

After reviewing the literature and research gap, the present research hypotheses are shown in Fig. 9.1 and are formulated as follows:

- *H1.* There is a statistically significant effect of adopting the proposed disclosure index for actual cybersecurity risks on enhancing the FR of financial information.
- *H2.* There is a statistically significant effect of adopting the proposed disclosure index for cybersecurity risk management on enhancing the FR of financial information.

4.2 Research Variables

The current research is based on two variables: the independent variable represented by the items of the proposed index for disclosing cyber implications (security risks) and the dependent variable represented by the FR of financial information (see Table 9.5).

Measurement of Study Variables:

4.3 Developing the Disclosure Index

Content analysis is used to identify and classify disclosure elements relating to cybersecurity and FR based on past research and reporting standards. Items were scored binary (1 = disclosed, 0 = not disclosed) to capture key disclosure quality factors.

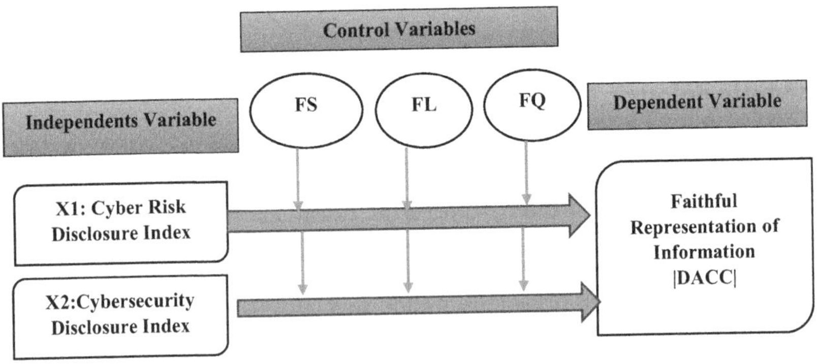

Fig. 9.1. Research Hypotheses.

Table 9.5. Study Variables and Their Measurement Methods (Proposed by the Researchers).

Variable	Measurement Method	Source
Independent variable (X):		
A Proposed Index for the Disclosure of Cyber-related Implications	The researchers' index of 54 equally weighted variables split into two sub-indices measures cybersecurity risk disclosure. If mentioned in the company's financial reports, each item is 1; otherwise, 0. For each organisation, the scores are combined and compared to the minimum 54 disclosure items to establish the cybersecurity risk disclosure ratio.	Proposed by authors, based on the study of (Abdelraouf & Hussainey, 2026; Basiouny et al., 2024; Chen et al., 2023; Cheng et al., 2022).
Dependent Variable (Y):		
The Faithful Representation of Financial Information	Quality discretionary accruals indicate earnings management and financial reporting reliability. Steps to estimate discretionary accruals using the Modified Jones Model: 1. Measuring Total Accruals Related to the Difference Between Net Operating Income and Cash Flow from Operating Activities Using the following equation: $TACC_{i,t} = ONI_{i,t} - CFO_{i,t}$ where: $TACC_{i,t}$: Total accruals (i) during period (t). $ONI_{i,t}$: Net operating income (i) during period (t). $CFO_{i,t}$: Cash flow from operating activities (i) during period (t).	(Shafakheibari & Oladi, 2015)

(Continued)

Table 9.5. *(Continued)*

Variable	Measurement Method	Source
	2. Estimating the Parameters (B_1, B_2, B_3) of the Model to Calculate Non-Discretionary Accruals (NDACC) Using the following regression equation for the sample companies for each year separately: $\frac{TACC_{i,t}}{A_{i,t}} = B_1\left(\frac{1}{A_{i,t}}\right) + B_2\left(\frac{\Delta REV_{i,t} - \Delta REC_{i,t}}{A_{i,t}}\right) + B_3\left(\frac{PPE_{i,t}}{A_{i,t}}\right) + \epsilon_{i,t}$ where: *TACC*: Total accruals, ΔREV: Change in revenues, ΔREC: Change in account receivable, PPE: Property, plant& equipment, *A*:Total assets, ϵ: Random error term. 3. Determining Normal Non-Discretionary Accruals ($NDACC_{i,t}$) For each company (i) in period (t) using the following equation: $NDACC_{i,t} = B^0 + B_1\left(\frac{1}{A_{i,t}}\right) + B_2\left(\frac{(\Delta REV_{i,t} - \Delta REC_{i,t})}{A_{i,t}}\right) + B_3\left(\frac{PPE_{i,t}}{A_{i,t}}\right) + \epsilon_{i,t}$	

	4. Calculating Discretionary Accruals ($DACC_{i,t}$) Represented by the difference between total accruals and non-discretionary accruals: $DACC_{i,t} = TACC_{i,t}\text{-}NDACC_{i,t}$ 5. Calculating the Absolute Value of Discretionary Accruals for sample firms throughout the research, by industry.	
Control Variables:		
Firm size (FS_{it})	ln(Total Assets)	Singh (2025)
Firm leverage (FL_{it})	Debt to equity	Singh (2025)
Firm liquidity (FQ_{it})	Current assets to current Liabilities	Singh (2025)

The index was designed using numerous theoretical features to assure its robustness. To ensure comparability across companies of any size, the index should be bounded ($0 \leq S \leq 1$), monotonic (scores cannot decrease with additional items), anonymous (order of disclosure items does not affect final score) and decomposable (weighted average of sub-group scores) (Cho, 2022). These features enhance the index's transparency, simplicity and impartiality in assessing disclosure.

4.4 Empirical Study

We analyse a set of major telecommunication and fintech companies operating in Egypt, including Raya, Fawry, Vodafone, WE (Telecom Egypt), Orange and Etisalat over 2020–2024. Financial statements and narrative disclosures were collected the available data from official company websites, Mubasher Misr and Investing.com. The outcome (FR) is $\text{FR}_{it} = |\text{DACC}_{it}|$, where DACC is derived via the Modified Jones Model (Ronen & Yaari, 2008). Where the Controls Firm Size (FS), Financial Leverage (FL) and FQ.

4.4.1 Statistical Models

We estimate the regression model using Ordinary Least Squares (OLS) with firm fixed effects(α_i)and year fixed effects (τ_t) to control for unobserved heterogeneity across firms and time periods. The model is specified as follows:

$$H_1 : \text{FR}_{i,t} = \beta_0 + \beta_1\, x_{1i,t} + \beta_2\, x_{2i,t} + \gamma' X_{i,t} + \alpha_i + \tau_t + \epsilon_{i,t},$$

where.

- $\text{FR}_{i,t}$ is the dependent variable (Faithful Representation)
- $x_{1i,t}$ and $x_{2i,t}$ are the independent variables (Risk Disclosure and cybersecurity management Disclosure),
- $X_{it} = (\text{FS}_{it}, \text{FL}_{it}, \text{FQ}_{it})$ are control variables (Firm Size, Financial Leverage, Firm Liquidity),
- α_i and τ_t represent firm and year fixed effects
- $\epsilon_{i,t}$ is the error term.

This model tests *H1* and *H2*, exploring the relationship between disclosure practices, firm characteristics and faithful representation |DACC|.

Although *H1* and *H2* are formulated as separate hypotheses, both are tested simultaneously within a single regression model. The coefficients β_1 and β_2 capture the partial effect of each disclosure dimension – cyber risk disclosure (x_1) and governance disclosure (x_2) respectively – after controlling for the other, thereby ensuring that the estimated effect of each variable is net of the other's influence (Greene, 2018).

4.4.2 Main Findings

The study uses a Panel Least Squares (PLS) regression with fixed effects for both cross-section and period to account for unobserved heterogeneity across firms and time periods to examine the determinants of FR, using Discretionary Accruals (|DACC|) as a proxy. The results from the Modified Johns model and the Kothari model (robustness check) are presented below.

4.4.2.1 Descriptive Statistics. Table 9.6 presents the descriptive statistics for the key variables in the study. The mean value of |DACC| is 78.39 with a standard deviation of 207.18, indicating significant variability in discretionary accruals across the firms. The mean value of Risk Disclosure (x_1) is 0.55 with a standard deviation of 0.12, suggesting moderate variation in risk disclosure practices among firms. Governance Disclosure (x_2) has a mean of 0.65 and a standard deviation of 0.14, indicating slightly higher consistency in governance disclosures. The mean of FS is 10.48, with a standard deviation of 1.96, suggesting some degree of variability in firm size. The mean of FQ is 1.24, with a higher standard deviation of 1.23, indicating considerable variation in liquidity levels across firms.

4.4.2.2 Covariance Matrix. Table 9.7 presents the covariance matrix, which reveals that Risk Disclosure (x_1) has a moderate positive correlation of 0.29 with |DACC|, suggesting that increased risk disclosure is associated with higher discretionary accruals, while Governance Disclosure (x_2) shows a weaker, yet positive correlation of 0.19 with |DACC|, indicating that stronger governance disclosure is linked to slightly higher accruals; FQ exhibits a notable positive correlation of 0.40 with |DACC|, highlighting that more liquid firms tend to report more discretionary accruals, and FS demonstrates a modest negative correlation of −0.27 with |DACC|, suggesting that larger firms may engage in less earnings management.

It is important to note that these bivariate correlations reflect unconditional associations and do not account for the joint influence of other covariates. The apparent positive correlation between x_1 and |DACC| is partly attributable to the confounding role of firm size (FS), which is positively associated with both

Table 9.6. Descriptive Statistics.

Variable	Mean	Median	Max	Min	Std. Dev.
|DACC|	78.39	7.69	1008.96	0.02	207.18
x_1(Risk Disclosure)	0.55	0.52	0.86	0.33	0.12
x_2(Governance Disclosure)	0.65	0.65	0.88	0.42	0.14
Financial Leverage (FL_{it})	1.67	1.66	3.31	0.50	0.57
Firm Size (FS_{it})	10.48	11.60	12.20	6.38	1.96
Firm liquidity (FQ_{it})	1.24	0.93	7.30	0.49	1.23

Table 9.7. Covariance Matrix.

	|DACC|	x_1	x_2	$\mathbf{FL}_{it}$	$\mathbf{FQ}_{it}$	$\mathbf{FS}_{it}$
|DACC|	1.00					
x_1	0.29	1.00				
x_2	0.19	0.70	1.00			
FL_{it}	−0.188	0.06	0.296	1.00		
FQ_{it}	0.40	−0.095	−0.099	−0.23	1.00	
FS_{it}	−0.27	0.009	0.267	0.26	−0.42	1.00

disclosure levels and discretionary accruals (r = 0.40). Once FS is held constant in the multivariate model, this suppression is removed and the true negative partial effect of risk disclosure emerges (Dechow et al., 1995; Kothari et al., 2005; Wooldridge, 2010).

4.4.2.3 OLS Regression Results. The results of the Modified Johns model and Robustness Check model Table 9.7 provide robust evidence on the determinants of FR. The regression analysis reveals that Risk Disclosure (x_1) is significantly negatively associated with |DACC| (coefficient = −807.47, p = 0.0204), suggesting that firms with more transparent risk disclosures tend to exhibit lower levels of discretionary accruals, thereby reducing earnings management This outcome reinforces the conclusions drawn in prior studies, including (Basiouny et al., 2024; Daoud & Serag, 2022; Rosati et al., 2022).

.While, governance disclosure (x_2) shows a positive relationship with |DACC| (coefficient = 943.60, p = 0.0776), indicating that higher governance disclosures are associated with higher discretionary accruals, potentially due to more complex internal controls and strategic reporting practices which is consistent with the findings of (Cortez & Dekker, 2022). Similarly, FS has a strong positive association with |DACC| (coefficient = 468.43, $p < 0.0001$), implying that larger firms, with their more complex operations, tend to report higher discretionary accruals; FL is negatively related to |DACC| (coefficient = −171.32, p = 0.0016), suggesting that firms with higher financial leverage engage in more conservative financial reporting, potentially due to increased scrutiny from stakeholders; FQ, however, does not have a statistically significant impact on |DACC| (coefficient = −27.35, p = 0.2333), indicating that liquidity does not substantially influence earnings management in this sample in agreement with (Singh, 2025). Another important finding is that The model explains about 89.36% of the variation in FR (R^2 = 0.8936; adjusted R^2 = 0.7943) and is statistically significant overall (F = 8.99, p = 0.000064).

4.4.2.4 Robustness Check. The robustness check model (Kothari model) provides similar results shown in Table 9.8, confirming the stability and reliability of the findings (Kothari et al., 2005). The Kothari model is specifically

Table 9.8. OLS Regression Results on Faithful Representation (FR).

Model	Modified Johns Model	Robustness Check Model
Dependent Variable	FR = |DACC|	
Intercept	−4692.70 (854.96), $p = 0.0001$**	−4685.98 (854.44), $p = 0.0001$**
H1: Risk Disclosure (x_1)	−807.54 (311.6), $p = 0.0204$**	−807.47 (311.41), $p = 0.0204$**
H2: Risk Management (x_2)	945.00 (498.32), $p = 0.0773$*	943.60 (498.02), $p = 0.0776$*
FS_{it}(Firm Size)	469.03 (79.69), $p = 0.0000$**	468.43 (79.64), $p = 0.0000$**
FL_{it}(Firm Leverage)	−171.53 (44.68), $p = 0.0016$**	−171.32 (44.65), $p = 0.0016$**
FQ_{it}(Firm liquidity)	−27.28 (22.03), $p = 0.2347$	−27.35 (22.02), $p = 0.2333$
R-squared	0.893,616	0.893,455
Adj. R-squared	0.794,324	0.794,013
F-statistic	8.999,902, $p = 0.000064$**	8.984,698, $p = 0.000064$**

Note: that Standard errors are presented in parentheses, *denotes statistical significance at $p \leq 0.1$, and **indicates significance at $p \leq 0.05$.

used to adjust for performance-related biases in discretionary accruals, providing a more accurate measure of earnings management by controlling for firm performance. In the robustness check model, the results remain consistent with the main findings. The coefficients for Risk Disclosure (x_1) (−807.47) and Governance Disclosure (x_2) (943.60) are slightly changed, confirming the robustness of these relationships. The FS and FL variables continue to exhibit strong statistical significance, reinforcing their importance in explaining |DACC|. The R-squared value of 0.8935 further supports the validity of the model.

The close similarity between the two models' coefficients (x_1: −807.54 vs −807.47; x_2: 945.00 vs 943.60) should be interpreted as evidence of result stability rather than model redundancy. With a small panel of six firms, performance-related variation – which the Kothari adjustment targets – is inherently limited, naturally reducing numerical differences between the two specifications (Kothari et al., 2005). This convergence across independently estimated models strengthens confidence in the findings (Gow et al., 2010).

5. Conclusion

This study develops and applies a 54-item Cybersecurity Disclosure Index, which includes risk/incident and management/governance sub-indices, to investigate how the quality of cybersecurity disclosures influences the FR of financial information, using Absolute Discretionary Accruals |DACC| as a proxy. The analysis focuses on a group of six leading telecommunications and fintech companies operating in Egypt over the period 2020–2024. The findings reveal that Risk Disclosure is negatively associated with |DACC|, suggesting that higher levels of cyber risk disclosure contribute to more accurate and reliable financial reporting. On the other hand, Cybersecurity Management Disclosure is positively related to higher levels of discretionary accruals, indicating that more detailed Management disclosures may introduce complexity, potentially leading to more aggressive earnings management practices. In fact, this means that clear risk disclosures enhance transparency and reduce financial manipulation, while detailed Cybersecurity Management disclosures could create opportunities for earnings management, potentially misleading stakeholders about a company's true financial position. The results from the questionnaire further validate the index's robustness, demonstrating its relevance and practical applicability in the context of cybersecurity disclosure.

Theoretical contributions include the development of a comprehensive Cybersecurity Disclosure Index that effectively distinguishes between actual cybersecurity risks and management responsibilities. This index fills a critical gap in the literature by offering a standardised, transparent framework for assessing cybersecurity-related disclosures, which is crucial for both financial reporting and stakeholder decision-making.

The study offers valuable insights for corporate managers, regulators and auditors. By improving the transparency and quality of cybersecurity risk disclosures, firms can enhance the FR of their financial statements, providing stakeholders with more reliable information. The findings also highlight the need for regulators to develop clearer guidelines for cybersecurity disclosure, as this will likely improve investor confidence and facilitate more informed decision-making. Furthermore, boards and auditors may use the index as a systematic checklist to direct oversight duties, assess the efficacy of internal controls and provide independent verification of cyber-related disclosures.

Despite the promising findings, it is important to note this study limitations, especially for the small panel (six firms over five years), sector-specific, and relies on the absolute value of discretionary accruals |DACC| as the primary outcome. While the findings are consistent with theoretical expectations, future work should broaden the time horizon and industry coverage, incorporate alternative measures of reporting quality (e.g., Dechow–Dichev accrual quality, restatements) and undertake formal validation of the index (Delphi CVR/CVI, inter-rater reliability and sensitivity ranges). Taken together, the evidence indicates that incident-focused disclosure improves FR contemporaneously, whereas governance-oriented disclosure may contribute with a lag.

To conclude, this study's findings imply that disclosure of cybersecurity risks, especially in relation to real occurrences, significantly affects the accuracy of financial statements. However, disclosures pertaining to cybersecurity governance seem to have a more subtle effect on reporting quality, highlighting the need for strategic governance with a focus on the long term to improve financial transparency. The importance of regulatory frameworks in promoting more thorough, open and prompt disclosures of cybersecurity risks cannot be overstated. Such disclosures are vital in improving the FR and guaranteeing that businesses' financial accounts fairly portray their activities and risks.

References

Abdel-khalik, A. R. (2019). Failing faithful representations of financial statements: Issues in reporting financial instruments. *Abacus*, *55*(4), 676–708.

Abdelraouf, M., & Hussainey, K. (2026). Systematic review of cyberrisk disclosure practices: Insights and implications. *The Journal of Risk Finance*, *27*(3), 349–367. https://doi.org/10.1108/JRF-07-2024-0210

Al Amosh, H., & Khatib, S. F. (2025). Cybersecurity transparency and firm success: Insights from the Australian landscape. *Australian Economic Papers*, *64*(2), 189–204.

Amani, F., Magnan, M., & Moldovan, R. (2025). Cybersecurity risks and incidents disclosure: A literature review. *Accounting Perspectives*, *24*(3), 605–667. https://doi.org/10.1111/1911-3838.12411

Amin, M. (2024). The importance of cybersecurity and protecting of digital assets and understanding the role of cybersecurity laws in safeguarding digital assets. *Journal of Public Administration*, *70*(3), 493–501.

Basiouny, M. M. M., Elnagar, S. M. A., & Ahmed, A. S. A. (2024). The impact of cybersecurity risk disclosure on the quality of financial reporting and market value: Evidence from Egyptian stock market. *Educational Administration: Theory and Practice*, *30*(5), 2504–2516.

Chen, J., Henry, E., & Jiang, X. (2023). Is cybersecurity risk factor disclosure informative? Evidence from disclosures following a data breach. *Journal of Business Ethics*, *187*(1), 199–224.

Chen, Z. (2020). Deep learning for cybersecurity: A review. In *Proceedings of the 2020 International Conference on Computing and Data Science (CDS)* (pp. 7–18). IEEE.

Cheng, X., Hsu, C., & Wang, T. D. (2022). Talk too much? The impact of cybersecurity disclosures on investment decisions. *Communications of the Association for Information Systems*, *50*(1), 26.

Cho, W. J. (2022). How to add apples and oranges: Aggregating performances of different nature. *Games and Economic Behavior*, *131*, 222–244.

Cloud Security Alliance (CSA). (2017). *Security guidance for critical areas of focus in cloud computing (Version 4.0)*. Cloud Security Alliance. https://cloudsecurityalliance.org

Cortez, E. K., & Dekker, M. (2022). A corporate governance approach to cybersecurity risk disclosure. *European Journal of Risk Regulation*, *13*(3), 443–463.

Daoud, M. M., & Serag, A. A. (2022). A proposed framework for studying the impact of cybersecurity on accounting information to increase trust in the

financial reports in the context of industry 4.0: An event, impact and response approach. *Journal of Commerce and Finance*, *42*(1), 20–61.
Dechow, P. M., Sloan, R. G., & Sweeney, A. P. (1995). Detecting earnings management. *The Accounting Review*, *70*(2), 193–225.
Foya, D., & Garikayi, V. (2021). Assessing cyber security awareness and organisational preparedness on cyber security in audit firms: A case of the big 4 audit firms (EY, Deloitte, KPMG, PWC) [2017–2020]. *Indiana Journal of Economics and Business Management*, *1*(1), 19–34.
Gow, I. D., Ormazabal, G., & Taylor, D. J. (2010). Correcting for cross-sectional and timeseries dependence in accounting research. *The Accounting Review*, *85*(2), 483–512.
Greene, W. H. (2018). *Econometric analysis* (8th ed.). Pearson.
Kävrestad, J., Burvall, F., & Nohlberg, M. (2025). A taxonomy of factors that contribute to organizational cybersecurity awareness (CSA). *Information & Computer Security*, *33*(2), 141–160.
Kothari, S. P., Leone, A. J., & Wasley, C. E. (2005). Performance matched discretionary accrual measures. *Journal of Accounting and Economics*, *39*(1), 163–197.
Lavion, D. (2018). *PwC's global economic crime and fraud survey 2018*. PwC.
Li, H., No, G., & Wang, T. (2018). SEC's cybersecurity disclosure guidance and disclosed cybersecurity risk factors. *International Journal of Accounting Information Systems*, *30*, 40–55.
Morshed, A., & Khrais, L. T. (2025). Cybersecurity in digital accounting systems: Challenges and solutions in the Arab gulf region. *Journal of Risk and Financial Management*, *18*(1), 41.
Ronen, J., & Yaari, V. (2008). Modifications to the Jones model and alternative methodologies. In *Earnings management: Emerging insights in theory, practice, and research* (Vol. 1, pp. 433-–461). Springer.
Rosati, P., Gogolin, F., & Lynn, T. (2022). Cyber-security incidents and audit quality. *European Accounting Review*, *31*(3), 701–728.
Schaffner, L. G., Tettamanzi, P., & Murgolo, M. (2023). Cyber security and risk disclosure: A literature review for theory and practice. *A Literature Review for Theory and Practice*, *6*, 1–21.
Shafakheibari, N., & Oladi, B. (2015). The effect of ERP system on relevance of accounting data and quality of financial reporting quality. *Management and Administrative Sciences Review*, *4*(3), 504–514.
Singh, H. (2025). Is corporate reputation associated with voluntary cybersecurity risk reporting? *Meditari Accountancy Research*, *33*(1), 198–219.
Smaili, N., Radu, C., & Khalili, A. (2023). Board effectiveness and cybersecurity disclosure. *Journal of Management and Governance*, *27*(4), 1049–1071.
Wooldridge, J. M. (2010). *Econometric analysis of cross section and panel data* (2nd ed.). MIT Press.

Chapter 10

Will AI Be a Key Solution to Sustainability Challenges? Rethinking the Measurement of Business Success in the AI Era

Angela Ya Gao

University of Sussex Business School, UK

Abstract

This chapter examines how artificial intelligence (AI), when developed and governed responsibly, can help redefine business success beyond short-term financial metrics by enabling multidimensional value measurement across the Six Capitals Framework: financial, manufactured, intellectual, human, social and relationship, and natural capitals. Drawing on systems thinking, stakeholder theory and integrated thinking, it highlights the limitations of traditional measurement methods, particularly for non-financial capitals, and explores how AI technologies, such as advanced analytics, natural language processing and real-time sensing, can address these gaps.

Following a Design Science Research (DSR) approach (Hevner et al., 2004), this chapter develops a conceptual artefact that integrates scenario analysis, conceptual synthesis and visual modelling to explore the interplay between AI maturity and sustainability performance. It shows how early-stage AI supports operational efficiency, while advanced AI can integrate data streams, model sustainability trade-offs and inform adaptive, long-term strategies. A forward-looking example illustrates a Level 5 AI-enabled 'Living Dashboard' ecosystem, where humans and AI co-create sustainable value in real time, enhancing decision-making without replacing human judgement.

The discussion also addresses ethical, equity and environmental concerns, including algorithmic bias, over-automation, uneven access and the energy footprint of AI systems. It emphasises that AI should complement, not substitute, human values-based leadership, and that governance must ensure transparency, inclusivity and ecological alignment.

Sustainability in Accounting and Finance Education, 165–182

Published under exclusive licence by Emerald Publishing Limited
doi:10.1108/978-1-80686-393-820261010

Ultimately, this chapter positions AI as a catalyst for transforming value creation and measurement, offering organisations the tools to align profitability with resilience, inclusivity and ecological regeneration, paving the way for a more balanced, future-ready model of enterprise.

Keywords: Artificial intelligence (AI); sustainability; six capitals framework; integrated reporting; value measurement; AI maturity model; sustainable value creation; multi-capital accounting; corporate governance; business performance metrics

1. Introduction: Rethinking Success in an Age of Crisis and Intelligence

We are living in an era defined by overlapping crises, from climate disasters and deepening social inequality to eroding trust in governance and the limits of short-term economic models. While traditional capitalism has delivered growth, its focus on financial performance is increasingly viewed as insufficient for addressing today's systemic challenges. In response, new movements are emerging that call for broader, more inclusive definitions of business success, ones that prioritise transparency, long term resilience and multi stakeholder value.

At the same time, we are entering the age of artificial intelligence (AI). From diagnostics to forecasting and automation, AI is transforming industries and decision-making at unprecedented speed. Yet this technological shift brings not only opportunity, but also complex questions around ethics, equity and the future of work.

This chapter explores how AI, when developed and governed responsibly, can support a more holistic vision of business success by transforming how we measure, manage and enrich value across the Six Capitals. Adopting a Design Science Research (DSR) methodology (Hevner et al., 2004), the analytical framework was iteratively developed through problem identification, conceptual synthesis and artefact design. Scenario analyses and visual frameworks were constructed through literature-informed reasoning and iterative reflection (Li, 2024; Wang et al., 2023; Yue & Hu, 2023). Throughout this process, the author critically guided the inquiry to ensure relevance, rigour and alignment with real-world strategic and sustainability challenges. The resulting artefact is a forward-looking, visually engaging and practically grounded model illustrating how AI may enable organisations to progress beyond short-term profit metrics towards multi-capital, long-term value creation.

2. Theoretical Foundation: The Six Capitals Framework

In an era where sustainability, resilience and long-term value creation have become central to strategic conversations, the Six Capitals Framework offers a more holistic lens through which business performance can be understood and communicated. Developed by the *International Integrated Reporting Council (IIRC)* and now embedded within the *IFRS Integrated Reporting Framework (2021)*, the six capitals extend beyond financial metrics to include other forms of value that organisations depend on, transform and affect over time.

> Integrated reporting aims to enhance accountability and stewardship for the broad base of capitals (financial, manufactured, intellectual, human, social and relationship, and natural) and promote understanding of their interdependencies. (IFRS Integrated Reporting Framework, 2021, p. 2)

The framework recognises that businesses operate within and draw from a broader ecosystem – economic, human, social and environmental – and that value creation must be assessed across multiple dimensions, not just the financial bottom line.

2.1 The Six Capitals Explained

Financial Capital refers to the traditional funds available to an organisation, such as equity, debt or retained earnings, used to support business operations and investments. This is the most familiar and measurable form of capital and remains central to organisational sustainability.

Manufactured Capital includes physical assets and infrastructure created by organisations to deliver goods and services, such as buildings, machinery and technologies. It reflects the organisation's capacity to produce and operate effectively in the physical world.

Intellectual Capital represents intangible assets such as knowledge, systems, procedures, intellectual property and brand reputation. It encompasses the innovation capacity of a company and underpins its ability to adapt, evolve and remain competitive.

Human Capital refers to the skills, experience, capabilities and well-being of employees. It includes organisational culture, motivation, diversity and leadership. This capital is increasingly seen as a core driver of productivity, creativity and innovation.

Social and Relationship Capital comprises the networks of relationships an organisation builds with customers, suppliers, regulators, communities and society at large. Trust, reputation and licence to operate are fundamental dimensions of this capital.

Natural Capital includes environmental resources such as air, water, land, biodiversity and ecosystems. It represents both the raw materials used and the ecological services (e.g. climate regulation) organisations depend on to survive and grow.

The IFRS Integrated Reporting Framework outlines these six capitals and provides an overview of how each capital contributes to value creation and interacts within an organisation's broader operating context (IIRC, 2021).

2.2 Why Six Capitals Are Not Interchangeable?

While the Six Capitals Framework offers a unified lens to understand value creation, it is essential to recognise that these capitals are *fundamentally distinctive and not interchangeable*. Each capital represents a unique dimension of value that contributes to organisational success in ways that cannot simply be bought, substituted or converted. *For example*, financial capital cannot purchase trust, loyalty or innovation in the same way that authentic relationships, reputation or talent development can. Similarly, natural capital such as clean air, fertile soil or biodiversity cannot be restored purely through monetary investment once it has been depleted or destroyed. Human capital, too, is not reducible to payroll; motivation, creativity and leadership cannot be mass-produced or instantly acquired. These distinctions highlight *the limits of traditional financial metrics and the risks of treating non-financial capitals as secondary*. Rather than viewing the capitals as interchangeable assets on a balance sheet, *the framework invites organisations to appreciate the interdependence and irreplaceability of each dimension, especially in the context of long-term resilience and sustainability.*

2.3 Underlying Theories

The Six Capitals Framework is underpinned by three complementary theoretical perspectives. *Systems thinking* emphasises that organisations are embedded within broader social, ecological and economic systems, where interconnections and externalities play a critical role (Scrieciu et al., 2021). *Stakeholder theory* calls for businesses to consider the interests of a wide range of stakeholders, not just shareholders, and the capitals help translate those interests into strategy and reporting (Harrison et al., 2019). *Integrated thinking* encourages organisations to understand and manage the relationships between different forms of capital, aligning decisions with long-term purpose and sustainable value creation. While each of these theories offers a rich academic foundation, this chapter does not explore them in depth but instead focuses on their practical relevance to AI-enabled value measurement (Herath et al., 2021).

3. Challenges in Capital Measurement and the Potential of AI

While conceptually robust, implementing the Six Capitals Framework raises important questions about measurement. Unlike financial capital, which is governed by established accounting standards, the other capitals are often difficult to quantify in consistent, comparable and credible ways. For instance:

- How do we assess the health of social capital: trust, influence or community engagement?
- Can we quantify intellectual capital in a way that reflects its value across industries?
- How can natural capital be priced without oversimplifying complex environmental systems?

Efforts have been made to address these questions through initiatives such as the Natural Capital Protocol, Sustainability Accounting Standards Board Standards and the Global Reporting Initiative (GRI). However, a major barrier remains, *much of this information is non-financial, unstructured and context-specific, making it difficult to standardise across sectors.*

This is precisely where AI offers significant potential to overcome existing measurement limitations. Traditional approaches to assessing non-financial capitals often struggle with subjectivity, fragmented data and the lack of standardised indicators. *AI technologies,* such as advanced analytics, natural language processing (NLP) and real-time sensing, *can help address these gaps* by enabling organisations to collect, interpret and report data in a more scalable, consistent and timely manner (Adeoye & Adams, 2024; Budde et al., 2024). For example, AI can analyse unstructured information from stakeholder feedback, sustainability reports or social media to quantify aspects of social and relationship capital. It can process satellite imagery and sensor data to track environmental impacts in real time, supporting more accurate assessments of natural capital. Similarly, machine learning (ML) can detect patterns in employee behaviour or innovation processes that reveal the health of human and intellectual capital (Rane et al., 2024). By making such insights more accessible and cost-effective, *AI has the potential to transform how organisations measure what matters, enabling a shift towards genuinely multidimensional value creation.*

Moreover, AI can play a vital role in assessing and navigating *the structural impacts* of sustainability transitions (Liu et al., 2025), such as the phasing out of fossil fuels or the transformation of labour markets through automation. These shifts involve complex, interconnected changes across sectors and timeframes, making them difficult to model with traditional tools. AI can support scenario analysis, risk forecasting and transition planning by processing vast datasets, from energy consumption patterns to workforce demographics, to simulate possible outcomes and stress-test business strategies.

For example, *ML models can help estimate the carbon impact of transitioning from fossil fuels to renewable energy sources,* including forecasting emissions reductions, financial implications and regulatory alignment across different geographies. This allows businesses to better plan decarbonisation pathways in line with climate targets and evolving market dynamics. Another example, *AI can be used to analyse workforce data to predict the likely effects of automation on employment, skills gaps, training needs and regional labour shifts* (Idoko et al., 2024). By identifying which roles are most at risk of being replaced and where new opportunities may emerge, businesses can proactively reskill employees, redesign roles and ensure a more just and strategic approach to digital transformation.

4. The Future of AI: A Framework for AI Development (Levels 1–5)

A widely cited framework (see Fig. 10.1) for understanding AI maturity, adapted from industry analyses and popularised through a Bloomberg article (Bloomberg, 2024) has been referenced across academic, policy and industry discussions for its clarity in illustrating how AI capabilities evolve over time.

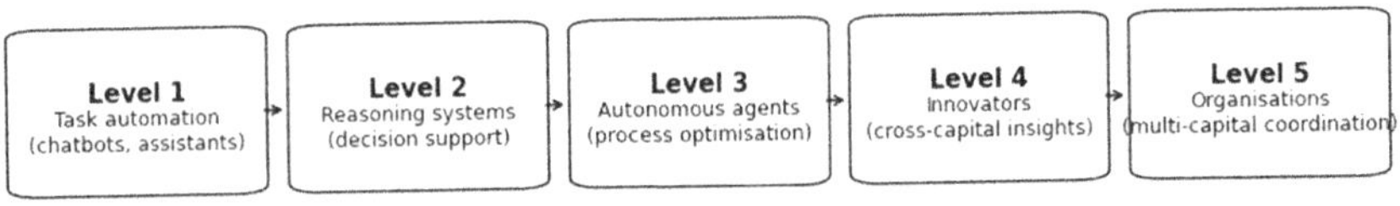

Fig. 10.1. Stages of AI Maturity and Capability Evolution. *Note:* This figure illustrates the progressive development of artificial intelligence capabilities from Level 1 to Level 5. Each stage reflects a higher degree of autonomy, reasoning and systemic integration, evolving from simple task automation (e.g., chatbots and digital assistants) to organisational-level intelligence that enables multi-capital coordination and strategic decision-making across multiple capitals. This framework supports a structured understanding of how AI maturity underpins sustainable value creation and measurement. *Source:* Author's conceptual visualisation based on literature on AI maturity and sustainability measurement.

To examine how AI may progressively influence value creation and measurement across the Six Capitals, a forward-looking narrative was developed through conceptual reasoning and synthesis of emerging literature. The ensuing staged analysis traces the evolution of AI capabilities from Level 1 to Level 5 maturity, providing a structured perspective on their potential strategic and systemic impacts.

At *Level 1–2 AI* maturity (approximately 2015–2023), AI mainly automates specific tasks such as customer support, basic decision aids and administrative workflows. Early examples include *chatbots like Apple's Siri, Amazon's Alexa and customer service bots like those used by banks and telecoms.* The impact of AI at these stages has been local and modest – helping individual workflows or departments become more efficient but without fundamentally restructuring how companies allocate attention across the Six Capitals. Strategic focus has remained overwhelmingly financial, with little systemic change to broader value creation models.

At *Level 3 AI* (emerging 2023–2026), AI begins acting autonomously to optimise isolated processes – such as *automated invoice management through platforms like UiPath or AI-driven recruitment filtering systems like HireVue.* Although this frees some human and organisational capacity, AI at this stage remains task-specific and operational. Deep, integrated shifts in company strategy across all six capitals are still limited because the AI mainly supports micro-decisions within silos.

At *Level 4 AI* (anticipated 2026–2032), businesses start to experience a more profound transformation. AI systems begin assisting not only with operations but also with *cross-functional innovation and sustainability strategy development.* Early prototypes include *Microsoft's Sustainability Manager AI tools and Google DeepMind's research on energy-saving AI.* Companies equipped with Level 4 AI can strategically use insights generated by these intelligent systems to rebalance their focus – investing not just in financial return, but in long-term human capital development, intellectual property generation and environmental stewardship.

Level 5 AI (envisioned from 2032 onward) will act as a fully functioning organisational layer. These advanced systems would autonomously coordinate and balance performance across financial, manufactured, intellectual, human, social and natural capitals simultaneously. Conceptually, *AI-driven* 'autonomous business units' or *entire* AI-managed impact portfolios could emerge. Pioneering experiments include Decentralised Autonomous Organisations (DAOs) in blockchain ecosystems, which hint at early forms of decentralised and autonomous organisational structures. Although DAOs are not necessarily AI-managed entities, they offer useful insights into how more autonomous organisational models may evolve. With Level 5 AI, companies would dynamically optimise not only shareholder returns but multi-capital outcomes in real time.

The above progression analysis of AI capabilities from Level 1 to Level 5, along with their potential strategic and systemic impacts, is summarised in Table 10.1.

Table 10.1. Conceptual Evolution of AI Maturity and Its Influence on Value Creation and Measurement Across the Six Capitals.

Approximate Period	**AI Maturity Level**	**Key Characteristics**	**Illustrative Examples**
2015–2023	*Level 1–2 (Chatbots, Reasoners)*	Focused on automating routine and repetitive tasks; improves efficiency in specific functions	Virtual assistants and customer service bots such as Siri and Alexa
2023–2026	*Level 3 (Agents)*	Capable of autonomous optimisation within defined processes; supports operational decision-making	Workflow automation tools like UiPath and AI-driven recruitment systems such as HireVue
2026–2032	*Level 4 (Innovators)*	Integrates across multiple business functions; enables strategic innovation in sustainability and ESG management	Platforms such as Microsoft Sustainability Manager and DeepMind's energy optimisation systems

(Continued)

(Continued)

Approximate Period	AI Maturity Level	Key Characteristics	Illustrative Examples
2032 onward	*Level 5 (Organisations)*	Fully autonomous, self-optimising systems capable of balancing performance and value across all Six Capitals	Early decentralised autonomous organisations (DAOs) and conceptual AI-managed enterprises

Source: Developed by the author through conceptual reasoning and literature synthesis.
Note: This table summarises the progressive development of AI maturity from Level 1 to Level 5 and its corresponding impact on how organisations create and measure value across the Six Capitals.

5. Mapping AI Maturity Levels to the Six Capitals: Opportunities and Transformations

To further explore how AI could address the persistent challenges in measuring the Six Capitals, the following conceptual table (see Table 10.2) analyses typical barriers to meaningful assessment and illustrates how different levels of AI maturity (Levels 1–5) may contribute to closing the measurement gap. As AI capabilities advance, from automation and pattern recognition to autonomous action and innovation, they enable new ways to collect, analyse and interpret data across capital domains. Nevertheless, these opportunities are accompanied by risks related to over-reliance, ethical misuse and data quality, all of which must be carefully managed as AI systems become integrated into performance measurement and reporting processes.

Table 10.2. Conceptual Mapping of Six Capitals Assessment Challenges, AI Maturity Level Contributions, and Associated Risks.

Capital	Current Challenges	AI Maturity (Levels 1–5) Contributions	Risks/ Considerations
Financial	Short-termism, poor forecasting	L2–L4: Predictive models, scenario analysis, cost-efficiency tools	Over-automation, bias
Manufactured	Asset underutilisation	L3–L5: Smart operations, digital twins, AI-led supply chains	Job displacement

(Continued)

Capital	**Current Challenges**	**AI Maturity (Levels 1–5) Contributions**	**Risks/ Considerations**
Intellectual	Measuring innovation and IP impact	L2–L4: AI-supported R&D tracking, IP generation tools	Misuse of proprietary data
Human	Talent engagement, well-being, skills gaps	L2–L5: AI in training, well-being monitoring, performance analytics	Surveillance, ethical risks
Social and relationship	Hard-to-measure trust and reputation	L1–L4: Sentiment AI, stakeholder mapping, automated transparency tools	Manipulation, PR bias
Natural	Sustainability metrics incomplete or costly	L2–L5: AI-powered ESG monitoring, satellite tracking, carbon modelling	Data reliability, greenwashing automation

Source: Developed by the author through conceptual reasoning and literature synthesis.
Note: This table outlines common barriers to effective measurement of the Six Capitals, illustrates how AI maturity levels (1–5) can help address these challenges, and highlights key ethical and operational risks that may arise.

To explore how AI can help address persistent measurement challenges across the Six Capitals, Table 10.3 maps AI maturity levels (1–5) to each capital. This conceptual framework, informed by contemporary discussions on AI maturity in industry and academic literature (e.g., Bloomberg, 2024), illustrates the evolution of AI from basic conversational tools (Level 1) to systems capable of performing complex organisational functions (Level 5). As AI capabilities advance, they enable increasingly sophisticated ways to automate customer interactions, analyse resource use, manage innovation pipelines and orchestrate circular economy systems. Collectively, these developments enhance how organisations gather, process and interpret data across all capital domains, particularly in areas where measurement remains limited, subjective or resource-intensive.

Beyond improving data collection, these AI capabilities have the potential to *reshape how we measure business success* altogether. Rather than relying solely on financial metrics, advanced AI systems enable organisations to generate more timely, consistent and multidimensional insights, capturing value in human well-being, intellectual property, stakeholder trust and environmental impact. This evolution paves the way for a more integrated, capital-balanced approach to performance evaluation, aligning business strategy with long-term sustainability and stakeholder outcomes.

Table 10.3. Conceptual Overview of AI-Enabled Solutions to Persistent Six Capitals Measurement Challenges.

AI Levels	Financial Capital	Manufactured Capital	Intellectual Capital	Human Capital	Social and Relationship Capital	Natural Capital
Level 1: Chatbots (Conversational AI)	Customer service automation	Product information chatbots	Knowledge bases and learning support	HR chatbots and onboarding	Customer interaction tools	Eco-impact FAQs and sustainability education
Level 2: Reasoners (Human-level problem-solving)	AI-enhanced decision-making	Design optimisation support	AI-assisted problem-solving	Well-being tracking and coaching	Stakeholder analysis and empathy engines	Resource consumption modelling
Level 3: Agents (Systems that can take actions)	Autonomous financial agents	Process automation agents	IP management and decision agents	Personalised career development systems	Community engagement bots	Real-time environmental monitoring
Level 4: Innovators (AI aiding invention)	AI-driven risk modelling and forecasting	Smart factories and digital twins	AI-supported patent generation and innovation discovery	AI-facilitated training and development systems	Transparency and accountability tools	Carbon scenario simulation and predictive ESG modelling

Level 5: Organisations (AI performing integrated functions)	End-to-end financial operations	Fully autonomous supply chains	Self-improving R&D ecosystems	Organisational knowledge orchestration	Network-building intelligent systems	AI-led circular economy management

Source: Developed by the author through conceptual reasoning and literature synthesis.
Note: This table maps the application of AI maturity levels (1–5) to each of the Six Capitals, illustrating how advancing AI capabilities, from chatbots to autonomous organisational systems, can support more integrated and sustainable performance evaluation.

Building on the approach popularised in recent industry analyses of AI maturity (e.g., Bloomberg, 2024), Chart 10.1 maps five progressive stages of AI development against the Six Capitals Framework *to examine how AI may help address persistent measurement challenges*. At the lower *levels (1 and 2)*, AI tools such as chatbots and rule-based systems provide limited support, primarily automating transactional processes and generating structured data – particularly within financial and manufactured capital. As AI advances into the stage of autonomous agents *(Level 3)*, it begins to assist with more dynamic data gathering and real-time monitoring across intellectual, human and social dimensions. By *Level 4*, AI becomes capable of contributing to creative problem-solving, environmental, social and governance (ESG) scenario modelling and predictive analysis, significantly enhancing the measurement of natural and social capital. Ultimately, at *Level 5*, AI systems operate with organisation-wide intelligence, enabling integrated and adaptive measurement systems across all capitals. These systems are not only more efficient and scalable but also capable of deriving

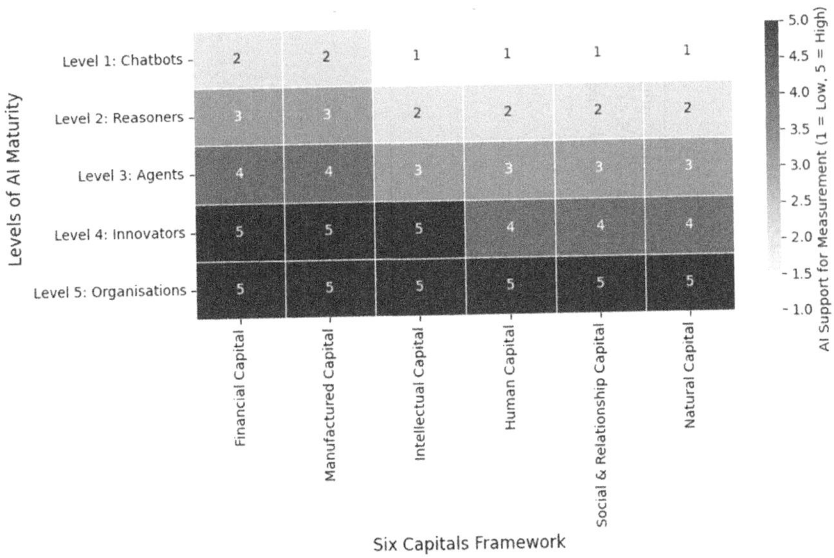

Chart 10.1. Mapping AI Levels to the Six Capitals: Addressing Measurement Challenges. *Note:* This conceptual chart is to illustrate how AI maturity levels (1–5) progressively enhance the capacity to measure and integrate the Six Capitals. The visual shows increasing systemic integration and multidimensional value creation as AI evolves from automation to organisational intelligence. *Source:* Author's conceptual visualisation created using Python, synthesising insights from scholarly work on AI maturity frameworks and sustainability measurement practices.

insights from unstructured data and complex interdependencies. This progression points towards a future in which AI plays a central role in enabling multidimensional, forward-looking business intelligence that supports sustainable value creation. The *1–5 scale* shown in the chart's legend indicates the *degree of AI support for measurement*, where *1* = *Low* (basic or minimal assistance) and *5* = *High* (comprehensive, advanced and integrated AI-driven measurement capabilities).

6. Rethinking Business Success: AI-Enabled Capital Accounting

Building on the AI maturity model and its growing role in addressing the measurement challenges across the Six Capitals, this section explores how AI, particularly at *Levels 4 and 5*, may fundamentally *reshape how we define and manage business success*. Traditionally, business performance has been viewed through a narrow financial lens, often overlooking equally vital yet less tangible capitals such as human well-being, intellectual assets, social trust and environmental health, largely because these dimensions have been difficult, costly and time-consuming to track, quantify, visualise and integrate into decision-making systems. AI offers a way to shift from fragmented, retrospective reporting to a more *integrated and forward-looking model of capital accounting* (Artene et al., 2024; Chekashova, 2025).

As businesses begin to adopt more advanced AI systems, success in the AI era could be defined by *dynamic value accounting: the ability to track, evaluate and respond to changes across all Six Capitals in real time*. AI-enabled platforms will support this shift by generating *multi-capital dashboards* that surface key trade-offs, such as balancing profit growth with emissions reduction or innovation gains with employee well-being. These tools allow decision-makers to visualise complex relationships, identify tensions and make choices that are aligned with long-term value, not just short-term efficiency.

At *Level 4*, AI begins to contribute to the design of *adaptive sustainability strategies*, supporting what-if modelling, ESG simulation and strategic foresight grounded in capital interdependencies. At *Level 5*, AI systems become capable of managing entire decision loops, monitoring capital inputs and outputs, self-assessing risks and opportunities and recommending course corrections, effectively enabling *self-evaluating organisations*. These AI-led systems do not simply track performance; they become partners in *steering the organisation towards balanced, regenerative value creation*.

Ultimately, this evolution reframes business success away from single-bottom-line metrics and towards a *continuous, AI-enhanced assessment of capital health and inter-capital performance*. It sets the stage for a more resilient, transparent and purpose-driven model of enterprise, one in which the measurement of success is as multidimensional as the challenges businesses now face.

As businesses move towards more integrated and intelligent systems of value management, AI is set to play a transformative role, not just in improving how performance is measured, but in reshaping how value is understood and acted upon. At Levels 4 and 5 of AI maturity, technology gains the ability to synthesise real-time data across all Six Capitals, support adaptive decision-making, and optimise for long-term, multidimensional outcomes. To illustrate this potential shift, the following radar chart (see Chart 10.2) presents *a conceptual vision of how AI-enhanced businesses could enrich value across the Six Capitals*, in contrast to the traditional single-bottom-line approach that prioritises financial capital above all else. This visual representation captures the essence of a future in which business success is redefined through AI integration, embedding sustainability, adaptability and stakeholder well-being at the core of strategic decision-making.

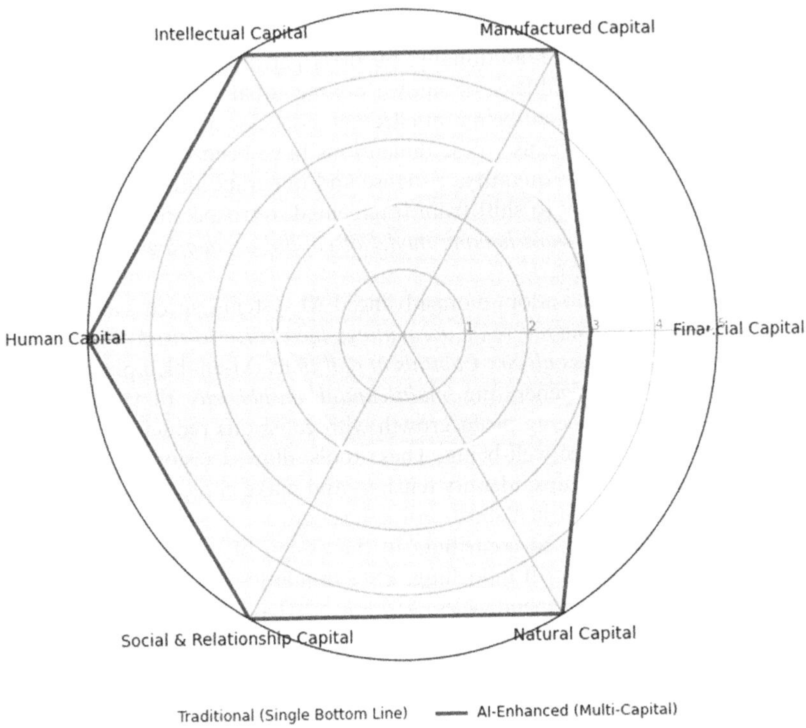

Chart 10.2. Conceptual Vision: How AI-Enhanced Businesses Could Enrich Value Across the Six Capitals Compared with the Traditional Single-Bottom-Line Approach. *Note:* This chart contrasts the traditional profit-centred model with a future vision of AI-enabled, multi-capital value creation. It illustrates how integrating AI into organisational strategy can enhance performance across financial, manufactured, intellectual, human, social and natural capitals, redefining business success in more sustainable and balanced terms. *Source:* Author's conceptual visualisation created using Python, synthesising insights from emerging literature and practice on AI-enabled sustainability and value creation.

7. Challenges and Cautions

While AI offers transformative potential for enhancing how businesses measure and manage value across the Six Capitals, it also raises important *ethical, environmental and systemic challenges* that must not be overlooked.

A key concern is *data ethics and algorithmic bias* (Rezaei et al., 2024). AI models are only as good as the data they are trained on, and if that data reflects historical inequalities or blind spots, it can lead to flawed, exclusionary outcomes. This is especially sensitive when measuring intangible capitals like human well-being or social trust, where subjective interpretations can embed bias into strategic decisions. Additionally, *overdependence on AI* poses strategic and ethical challenges. As AI systems grow more autonomous, especially at Levels 4 and 5, human oversight and values-based decision-making become increasingly important to ensure that organisational actions remain context-sensitive and socially responsible.

There are also risks of *capital substitution* (Ricciardi Celsi & Zomaya, 2025), where one form of value is enhanced at the cost of another. For instance, increased efficiency in manufactured or financial capital through automation may come at the expense of human capital, reducing workforce resilience or well-being. Without a holistic governance approach, AI may inadvertently deepen the very imbalances the Six Capitals Framework aims to address.

Equity in access also remains a significant issue. *Not all businesses or regions have equal access to advanced AI tools*, creating a risk that digital transformation will further widen gaps between large and small enterprises, or between developed and emerging economies.

Finally, the *energy demands of AI* present a growing sustainability challenge. Large-scale models require high computational power, placing pressure on existing infrastructure and raising questions about the environmental footprint of powering AI, especially if powered by non-renewable sources. As organisations increasingly depend on AI to support sustainability goals, they must also *ensure that the deployment of AI itself is energy-efficient and aligned with green energy transitions.*

8. Conclusion: Towards AI-Supported Sustainable Value Creation

As this chapter has explored, AI, when developed and deployed responsibly, holds significant promise for transforming how we define and measure business success. By enabling more timely, scalable and multidimensional insights across the Six Capitals, AI can help organisations move beyond narrow financial metrics and towards a broader, more sustainable conception of value. Particularly at Levels 4 and 5 of maturity, AI is no longer just a tool for automation. It becomes a strategic partner capable of supporting adaptive, system-wide optimisation across financial, human, social, intellectual, natural and manufactured capitals.

However, this shift must be approached with caution. AI should *support, not replace, human-centred judgement and long-term thinking*. While algorithms can identify patterns, simulate scenarios and flag trade-offs, it is human values, ethics and contextual understanding that ensure technology serves the public good. The risk of data bias, over-automation, unequal access and environmental burden must be addressed through thoughtful design, inclusive policy and transparent governance.

Looking ahead, realising the full potential of AI for sustainable value creation will require collaboration across sectors. *Business leaders, policymakers, AI designers and educators* must come together to ensure that future AI systems are not only technically capable but also *socially attuned, ethically guided and inclusively accessible*. This includes investing in digital infrastructure, embedding ethical frameworks into development processes and rethinking education and regulation to match the speed of technological change.

Ultimately, AI is not a solution in itself but a catalyst. Its real power lies in enabling us to better understand and act on what truly matters. In doing so, it opens the door to a more balanced, resilient and purpose-driven model of enterprise, one capable of creating value for business, society and the planet alike.

9. Designing the Future Firm: A Level 5 AI Ecosystem Where Humans and Machines Co-Create Sustainable Value

I would like to end this chapter with a forward-looking example that illustrates how a Level 5 AI-enabled business ecosystem might operate, not as a replacement for human work, but as a collaborative system where intelligent technology and human values co-create sustainable, multi-capital value in real time.

Imagine a global apparel company operating at *Level 5 AI maturity*, where AI acts not merely as a tool but as an intelligent organisational layer: orchestrating decisions, predicting outcomes and balancing performance across the Six Capitals in real time.

At the centre of this ecosystem is a *Living Dashboard*, a fully integrated monitoring and reporting system powered by AI. This system continuously gathers data from across the value chain: satellite and sensor data from regenerative cotton farms (natural capital), digital twins of supply chains and manufacturing assets (manufactured capital), employee well-being trackers (human capital), R&D innovation logs (intellectual capital) and stakeholder sentiment analysis drawn from real-time media scans (social capital). With reduced latency and increasingly efficient data processing, the dashboard provides decision-makers with a dynamic, system-level view of capital health and trade-offs.

A critical concern with this future scenario is the fear that highly autonomous AI systems will eliminate most jobs. But in this *co-creative ecosystem*, AI is not designed to replace human input – it is designed to *amplify it*. Routine and data-heavy tasks are indeed automated, but humans shift into roles that require *ethical judgement, creativity, empathy, cross-cultural leadership and purpose-driven innovation.* New job categories emerge: *Capital Stewards, Sustainability Strategists, AI Ethicists and Community Value Designers*, professionals who work alongside intelligent systems to steer the business through uncertainty and complexity.

Rather than displacing work, the Level 5 ecosystem enables a *reallocation of human potential.* AI takes over the repetitive and predictive; humans take the lead in shaping organisational purpose, resolving tensions between capitals and engaging meaningfully with diverse stakeholders. In this model, *success is no longer measured solely in profit*, but in the business's ability to co-create value that is financially viable, socially inclusive and ecologically regenerative.

References

Adeoye, S., & Adams, R. (2024). Leveraging artificial intelligence for predictive healthcare: A data-driven approach to early diagnosis and personalized treatment. *Cognizance Journal of Multidisciplinary Studies*, *4*, 80–97.

Artene, A. E., Domil, A. E., & Ivascu, L. (2024). Unlocking business value: Integrating AI-driven decision-making in financial reporting systems. *Electronics*, *13*(15).

Bloomberg. (2024). https://www.bloomberg.com/news/articles/2024-07-11/openai-sets-levels-to-track-progress-toward-superintelligent-ai?utm_source=chatgpt.com&embedded-checkout=true

Budde, M., Hilbring, D., Vogl, J., Dittmar, D., & Abecker, A. (2024). NiMo 4.0–Enabling advanced data analytics with AI for environmental governance in the water domain. *at-Automatisierungstechnik*, *72*(6), 564–578.

Chekashova, A. (2025). Integrated AI FP&A: Unlocking the highest stage of FP&A maturity. *The American Journal of Management and Economics Innovations*. https://api.semanticscholar.org/CorpusID:279737083

Harrison, J. S., Barney, J. B., Freeman, R. E., & Phillips, R. A. (Eds.). (2019). *The Cambridge handbook of stakeholder theory*. Cambridge University Press. https://doi.org/10.1017/9781108123495

Herath, R., Senaratne, S., & Gunarathne, N. (2021). Integrated thinking, orchestration of the six capitals and value creation. *Meditari Accountancy Research*, *29*(4), 873–907. https://doi.org/10.1108/MEDAR-01-2020-0676

Hevner, A. R., March, S. T., Park, J., & Ram, S. (2004). Design science in information systems research. *MIS Quarterly*, *28*(1), 75–105.

Idoko, I. P., Igbede, M. A., Manuel, H. N. N., Adeoye, T. O., Akpa, F. A., & Ukaegbu, C. (2024). Big data and AI in employment: The dual challenge of workforce replacement and protecting customer privacy in biometric data usage. *Global Journal of Engineering and Technology Advances*, *19*(02), 89–106.

International Integrated Reporting Council (IIRC). (2021). *The International <IR> Framework*. IFRS Foundation. https://integratedreporting.ifrs.org/

Li, Z. (2024). A design trajectory map of Human-AI collaborative reinforcement learning systems: Survey and taxonomy. *arXiv.org*. https://doi.org/10.48550/arxiv.2405.10214

Liu, Z., Wu, C., & Xu, X. (2025). The role of artificial intelligence in sustainable development and industrial transformation. *Asia Pacific Economic and Management Review*. https://api.semanticscholar.org/CorpusID:277200710

Rane, N., Choudhary, S., & Rane, J. (2024, May 27). Artificial intelligence driven approaches to strengthening Environmental, Social, and Governance (ESG) criteria in sustainable business practices: A review. https://ssrn.com/abstract=4843215

Rezaei, M., Pironti, M., & Quaglia, R. (2024). AI in knowledge sharing, which ethical challenges are raised in decision-making processes for organisations? *Management Decision*, *63*(10), 3369–3388.

Ricciardi Celsi, L., & Zomaya, A. Y. (2025). Perspectives on managing AI ethics in the digital age. *Information*, *16*(4), 318.

Scrieciu, S. Ş., Zimmermann, N., Chalabi, Z., & Davies, M. (2021). Linking complexity economics and systems thinking, with illustrative discussions of urban sustainability. *Cambridge Journal of Economics*, *45*(4), 695–722.

Wang, S., Yuan, H., Zhou, L., Ni, L. M., Shum, H. Y., & Guo, J. (2023). Alpha-GPT: Human-AI interactive alpha mining for quantitative investment. *arXiv:2308.00016*. https://doi.org/10.48550/arxiv.2308.00016

Yue, B., & Hu, L. (2023). The impact of human-AI collaboration types on consumer evaluation and usage intention: A perspective of responsibility attribution. *Frontiers in Psychology*, *14*. https://doi.org/10.3389/fpsyg.2023.1277861

Section 3

ESG, Governance and Performance

Chapter 11

Does Corporate Governance Moderate the Relationship Between ESG Performance and the Financial Performance of Indian Companies?

Sampadaa Saxena, Vrinda Santhosh and Ranjeet Kumar Mishra

CHRIST (Deemed to be University), Delhi NCR Campus, India

Abstract

Our study aims to empirically investigate the moderating role of corporate governance factors in the relationship between ESG performance and the financial performance of Indian firms. For this purpose, we have collected five years of data from 2018 to 2022 of the top 100 Bombay Stock Exchange (BSE)-listed companies through Centre for Monitoring Indian Economy (CMIE) prowess and the Bloomberg database. Firm performance is assessed through profitability and value measures, while ESG performance is measured using Bloomberg's overall ESG score. Board size, frequency of board meetings, independent board, board gender diversity, CEO duality and ownership structure are used as a proxy of corporate governance. We use firm age, firm size, leverage and short-term solvency as control variables. Employing Pooled Ordinary Least Square (OLS), our result shows that out of the different corporate governance variables, only board size significantly moderates the relationship between ESG performance and the financial performance of Indian firms. To the best of our knowledge, this study is one of the limited existing literature that explored the moderating role of corporate governance in the relationship between ESG performance and the financial performance of firms. The findings obtained from our study have practical implications for accounting education and sustainability reporting training, highlighting the need to integrate governance complexity and ESG analysis into accounting curricula. By equipping future professionals with nuanced understanding of ESG dynamics,

Sustainability in Accounting and Finance Education, 185–203

Published under exclusive licence by Emerald Publishing Limited
doi:10.1108/978-1-80686-393-820261011

educators can better prepare students to evaluate non-financial disclosures and governance mechanisms in financial decision-making contexts.

Keywords: ESG; BSE; Sustainability; corporate governance; firm performance

1. Introduction

Environmental, Social and Governance (ESG) performance has received attention in the past few years from investors, firm managers and other stakeholders as it is an increasingly known way to increase the value of a firm (Ahmad et al., 2021). An article published by McKinsey & Company underscores the importance of ESG in a firm and how it can lead to top-line growth, cost reduction, reduced regulatory and legal interventions, employee productivity uplift and lastly, investment and asset optimisation (Henisz et al., 2019).

Similarly, corporate governance plays an important role, including improving corporate accountability, building a corporate reputation and providing valuable investment decision-making information. Corporate governance focuses on resolving the issue of the agency's alignment between the interests of management and shareholders.

With this paper, we first attempt to investigate the relationship between ESG performance and a firm's performance and subsequently, examine the moderating role of corporate governance on the performance of ESG and firm performance, which has not yet been explored in any of the existing literature.

Although the relationship between ESG performance and firm performance has been investigated in numerous empirical/past studies, the result is not conclusive (Ahmad et al., 2021; Atan et al., 2016; Dahal et al., 2023; Jaiwani & Gopalkrishnan, 2023; Khanchel et al., 2023; Maji & Lohia, 2022; Minutolo et al., 2019; Morri et al., 2024; Mukherjee & Nuñez, 2019; Lee & Isa, 2022; Carnini Pulino et al., 2022; Ruan & Liu, 2021; Shaikh, 2022; Velte, 2017; Yoon et al., 2024). Some of the authors have found positive relationships between these two variables (Ahmad et al., 2021; Khancel et al., 2023; Maji & Lohia, 2022; Minutolo et al., 2019; Lee & Isa, 2022; Carnini Pulino et al., 2022; Velte, 2017), while on the other hand, studies have found negative relationships (Jaiwani & Gopalkrishnan, 2023; Shaikh, 2022; Ruan & Liu, 2021; Yoon et al., 2024), and some have found evidence of insignificance relations (Atan et al, 2016; Dahal et al., 2023; Mukherjee & Nuñez, 2019).

The scope for more research in this field is expanded by the inconclusive findings of earlier investigations. In addition to this restriction of earlier research, we have discovered that no study has looked into the moderating role of corporate governance in the context of a firm's performance and ESG performance. We attempted to investigate in our study how corporate governance influences the relationship between ESG and firm performance in a moderating way.

This study aims to identify the ESG performance of selected Indian companies and to empirically investigate the impact of ESG on their financial outcomes, exploring whether strong ESG practices relate to better financial performance. Also, the study examines the moderating role of corporate governance in this relationship, seeking to determine whether strong corporate governance practices enhance or worsen the effect of ESG on a company's profitability.

This study would help in making policy for the companies to help them in sustainable economic growth. Corporate governance ensures that companies are running transparently, ethically and efficiently, protecting the interests of both internal and external stakeholders. ESG scores offer insights into how well a company is managing its impact on the environment, their social responsibilities and corporate governance practices. Together, they help policymakers create strategies that enhance a company's reputation, attract investors, reduce risks and ensure long-term sustainability and success.

The research is subject to certain limitations, the study is constrained by the specific time frame of five years from 2018 to 2023 and the geographical focus on India, which may limit the generalisation of the findings.

2. Literature Review

Various theoretical frameworks exist in relation to ESG which helps in organising and understanding complex phenomena alongside with facilitating prediction of ESG risks which can help entities to address related risks and opportunities. Additionally, these frameworks add more credibility to the research and analysis of ESG performance (Martiny et al., 2024). Notable frameworks include stakeholder theory, agency theory, institutional theory and resource theory. Stakeholder theory states that the capacity of a firm to generate sustainable wealth is determined by its relationships with its various stakeholders. Therefore, it should disclose financial and non-financial information in order to increase transparency (Garcia et al., 2017). Agency theory underscores the importance of independence of the board from management and leadership structure duality or separation of the functions of CEO and chairman of the board (Hafsi & Turgut, 2013). Likewise, institutional theory states how institutional investors significantly influence strategic firm decisions through their voting power and superior skills in information acquisition and management monitoring and resource-based view theory emphasises the importance of company's internal resources and capabilities in achieving a competitive advantage which can have a direct impact on ESG performance.

2.1 Impact of Overall ESG Score on Firm Performance

The existing studies with respect to the relation between ESG score and Firm performance provide mixed results. On one hand, in line with the stakeholder theory, it's seen that the adoption of ESG practices ensures the well-being of the diverse stakeholders associated with a firm while also elevating the market value of firms (Maji & Lohia, 2022). Positive impact of ESG performance on firm performance indicates that disclosing ESG performance is positively perceived by stakeholders and helps build bonds and trust amongst the market players (Ademi & Klungseth, 2022; Qureshi et al., 2021). A significant and positive impact of ESG performance on firm performance was found in the Chinese manufacturing industry (Tao, 2023) while a mild but significant positive effect was found between ESG ratings and financial performance in the European food industry (Sandberg et al., 2022). Various other studies have concluded that there exists a positive relation between the overall ESG score and firm performance (Ahmad et al., 2021; Alareeni & Hamdan, 2020; Friede et al., 2015; Jung & Yoo, 2023; Kalia & Aggarwal, 2022; Kim & Li, 2021; Maji & Lohia, 2024; Melinda & Wardhani, 2020; Minutolo et al., 2019; Naeem et al., 2022; Pinheiro et al., 2023; Carnini Pulino et al., 2022; Velte, 2017; Xie et al., 2018). On the other hand, few studies have implied that there exists a negative relationship – contradicting the stakeholder theory and resources based view (Candio, 2024; Firmansyah et al., 2023; Jaiwani & Gopalkrishnan, 2023; Makridou et al., 2023; Ruan & Liu, 2021; Shaikh, 2022; Sharma & Thakural, 2015; Yoon et al., 2024). There also exists a pool of literature that justifies that there is neither a positive nor negative relationship between ESG performance and firm performance (Atan et al., 2016, 2018; Mukherjee & Nuñez, 2019).

On the basis of the above discussion, we have developed the first hypothesis of our study as follows:

H1. There is a significant impact of ESG performance on a firm's financial performance.

2.2 Moderating Role of Corporate Governance in the Relationship Between ESG and Financial Performance

There exists a very scarce pool of literature on the moderating effect of corporate governance on the relationship between ESG and financial performance. But the ones that exist, affirms that board size, one of the measures of corporate governance, positively moderates the relationship between ESG and financial performance. (Achdi & Ameur, 2011; Belkhir, 2009; Juras & Hinson, 2008; Rossi et al., 2021). Similarly, studies have also established that board independence and CEO duality plays a moderating role ensuring transparency and creating a sustainable financial value for the firms, reinforcing their competitive advantage. (Chen & Bikki, 2000; Rossi et al., 2021; Xiao & Yuan, 2007). Hence, we arrive at our final hypothesis:

H2. Corporate Governance factors moderate the relationship between ESG performance and firm's financial performance.

3. Methodology

This section talks about data sources, period of study, selection of companies and formulation of empirical models for examining the relationship between ESG and firm performance along with the moderating effect of corporate governance factors between the relation of the aforementioned variables.

3.1 Data

This study investigates the relationship between ESG performance and the financial performance of Indian firms, taking into consideration the moderating effect of corporate governance. For that purpose, we have taken 100 BSE companies on the basis of market capitalisation and availability of ESG data. We have taken 5 years of data during the period of 2018–2022. The data was taken from three different sources. ESG data was taken from Bloomberg, a leading provider of comprehensive financial and sustainability-related information, while the financial data was taken from CMIE Prowess and Annual Report of the selected companies for the selected time period.

3.2 Variables

In our study, we have used four sets of variables: dependent variables, independent variables, moderating variables and control variables. The dependent variable used in this study is the financial performance of the selected firms. This is measured in two ways, i.e. through profitability ratios, namely Return on Assets (ROA) and Return on Equity (ROE) and through market value measures, namely Tobin's Q and Market to Book Value ratio. Overall ESG Score forms part of independent variables. Moderating variables consist of corporate governance factors, i.e. board size, independent board, board meeting, board gender diversity, CEO duality and ownership structure. Lastly, firm age, firm size, leverage and current ratio form part of control variables. Table 11.1 describes the measurement of variables.

3.3 Empirical Models and Estimation Techniques

To test the impact of ESG performance on financial performance of companies and moderating role of corporate governance factors in the relationship between these two variables, we have formulated the following models:

Model 1:

$$\mathrm{FP} = \alpha_0 + \beta_1 \mathrm{ESG}_{it} + \beta_2 \mathrm{SIZE}_{it} + \beta_3 \mathrm{AGE}_{it} + \beta_4 \mathrm{CR}_{it} + \beta_5 \mathrm{LEV}_{it} + \mathrm{e}_{it}$$

Model 2:

$$\mathrm{FP} = \alpha_0 + \beta_1 \mathrm{ESG}_{it} + \beta_2 \mathrm{BS}_{it} + \beta_3 \mathrm{ESG}_{it} \times \mathrm{BS}_{it} + \beta_4 \mathrm{SIZE}_{it} + \beta_5 \mathrm{AGE}_{it} + \beta_6 \mathrm{CR}_{it} + \beta_7 \mathrm{LEV}_{it} + \mathrm{e}_{it}$$

Table 11.1. Measurement of Variables

Variable	Symbol	Measurement
Return on assets	ROA	Net income/Total assets
Return on equity	ROE	Net income/Shareholder's equity
Market to book value ratio	MBVR	Market capitalisation/Book value of shares
Tobin's Q	TQ	(Market capitalisation + short term debts + long term debts)/Total assets
Overall ESG score	ESG	Bloomberg's overall environmental, social and governance score
Board size	BS	No. of directors
Independent board	IB	(No. Of independent directors/Board size) × 100
Board meeting	BM	No. of board meeting
Board gender diversity	GEND	(No. Of female director/Board size) × 100
CEO duality	DUAL	1 – if CEO is chairman; 0 – otherwise
Promoter holding	PROMOWN	Percentage of shares held by promoters
Domestic institutional investor	DINSTOWN	Percentage of shares held by domestic institutional investors
Foreign institutional holding	FINSTOWN	Percentage of shares held by foreign institutional investors
Firm age	AGE	No. of years from incorporation
Firm size	SIZE	Natural log of total assets
Leverage	LEV	(Short term debts + Long term debts)/Total assets
Current ratio	CR	Current assets/Current liabilities

Model 3:

$$\mathrm{FP} = \alpha_0 + \beta_1 \mathrm{ESG}_{it} + \beta_2 \mathrm{IB}_{it} + \beta_3 \mathrm{ESG}_{it} \times \mathrm{IB}_{it} + \beta_4 \mathrm{SIZE}_{it} + \beta_5 \mathrm{AGE}_{it} + \beta_6 \mathrm{CR}_{it} + \beta_7 \mathrm{LEV}_{it} + \mathrm{e}_{it}$$

Model 4:

$$\mathrm{FP} = \alpha_0 + \beta_1 \mathrm{ESG}_{it} + \beta_2 \mathrm{BM}_{it} + \beta_3 \mathrm{ESG}_{it} \times \mathrm{BM}_{it} + \beta_4 \mathrm{SIZE}_{it} + \beta_5 \mathrm{AGE}_{it} + \beta_6 \mathrm{CR}_{it} + \beta_7 \mathrm{LEV}_{it} + \mathrm{e}_{it}$$

Model 5:

$$\mathrm{FP} = \alpha_0 + \beta_1 \mathrm{ESG}_{it} + \beta_2 \mathrm{GEND}_{it} + \beta_3 \mathrm{ESG}_{it} \times \mathrm{GEND}_{it} + \beta_4 \mathrm{SIZE}_{it} + \beta_5 \mathrm{AGE}_{it} + \beta_6 \mathrm{CR}_{it} + \beta_7 \mathrm{LEV}_{it} + \mathrm{e}_{it}$$

Model 6:

$$\mathrm{FP} = \alpha_0 + \beta_1 \mathrm{ESG}_{it} + \beta_2 \mathrm{DUAL}_{it} + \beta_3 \mathrm{ESG}_{it} \times \mathrm{DUAL}_{it} + \beta_4 \mathrm{SIZE}_{it} + \beta_5 \mathrm{AGE}_{it} + \beta_6 \mathrm{CR}_{it} + \beta_7 \mathrm{LEV}_{it} + \mathrm{e}_{it}$$

Model 7:

$$FP = \alpha_0 + \beta_1 ESG_{it} + \beta_2 PROMOWN_{it} + \beta_3 ESG_{it} \times PROMOWN_{it} + \beta_4 DINSTOWN_{it} + \beta_5 ESG_{it} \times DINSTOWN_{it} + \beta_6 FINSTOWN_{it} + \beta_7 ESG_{it} \times FINSTOWN_{it} + \beta_8 SIZE_{it} + \beta_9 AGE_{it} + \beta_{10} CR_{it} + \beta_{11} LEV_{it} + e_{it}$$

Model 8:

$$FP = \alpha_0 + \beta_1 ESG_{it} + \beta_2 BS_{it} + \beta_3 BM_{it} + \beta_4 GEND_{it} + \beta_5 DUAL_{it} + \beta_6 PROMOWN_{it} + \beta_7 DINSTOWN_{it} + \beta_8 FINSTOWN_{it} + \beta_9 SIZE_{it} + \beta_{10} AGE_{it} + \beta_{11} CR_{it} + \beta_{12} LEV_{it} + e_{it}$$

Model 9:

$$FP = \alpha_0 + \beta_1 ESG_{it} + \beta_2 BS_{it} + \beta_3 ESG_{it} \times BS_{it} + \beta_4 IB_{it} + \beta_5 ESG_{it} \times IB_{it} + \beta_6 BM_{it} + \beta_7 ESG_{it} \times BM_{it} + \beta_8 GEND_{it} + \beta_9 ESG_{it} \times GEND_{it} + \beta_{10} DUAL_{it} + \beta_{11} ESG_{it} \times DUAL_{it} + \beta_{12} PROMOWN_{it} + \beta_{13} ESG_{it} \times PROMOWN_{it} + \beta_{14} DINSTOWN_{it} + \beta_{15} ESG_{it} \times DINSTOWN_{it} + \beta_{16} FINSTOWN_{it} + \beta_{17} ESG_{it} \times FINSTOWN_{it} + \beta_{18} SIZE_{it} + \beta_{19} AGE_{it} + \beta_{20} CR_{it} + \beta_{21} LEV_{it} + e_{it}$$

Here, FP indicates Firm Performance, β is a regression coefficient, and α and e are constant and error terms respectively, i indicate firm and t stands for time.

Pooled Ordinary Least Square (OLS) regression is used to estimate the result.

4. Analysis and Interpretation

In this section, we demonstrate the result of data analysis. First of all descriptive statistics of data is presented followed by the result of regression analysis.

4.1 Descriptive Statistics

Table 11.2 represents the mean, standard deviation, maximum and minimum value of each variable.

Table 11.2 shows descriptive statistics of sample companies over a period of five years. The average ROA is approximately 10%, with standard deviation of 10.81. The highest and lowest ROA values are 60.17% and −86,98%, respectively. Similarly, average ROE stands at 16.85% and has standard deviation of 23.31.

For Tobin's q, average value over five years is 4.39, with a standard deviation of 6.39. When examining ESG performance of companies, the overall ESG score has an average of 43.16, ranging from minimum of 16.04 to maximum of 76.98, with standard deviation of 10.52.

Table 11.2. Descriptive Statistics

	N	Min	Max	Mean	Std. Dev.
ROA	500	−86.98	60.17	9.8168	10.81554
ROE	500	−326.95	103.12	16.8546	23.31316
TQ	500	0.12	64.88	4.3944	6.39081
MBVR	500	−2.16	91.16	6.6095	10.56818
ESGSCORE	500	16.04	76.98	43.1591	10.52750
BS	500	4.00	24.00	11.0640	2.77621
BM	500	4.00	22.00	6.4340	2.85200
IB	500	0.00	83.33	50.0737	11.04607
GEND	500	0.00	50.00	15.7611	8.59732
DUAL	500	0.00	1.00	0.2260	0.41866
FINSTOWN	500	0.00	41.92	13.3374	8.57420
PROMOWN	500	15.85	88.58	56.3065	13.99262
DINSTOWN	500	0.30	33.93	13.2147	6.86256
SIZE	500	6.89	13.79	9.4386	1.40764
AGE	500	2.64	5.38	3.9156	0.53717
LEV	500	0.00	0.80	0.1287	0.15644
CR	500	0.05	8.21	1.7354	1.18644

It can also be seen that high standard deviation across these variables shows substantial variability in company performance, which may be a point of concern. However, our study does not incorporate any corrective measures to address this issue.

4.2 Regression Analysis

This section presents the estimation results of the Pooled OLS regression models. Our study employs a total of nine models. Model 1 examines the direct impact of the overall ESG score on firm performance. Model 2 to 7 assesses the moderating role of individual corporate governance factors in the relationship between ESG performance and firm performance. Model 8 evaluates the combined effect of ESG performance and corporate governance factors on firm performance. At last, Model 9 analyses the moderating influence of all corporate governance factors on the relationship between ESG performance and financial performance. OLS regression analysis was conducted for all nine models, incorporating four different measures of firm performance. The estimation results for ROA, ROE, Tobin's q (TQ) and Market-to-Book Value Ratio (MBVR) are presented in Tables 11.3–11.6 respectively.

Table 11.3 shows that ESG performance does not have a significant impact on ROA for selected companies. However, when examining the moderating effect of corporate governance factors on the relationship between ESG performance and

Table 11.3. ESG Performance, Corporate Governance and ROA

	Model 1		Model 2		Model 3		Model 4		Model 5		Model 6		Model 7		Model 8		Model 9	
	Std. Coeff. Beta	Sig.	Std. Coeff. Beta	Sig.	Std. Coeff. Beta	Sig.	Std. Coeff. Beta	Sig.	Std. Coeff. Beta	Sig.	Std. Coeff. Beta	Sig.	Std. Coeff. Beta	Sig.	Std. Coeff. Beta	Sig.	Std. Coeff. Beta	Sig.
(Constant)		0.486		0.026		0.174		0.802		0.396		0.713		0.462		0		0.019
ESGSCORE	−0.048	0.267	**0.382**	**0.02**	−0.1	0.09	0.073	0.424	−0.079	0.139	−0.019	0.692	−0.243	0.475	−0.073	0.075	0.24	0.533
LEV	**−0.282**	**0.000**	**−0.268**	**0.000**	**−0.276**	**0.000**	**−0.293**	**0.000**	**−0.279**	**0.000**	**−0.287**	**0.000**	**−0.212**	**0.000**	**−0.215**	**0.000**	**−0.205**	**0.000**
CR	**0.258**	**0.000**	**0.247**	**0.000**	**0.257**	**0.000**	**0.212**	**0.000**	**0.256**	**0.000**	**0.259**	**0.000**	**0.257**	**0.000**	**0.214**	**0.000**	**0.214**	**0.000**
SIZE	−0.06	0.195	**−0.102**	**0.03**	−0.079	0.105	**−0.161**	**0.002**	−0.065	0.166	−0.054	0.248	**−0.118**	**0.011**	**−0.231**	**0.000**	**−0.235**	**0.000**
AGE	**0.146**	**0.000**	**0.158**	**0.000**	**0.145**	**0.000**	**0.142**	**0.000**	**0.149**	**0.000**	**0.145**	**0.000**	**0.178**	**0.000**	**0.181**	**0.000**	**0.192**	**0.000**
BS			**0.524**	**0.001**											**0.101**	**0.008**	**0.449**	**0.005**
ESGXBS			**−0.622**	**0.007**													−0.213	0.434
IB					−0.071	0.183									0.048	0.229	0.219	0.049
ESGXIB					0.09	0.176											−0.331	0.101
BM							0.396	0.011							**0.178**	**0.000**	0.096	0.545
ESGXBM							0.251	0.174									0.102	0.601
GEND									−0.042	0.569					0.078	0.036	0.116	0.341
ESGXGEND									0.078	0.338							−0.056	0.688
DUAL											0.165	0.329			−0.004	0.911	0.21	0.222
ESGXDUAL											−0.2	0.251					−0.236	0.195
PROMOWN													0.198	0.383	**0.341**	**0.000**	0.264	0.285
DINSTAOWN													0.225	0.198	**0.162**	**0.000**	0.34	0.067
FINSTAOWN													0.183	0.377	**0.304**	**0.000**	0.127	0.539
ESGXPROMOWN													0.209	0.476			0.095	0.77
ESGXDINSTOWN													−0.09	0.659			−0.234	0.288
ESGXFINSTAOWN													0.134	0.585			0.209	0.393

Table 11.4. ESG Performance, Corporate Governance and ROE

	Model 1		Model 2		Model 3		Model 4		Model 5		Model 6		Model 7		Model 8		Model 9	
	Std. Coeff. Beta	Sig.	Std. Coeff. Beta	Sig.	Std. Coeff. Beta	Sig.	Std. Coeff. Beta	Sig.	Std. Coeff. Beta	Sig.	Std. Coeff. Beta	Sig.	Std. Coeff. Beta	Sig.	Std. Coeff. Beta	Sig.	Std. Coeff. Beta	Sig.
(Constant)		0.89		0.432		0.979		0.873		0.693		0.86		0.004		0.009		0.000
ESGSCORE	0.000	0.996	0.18	0.336	0.029	0.656	0.074	0.469	0.025	0.669	−0.005	0.931	0.798	0.042	−0.016	0.735	1.162	0.01
LEV	**−0.16**	**0.002**	**−0.16**	**0.002**	**−0.164**	**0.002**	**−0.173**	**0.001**	**−0.167**	**0.001**	**−0.159**	**0.003**	**−0.115**	**0.027**	**−0.126**	**0.016**	**−0.112**	**0.036**
CR	0.08	0.109	0.076	0.128	0.079	0.114	0.038	0.45	0.079	0.116	0.081	0.109	0.073	0.14	0.042	0.405	0.035	0.495
SIZE	−0.069	0.185	−0.077	0.152	−0.067	0.217	−0.168	0.004	−0.057	0.276	−0.07	0.179	−0.124	0.02	−0.199	0.001	−0.221	0.000
AGE	**0.155**	**0.001**	**0.159**	**0.000**	**0.155**	**0.001**	**0.151**	**0.001**	**0.154**	**0.001**	**0.156**	**0.001**	**0.181**	**0.000**	**0.177**	**0.000**	**0.187**	**0.000**
BS			0.185	0.301											−0.005	0.91	0.079	0.675
ESGXBS			−0.262	0.32													0.364	0.253
IB					0.009	0.88									0.055	0.236	**0.307**	**0.018**
ESGXIB					−0.047	0.527											**−0.5**	**0.034**
BM							0.307	0.079							**0.197**	**0.000**	0.15	0.422
ESGXBM							−0.146	0.482									0.046	0.841
GEND									0.121	0.14					**0.099**	**0.023**	0.188	0.187
ESGXGEND									−0.075	0.409							−0.13	0.423
DUAL											−0.015	0.935			0.03	0.495	0.127	0.527
ESGXDUAL											0.026	0.893					−0.104	0.626
PROMOWN													**0.765**	**0.004**	**0.292**	**0.000**	**0.917**	**0.002**
DINSTOWN													0.384	0.057	**0.109**	**0.029**	**0.555**	**0.011**
FINSTOWN													**0.633**	**0.008**	**0.214**	**0.000**	**0.679**	**0.005**
ESGXPROMOWN													−0.618	0.068			**−0.834**	**0.028**
ESGXDINSTOWN													−0.348	0.137			**−0.549**	**0.033**
ESGXFINSTOWN													−0.522	0.064			**−0.566**	**0.048**

Table 11.5. ESG Performance, Corporate Governance and MBVR

	Model 1		Model 2		Model 3		Model 4		Model 5		Model 6		Model 7		Model 8		Model 9	
	Std. Coeff. Beta	Sig.	Std. Coeff. Beta	Sig.	Std. Coeff. Beta	Sig.	Std. Coeff. Beta	Sig.	Std. Coeff. Beta	Sig.	Std. Coeff. Beta	Sig.	Std. Coeff. Beta	Sig.	Std. Coeff. Beta	Sig.	Std. Coeff. Beta	Sig.
(Constant)		0.000		0.115		0.013		0		0.004		0.000		0.497		0.686		0.03
ESGSCORE	−0.035	0.448	0.178	0.322	0.025	0.691	−0.052	0.606	0.034	0.546	−0.014	0.79	0.439	0.246	−0.077	0.092	0.745	0.082
LEV	**−0.244**	**0.000**	**−0.25**	**0.000**	**−0.25**	**0.000**	**−0.248**	**0.000**	**−0.261**	**0.000**	**−0.227**	**0.000**	**−0.201**	**0.000**	**−0.188**	**0.000**	**−0.186**	**0.000**
CR	**−0.162**	**0.001**	**−0.166**	**0.001**	**−0.16**	**0.001**	**−0.172**	**0.001**	**−0.167**	**0.000**	**−0.148**	**0.002**	**−0.144**	**0.003**	**−0.157**	**0.001**	**−0.145**	**0.003**
SIZE	**−0.244**	**0.000**	**−0.24**	**0.000**	**−0.216**	**0.000**	**−0.272**	**0.000**	**−0.213**	**0.000**	**−0.253**	**0.000**	**−0.266**	**0.000**	**−0.298**	**0.000**	**−0.304**	**0.000**
AGE	**0.101**	**0.02**	**0.102**	**0.018**	**0.101**	**0.019**	**0.099**	**0.022**	**0.097**	**0.022**	**0.102**	**0.018**	**0.138**	**0.001**	**0.139**	**0.001**	**0.138**	**0.001**
BS			0.174	0.313											−0.015	0.717	0.176	0.322
ESGXBS			−0.312	0.218													0.254	0.4
IB					0.103	0.072									0.048	0.282	0.228	0.065
ESGXIB					−0.107	0.135											−0.332	0.138
BM							0.017	0.922							0.084	0.09	−0.099	0.574
ESGXBM							0.044	0.827									0.204	0.344
GEND									**0.321**	**0.000**					**0.17**	**0.000**	**0.526**	**0.000**
ESGXGEND									**−0.202**	**0.019**							**−0.451**	**0.004**
DUAL											0.325	0.074			**0.104**	**0.015**	0.347	0.069
ESGXDUAL											−0.251	0.181					−0.268	0.185
PROMOWN													0.445	0.078	**0.234**	**0.000**	**0.589**	**0.032**
DINSTOWN													0.074	0.705	0.019	0.692	0.154	0.455
FINSTOWN													**0.681**	**0.003**	**0.233**	**0.000**	**0.728**	**0.002**
ESGXPROMOWN													−0.325	0.32			−0.492	0.171
ESGXDINSTOWN													−0.115	0.61			−0.184	0.451
ESGXFINSTOWN													**−0.558**	**0.041**			**−0.606**	**0.026**

Table 11.6. ESG Performance, Corporate Governance and TQ

	Model 1		Model 2		Model 3		Model 4		Model 5		Model 6		Model 7		Model 8		Model 9	
	Std. Coeff. Beta	Sig.	Std. Coeff. Beta	Sig.	Std. Coeff. Beta	Sig.	Std. Coeff. Beta	Sig.	Std. Coeff. Beta	Sig.	Std. Coeff. Beta	Sig.	Std. Coeff. Beta	Sig.	Std. Coeff. Beta	Sig.	Std. Coeff. Beta	Sig.
(Constant)		0.000		0.955		0.053		0.002		0.099		0.001		0.139		0.689		0.001
ESGSCORE	0.033	0.461	**0.485**	**0.005**	**0.154**	**0.011**	0.01	0.913	**0.172**	**0.001**	0.05	0.321	0.568	0.11	−0.004	0.932	**1.219**	**0.002**
LEV	**−0.197**	**0.000**	**−0.211**	**0.000**	**−0.211**	**0.000**	**−0.199**	**0.000**	**−0.219**	**0.000**	**−0.202**	**0.000**	**−0.131**	**0.006**	**−0.148**	**0.002**	**−0.141**	**0.003**
CR	−0.078	0.09	−0.086	0.062	−0.08	0.082	−0.081	0.088	−0.077	0.085	−0.079	0.09	−0.057	0.206	−0.068	0.138	−0.059	0.188
SIZE	**−0.34**	**0.000**	**−0.328**	**0.000**	**−0.317**	**0.000**	**−0.352**	**0.000**	**−0.299**	**0.000**	**−0.335**	**0.000**	**−0.37**	**0.000**	**−0.374**	**0.000**	**−0.393**	**0.000**
AGE	**0.2**	**0.000**	**0.203**	**0.000**	**0.198**	**0.000**	**0.199**	**0.000**	**0.189**	**0.000**	**0.2**	**0.000**	**0.25**	**0.000**	**0.245**	**0.000**	**0.244**	**0.000**
BS			**0.355**	**0.031**											−0.058	0.153	**0.391**	**0.019**
ESGXBS			**−0.663**	**0.006**													0.043	0.879
IB					0.093	0.089									−0.019	0.653	0.169	0.144
ESGXIB					**−0.201**	**0.003**											−0.369	0.078
BM							−0.022	0.892							0.05	0.292	−0.268	0.105
ESGXBM							0.054	0.783									0.369	0.067
GEND									**0.405**	**0.000**					**0.113**	**0.004**	**0.654**	**0.000**
ESGXGEND									**−0.375**	**0.000**							**−0.667**	**0.000**
DUAL											0.085	0.628			0.003	0.95	0.228	0.201
ESGXDUAL											−0.114	0.529					−0.273	0.148
PROMOWN													**0.516**	**0.03**	**0.238**	**0.000**	**0.728**	**0.005**
DINSTOWN													0.238	0.192	−0.012	0.795	0.322	0.094
FINSTOWN													**0.674**	**0.002**	**0.299**	**0.000**	**0.663**	**0.002**
ESGXPROMOWN													−0.352	0.251			**−0.694**	**0.039**
ESGXDINSTOWN													−0.312	0.142			−0.442	0.053
ESGXFINSTOWN													−0.459	0.073			−0.458	0.072

financial performance, the findings reveal that, apart from board size, no other corporate governance factors significantly influence this relationship. The results suggest that board size negatively affects the relationship between ESG performance and the firm's financial performance, as measured by ROA. Additionally, regarding the impact of control variables on firm performance, the study finds that leverage and firm size negatively affect firm performance, whereas short term solvency (measured by Current Ratio (CR)) and firm age have a positive impact.

Table 11.4 shows that ESG performance does not have a significant impact on ROE for selected companies. However, when examining the moderating effect of corporate governance factors on the relationship between ESG performance and financial performance, the findings reveal that, apart from independent board, promoter's shareholdings and institutional investors shareholding, no other corporate governance factors significantly influence this relationship. Although, these variables individually are not able to moderate the relationship between ESG performance and firms' financial performance. The results suggest that independent board, promoter's shareholdings and institutional investors shareholding negatively affect the relationship between ESG performance and the firm's financial performance, as measured by ROE. Additionally, regarding the impact of control variables on firm performance, the study finds that leverage and firm size negatively affect firm performance, whereas short term solvency (measured by CR) and firm age have a positive impact.

Table 11.5 shows that ESG performance does not have a significant impact on MBVR for selected companies. However, when examining the moderating effect of corporate governance factors on the relationship between ESG performance and financial performance, the findings reveal that, apart from gender diversity and foreign institutional investors shareholding, no other corporate governance factors significantly influence this relationship. The results suggest that gender diversity and foreign institutional investors shareholding negatively affects the relationship between ESG performance and the firm's financial performance, as measured by MBVR. Additionally, regarding the impact of control variables on firm performance, the study finds that leverage, short term solvency (measured by CR) and firm size negatively affect firm performance, whereas firm age have a positive impact.

Table 11.6 shows that ESG performance does not have a significant impact on TQ for selected companies. However, when examining the moderating effect of corporate governance factors on the relationship between ESG performance and financial performance, the findings reveal that, apart from board size, independent board, gender diversity and promoters' shareholding no other corporate governance factors significantly influence this relationship. The results suggest that board size, independent board, gender diversity and promoter's shareholding negatively affect the relationship between ESG performance and the firm's financial performance, as measured by TQ. Although, promoter's shareholding individually is not able to moderate the relationship between ESG performance and firms' financial performance. Additionally, regarding the impact of control variables on firm performance, the study finds that leverage, short term solvency (measured by CR) and firm size negatively affect firm performance, whereas firm age have a positive impact.

5. Result and Discussion

5.1 Impact of ESG Performance on Financial Performance

The findings of this study suggest that the ESG performance does not have a significant impact on either of the financial performance indicators i.e. ROA, ROE, MBVR and TQ. This contradicts with the stakeholder theory which suggests that firms with strong ESG practices should experience better financial outcomes (Garcia et al., 2017). This finding is consistent with results of Mukherjee and Nuñez (2019), Atan et al. (2016, 2018).

5.2 The Moderating Effect of Corporate Governance on Firm Performance

This study highlights that while ESG performance does not directly impact financial performance indicators, few corporate governance factors play a crucial moderating role. However, these governance mechanisms, instead of strengthening the relationship between ESG and financial performance, negatively moderate the relationship.

Firstly, our study suggests that board size has a significant negative moderating effect on the relationship between ESG and financial performance indicators, specifically on ROA and TQ, which is contrary to the agency theory which suggests that larger the board size, better policy monitoring process that takes place. Secondly, the study found out that, when combined together independent boards, promoter shareholding and institutional investors have a negative moderating impact on the relationship between ESG and ROE but they individually do not moderate the relationship. Moreover, the study also found out that gender diversity negatively moderates the relation between ESG and variables of financial performance namely both MBVR and TQ. Additionally, foreign institutional investors exhibit a negative moderating effect on ESG and MBVR, but have no significant effect when other financial performance indicators are in play. Lastly, our study establishes that independent board has a negative moderating effect on the ESG-financial performance relationship. These findings contradict with existing literature that have found a positive moderating effect of corporate governance on the ESG-firm performance relationship (Achdi & Ameur, 2011; Albitar et al., 2020; Belkhir, 2009; Chen & Bikki, 2000; Jung, 2024; Juras Hinson,. 2008; Rossi et al., 2021; Xiao & Yuan, 2007).

6. Conclusion

This study examines the impact of ESG performance on the financial performance of Indian companies, with a particular focus on the moderating role of corporate governance. Using data from 100 BSE-listed companies between 2018 and 2022, analysed through Pooled OLS, the findings reveal that ESG performance alone does not have a significant impact on key financial metrics such as ROA, ROE, Tobin's *Q* and MBVR. However, corporate governance factors – specifically board size, gender diversity and foreign institutional shareholding – appear to weaken the relationship between ESG and financial performance, highlighting the complexity of governance structures in this context. Several factors could explain why corporate governance weakens this relationship. Larger board sizes may hinder the effectiveness of ESG-driven strategies due to coordination difficulties, conflicting interests and sluggish decision-making processes. Similarly, while gender diversity is generally considered beneficial, in this study, it appears to dilute the impact of ESG on financial performance, possibly due to challenges in influencing firm strategies. Foreign institutional investors may also contribute to this weakening effect, as their preference for short-term financial gains might conflict with the long term sustainability objectives of ESG initiative. Independence boards, despite being expected to enhance transparency, were found to negatively moderate the ESG-financial performance link, suggesting a misalignment between governance structures and ESG goals. Additionally, high promoter shareholding may prioritise personal or family interests over broader ESG goals. These findings have several implications for accounting education.

Educators and accounting programmes can consider incorporating case-based discussions, empirical methods and governance analysis into ESG and financial performance modules. Students can be taught to critically assess how governance mechanisms interact with sustainability metrics and thereby enhance their ability to interpret ESG disclosures and develop integrated financial strategies. Moreover, the observed disconnect between board independence and ESG goals highlights the importance of training future accountants to navigate tensions between short-term profitability and long-term sustainability. This finding also presents valuable opportunities for educators engaged in academic research. Educators can explore how specific corporate governance mechanisms influence ESG integration across sectors and contribute further to the growing body of literature on sustainability accounting and reporting. Integrating empirical insights like these into research projects can strengthen the link between academic inquiry and real-world application, enriching both teaching and scholarly output.

However, there are some limitations. The statistical methods used have certain flaws and stronger analytical tools could improve accuracy. The study also has a small sample size and used a time period based on data availability, which might limit generalisation of the results. Given these challenges, future research should employ more advanced statistical techniques, expand the sample size, extend the study period and focus on specific industries to gain deeper insights into how ESG performance impacts financial outcomes.

References

Achdi, H., & Ameur, I. G. B. (2011). Board characteristics, performance and risk taking behaviour in Tunisian banks. *International Journal of Business and Management*, *6*, 88–97.

Ademi, B., & Klungseth, N. J. (2022). Does it pay to deliver superior ESG performance? Evidence from US S&P 500 companies. *Journal of Global Responsibility*, *13*(4), 421–449. https://doi.org/10.1108/jgr-01-2022-0006

Ahmad, N., Mobarek, A., & Roni, N. N. (2021). Revisiting the impact of ESG on financial performance of FTSE350 UK firms: Static and dynamic panel data analysis. *Cogent Business & Management*, *8*(1). https://doi.org/10.1080/23311975.2021.1900500

Alareeni, B. A., & Hamdan, A. (2020). ESG impact on performance of US S&P 500-listed firms. *Corporate Governance: International Journal of Business in Society*, *20* (7), 1409–1428. https://doi.org/10.1108/cg-06-2020-0258

Albitar, K., Hussainey, K., Kolade, N., & Gerged, A. M. (2020). ESG disclosure and firm performance before and after IR. *International Journal of Accounting and Information Management*, *28*(3), 429–444. https://doi.org/10.1108/ijaim-09-2019-0108

Atan, R., Alam, M. M., Said, J., & Zamri, M. (2018). The impacts of environmental, social, and governance factors on firm performance: Panel study of Malaysian companies. *Management of Environmental Quality: An International Journal*, *29*(2), 182–194. https://doi.org/10.1108/MEQ-03-2017-0033

Atan, R., Said, J., Razali, F. A., & Saunah, Z. (2016). Environmental, Social and governance disclosure performance: A comparative study. *International Journal of Economics and Management*, 355–375. http://www.econ.upm.edu.my/ijem

Belkhir, M. (2009). Board of directors' size and performance in the banking industry. *International Journal of Managerial Finance*, *5*, 201–222.

Candio, P. (2024). The effect of ESG and CSR attitude on financial performance in Europe: A quantitative re-examination. *Journal of Environmental Management*. https://doi.org/10.1016/j.jenvman.2024.120390

Carnini Pulino, S., Ciaburri, M., Magnanelli, B. S., & Nasta, L. (2022). Does ESG disclosure influence firm performance? *Sustainability*, *14*(13), 7595. https://doi.org/10.3390/su14137595

Chen, C. J. P., & Bikki, J.. (2000). Association between independent non-executive directors, family control and financial disclosures in Hong Kong. *Journal of Accounting and Public Policy*, *19*, 285–310.

Dahal, M., Sangma, A., Das, J., & Ray, P. (2023). Mandatory CSR spending, ESG and firm performance: Evidence from Bombay stock exchange. *Rajagiri Management Journal*, *18*(2), 137–150. https://doi.org/10.1108/ramj-08-2022-0132

Firmansyah, E. A., Umar, U. H., & Jibril, R. S. (2023). Investigating the effect of ESG disclosure on firm performance: The case of Saudi Arabian listed firms. *Cogent Economics & Finance*, *11*(2). https://doi.org/10.1080/23322039.2023.2287923

Friede, G., Busch, T., & Bassen, A. (2015). ESG and financial performance: Aggregated evidence from more than 2000 empirical studies. *Journal of Sustainable Finance & Investment*, *5*(4), 210–233. https://doi.org/10.1080/20430795.2015.1118917

Garcia, A. S., Mendes-Da-Silva, W., & Orsato, R. J. (2017). Sensitive industries produce better ESG performance: Evidence from emerging markets. *Journal of Cleaner Production*. https://doi.org/10.1016/j.jclepro.2017.02.180

Hafsi, T., & Turgut, G. (2013). Boardroom diversity and its effect on social performance: Conceptualization and empirical evidence. *Journal of Business Ethics*. https://doi.org/10.1007/s10551-012-1272-z

Henisz, W., Koller, T., & Nuttall, R. (2019). Five ways that ESG creates value. *McKinsey Quarterly*, *4*, 1–12.

Jaiwani, M., & Gopalkrishnan, S. (2023). Do private and public sector banks respond to ESG in the same way? Some evidences from India. *Benchmarking: An International Journal*. https://doi.org/10.1108/bij-05-2023-0340

Jung, H. (2024). The moderating effect of board characteristics in the relationship between ESG and corporate financial performance. *Studies in Business and Economics*, *19*(2), 110–119. https://doi.org/10.2478/sbe-2024-0028

Jung, Y. L., & Yoo, H. S. (2023). Environmental, social, and governance activities and firm performance: Global evidence and the moderating effect of market competition. *Corporate Social Responsibility and Environmental Management*, *30*(6), 2830–2839. https://doi.org/10.1002/csr.2518

Juras, P. E., & Hinson, Y. L. (2008). Examining the effect of board characteristics on agency costs and selected performance measures in banks. *Academy of Banking Studies Journal*, *7*, 87.

Kalia, D., & Aggarwal, D. (2022). Undefined. *Journal of Global Responsibility*, *14*(1), 155–176. https://doi.org/10.1108/jgr-05-2022-0045

Khanchel, I., Lassoued, N., & Baccar, I. (2023). Sustainability and firm performance: The role of environmental, social and governance disclosure and green innovation. *Management Decision*, *61*(9), 2720–2739. https://doi.org/10.1108/md-09-2021-1252

Kim, S., & Li, Z. (2021). Understanding the impact of ESG practices in corporate finance. *Sustainability*, *13*(7), 3746. https://doi.org/10.3390/su13073746

Lee, S., & Isa, M. (2022). Environmental, social and governance (ESG) practices and financial performance of shariah-compliant companies in Malaysia. *Journal of Islamic Accounting and Business Research*, *14*(2), 295–314. https://doi.org/10.1108/jiabr-06-2020-0183

Maji, S. G., & Lohia, P. (2022). Environmental, social and governance (ESG) performance and firm performance in India. *Society and Business Review*, *18*(1), 175–194. https://doi.org/10.1108/sbr-06-2022-0162

Maji, S. G., & Lohia, P. (2024). Unveiling the financial effect of ESG disclosure on financial performance in India: Climate-sensitive corporates' perspective. *International Journal of Ethics and Systems*. https://doi.org/10.1108/ijoes-02-2024-0039

Makridou, G., Doumpos, M., & Lemonakis, C. (2023). Relationship between ESG and corporate financial performance in the energy sector: Empirical evidence from European companies. *International Journal of Energy Sector Management*, *18*(4), 873–895. https://doi.org/10.1108/ijesm-01-2023-0012

Martiny, A., Taglialatela, J., Testa, F., & Iraldo, F. (2024). Determinants of environmental social and governance (ESG) performance: A systematic literature review. *Journal of Cleaner Production*. https://doi.org/10.1016/j.jclepro.2024.142213

Melinda, A., & Wardhani, R. (2020). The effect of environmental, social, governance, and controversies on firms' value: Evidence from Asia. *International Symposia in Economic Theory and Econometrics*, 147–173. https://doi.org/10.1108/s1571-038620200000027011

Minutolo, M. C., Kristjanpoller, W. D., & Stakeley, J. (2019). Exploring environmental, social, and governance disclosure effects on the S&P 500 financial performance. *Business Strategy and the Environment*, *28*(6), 1083–1095. https://doi.org/10.1002/bse.2303

Morri, G., Yang, F., & Colantoni, F. (2024). Green investments, green returns: Exploring the link between ESG factors and financial performance in real estate. *Journal of Property Investment & Finance*, *42*(5), 435–452. https://doi.org/10.1108/jpif-09-2023-0084

Mukherjee, A., & Nuñez, R. (2019). Doing well by doing good: Can voluntary CSR reporting enhance financial performance? *Journal of Indian Business Research*, *11*(2), 100–119. https://doi.org/10.1108/jibr-07-2018-0199

Naeem, N., Cankaya, S., & Bildik, R. (2022). Does ESG performance affect the financial performance of environmentally sensitive industries? A comparison between emerging and developed markets. *Borsa Istanbul Review*, *22*, S128–S140. https://doi.org/10.1016/j.bir.2022.11.014

Pinheiro, A. B., Panza, G. B., Berhorst, N. L., Toaldo, A. M., & Segatto, A. P. (2023). Exploring the relationship among ESG, innovation, and economic and financial performance: Evidence from the energy sector. *International Journal of Energy Sector Management*, *18*(3), 500–516. https://doi.org/10.1108/ijesm-02-2023-0008

Qureshi, M. A., Akbar, M., Akbar, A., & Poulova, P. (2021). Do ESG endeavors assist firms in achieving superior financial performance? A case of 100 best corporate citizens. *Sage Open*, *11*(2). https://doi.org/10.1177/21582440211021598

Rossi, M., Chouaibi, J., Chouaibi, S., Jilani, W., & Chouaibi, Y. (2021). Does a board characteristic moderate the relationship between CSR practices and financial performance? Evidence from European ESG firms. *Journal of Risk and Financial Management*, *14*. https://doi.org/10.3390/jrfm14080354

Ruan, L., & Liu, H. (2021). Environmental, social, governance activities and firm performance: Evidence from China. *Sustainability*, *13*(2), 767. https://doi.org/10.3390/su13020767

Sandberg, H., Alnoor, A., & Tiberius, V. (2022). Environmental, social, and governance ratings and financial performance: Evidence from the European food industry. *Business Strategy and the Environment*, *32*(4), 2471–2489. https://doi.org/10.1002/bse.3259

Shaikh, I. (2022). Environmental, social, and governance (Esg) practice and firm performance: An international evidence. *Journal of Business Economics and Management*, *23*(1), 218–237. https://doi.org/10.3846/jbem.2022.16202

Tao, J. (2023). Study on the impact of ESG performance on firm performance. *SHS Web of Conferences*, *165*, 01016. https://doi.org/10.1051/shsconf/202316501016

Velte, P. (2017). Does ESG performance have an impact on financial performance? Evidence from Germany. *Journal of Global Responsibility*, *8*(2), 169–178. https://doi.org/10.1108/jgr-11-2016-0029

Xiao, H., & Yuan, J. (2007). Ownership structure, board composition and corporate voluntary disclosure. *Managerial Auditing Journal*, *22*, 604–619.

Xie, J., Nozawa, W., Yagi, M., Fujii, H., & Managi, S. (2018). Do environmental, social, and governance activities improve corporate financial performance?. *Business Strategy and the Environment*, *28*(2), 286–300. https://doi.org/10.1002/bse.2224

Yoon, B., Lee, J. H., & Cho, J. H. (2024). Corporate social responsibility and financial performance: New evidence from the Korean market. *Sage Open*, *14*(2). https://doi.org/10.1177/21582440241255196

Chapter 12

Innovation for Sustainability? Linking R&D to ESG Performance Through Disclosure Analysis

Asma Mechta[a], *Zsuzsanna Szeles*[a] *and Agnes Siklosi*[b]

[a]University of Sopron, Hungary
[b]Budapest University of Economics and Business, Hungary

Abstract

This study investigates how research and development (R&D) investment influences firms' environmental, social and governance (ESG) performance. While prior literature provides mixed evidence, little is known about this relationship when combining academic insights with disclosure-based analysis. The authors address this gap through a systematic review of peer-reviewed studies and a qualitative content analysis of Tesco's annual reports from 2022 to 2024. Using a keyword-driven approach, R&D-related disclosures were coded into ESG categories, and textual similarity measures were applied to detect year-on-year repetition and potential 'cheap talk'. The findings show that R&D contributes positively to environmental performance through low-carbon technologies and process innovations, while social outcomes remain limited and largely framed through workforce and customer engagement. Governance disclosures emphasise oversight but display high textual similarity across years, suggesting templated reporting. Overall, the study highlights the dual role of R&D as both a driver of sustainable innovation and a source of disclosure complexity. By linking the R&D–ESG literature with empirical evidence from corporate reporting, the paper provides theoretical and managerial insights into how innovation strategies can be aligned with sustainability objectives while avoiding symbolic communication.

Keywords: Research and development (R&D); environmental, social and governance (ESG); corporate sustainability; disclosure analysis; cheap talk

Sustainability in Accounting and Finance Education, 205–223

doi:10.1108/978-1-80686-393-820261012

1. Introduction

Innovation has long been recognised as a central driver of corporate growth and competitiveness (Kogan et al., 2017; Romer, 1994). More recently, environmental, social and governance (ESG) considerations have emerged as critical determinants of long-term corporate value, reflecting both financial and non-financial risks (Gillan et al., 2021; Pollman, 2019) Management increasingly views both ESG practices and research and development (R&D) investment as intangible assets capable of generating sustained competitive advantage (McGrath et al., 1996; Wernerfelt, 1984). However, managers face difficult trade-offs in allocating resources between ESG and innovation, as both require significant long-term commitments and often compete for limited capital (Yu et al., 2024).

R&D is widely regarded as a core intangible investment that enables firms to generate new knowledge, technologies and business models (Corrado et al., 2005; Lev & Sougiannis, 1996). Unlike routine expenditures, R&D creates long-term innovation capacity, supporting both financial performance and non-financial outcomes such as environmental and social improvements. Recent studies emphasise that R&D not only drives competitiveness but also underpins corporate transitions towards sustainability by fostering eco-innovation, cleaner production methods and socially beneficial technologies (Alam et al., 2019; Fu et al., 2020). As such, R&D can be viewed as a strategic enabler of ESG performance: environmentally, by reducing emissions and resource use; socially, by generating safer products and services; and from a governance perspective, by requiring forward-looking oversight and transparent disclosure. This study therefore investigates the role of R&D as a bridge between corporate innovation and ESG outcomes, focusing on how such investments are represented in the literature and in corporate reporting.

Prior research demonstrates that R&D can enhance ESG outcomes by driving technological innovation, reducing environmental footprints and fostering social and organisational improvements (Fu et al., 2020; Padgett & Galan, 2010). Yet evidence is mixed: while some studies highlight positive synergies, others identify resource trade-offs, diminishing returns and uneven effects across industries (Erhemjamts et al., 2013; Xu et al., 2020). At the same time, governance-related outcomes of R&D remain less understood, with studies suggesting both enhanced transparency and increased managerial complexity (Honoré et al., 2015; Zhong, 2018). Thus, the relationship between R&D and ESG performance remains contested and underexplored.

A further challenge lies in the disparity between ESG disclosure and actual ESG performance, often labelled as 'decoupling' or 'greenwashing' (Cho et al., 2015; Kim & Lyon, 2015). While companies increasingly disclose sustainability-related activities, disclosure may not fully capture the substance of corporate practices. Content analysis of corporate reporting has therefore become an important methodological tool for investigating how firms portray ESG-related activities and how these align with underlying strategies (Beattie & Thomson, 2007).

Against this backdrop, this study seeks to advance the literature in two ways. First, conceptually, it reviews and synthesises prior studies on the interplay between R&D investment and ESG performance, addressing the dual potential of R&D to generate sustainability synergies while also producing unintended costs. Second, methodologically, it employs a content analysis of Tesco Public Limited Company (PLC) annual report to provide an illustrative example of how R&D-related activities are represented within ESG disclosure. By combining insights from both literature and disclosure analysis, this study contributes to sustainability accounting scholarship by clarifying the nuanced role of R&D in shaping ESG outcomes and offering practical insights for aligning innovation strategies with sustainability objectives.

The remainder of this paper is structured as follows. Section 2 reviews the relevant literature on R&D and ESG performance. Section 3 outlines the methodological approach. Section 4 presents the findings from the content analysis of Tesco's annual reports and the literature synthesis. Section 5 discusses the implications and concludes with limitations and suggestions for future research.

2. Systematic Literature Review

The connection between R&D and ESG outcomes has been explained through several theoretical perspectives. The resource-based view (RBV) highlights R&D as an intangible resource providing sustainable advantage when effectively leveraged (Wernerfelt, 1984). Extending this, the natural resource-based view (NRBV) argues that environmentally oriented innovation can create enduring advantages by addressing ecological constraints (Hart, 1995). The Porter Hypothesis suggests that external pressures, such as environmental regulations, can stimulate innovation that offsets compliance costs (Porter & van der Linde, 1995). Finally, stakeholder theory (Freeman, 2010) emphasises the role of R&D in addressing societal and governance expectations. Together, these frameworks suggest that R&D has the potential to enhance ESG performance, but that outcomes depend on the strategic alignment of investments and governance mechanisms.

2.1 R&D and Environmental Outcomes

Environmental sustainability has emerged as the most widely studied dimension of ESG, reflecting growing policy and investor pressure to reduce firms' ecological footprints (Porter & van der Linde, 1995). Prior research consistently links R&D intensity with eco-innovation, environmental efficiency and green technological transformation. For example, Alam et al. (2019) find that R&D investment reduces firms' carbon intensity by improving energy efficiency, Kong et al. (2024) show that green-oriented R&D fosters innovation in Chinese firms. Similarly, Lee and Min (2015) demonstrate that green R&D initiatives reduce emissions and enhance firm performance. More recent studies extend this evidence: Zhang et al. (2025) highlight that technological collaboration, when coupled with high R&D intensity, significantly improves green innovation efficiency. In addition, Liao (2025) reveals that fintech adoption supports environmental innovation, with R&D serving as a critical mediator. Finally, Yousaf et al. (2025) show that CEOs with R&D experience are more likely to direct resources towards green innovation, underscoring the importance of managerial background.

However, the environmental benefits of R&D are not guaranteed. Some innovations are resource-intensive, producing rebound effects that undermine environmental gains (Lee & Min, 2015). Moreover, firms may pursue environmental R&D symbolically to satisfy external legitimacy pressures, while the actual sustainability benefits remain limited (Cho et al., 2015). Despite these limitations, the literature broadly supports the argument of the natural RBV (Hart, 1995): when strategically aligned with sustainability goals, R&D investment plays a pivotal role in advancing firms' environmental ESG performance.

2.2 R&D and Social Outcomes

ESG performance of firms has become increasingly important for both policymakers and investors (Nekhili et al., 2019; Velte, 2017). Although ESG reflects the modern dimensions of corporate social responsibility (CSR) (Miralles-Quirós et al., 2019), the two concepts are not identical. CSR refers broadly to 'policies and practices of corporations that reflect business responsibility for some of the wider societal good' (Matten & Moon, 2008), while ESG focuses more narrowly on measurable outcomes in three domains: ESG issues. Prior studies show that CSR commitments can reduce business risk and the cost of capital (Bassen et al., 2006; Orlitzky & Benjamin, 2001), suggesting that firms' social and ethical behaviour has tangible financial implications. Within this context, R&D investment has been increasingly linked to social outcomes and CSR performance. Padgett and Galan (2010) demonstrate that firms with higher R&D intensity are more engaged in CSR activities, Fu et al. (2020) find that R&D-intensive firms often specialise in CSR domains that align with their innovation strategies. More recent evidence confirms these complementarities. For instance, a study in India shows that mandatory CSR regulation increases corporate R&D investments, reflecting synergies between regulatory-driven social responsibility and innovation (Jadiyappa & Chauhan, 2023). Similarly, CSR communication has been shown to amplify the strategic impact of R&D, with advertising of CSR initiatives strengthening the market value of innovation (Bae et al., 2023).

Nevertheless, the relationship is not without tensions. Hull and Rothenberg (2008) argue that CSR contributes more to firm performance in less innovative firms, pointing to potential substitution effects between social responsibility and innovation. Furthermore, R&D-driven technological change, particularly automation, has raised concerns about inequality and worker displacement. As highlighted in recent studies of R&D, ESG and green innovation performance in

China, innovation may deliver environmental and social benefits, but these are contingent on governance structures and corporate strategies (Xu et al., 2020). Taken together, the literature suggests that while R&D has the potential to foster positive social outcomes, it also introduces risks that require careful governance and stakeholder engagement.

2.3 R&D and Governance Outcomes

Governance is a critical factor shaping the effectiveness of R&D investments in advancing ESG outcomes. Strong governance mechanisms 'including independent boards, institutional ownership, and ESG committees' create the oversight necessary to sustain long-term innovation strategies (Chen et al., 2024). Recent evidence also points to reciprocal effects: ESG practices can stabilise R&D. Chen (2024), for instance, find that firms with stronger ESG performance are less likely to engage in misconduct, which indirectly supports consistent R&D investment. Sun et al. (2025) further argue that disclosure of R&D activities enhances corporate transparency and fosters improved governance practices.

At the same time, risks persist. R&D does not automatically translate into stronger governance outcomes, as opportunistic managers may exaggerate or misrepresent the ESG contributions of innovation (Kim & Lyon, 2015). Furthermore, governance failures can weaken innovation outcomes, leaving firms vulnerable to both environmental and social risks. These findings align with stakeholder theory (Freeman, 2010), which emphasises that effective governance and accountability mechanisms are essential for ensuring that innovation contributes to long-term corporate sustainability. Overall, the literature suggests that governance outcomes depend less on the volume of R&D spending and more on the institutional structures that direct and monitor those investments.

2.4 ESG Disclosure, Cheap Talk and Content Analysis

An enduring challenge is the divergence between disclosure and performance, often described as decoupling. Firms may overstate positive practices (greenwashing) or understate them (brown-washing) (Kim & Lyon, 2015). Cho et al. (2015) demonstrate that sustainability reporting often serves symbolic rather than substantive purposes, obscuring the real ESG impact of activities. A related concept is cheap talk, where disclosures rely on vague or repetitive language that signals commitment to stakeholders without corresponding evidence of new actions (Bochkay et al., 2023; Li, 2011). In such cases, similarity across successive reports may indicate that disclosures are templated rather than reflecting genuine progress.

Although few recent studies explicitly analyse R&D in this context, related findings are relevant. For example, environmental R&D has been shown to mediate the ESG–firm efficiency link in BRICS firms, suggesting that disclosure itself plays a role in shaping market perceptions (Farooq & Thavorn, 2025). Methodologically, content analysis is central for examining these dynamics.

Beattie and Thomson (2007) advocate its use in systematically studying corporate reports, and contemporary ESG research has applied it to evaluate how firms frame innovation. In line with this, our study applies content analysis to Tesco's 2022–2024 annual reports, combining coding with textual similarity analysis to illustrate how R&D is positioned within ESG disclosure and to assess whether repetition signals substantive innovation or cheap talk.

The systematic review highlights the central but complex role of R&D in shaping ESG performance. On the environmental side, R&D frequently enhances eco-innovation and reduces carbon emissions, yet some studies warn of rebound effects when innovation itself is resource intensive. On the social dimension, R&D supports CSR activities and stakeholder engagement, particularly under regulatory or reputational pressures, though it can also generate unintended consequences such as labour displacement and inequality. Governance research shows that R&D is both influenced by board oversight and investor monitoring, while simultaneously promoting transparency through disclosure. Collectively, these findings underscore that R&D is a double-edged sword: a critical enabler of sustainability, but also a potential source of symbolic communication and new risks when embedded in disclosure strategies.

To integrate these insights, Table 12.1 summarises 18 representative studies across ESG and disclosure dimensions. The evidence confirms that most prior research has concentrated on environmental outcomes, while social and governance dimensions remain comparatively underexplored. In addition, studies of ESG disclosure and decoupling emphasise that the relationship between R&D and ESG is not only material but also perceptual, shaped by how firms frame innovation in communications with stakeholders. The dominance of findings in the environmental domain highlights a gap in understanding the broader ESG implications of R&D.

From this integrated perspective, four guiding propositions emerge. First, R&D investment tends to enhance environmental and social performance when strategically aligned with sustainability objectives, though rebound effects and social trade-offs remain possible. Second, robust governance mechanisms including board oversight and investor monitoring are required to ensure that R&D supports long-term ESG objectives rather than creating new risks. Third, ESG disclosure strategies mediate the relationship between R&D and perceived performance, with higher risks of decoupling when reports rely on repetitive or vague language. Finally, similarity across successive reports may indicate cheap talk, raising questions about whether R&D-related disclosures reflect substantive innovation or symbolic communication. These propositions frame the subsequent analysis, where prior research is combined with content analysis of Tesco's 2022–2024 annual reports to illustrate how R&D is embedded in ESG disclosure and to assess the extent of substantive versus symbolic reporting.

Table 12.1. Selected Literature on R&D and ESG Performance.

Author(s) and Year	ESG Dimension	Method	Key Findings
Alam et al. (2019)	Environmental	Panel regression	R&D investment reduces carbon intensity.
Xu et al. (2020)	Environmental	Firm-level study	Green-oriented R&D fosters eco-innovation.
Lee and Min (2015)	Environmental	Panel regression	Green R&D reduces emissions and improves firm performance.
Liu et al. (2025)	Environmental	Empirical (China)	Collaboration + R&D intensity improve green innovation efficiency.
Liao (2025)	Environmental	Econometric analysis	Fintech adoption boosts green innovation via R&D mediation.
Yousaf et al. (2025)	Environmental	Firm-level	CEOs with R&D experience promote green innovation.
Padgett and Galan (2010)	Social	Regression	R&D intensity linked to CSR engagement.
Fu et al. (2020)	Social	Multi-country study	R&D-intensive firms specialise in CSR domains.
Jadiyappa and Chauhan (2023)	Social	Policy analysis (India)	Mandatory CSR regulation increases corporate R&D.
Bae et al. (2023)	Social	Theoretical model	CSR communication strengthens R&D's market impact.
Hull and Rothenberg (2008)	Social	Panel data	CSR is most valuable in less innovative firms.
Chen et al. (2024)	Governance	Governance study	Independent boards stabilise long-term R&D.
Chen (2024)	Governance	Econometric	ESG performance reduces misconduct, stabilises R&D.
Sun et al. (2025)	Governance	Empirical	R&D disclosure improves transparency and oversight.

(Continued)

Table 12.1. *(Continued)*

Author(s) and Year	ESG Dimension	Method	Key Findings
Cho et al. (2015)	Disclosure	Case study	ESG reporting is often symbolic (organisational façade).
Kim and Lyon (2015)	Disclosure	Empirical	Greenwashing vs. brown-washing in sustainability disclosure.
Beattie and Thomson (2007)	Disclosure	Content analysis	Framework for studying corporate disclosure.
Farooq and Thavorn (2025)	Disclosure	Panel data (BRICS)	Environmental R&D mediates ESG–efficiency link.

Source: Authors' own work.

3. Methodological Approach

This study adopts a mixed-method design that combines a systematic literature review with a case-based content analysis. The approach is motivated by the contradictory evidence in prior research: while some studies argue that R&D investment strengthens ESG outcomes through green innovation and social responsibility (Fu et al., 2020; Xu et al., 2020), others highlight trade-offs, including resource-intensive technologies, social risks of automation and the possibility of symbolic rather than substantive disclosure (Cho et al., 2015; Hull & Rothenberg, 2008). To address these tensions, the study synthesises academic findings and examines how they are reflected in corporate reporting.

3.1 Systematic Literature Review Method

To investigate the relationship between R&D and ESG performance, a systematic literature review was conducted following established guidelines for evidence synthesis in management research (Page et al., 2021; Tranfield et al., 2003). The search was performed in Scopus, using keywords that directly relate to the research focus and the main debates in the literature 'R&D' or 'research and development' combined with 'ESG', 'sustainability performance', or 'CSR'. Filters were applied to include only peer-reviewed journal articles and reviews, published in English at the final stage of publication. Editorials, purely technical studies without a corporate ESG dimension, and non-English texts were excluded. The initial search produced 43 records, which were screened by title, abstract and full text against inclusion criteria. After quality assessment, 34 studies were retained for analysis. Foundational works on corporate responsibility and disclosure were added to ensure theoretical completeness. The selected articles were then grouped into four categories: environmental, social, governance and disclosure/decoupling, which informed the organisation of the literature review. This structure allows the review to capture both empirical findings and theoretical contributions relevant to the R&D–ESG nexus.

3.2 Content Analysis Approach

The empirical analysis draws on qualitative content analysis of Tesco's 2022–2024 annual reports. A keyword-driven search was applied to identify passages that referred to 'R&D', 'research and development', 'innovation', 'technology' or 'digital' investment. These excerpts were then coded into ESG categories, depending on the context in which R&D was presented. To ensure reliability, the coding framework was informed by prior studies that have used content analysis to examine corporate disclosure (Beattie & Thomson, 2007; Cho et al., 2015).

In addition to thematic coding, the study also tested for repetition in disclosure, a phenomenon often described as cheap talk (Kim & Lyon, 2015). For this purpose, all R&D-related passages were extracted from Tesco's annual reports for 2022–2024 and compared across years. Instead of relying solely on automated text mining, a manual similarity test was conducted. Passages were grouped by year, and identical or near-identical sentences and phrases were identified through direct comparison. The proportion of overlapping text between years was then calculated, providing a measure of disclosure repetition. This manual coding approach follows established practices in textual analysis (Li, 2011) and aligns with recent work on boilerplate detection in financial reporting (Bochkay et al., 2023), offering a robust framework for applying cheap talk analysis to ESG and R&D disclosures.

4. Empirical Analysis: Tesco's ESG Disclosure and R&D Framing

4.1 Rationale for Case Selection

Tesco PLC provides a compelling case for examining the intersection of R&D investment and ESG disclosure. As the United Kingdom's largest retailer and one of Europe's most influential multinational corporations, Tesco has long been at the forefront of sustainability initiatives in the retail sector. Its market position, extensive supply chain and stakeholder visibility make it a reference point for how large corporations integrate innovation into sustainability strategies. Prior research suggests that retail firms face distinctive ESG challenges, including carbon-intensive logistics, food waste management and labour-intensive operations (e.g., Nekhili et al., 2019; Velte, 2017). In this context, innovation and

R&D are expected to play a critical role in addressing environmental and social risks while reinforcing governance mechanisms.

A further justification for focusing on Tesco is the consistency and transparency of its annual reporting. Over the past decade, Tesco has significantly expanded the scope of its sustainability disclosures, aligning with frameworks such as the Global Reporting Initiative (GRI) and Task Force on Climate-related Financial Disclosures (TCFD). The analysis focuses on the company's annual reports from 2022 to 2024, enabling a longitudinal perspective on how R&D and innovation are framed within ESG narratives. This design allows us not only to assess the extent to which R&D contributes to sustainability objectives but also to explore whether recurring patterns in disclosure signal substantive progress or potential 'cheap talk' (Kim & Lyon, 2015).

4.2 Findings by ESG Dimension

Tesco's annual reports from 2022 to 2024 reveal that R&D and innovation are consistently tied to ESG performance, though the emphasis varies across the three dimensions. Environmental and governance disclosures are the most explicit, while social outcomes are present but often framed more indirectly. Table 12.2 provides a shortlist of the strongest Tesco quotes classified by ESG dimension.

4.2.1 Environmental

Innovation is most prominently linked to environmental commitments. In 2022, Tesco described efforts to 'reduce our carbon footprint e.g., technology for energy efficiency' (Tesco, 2022, p. 36). The 2023 report presented R&D as part of trial-based experimentation, noting that the company was 'trialling agricultural innovations such as low-carbon fertilisers' (Tesco, 2023, p. 13) and implementing initiatives related to 'packaging and food waste; innovation initiatives…' (Tesco, 2023, p. 72). By 2024, the disclosures suggest greater integration of sustainability into operations: 'support the reduction of our carbon footprint… non-green technology to have been phased out' (Tesco, 2024, pp. 35, 44). These statements illustrate a trajectory from pilot projects to embedding low-carbon innovation into the core of the business.

4.2.2 Social

R&D's social role is less explicit but emerges through human capital and consumer-oriented innovations. In 2022, Tesco stressed investment in its workforce, highlighting the use of 'technology to upskill colleagues, giving them new capabilities' (Tesco, 2022, p. 20). By 2023, the emphasis shifted towards customers, with the report citing 'customer insight and product innovation outcomes' that supported affordability and healthy choices (Tesco, 2023, p. 66). In 2024, social outcomes were framed through partnerships and community

Table 12.2. Shortlist of the Strongest Tesco Quotes.

Year	Page	Text	ESG
2022	36	reduction of our carbon footprint e.g. technology investments	Environmental
2022	74	in relation to technology-related risks and sustainability reporting,	Environmental
2022	115	Further details are set out in the Retail technology environment,	Environmental
2022	34	ethics and compliance, safety, responsible sourcing, technology	Governance
2022	71	programmes across Risk & Audit, People and Technology. This	Governance
2022	101	relating to corporate tax compliance, technology consulting, internal	Governance
2022	20	have supported our colleagues in UK stores to develop their digital	Social
2022	20	to support our colleagues to build their digital confidence. Since	Social
2022	20	technology to upskill colleagues, giving them more flexibility in	Social
2023	13	trialling agricultural innovations such as low-carbon fertilisers,	Environmental
2023	72	to packaging and food waste; innovation initiatives; and the roll	Environmental
2023	119	Further details are set out in the Retail technology environment,	Environmental
2023	41	compliance, safety, responsible sourcing, technology compliance,	Governance
2023	49	impact on the Group of three key risk areas, covering consumer sentiment, technology write	Governance
2023	73	the Chief Audit and Risk Officer, the Chief Technology Officer	Governance
2023	11	out individualised digital coupons to four million customers in	Social
2023	66	Customer insight and product innovation	Social
2024	35	support the reduction of our carbon footprint e.g. technology investments	Environmental

(Continued)

Table 12.2. *(Continued)*

Year	Page	Text	ESG
2024	44	non-green technology to have been phased out, whereas in our 3°C scenario green technology uptake will continue to grow, but carbon-	Environmental
2024	124	The Group's retail technology environment is complex and a significant element of its financial processes and business operations are	Environmental
2024	39	of supply risks. This also includes developing a technology solution for	Governance
2024	87	technology tools. In the year, members of the Board and Executive	Governance
2024	91	and Risk Officer, the Chief Technology Officer and representatives of	Governance
2024	67	Customers: the exclusive partnership will, for the initial 10-year period, combine Tesco's market-leading brand, physical and digital reach and	Social
2024	68	The Board regularly receives updates on customer behaviours. Innovation in	Social
2024	73	and Tesco colleagues; and trial innovations that can help reduce on-farm	Social

Source: Authors' own work.

innovation, for instance: 'Customers – the exclusive partnership will… trial innovations that benefit Tesco colleagues' (Tesco, 2024, pp. 67, 73). These passages suggest that R&D is positioned less as direct 'social R&D' and more as an enabler of workforce development, affordability and community engagement.

4.2.3 Governance

Governance disclosures consistently highlight oversight of innovation and technology risks. In 2022, Tesco described 'programmes across Risk & Audit, People and Technology' (Tesco, 2022, p. 71) and noted board engagement with corporate tax and technology compliance (Tesco, 2022, p. 101). In 2023, risk framing became sharper, with attention to 'the impact on the Group of three key risk areas, compliance, safety, responsible sourcing, technology' (Tesco, 2023, p. 49), alongside the role of 'the Chief Audit and Risk Officer, the Chief Technology Officer…' in governance (Tesco, 2023, p. 73). By 2024, disclosures emphasised formal board oversight: 'The Board regularly receives updates on customer and technology innovation' (Tesco, 2024, p. 68) and detailed reporting to the Audit and Risk Committee (Tesco, 2024, p. 91). These examples demonstrate that Tesco's governance framing positions R&D as a strategic issue requiring continuous monitoring.

Together, these findings indicate that environmental and governance dimensions are most frequently tied to R&D, while social outcomes are referenced more indirectly. This pattern mirrors broader research suggesting that firms tend to foreground environmental and governance innovation in disclosure, while social issues are often integrated more symbolically or operationally (Fu et al., 2020; Padgett & Galan, 2010).

4.3 Comparative Trends

A comparative view of Tesco's 2022–2024 reports highlights both continuity and gradual change in how R&D is linked to ESG. The environmental dimension shows the clearest trajectory. In 2022, the focus was on operational improvements such as 'reduce our carbon footprint e.g. technology for energy efficiency' (Tesco, 2022, p. 36). By 2023, this developed into targeted experimentation, with the company 'trialling agricultural innovations such as low-carbon fertilisers' (Tesco, 2023, p. 13). In 2024, the narrative shifted towards integration, asserting that 'non-green technology [is] to have been phased out' (Tesco, 2024, p. 44). The sequence suggests a progression from incremental measures, through pilot trials, to more embedded sustainability practices.

Social disclosures show much less dynamism. Across all three reports, the themes of workforce development, affordability and community engagement are repeated, often in similar terms. The 2022 emphasis on 'technology to upskill colleagues' (Tesco, 2022, p. 20) was followed by 2023s framing of 'customer insight and product innovation outcomes' (Tesco, 2023, p. 66), and in 2024, the narrative again stressed partnerships and community impact. While the emphasis shifted slightly across stakeholder groups, the underlying language remained broadly stable, suggesting that social innovation is more often framed as ongoing operational practice than as a site of novel R&D investment.

Governance disclosures are the most formulaic. Each year, innovation is presented through board oversight, audit committees and risk management processes. In 2022, governance referred to 'programmes across Risk & Audit, People and Technology' (Tesco, 2022, p. 71). In 2023, this was reframed around 'the impact on the Group of three key risk areas, compliance, safety, responsible sourcing, technology' (Tesco, 2023, p. 49). By 2024, the Audit & Risk Committee was again cited as receiving 'detailed reports on sustainability innovation' (Tesco, 2024, p. 91). The repetition across years points to a reporting template more than to substantive change.

The textual similarity analysis reinforces this impression. Using bigram and trigram comparisons, R&D-related disclosures were evaluated across Tesco's 2022–2024 reports. Similarity scores were high between adjacent years (2022–2023 = 0.82; 2023–2024 = 0.83), indicating substantial reuse of phrasing.

Over the full interval (2022–2024), the similarity remained high (0.80), confirming that much of the disclosure language is repeated year-on-year. This reliance on near-identical wording highlights the risk of boilerplate reporting, a practice frequently associated with *cheap talk* in sustainability communication (Bochkay et al., 2023; Kim & Lyon, 2015; Li, 2011). At the same time, qualitative coding shows that while environmental disclosures exhibit incremental development particularly around low-carbon and digital initiatives – the social and governance dimensions remain comparatively static and templated. This mixed pattern echoes wider debates in the ESG literature about how to distinguish genuine innovation from symbolic disclosure (Cho et al., 2015).

5. Discussion and Conclusion

The findings from Tesco's annual reports highlight the dual role of R&D as both an enabler of sustainability outcomes and a potential source of symbolic communication. This section situates these results within the wider literature, drawing out theoretical contributions and practical implications.

5.1 Discussion, Theoretical Contributions

First, the analysis supports prior research that links R&D to environmental innovation, showing how corporate disclosures frame such investment as a pathway to reducing carbon emissions and improving resource efficiency (Fu et al., 2020; Xu et al., 2020). Tesco's trajectory from energy-efficiency measures in 2022 to low-carbon fertiliser trials in 2023 and non-green technology phase-outs in 2024 illustrate this process. Yet the textual similarity across reports suggests that these innovations are narrated in formulaic ways, echoing Cho et al.'s (2015) critique that ESG disclosures often function symbolically. The contribution here is to demonstrate that R&D often assumed to be substantively innovative can also be subject to disclosure routinisation, blurring the line between genuine innovation and cheap talk.

Second, the social dimension reveals a less dynamic relationship between R&D and ESG. Consistent with Padgett and Galan (2010), Tesco's disclosures show that R&D-intensive firms engage with CSR issues but often through alignment with core business activities rather than through dedicated social innovation. The limited evolution in Tesco's social reporting across three years illustrates the difficulty of achieving synergies between technological innovation and social outcomes. This finding contributes to the literature by highlighting the unevenness of R&D's impact across ESG dimensions.

Finally, the governance dimension underscores the role of institutional oversight. Tesco consistently frames innovation within the remit of its board, audit and risk committees, reflecting Bozec and Di Vito's (2019) argument that governance mechanisms can channel R&D towards long-term objectives. However, the repetitive language across years suggests that governance may also reinforce disclosure templates, thereby institutionalising symbolic communication. This insight extends prior work by showing that governance does not simply stabilise R&D investment (Liu et al., 2024) but may also stabilise the way R&D is reported, for better or worse.

5.2 Conclusion

This study examined the relationship between R&D investment and ESG performance by combining a systematic literature review with a content analysis of Tesco's 2022–2024 annual reports. The review revealed both synergies and tensions in the R&D–ESG nexus, with evidence that R&D can enable green innovation and social responsibility but may also generate trade-offs, costs or symbolic reporting. The case analysis of Tesco illustrated these dynamics in practice. Environmental disclosures suggested a gradual progression from efficiency measures to low-carbon trials and phase-outs, while social disclosures remained relatively static and governance disclosures were highly repetitive. The textual similarity analysis confirmed a reliance on templated language, raising the possibility that some of Tesco's reporting functions as 'cheap talk'. The paper contributes to the literature by showing that even when firms invest in R&D, the ESG outcomes reported may not always reflect substantive innovation. It also highlights that the impact of R&D is uneven across ESG dimensions and that disclosure practices may obscure as much as they reveal. For managers, the findings underline the need to align R&D portfolios more closely with sustainability goals and to complement disclosure with measurable outcomes. For policymakers, the results suggest that ESG disclosure regulation should consider both content and year-on-year differentiation to discourage boilerplate reporting.

At the same time, the study is not without limitations. Focusing on a single case necessarily restricts generalisability, and reliance on annual reports means the analysis captures only what firms choose to disclose. While the similarity test highlights patterns of repetition, it cannot establish whether reported initiatives reflect substantive innovation or symbolic narrative. Moreover, the literature review was limited to peer-reviewed English-language sources, excluding potentially relevant perspectives from grey literature and non-English scholarship. These constraints should be borne in mind when interpreting the findings. Future research could extend this work by examining cross-sectoral cases, triangulating disclosures with performance indicators such as patents or emissions data and applying more advanced text mining techniques to capture the subtleties of ESG communication. In doing so, scholars can continue to refine understanding of how R&D shapes, and is shaped by, the evolving landscape of corporate sustainability.

Acknowledgements

We gratefully acknowledge Professor Khaled Hussainey for his invaluable guidance, constructive feedback and continuous support throughout this chapter.

References

Alam, Md. S., Atif, M., Chien-Chi, C., & Soytaş, U. (2019). Does corporate R&D investment affect firm environmental performance? Evidence from G-6 countries. *Energy Economics*, *78*, 401–411. https://doi.org/10.1016/j.eneco.2018.11.031

Bae, J., Oh, H., & Kim, S. (2023). Advertising role of CSR and strategic investment in R&D: Evidence from the biohealth industry. *Journal of Current Issues and Research in Advertising*, *44*(1), 105–121. https://doi.org/10.1080/10641734.2022.2131655

Bassen, A., Meyer, K., & Schlange, J. (2006). *The influence of corporate responsibility on the cost of capital* (SSRN Scholarly Paper 984406). Social Science Research Network. https://doi.org/10.2139/ssrn.984406

Beattie, V., & Thomson, S. J. (2007). Lifting the lid on the use of content analysis to investigate intellectual capital disclosures. *Accounting Forum*, *31*(2), 129–163. https://doi.org/10.1016/j.accfor.2007.02.001

Bochkay, K., Brown, S. V., Leone, A. J., & Tucker, J. W. (2023). Textual analysis in accounting: What's next? *Contemporary Accounting Research*, *40*(2), 765–805. https://doi.org/10.1111/1911-3846.12825

Bozec, Y., & Di Vito, J. (2019). Founder-controlled firms and R&D investments: New evidence from Canada. *Family Business Review*, *32*(1), 76–96. https://doi.org/10.1177/0894486518793237

Chen, M. (2024). ESG performance and firm misconduct: Evidence from R&D manipulation. *Economics Letters*, *237*, 111668. https://doi.org/10.1016/j.econlet.2024.111668

Chen, W., Xie, Y., & He, K. (2024). Environmental, social, and governance performance and corporate innovation novelty. *International Journal of Innovation Studies*, *8*(2), 109–131. https://doi.org/10.1016/j.ijis.2024.01.003

Cho, C. H., Laine, M., Roberts, R. W., & Rodrigue, M. (2015). Organized hypocrisy, organizational façades, and sustainability reporting. *Accounting, Organizations and Society*, *40*, 78–94. https://doi.org/10.1016/j.aos.2014.12.003

Corrado, C., Hulten, C., & Sichel, D. (2005). Measuring capital and technology: An expanded framework. In C. Corrado, J. Haltiwanger, & D. Sichel (Eds.), *Measuring capital in the new economy* (pp. 11–46). University of Chicago Press. https://doi.org/10.7208/chicago/9780226116174.003.0002

Erhemjamts, O., Li, Q., & Venkateswaran, A. (2013). Corporate social responsibility and its impact on firms' investment policy, organizational structure, and performance. *Journal of Business Ethics*, *118*(2), 395–412. https://doi.org/10.1007/s10551-012-1594-x

Farooq, U., & Thavorn, J. (2025). Exploring the impact of environmental, social, and governance (ESG) performance on firm efficiency: The mediating role of environmental R&D investment in BRICS economies. *Corporate Social Responsibility and Environmental Management*, *32*(3), 3978–3996. https://doi.org/10.1002/csr.3165

Freeman, R. E. (2010). *Strategic management: A stakeholder approach*. Cambridge University Press.

Fu, L., Boehe, D., & Orlitzky, M. (2020). Are R&D-intensive firms also corporate social responsibility specialists? A multicountry study. *Research Policy*, *49*(8), 104082. https://doi.org/10.1016/j.respol.2020.104082

Gillan, S. L., Koch, A., & Starks, L. T. (2021). Firms and social responsibility: A review of ESG and CSR research in corporate finance. *Journal of Corporate Finance*, *66*, 101889. https://doi.org/10.1016/j.jcorpfin.2021.101889

Hart, S. L. (1995). A natural-resource-based view of the firm. *Academy of Management Review*, *20*(4), 986–1014. https://doi.org/10.2307/258963

Honoré, F., Munari, F., & van Pottelsberghe de La Potterie, B. (2015). Corporate governance practices and companies' R&D intensity: Evidence from European countries. *Research Policy*, *44*(2), 533–543. https://doi.org/10.1016/j.respol.2014.10.016

Hull, C. E., & Rothenberg, S. (2008). Firm performance: The interactions of corporate social performance with innovation and industry differentiation. *Strategic Management Journal*, *29*(7), 781–789. https://doi.org/10.1002/smj.675

Jadiyappa, N., & Chauhan, Y. (2023). Mandatory CSR regulation and R&D investments: Evidence from a quasi-natural experiment. *Finance Research Letters*, *55*, 103822. https://doi.org/10.1016/j.frl.2023.103822

Kim, E.-H., & Lyon, T. P. (2015). Greenwash vs. Brownwash: Exaggeration and undue modesty in corporate sustainability disclosure. *Organization Science*, *26*(3), 705–723. https://doi.org/10.1287/orsc.2014.0949

Kogan, L., Papanikolaou, D., Seru, A., & Stoffman, N. (2017). Technological innovation, resource allocation, and growth. *Quarterly Journal of Economics*, *132*(2), 665–712. https://doi.org/10.1093/qje/qjw040

Kong, D., Xiang, G., & Zhu, L. (2024). Innovation-driven development and corporate green innovation. *Finance Research Letters*, *68*, 106008. https://doi.org/10.1016/j.frl.2024.106008

Lee, K.-H., & Min, B. (2015). Green R&D for eco-innovation and its impact on carbon emissions and firm performance. *Journal of Cleaner Production*, *108*, 534–542. https://doi.org/10.1016/j.jclepro.2015.05.114

Lev, B., & Sougiannis, T. (1996). The capitalization, amortization, and value-relevance of R&D. *Journal of Accounting and Economics*, *21*(1), 107–138. https://doi.org/10.1016/0165-4101(95)00410-6

Li, F. (2011). *Textual analysis of corporate disclosures: A survey of the literature* (SSRN Scholarly Paper 1756926). Social Science Research Network. https://papers.ssrn.com/abstract=1756926

Liao, C.-S. (2025). Does Fintech improve green innovation efficiency in China? Insight from R&D activities, green finance, and government environmental awareness. *The Quarterly Review of Economics and Finance*, *103*, 102035. https://doi.org/10.1016/j.qref.2025.102035

Liu, W., Wang, Z., Shi, Q., & Bao, S. (2024). Impact of the digital transformation of Chinese new energy vehicle enterprises on innovation performance. *Humanities and Social Sciences Communications*, *11*(1). https://doi.org/10.1057/s41599-024-03109-y

Liu, Y., Song, J., Zhou, B., & Liu, J. (2025). Artificial intelligence applications and corporate ESG performance. *International Review of Economics & Finance*, *104*, 104559. https://doi.org/10.1016/j.iref.2025.104559

Matten, D., & Moon, J. (2008). "Implicit" and "Explicit" CSR: A conceptual framework for a comparative understanding of corporate social responsibility. *Academy of Management Review*, *33*(2), 404–424. https://doi.org/10.5465/amr.2008.31193458

McGrath, R. G., Tsai, M.-H., Venkataraman, S., & MacMillan, I. C. (1996). Innovation, competitive advantage and rent: A model and test. *Management Science*, *42*(3), 389–403. https://doi.org/10.1287/mnsc.42.3.389

Miralles-Quirós, M. M., Miralles-Quirós, J. L., & Redondo Hernández, J. (2019). ESG performance and shareholder value creation in the banking industry: International differences. *Sustainability*, *11*(5), 1404. https://doi.org/10.3390/su11051404

Nekhili, M., Boukadhaba, A., Nagati, H., & Chtioui, T. (2019). ESG performance and market value: The moderating role of employee board representation. *International Journal of Human Resource Management*, *32*(14), 3061–3087. https://doi.org/10.1080/09585192.2019.1629989

Orlitzky, M., & Benjamin, J. D. (2001). Corporate social performance and firm risk: A meta-analytic review. *Business & Society*, *40*(4), 369–396. https://doi.org/10.1177/000765030104000402

Padgett, R. C., & Galan, J. I. (2010). The effect of R&D intensity on corporate social responsibility. *Journal of Business Ethics*, *93*(3), 407–418. https://doi.org/10.1007/s10551-009-0230-x

Page, M. J., Moher, D., Bossuyt, P. M., Boutron, I., Hoffmann, T. C., Mulrow, C. D., Shamseer, L., Tetzlaff, J. M., Akl, E. A., Brennan, S. E., Chou, R., Glanville, J., Grimshaw, J. M., Hróbjartsson, A., Lalu, M. M., Li, T., Loder, E. W., Mayo-Wilson, E., McDonald, S., … McKenzie, J. E. (2021). PRISMA 2020 explanation and elaboration: Updated guidance and exemplars for reporting systematic reviews. *BMJ*, *372*, n160. https://doi.org/10.1136/bmj.n160

Pollman, E. (2019). *Corporate social responsibility, ESG, and compliance* (SSRN Scholarly Paper 3479723). Social Science Research Network. https://doi.org/10.2139/ssrn.3479723

Porter, M. E., & van der Linde, C. (1995). Toward a new conception of the environment-competitiveness relationship. *The Journal of Economic Perspectives*, *9*(4), 97–118. https://doi.org/10.1257/jep.9.4.97

Romer, P. M. (1994). The origins of endogenous growth. *The Journal of Economic Perspectives*, *8*(1), 3–22. https://doi.org/10.1257/jep.8.1.3

Sun, Y., Tao, Q., Wang, D., & Zhang, W. (2025). Corporate ESG decoupling and R&D investment. *The North American Journal of Economics and Finance*, *75*, 102278. https://doi.org/10.1016/j.najef.2024.102278

Tesco PLC. (2022). *Annual report and financial statements 2022*. Tesco PLC.

Tesco PLC. (2023). *Annual report and financial statements 2023*. Tesco PLC.

Tesco PLC. (2024). *Annual report and financial statements 2024*. Tesco PLC.

Tranfield, D., Denyer, D., & Smart, P. (2003). Towards a methodology for developing evidence-informed management knowledge by means of systematic review. *British Journal of Management*, *14*(3), 207–222. https://doi.org/10.1111/1467-8551.00375

Velte, P. (2017). Does ESG performance have an impact on financial performance? Evidence from Germany. *Journal of Global Responsibility*, *8*(2), 169–178. https://doi.org/10.1108/JGR-11-2016-0029

Wernerfelt, B. (1984). A resource-based view of the firm. *Strategic Management Journal*, *5*(2), 171–180. https://doi.org/10.1002/smj.4250050207

Xu, J., Liu, F., & Shang, Y. (2020). R&D investment, ESG performance and green innovation performance: Evidence from China. *Kybernetes, 50*(3), 737–756. https://doi.org/10.1108/K-12-2019-0793

Yousaf, U. B., Yousaf, I., Hussain, H., & Hussain, M. J. (2025). CEO's R&D experience and green innovation: Evidence from China. *Journal of International Money and Finance, 157*, 103374. https://doi.org/10.1016/j.jimonfin.2025.103374

Yu, Z., Farooq, U., Alam, M. M., & Dai, J. (2024). How does environmental, social, and governance (ESG) performance determine investment mix? New empirical evidence from BRICS. *Borsa Istanbul Review, 24*(3), 520–529. https://doi.org/10.1016/j.bir.2024.02.007

Zhang, Y., Li, W., & Yang, L. (2025). The impact of environmental regulation on green innovation of environmental enterprises in China: The moderating effect of R&D investment and government green subsidies. *Polish Journal of Environmental Studies, 34*(1), 447–461. https://doi.org/10.15244/pjoes/185700

Zhong, R. (Irene). (2018). Transparency and firm innovation. *Journal of Accounting and Economics, 66*(1), 67–93. https://doi.org/10.1016/j.jacceco.2018.02.001

Chapter 13

The Double-Edged Role of CSR Awards: Value Creation or Market Penalty?

Rabia Najaf[a] *and Khakan Najaf*[b]

[a]Sunway University, Malaysia
[b]Canadian University Dubai, UAE

Abstract

This research explores how corporate social responsibility (CSR) awards influence firm performance, using data from 397 Malaysian companies across 13 sectors between 2018 and 2021. Although CSR awards are frequently seen as evidence of ethical excellence, their economic impact remains unclear. Building on Agency Theory, we argue that managers may prioritise CSR recognition to advance personal reputations rather than shareholder wealth, creating costs that reduce market valuation. Social role theory views firms as social actors, suggesting that awards can strengthen legitimacy, morale and reputation among stakeholders. In contrast, Signalling theory implies that awards may function as symbolic gestures, potentially interpreted as greenwashing. To separate true effects from confounding factors, the study applies the potential outcomes framework. Empirical findings reveal that while CSR awards are associated with a decline in market value, strong Environmental, Social and Governance (ESG) performance and female Chief Financial Officer (CFO) leadership improve operational returns (Return on Assets [ROA]). The results underscore a paradox: CSR awards can foster internal efficiency and credibility but do not reliably enhance market performance. This study advances CSR research by integrating multiple theoretical perspectives and highlighting the importance of transparent communication to align social recognition with investor expectations.

Keywords: Corporate social responsibility (CSR) awards; ESG performance; agency theory; signalling theory; firm performance; female CFOs

Sustainability in Accounting and Finance Education, 225–245

doi:10.1108/978-1-80686-393-820261013

1. Introduction

Corporate social responsibility (CSR) has significantly evolved for corporations over recent decades since (Bowen, 1953). Initially characterised by sporadic acts of kindness aimed at promoting social good, CSR has now become a central theme and a critical priority for corporations (Najaf and Najaf, 1988; Zolotoy et al., 2019). Many leading firms view CSR as an opportunity to enhance their business and consider it a vital component of their success (Najaf et al., 2024; Valet, 2019). In light of this context, we concentrate on CSR awards to contribute to the ongoing debate and pose the following question: Is there a significant connection between receiving a CSR award and financial performance or, ultimately, firm value? Therefore, this study hypothesises that award-winning companies may experience a negative impact on firm performance. We focus on CSR awards for two reasons. Firstly, if CSR indeed leads to improved financial performance or increased firm value, then receiving a CSR award should correlate with a rise in firm value. This is because CSR awards are typically organised by reputable media outlets and are given to firms in recognition of their exceptional, innovative and world-class CSR practices (Yang et al., 2024; Zhou et al., 2024).

Despite the importance of this topic, there is a notable gap in empirical research dedicated specifically to CSR awards. This is a significant omission, considering the importance of CSR for corporations and the credibility and favourable reputation that CSR award-winning firms gain. Apart from one recent study examining how winning CSR awards incentivises non-winners to improve their CSR performance, there is a lack of comprehensive research on this topic (Li et al., 2022). Previous research indicates that shareholders generally respond positively to news about corporate awards (Awaysheh et al., 2020).

In this study, we gathered data from 2018 to 2021, focusing on the top revenue-generating firms in Malaysia (Najaf et al., 2025). Our sample includes both financial and non-financial firms across 13 sectors. The potential negative impact of CSR awards on firm performance can be explained through Agency theory suggests conflicts of interest may arise between a company's management (agents) and its shareholders (principals). Management might pursue CSR activities and awards to enhance their reputation or align with personal values, rather than to maximise shareholder value. These CSR initiatives can be costly and might not yield immediate financial returns, creating a perception of reduced profitability (Fu et al., 2024; Najaf & Najaf, 2021a; Zhou et al., 2024).

Furthermore, shareholders might see the allocation of resources to CSR efforts as a diversion from the firm's core profit-generating activities, leading to concerns about the firm's focus and efficiency. This misalignment between management's actions and shareholders' expectations can negatively impact the firm's market performance (Alatawi et al., 2023; Bhandari & Javakhadze, 2017). While CSR awards aim to signal a firm's commitment to social and environmental responsibilities, they can also raise scepticism about the firm's true motivations. If stakeholders perceive these awards as superficial attempts at enhancing image (greenwashing), the intended positive signal might backfire, resulting in increased scrutiny and a negative perception of the firm's genuine commitment to CSR (Li et al., 2023; Montgomery et al., 2023).

Our initial regression results indicate that CSR awards have a significant negative impact on both market and firm performance. Despite the positive impact of Environmental, Social, and Governance (ESG) scores on Return on Assets (ROA), this effect may not necessarily translate to market value. Market valuations are influenced by a broader range of factors, including investor perceptions, market trends and external economic conditions. High ESG scores often reflect enhanced operational efficiency, ethical practices and effective risk management, which directly improve ROA by optimising resource utilisation and reducing costs (Aydoğmuş et al., 2022).

Additionally, companies with high ESG scores tend to have better risk management, reducing unexpected costs and liabilities. Operational efficiencies gained from sustainable practices, such as energy savings and waste reduction, directly enhance asset efficiency (Aldieri et al., 2023; Wong and Li, 2024). Our results demonstrate that having a female CFO positively impacts ROA. Prior studies prove that female CFO significant impact on the investment efficiency (Ali and Khan, 2024; Ismail & Abdul Wahab, 2024).

Consequently, even if a female CFO drives better ROA through efficient management, market value might not increase proportionally if investors focus on immediate returns or external conditions (Bradbury et al., 2022; Xing et al., 2021). The study's findings have important social and practical implications. CSR award-winning companies must recognise that while these awards enhance operational efficiency and internal processes, they might not immediately translate to increased market value due to investor biases and short-term focus.

By addressing these gaps in the literature, we provide new insights into the outcomes of CSR awards and contribute to the broader CSR literature. Our research highlights the complexities of measuring the impact of CSR awards on firm performance and underscores the need for more comprehensive and nuanced analyses in this area. The structure of this paper is organised as follows. We next present the literature and discuss the hypotheses. The third section presents the methodology, sample selection and empirical design. The results section discusses the main findings, additional analyses and robustness tests. The final section concludes the paper.

2. Theoretical Background

CSR awards are widely perceived as indicators of ethical excellence, but their actual influence on firm performance is subject to debate. Drawing on social role theory, firms can be understood as social actors that adopt behaviours aligning with societal expectations (Misani, 2010). Under this lens, receiving a CSR award may strengthen a company's socially responsible image, encouraging stakeholders – such as employees, customers and investors – to engage more positively with the firm. This can enhance morale, trust and brand reputation. However, signalling theory presents a more sceptical viewpoint. It suggests that some companies may pursue CSR awards primarily to project a favourable image rather than to reflect meaningful ethical change (Pomering & Johnson, 2009). In such cases, the award serves as a strategic signal to stakeholders, potentially obscuring deeper issues. Firms with greater resources or visibility may be more likely to win awards, regardless of the authenticity or impact of their CSR initiatives (Gallus & Frey, 2016) This raises concerns about selection bias, where differences in outcomes between awarded and non-awarded firms may reflect pre-existing characteristics rather than the effect of the award itself. As a result, to accurately evaluate the impact of CSR recognition, rigorous causal analysis – such as the Potential Outcomes Framework – is necessary to distinguish genuine effects from confounding factors.

2.1 CSR Award and Firm Performance

According to Eberhard-Harribey (2006), CSR involves not only adhering to legal obligations but also investing in human capital, the environment and stakeholder relations. This entails the voluntary incorporation of social and environmental considerations into business operations and interactions with stakeholders. The primary theories commonly used in the literature to explain why companies voluntarily engage in CSR practices and sustainability assurance include stakeholder theory, legitimacy theory and signalling theory (Lee et al., 2018; Velte, 2020). According to stakeholder theory, adopting sustainability practices allows companies to address the diverse needs of their stakeholders, including employees, customers, shareholders and the local community. This commitment to CSR activities helps resolve conflicts between shareholders, managers and various internal and external stakeholders. Additionally, utilising CSR rewards can encourage managers to engage in responsible actions, thereby reducing information asymmetry and limiting conflicts of interest among the involved parties (Freeman, 2010).

> *H1.* Ceteris paribus, companies that win CSR awards have a negative impact on firm performance (due to the additional expenses and potential misalignment with shareholder interests).

2.2 ESG Score and Firm Performance

Pressure from stakeholders has driven organisations to widely adopt sustainable practices (Tate et al., 2012). Given the necessity for organisations to reduce their environmental impact and enhance their overall sustainability efforts, they are seeking ways to collaborate with suppliers and customers to jointly pursue ESG goals. Consequently, ESG collaboration has recently garnered attention from both academics and practitioners. Indeed, ESG collaboration can enable firms to capitalise on emerging markets and achieve a first-mover advantage, leading to sustainable competitive advantages and ultimately enhancing firm performance (Grekova et al., 2016; Hassoun et al., 2022). When making investment decisions, shareholders are now required to evaluate and can easily monitor a firm's financial performance as well as its environmental and social (E&S) metrics, which are key components of CSR. The debate continues over whether E&S performance is advantageous to the average shareholder.

H2. Ceteris paribus, ESG score positive impact on the firm performance (supporting evidence market reputation).

2.3 Female Chief Financial Officers (CFOs) and Firm Performance

Chief Financial Officers (CFOs), while typically viewed as secondary to Chief Executive Officers (CEOs) in the corporate hierarchy, play a crucial role in strategic decision-making by integrating essential financial data into business deliberations (Cragun et al., 2020; Habib et al., 2022; Ham et al., 2017). Managerial characteristics significantly influence the decision-making processes within an organisation (Hambrick & Mason, 1984). Thus, existing research suggests that gender impacts corporate results, as attitudes towards risk associated with gender affect managerial actions (Francis et al., 2015). Women generally display more careful and meticulous decision-making behaviours, often characterised by less overconfidence, largely because of their tendency towards risk aversion. This behaviour is reflected in their typically smaller investments in high-risk assets compared to men (Charness & Gneezy, 2012; Gopalakrishna et al., 2022). Women tend to manage their pension funds more cautiously compared to men. Additionally, women generally show less overconfidence than men by favouring shorter-term debt options (La Rocca et al., 2020).

H3. Ceteris paribus, female CFO positive impact on the firm performance (supporting evidence more transparent financial reporting).

3. Sample and Data

This study investigates the association between sustainability practices and company performance in Malaysia from 2018 to 2021 (Jan et al., 2023). The analysis utilises secondary data sourced from ESG ratings and information reported in company-issued documents, including annual and sustainability reports. The sample consists of companies adhering to the revised national corporate governance framework introduced in 2017. Company performance is assessed using two indicators: one capturing internal financial efficiency and another reflecting valuation by the market. Main explanatory variables include whether a company received recognition for sustainability efforts and whether it appointed a female CFO, based on publicly available disclosures. The model includes various firm-level control variables and incorporates both time and industry effects to address potential variation across years and sectors (Guo, 2017). For further details on variable definitions, data sources and additional robustness checks, see Appendix A.

4. Empirical Results

4.1 Descriptive Statistics

Table 13.1 presents descriptive statistics for 397 firms. Tobin's *Q* averages 2.017, while ROA has a mean of 4.535, ranging from −506.623 to 83.963. ESG scores average 46.706, and 'Award Winning' is 0.181. Firm attributes include 10.936 analysts, leverage of 3.271 and firm size of 7.879. Board size and Big four auditors also show notable variations, with the latter averaging 0.678 (Najaf & Najaf, 2021b).

4.2 Correlation

Table 13.2 presents Spearman's rank correlations. Tobin's *Q* strongly correlates with ROA (0.759) but negatively with award-winning (−0.209) and firm size (−0.587). ESG scores show slight positive correlations with Tobin's *Q* (0.081) and ROA (0.091). Female CFO presence and analyst coverage have weak correlations, while loss negatively correlates with Tobin's *Q* and ROA. Board size and industry show moderate positive relationships. The overall Spearman rho is 0.130, indicating low general correlation (Najaf et al., 2021b).

Table 13.1. Descriptive Statistics (n/397).

Variables	**Variable Type**	**Mean**	**Std. Dev.**	**Min**	**Max.**
Tobin's Q	Continuous	2.017	2.779	−15.567	26.593
ROA	Continuous	4.535	27.463	−506.623	83.963
Panel B: Independent Variables of Interest					
ESG Score	Continuous	2.017	2.779	−15.567	26.593
Award winning	Dichotomous	0.181	0.386	0	1
Female CFO	Dichotomous	0.98	0.141	0	1
Panel C: Firm Attributes – Control Variables					
Analyst	Continuous	10.936	7.134	−5.041	24
Leverage	Continuous	3.271	2.698	1.117	12.844
Loss	Dichotomous	0.118	0.323	0	1
Firm Size	Continuous	7.879	1.591	3.065	12.272
Board size	Continuous	4.866	3.909	1	15
IND	Continuous	9.227	2.226	0	8
Big 4	Dichotomous	0.678	0.468	0	1

Table 13.2. Spearman's Rank Correlation Coefficients.

Variables	**(1)**	**(2)**	**(3)**	**(4)**	**(5)**	**(6)**	**(7)**	**(8)**	**(9)**	**(10)**	**(11)**
Tobin's Q	1.000										
ROA	0.759	1.000									
Award winning	−0.209	−0.167	1.000								
ESG Score	0.081	0.091	−0.074	1.000							
Female CFO	0.025	0.038	0.077	0.064	1.000						
Analyst	0.234	0.098	0.099	0.306	0.114	1.000					
Loss	−0.276	−0.473	0.013	0.038	−0.102	−0.117	1.000				
Firm size	−0.587	−0.658	0.096	0.019	0.023	0.218	0.144	1.000			
Board size	0.019	−0.048	0.075	0.233	0.102	0.265	−0.030	0.150	1.000		
IND	−0.168	−0.193	0.180	0.190	0.161	0.259	−0.024	0.312	0.542	1.000	
Big 4	−0.102	−0.101	−0.090	0.074	0.035	0.026	0.074	0.074	0.134	0.130	1.000

Note: Spearman rho = 0.130

4.3 Regression Analyses: Impact of CSR Award on the Firm Performance

The regression results in Table 13.3 indicate that ESG score has no significant effect on Tobin's Q (−0.003), but it shows a positive association with ROA (0.071*), statistically significant at the 10% level. The control variables such as analyst coverage (0.030***, 0.271***), leverage (0.054***, 0.497***) and firm size (−0.335***, −3.701***) show strong effects on performance, while others like loss (−0.206*, −7.351***) and board size (−0.038*, −0.444*) also display significant relationships (Karim et al., 2024). The significance notations represent different levels of statistical significance: * for 10% ($p < 0.10$), ** for 5% ($p < 0.05$), and *** for 1% ($p < 0.01$). The models show good fit, with adjusted R^2 values of 0.404 (40.4%) for Tobin's Q and 0.436 (43.6%) for ROA, indicating meaningful explanatory power.

4.4 Regression Analyses: Impact of ESG Score on the Firm Performance

The regression results in Table 13.4 indicate that ESG score has no statistically significant effect on Tobin's Q (−0.003), but it shows a weak positive effect on ROA (0.071*), significant at the 10% level. Several control variables demonstrate strong effects: analyst coverage (0.030***, 0.271***), leverage (0.054***, 0.497***) and firm size (−0.335***, −3.701***) are all significant at the 1% level. Loss (−0.206*, −7.351***), board size (−0.038*, −0.444*) and industry effects (0.048***) also show statistical significance at varying levels. The models explain a meaningful proportion of firm performance, with adjusted R^2 values of 0.404 (40.4%) for Tobin's Q and 0.436 (43.6%) for ROA (Najaf et al., 2021a).

4.5 Regression Analyses: Impact of Female CFO on the Firm Performance

The regression results in Table 13.5 indicate that having a female CFO has no statistically significant effect on Tobin's Q (0.103), but it is positively associated with ROA (1.500*), significant at the 10% level (Ali & Khan, 2024). Several control variables, including analyst coverage (0.033***, 0.300***), leverage (0.049***, 0.286*), loss (−0.312***, −7.608***) and firm size (−0.291***, −3.149***) show strong statistical significance, reinforcing the reliability of the model. The significance notations represent different levels of statistical significance: * indicates significance at the 10% level ($p < 0.10$), ** at the 5% level ($p < 0.05$), and *** at the 1% level ($p < 0.01$). The models also demonstrate solid explanatory power, with adjusted R^2 values of 0.365 (36.5%) for Tobin's Q and 0.401 (40.1%) for ROA (Najaf et al., 2020).

4.6 Margin Plots Impact of CSR Award on the Firm Performance

Fig. 13.1 shows that as the likelihood of a company being award-winning increases, the average predicted Tobin's Q, which measures firm performance, decreases. This suggests a negative relationship between winning awards and firm performance. The error bars indicate some variability in the predictions.

Table 13.3. Regression Analysis Impact of CSR Award Winning on the Firm Performance Test for First Hypothesis

Performance$_{it} = \alpha$ **+ CSR Award winning** $_{it}$ + $\sum_{i=1}^{n=7}$ **Controls**$_{it}$ + $\delta 1$**IND** + $\delta 2$**YE**$_{it} + \epsilon_{it}(1)$

Where Tobin's Q_{it} and ROA$_{it}$ are a continuous variable proxied by the performance of a firm (i) in the year (t). CSR Award winning$_{it}$ is a dichotomous variable (i) in year (t). We control for the Firm-level (Analyst, leverage, loss, firm size, board size, IND, Big 4). The data sample is from year 2018–2021.

Variables	*Tobin's Q*	*ROA*
	Model 1	***Model 2***
CSR Award winning	**−0.291*****	**−2.619*****
	[0.064]	**[0.655]**
Analyst	0.035***	0.316***
	[0.005]	[0.054]
Leverage	0.053***	0.334**
	[0.016]	[0.165]
Loss	−0.335***	−7.935***
	[0.085]	[0.792]
Firm Size	−0.295***	−3.203***
	[0.037]	[0.400]
Board size	0.002	−0.028
	[0.003]	[0.053]
IND	0.020*	0.061
	[0.011]	[0.144]
Big 4	0.047	−0.516

(Continued)

Table 13.3. *(Continued)*

Performance$_{it}$ = α + CSR Award winning $_{it}$ + $\sum_{i=1}^{n=7}$ Controls$_{it}$ + δ1IND + δ2YE$_{it}$ + ϵ_{it}(1)
Where Tobin's Q_{it} and ROA$_{it}$ are a continuous variable proxied by the performance of a firm (*i*) in the year (*t*). CSR Award winning$_{it}$ is a dichotomous variable (*i*) in year (*t*). We control for the Firm-level (Analyst, leverage, loss, firm size, board size, IND, Big 4). The data sample is from year 2018–2021.

	[0.061]	[0.753]
Constant	2.020***	27.652***
	[0.256]	[2.971]
IND, Y.E. Fixed Effect	Yes	Yes
Cluster	Firm	Firm
Observations	397	397
R2	0.400	0.422
Adjusted R2	0.387	0.410

Note: *$p < 0.10$, **$p < 0.05$, ***$p < 0.01$.

Table 13.4. Regression Analysis Impact of ESG Score on the Market and Financial Performance Test for Second Hypothesis.

$\text{Performance}_{it} = \alpha + \text{ESG score}_{it} + \sum_{i=1}^{n=7} \text{Controls}_{it} + \delta 1\text{IND} + \delta 2\text{YE}_{it} + \epsilon_{it}(2)$

Where Tobin's Q_{it} and ROA_{it} are a continuous variable proxied by the performance of a firm (*i*) in the year (*t*). ESG $score_{it}$ is a dichotomous variable (*i*) in year (*t*). We control for the Firm-level (Analyst, leverage, loss, firm size, board size, IND, Big4). The data sample is from year 2018–2021.

Variables	*Tobin's Q*	*ROA*
	Model 1	*Model 2*
ESG score	−0.003	**0.071***
	[0.003]	**[0.037]**
Analyst	0.030***	0.271***
	[0.005]	[0.058]
Leverage	0.054***	0.497***
	[0.014]	[0.155]
Loss	−0.206*	−7.351***
	[0.112]	[1.041]
Firm Size	−0.335***	−3.701***
	[0.028]	[0.422]
Board size	−0.038*	−0.444*
	[0.022]	[0.262]
IND	0.048***	0.129
	[0.018]	[0.236]

(Continued)

Table 13.4. *(Continued)*

$\text{Performance}_{it} = \alpha + \text{ESG score}_{it} + \sum_{i=1}^{n=7} \text{Controls}_{it} + \delta 1\text{IND} + \delta 2\text{YE}_{it} + \epsilon_{it}$ (2)

Where Tobin's Q_{it} and ROA_{it} are a continuous variable proxied by the performance of a firm (i) in the year (t). ESG score_{it} is a dichotomous variable (i) in year (t). We control for the Firm-level (Analyst, leverage, loss, firm size, board size, IND, Big4). The data sample is from year 2018–2021.

Big 4	0.028	0.055
	[0.069]	[0.841]
Constant	2.482***	29.376***
	[0.256]	[3.423]
IND, Y.E. Fixed Effect	Yes	Yes
Cluster	Firm	Firm
Observations	397	397
R2	0.420	0.451
Adjusted R2	0.404	0.436

Note: *$p < 0.10$, **$p < 0.05$, ***$p < 0.01$.

Table 13.5. Regression Analysis Impact of Female CFO on the Market and Financial Performance.

$\text{Performance}_{it} = \alpha + \text{Female CFO}_{it} + \sum_{i=1}^{n=7} \text{Controls}_{it} + \delta 1\text{IND} + \delta 2\text{YE}_{it} + \epsilon_{it} (3)$

Where Tobin's Q_{it} and ROA_{it} are a continuous variable proxied by the performance of a firm (*i*) in the year (*t*). Female CFO_{it} is a dichotomous variable (*i*) in year (*t*). We control for the Firm-level (Analyst, leverage, loss, firm size, board size, IND, Big4). The data sample is from year 2018–2021.

Variables	***Tobin's Q***	***ROA***
	Model 1	***Model 2***
Female CFO	0.103	**1.500***
	[0.070]	**[0.825]**
Analyst	0.033***	0.300***
	[0.004]	[0.052]
Leverage	0.049***	0.286*
	[0.013]	[0.149]
Loss	−0.312***	−7.608***
	[0.091]	[1.079]
Firm Size	−0.291***	−3.149***
	[0.023]	[0.272]
Board size	−0.001	−0.059
	[0.007]	[0.086]
IND	0.012	−0.052
	[0.014]	[0.166]
Big 4	0.047	−0.583

(*Continued*)

Table 13.5. *(Continued)*

$\text{Performance}_{it} = \alpha + \text{Female CFO}_{it} + \sum_{i=1}^{n=7} \text{Controls}_{it} + \delta 1\text{IND} + \delta 2\text{YE}_{it} + \epsilon_{it}(3)$

Where Tobin's Q_{it} and ROA_{it} are a continuous variable proxied by the performance of a firm (*i*) in the year (*t*). Female CFO_{it} is a dichotomous variable (*i*) in year (*t*). We control for the Firm-level (Analyst, leverage, loss, firm size, board size, IND, Big4). The data sample is from year 2018–2021.

	[0.061]	[0.722]
Constant	1.980^{***}	27.189^{***}
	[0.179]	[2.113]
IND, Y.E. Fixed Effect	Yes	Yes
Cluster	Firm	Firm
Observations	397	397
R2	0.378	0.413
Adjusted R2	0.365	0.401

Note: $^{*}p < 0.10$, $^{**}p < 0.05$, $^{***}p < 0.01$.

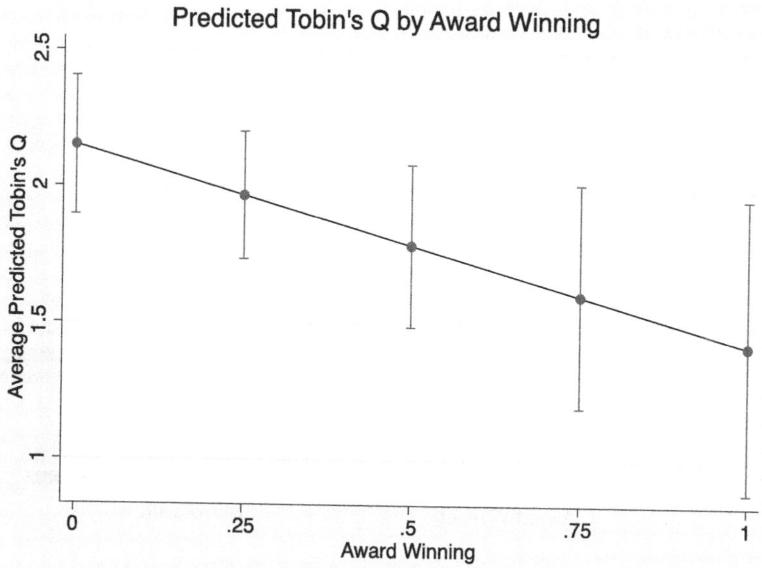

Fig. 13.1. Margin Plots Tobin's Q by Award Winning.
Source(s): Authors' own work.

4.7 Distribution of Firm-Year Observations by CSR Award Status

Fig. 13.2 displays the distribution of firm-year observations for award-winning and non-award firms. Non-award firms show a higher concentration and variability in frequency across years compared to award-winning firms. This suggests greater representation or activity among firms that did not receive CSR awards during the study period.

5. Conclusion, Policy Implications and Future Research

This research assessed the influence of CSR awards, ESG scores and female CFO presence on firm performance in Malaysia from 2018 to 2021 (Kampoowale et al., 2024). The analysis finds that firms receiving CSR awards tend to underperform in both market valuation and accounting returns, possibly due to investor concerns about authenticity or symbolic CSR practices. ESG scores appear to improve operational performance (ROA), though they show no significant link to market value, which may reflect investors' short-term priorities. Appointing female CFOs correlates with higher ROA, suggesting stronger internal performance, but has limited impact on market perception – potentially due to persistent biases or lag in recognition (Abdullah et al., 2023).

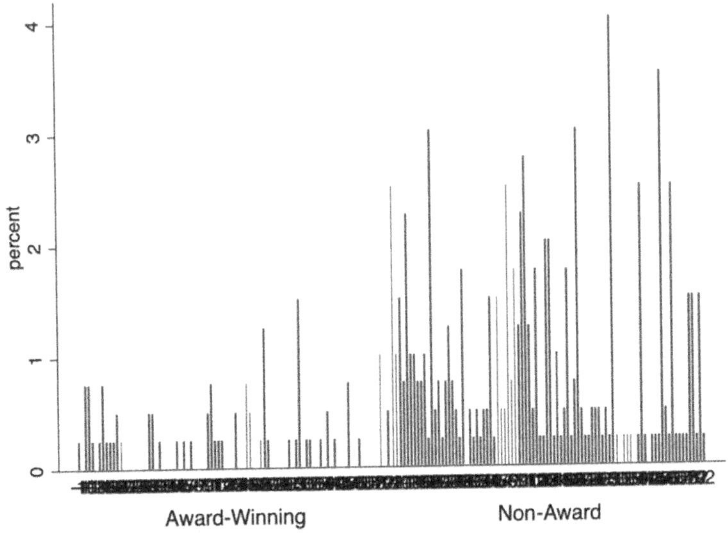

Fig. 13.2. Distribution of Firm-Year Observations by CSR Award Status. *Source(s):* Authors' own work.

To enhance the effectiveness and credibility of CSR initiatives, policymakers should consider introducing stricter reporting standards and assurance mechanisms to prevent greenwashing (Kurpierz & Smith, 2020). Promoting transparency in ESG disclosures and integrating them into regulatory frameworks can also improve stakeholder trust (Shalhoob, 2025). Moreover, corporate governance reforms that actively support gender diversity in executive roles could contribute to more inclusive and high-performing leadership structures. Investor education campaigns may help shift biases and promote more balanced evaluation of leadership and sustainability factors.

Subsequent studies should expand beyond the Malaysian context to determine whether these findings hold in different economic, cultural and regulatory environments. Longer time horizons could offer insights into the sustained effects of CSR and ESG practices on firm value. Additionally, future work should explore other aspects of executive and board diversity and examine how these dynamics interact with firm strategy and performance across industries (Murphy & McIntyre, 2007).

Acknowledgements

The authors received no financial or institutional support for this research.

References

Abdullah, Z., Qaderi, S. A., Binti Mohd Ariff, A. H., Chandren, S., & Abdul Latif, R. (2023). CEO, CFO, and board attributes' effect on fair value agriculture disclosure. *Cogent Business & Management*, *10*, 2275867.

Alatawi, I. A., Ntim, C. G., Zras, A., & Elmagrhi, M. H. (2023). CSR, financial and non-financial performance in the tourism sector: A systematic literature review and future research agenda. *International Review of Financial Analysis*, 102734.

Aldieri, L., Amendola, A., & Candila, V. (2023). The impact of ESG scores on risk market performance. *Sustainability*, *15*, 7183.

Ali, A., & Khan, M. (2024). Impact of female CFO board membership on firm investment efficiency: Does institutional gender parity matter? Evidence from emerging economies. *Journal of Economic and Administrative Sciences*. https://doi.org/10.1108/JEAS-08-2023-0221

Awaysheh, A., Heron, R. A., Perry, T., & Wilson, J. I. (2020). On the relation between corporate social responsibility and financial performance. *Strategic Management Journal*, *41*, 965–987. https://doi.org/10.1002/smj.3122

Aydoğmuş, M., Gülay, G., & Ergun, K. (2022). Impact of ESG performance on firm value and profitability. *Borsa Istanbul Review*, *22*, S119–S127.

Bhandari, A., & Javakhadze, D. (2017). Corporate social responsibility and capital allocation efficiency. *Journal of Corporate Finance*, *43*, 354–377.

Bowen, H. R. (1953). *Social responsibility of the businessman*. Harper & Row.

Bradbury, M., Jia, J., & Li, Z. (2022). Corporate social responsibility committees and the use of corporate social responsibility assurance services. *Journal of Contemporary Accounting and Economics*, *18*, 100317.

Charness, G., & Gneezy, U. (2012). Strong evidence for gender differences in risk taking. *Journal of Economic Behavior & Organization*, *83*, 50–58.

Cragun, O. R., Olsen, K. J., & Wright, P. M. (2020). Making CEO narcissism research great: A review and meta-analysis of CEO narcissism. *Journal of Management*, *46*, 908–936.

Eberhard-Harribey, L. (2006). Corporate social responsibility as a new paradigm in the European policy: How CSR comes to legitimate the European regulation process. *Corporate Governance: International Journal of Business in Society*, *6*, 358–368.

Francis, B., Hasan, I., Park, J. C., & Wu, Q. (2015). Gender differences in financial reporting decision making: Evidence from accounting conservatism. *Contemporary Accounting Research*, *32*, 1285–1318.

Freeman, R. E. (2010). *Strategic management: A stakeholder approach*. Cambridge University Press.

Fu, X., Bernard, P., Magan, R. G., Plaisent, M., & Liu, G. (2024). Corporate social responsibility as perceived by business people. In *Corporate Governance and CSR Strategies for Sustainability*. IGI Global.

Gallus, J., & Frey, B. S. (2016). Awards: A strategic management perspective. *Strategic Management Journal*, *37*, 1699–1714.

Gopalakrishna, G., Ter Riet, G., Vink, G., Stoop, I., Wicherts, J. M., & Bouter, L. M. (2022). Prevalence of questionable research practices, research misconduct and their potential explanatory factors: A survey among academic researchers in The Netherlands. *PLoS One*, *17*, e0263023.

Grekova, K., Calantone, R. J., Bremmers, H. J., Trienekens, J. H., & Omta, S. (2016). How environmental collaboration with suppliers and customers influences firm performance: Evidence from Dutch food and beverage processors. *Journal of Cleaner Production*, *112*, 1861–1871.

Guo, G. (2017). Demystifying variance in performance: A longitudinal multilevel perspective. *Strategic Management Journal*, *38*, 1327–1342.

Habib, A., Ranasinghe, D., Wu, J. Y., Biswas, P. K., & Ahmad, F. (2022). Real earnings management: A review of the international literature. *Accounting and Finance*, *62*, 4279–4344.

Hambrick, D. C., & Mason, P. A. (1984). Upper echelons: The organization as a reflection of its top managers. *Academy of Management Review*, *9*, 193–206.

Ham, C., Lang, M., Seybert, N., & Wang, S. (2017). CFO narcissism and financial reporting quality. *Journal of Accounting Research*, *55*, 1089–1135.

Hassoun, A., Prieto, M. A., Carpena, M., Bouzembrak, Y., Marvin, H. J., Pallarés, N., Barba, F. J., Bangar, S. P., Chaudhary, V., & Ibrahim, S. (2022). Exploring the role of green and Industry 4.0 technologies in achieving sustainable development goals in food sectors. *Food Research International*, *162*, 112068.

Ismail, I., & Abdul Wahab, E. A. (2024). Do female chief financial officers and female directors cooperate? Evidence from investment efficiency. *Meditari Accountancy Research*.

Jan, A., Rahman, H. U., Zahid, M., Salameh, A. A., Khan, P. A., Al-Faryan, M. A. S., Aziz, R. B. C., & Ali, H. E. (2023). Islamic corporate sustainability practices index aligned with SDGs towards better financial performance: Evidence from the Malaysian and Indonesian Islamic banking industry. *Journal of Cleaner Production*, *405*, 136860.

Kampoowale, I., Kateb, I., Salleh, Z., & Alahdal, W. M. (2024). Board gender diversity and ESG performance: Pathways to financial success in Malaysian emerging market. *International Journal of Emerging Markets*.

Karim, S., Vigne, S. A., Lucey, B. M., & Naeem, M. A. (2024). Discretionary impacts of the risk management committee attributes on firm performance: Do board size matter? *International Journal of Emerging Markets*, *19*, 2222–2240.

Kurpierz, J. R., & Smith, K. (2020). The greenwashing triangle: Adapting tools from fraud to improve CSR reporting. *Sustainability Accounting, Management and Policy Journal*, *11*, 1075–1093.

La Rocca, M., Neha, N., & La rocca, T. (2020). Female management, overconfidence and debt maturity: European evidence. *Journal of Management & Governance*, *24*, 713–747.

Lee, W. S., Sun, K.-A., & Moon, J. (2018). Application of upper echelon theory for corporate social responsibility dimensions: Evidence from the restaurant industry. *Journal of Quality Assurance in Hospitality & Tourism*, *19*, 387–414.

Li, W., Li, W., Seppänen, V., & Koivumäki, T. (2023). Effects of greenwashing on financial performance: Moderation through local environmental regulation and media coverage. *Business Strategy and the Environment*, *32*, 820–841.

Li, J., Yin, J., Shi, W., & Yi, X. (2022). Keeping up with the Joneses: Role of CSR awards in incentivizing non-winners' CSR. *Business & Society*, *61*, 649–689. https://doi.org/10.1177/0007650320982271

Misani, N. (2010). The convergence of corporate social responsibility practices. *Management Research Review*, *33*, 734–748.

Montgomery, A. W., Lyon, T. P., & Barg, J. (2023). No end in sight? A greenwash review and research agenda. *Organization & Environment*. https://doi.org/10.1177/10860266231168905

Murphy, S. A., & MCINTYRE, M. L. (2007). Board of director performance: A group dynamics perspective. *Corporate Governance: International Journal of Business in Society*, *7*, 209–224.

Najaf, K., Chin, A., & Najaf, R. (2021a). Conceptualising the corporate governance issues of fintech firms. In *The fourth industrial revolution: Implementation of artificial intelligence for growing business success*. Springer.

Najaf, K., Mostafiz, M. I., & Najaf, R. (2021b). Fintech firms and banks sustainability: Why cybersecurity risk matters? *International Journal of Financial Engineering*, *8*, 2150019.

Najaf, K., Schinckus, C., Mostafiz, M. I., & Najaf, R. (2020). *Conceptualising cybersecurity risk of fintech firms and banks sustainability*.

Najaf, R., Chin, A., Chin, A., Najaf, K., & Thuraisingham, J. (2024). *Women on board and business performance*. foresight.

Najaf, R., & Najaf, K. (1988). CSR and board gender diversity impact on the corporate performance. In *Annual International Conference on the Theory and Applications of Cryptographic Techniques* (pp. 21–55). Springer.

Najaf, R., & Najaf, K. (2021a). Nexus of political connections with green finance and financial performance. *Journal of Environmental Treatment Techniques*, *9*, 305–309.

Najaf, R., & Najaf, K. (2021b). Political ties and corporate performance: Why efficiency matters? *Journal of Business and Socio-economic Development*, *1*, 182–196.

Najaf, R., Najaf, K., & Elshareif, E. (2025). Impact of female PhDs, sustainability committees, and industry-specific government experience directors on Malaysian firm performance: A human capital and social role theory perspective. *Studies in Economics and Finance*. https://doi.org/10.1108/SEF-11-2024-0765

Pomering, A., & Johnson, L. W. (2009). Constructing a corporate social responsibility reputation using corporate image advertising. *Australasian Marketing Journal*, *17*, 106–114.

Shalhoob, H. (2025). ESG disclosure and financial performance: Survey evidence from accounting and Islamic finance. *Sustainability*, *17*, 1582.

Tate, W. L., Ellram, L. M., & Dooley, K. J. (2012). Environmental purchasing and supplier management (EPSM): Theory and practice. *Journal of Purchasing and Supply Management*, *18*, 173–188.

Valet, V. (2019). The world's most reputable companies for corporate responsibility 2019. *Forbes*. https://www.forbes.com/sites/vickyvalet/2019/09/17/the-worlds-most-reputable-companies-for-corporate-responsibility-2019/

Velte, P. (2020). Do CEO incentives and characteristics influence corporate social responsibility (CSR) and vice versa? A literature review. *Social Responsibility Journal*, *16*, 1293–1323.

Wong, M. C., & Li, W. (2024). Investigating ESG funds in China: Management fees and investment performance. *International Journal of Financial Studies*, *12*, 38.

Xing, L., Gonzalez, A., & Sila, V. (2021). Does cooperation among women enhance or impede firm performance? *The British Accounting Review*, *53*, 100936.

Yang, H., Shi, X., Bhutto, M. Y., & Ertz, M. (2024). Do corporate social responsibility and technological innovation get along? A systematic review and future research agenda. *Journal of Innovation & Knowledge*, *9*, 100462.
Zhou, Z., Wu, Y., & Xie, Q. (2024). Social responsibility, information technology, and high-quality development of mining enterprise using structural equation modeling (SEM). *Resources Policy*, *91*, 104925.
Zolotoy, L., O'sullivan, D., & Chen, Y. (2019). Local religious norms, corporate social responsibility, and firm value. *Journal of Banking & Finance*, *100*, 218–233.

Appendix A: Variables Definition

Dependent Variables		
Variable	**Definition**	**Source**
Tobin's Q	Market capitalisation + Total liabilities + Preferred Equity + Minority interest divided by Total Fixed assets + Current assets	Bloomberg
ROA	Net income divided by total assets	Bloomberg
Focus Independent Variables		
Variable	*Definition*	*Source*
ESG score	*ESG score is measured Environmental, social and governance pillar.*	*Bloomberg*
Awarding winning	*Assign '1' if a companies received any CSR award or sustainability award in 2018 to 2021; otherwise, assign '0'.*	Annual reports, sustainability reports and integrated reports
Female CFO	*Assign '1' if a CFO is female; otherwise, assign '0'*	Annual reports, sustainability reports and integrated reports
Control Variables		
Variable	*Definition*	*Source*
Leverage	*Ratio of a firm's debt to its equity.*	*Bloomberg*
Loss	*Negative net income used to capture financial distress or underperformance of firms*	*Bloomberg*

(Continued)

Dependent Variables		
Variable	**Definition**	**Source**
Firm Size	*Log of total assets*	*Bloomberg*
Board size	*Board size was measured as the total number of directors on the board*	*Bloomberg*
IND	*Number of independent directors*	*Bloomberg*
Big 4	*Audit by Big4 auditor = 1, otherwise "0"*	*Bloomberg*
Analyst	*Number of Analyst*	*Bloomberg*
Fixed Effect Control Variables		
Variable	*Definition*	
Year	1 (0) for observations from year *t* and 0 for other observations.	This study
IND	1 (0) if during year *t*, company *i* operating in industry *j* and 0 Otherwise	This study

Source(s): Authors' own work.

Chapter 14

Greener Futures: How Sustainability Performance Moderates CSR and Carbon Emissions in Chinese Companies

Rakia Riguen[a] *and Maali Kachouri*[b]

[a]University of Sfax, Tunisia
[b]Sousse University, Tunisia

Abstract

This chapter empirically examines how sustainability performance (SP) moderates the relationship between corporate social responsibility (CSR) and carbon emissions through Chief Sustainability Performance (CSP). While prior studies have explored the CSR environmental performance link, the moderating role of SP remains underexplored. Using a sample of 300 Chinese listed companies from 2010 to 2024, this study addresses this gap by analysing the dynamic interaction between sustainability practices, CSR and carbon emissions. Structural equation modelling (SEM) is employed to investigate the complex relationships among these variables. By considering SP as a key factor influencing both CSR activities and environmental outcomes, this study explores whether firms with strong SP are more effective in reducing carbon emissions and enhancing CSR practices. The findings reveal that SP significantly moderates the CSR carbon emissions relationship. Specifically, firms with higher SP are better positioned to implement CSR activities that lead to more substantial emission reductions. These results underscore the critical role of sustainability practices in shaping corporate environmental strategies. They suggest that firms with strong SP tend to adopt practices aligned with long-term environmental goals and broader societal benefits. This study contributes to the literature by establishing both direct and moderating links between SP, CSR and carbon emissions. It also emphasises the importance of integrating sustainability as a strategic priority for Chinese firms in an era of growing environmental awareness and regulatory scrutiny.

Sustainability in Accounting and Finance Education, 247–275

Published under exclusive licence by Emerald Publishing Limited
doi:10.1108/978-1-80686-393-820261014

Keywords: Carbon emissions; corporate social responsibility; sustainability performance; chief sustainability performance; environmental performance

1. Introduction

In recent years, sustainability has become a central concern for businesses, policymakers and societies worldwide due to the increasing risks posed by climate change. Companies are under growing pressure to align their operations with environmental, social and governance (ESG) principles, particularly in reducing carbon emissions and enhancing corporate social responsibility (CSR) practices. China, as the world's largest emitter of carbon dioxide (World Bank, 2022), has made significant policy commitments towards carbon neutrality by 2060 (Wang & Zhang, 2022), emphasising the need for firms to integrate sustainability performance (SP) into their strategies. SP plays a crucial role in shaping CSR effectiveness and mitigating environmental harm (Eccles et al., 2014). Previous studies suggest that firms with strong SP can better manage carbon emissions by implementing proactive environmental strategies and fostering transparency in CSR activities (Luo et al., 2017). Furthermore, the presence of a Chief Sustainability Officer (CSO) or a well-defined sustainability governance structure enhances corporate accountability and aligns CSR efforts with long-term environmental goals (Menz, 2010). In the Chinese corporate context, the interplay between CSR, carbon emissions and SP remains a critical yet underexplored area. While research has acknowledged the positive impact of CSR on carbon management (Luo & Tang, 2014), limited attention has been given to how SP moderates this relationship. Investigating this dynamic can provide valuable insights into how firms can effectively leverage CSR to achieve environmental sustainability while maintaining economic performance.

The relationship between CSR, carbon emissions and SP is a critical topic in corporate governance, accounting and finance, given the rising global focus on climate change. Firms with strong SP can enhance CSR effectiveness, reduce environmental risks and improve financial stability (Eccles et al., 2014). Understanding this relationship is essential for regulators, investors and policymakers, particularly in high-emission economies like China (Wang & Zhang, 2022). This study contributes to sustainability accounting by exploring how corporate strategies influence carbon management, aligning with stakeholder and legitimacy theories (Freeman, 1984; Suchman, 1995).

Extensive research has explored the relationship between CSR, carbon emissions and SP, highlighting the role of corporate governance and environmental strategies in mitigating climate risks (Eccles et al., 2014; Kolk, 2008). Previous studies have examined how CSR initiatives influence carbon performance (Luo & Tang, 2014), the impact of board diversity and sustainability governance on environmental disclosures (Luo et al., 2017), and the financial implications of sustainability practices (Clark et al., 2015).

However, while prior research acknowledges the positive role of SP in reducing carbon footprints, few studies have empirically tested its moderating effect on the CSR–carbon emissions relationship, particularly in emerging economies like China. The unique regulatory and institutional settings in China, combined with its dual carbon reduction goals (Wang & Zhang, 2022), create a pressing need for deeper insights into how sustainability governance can strengthen CSR effectiveness.

This study fills this gap by examining Chief Sustainability Performance (CSP) as a mediating mechanism, providing novel empirical evidence on how firms can enhance their environmental impact through strategic sustainability integration. This paper examines how SP moderates the relationship between CSR and carbon emissions in Chinese companies. Given China's ambitious dual carbon reduction goals, understanding the role of CSP in strengthening CSR effectiveness is crucial. The aim of this study is to empirically investigate whether higher SP enhances the impact of CSR initiatives on reducing carbon emissions, providing insights into corporate environmental strategies. The central argument is that firms with strong SP are better positioned to translate CSR efforts into meaningful carbon reductions. By integrating sustainability principles into their business models, these companies can bridge the gap between CSR commitments and actual environmental impact, thereby aligning with stakeholder and legitimacy theories. The purpose of this research is to investigate how SP moderates the relationship between CSR and carbon emissions in Chinese companies. Specifically, this study aims to examine whether firms with strong SP can better translate CSR initiatives into effective carbon reduction strategies.

By focusing on the role of CSP, this research seeks to provide empirical evidence on how sustainability-oriented governance can enhance environmental impact. The findings will contribute to the literature on corporate governance, sustainability accounting, and environmental management, offering insights for policymakers, investors and corporate leaders aiming to align CSR practices with climate change mitigation goals. This paper seeks to answer the following key question:

How does SP moderate the mediating role of the CSO on the relationship between CSR and carbon emissions in Chinese companies?

More specifically, the study explores the below:

- *Does strong sustainability performance enhance the effectiveness of CSR initiatives in reducing carbon emissions?*
- *What role do Chief Sustainability officers (CSOs) play in this relationship?*
- *How do firms with high sustainability performance differ from others in their environmental impact?*

Using a sample of 300 Chinese listed firms in the Shanghai and Shenzhen Stock Exchanges from 2010 to 2024, this study aims to provide a unique perspective on the moderating role of SP in the relationship between CSR and carbon emissions. By examining firms across multiple industries and regions within China, the study will also contribute to understanding how sustainability governance influences CSR effectiveness and carbon management in different economic sectors. The data on SP and CSR will be gathered from corporate sustainability reports, ESG ratings, financial reports and publicly available data from sources like Bloomberg, Thomson Reuters and the DataStream Database. Carbon emissions data will be collected from company environmental disclosures and industry-specific environmental reports. Information regarding carbon emissions will also be obtained from audit firm reports, regulatory filings and publicly available corporate filings to ensure a comprehensive analysis of CSR practices and carbon management. By leveraging structural equation modelling (SEM), the study will analyse the direct and indirect effects of the CSO on CSR outcomes and carbon reduction, offering valuable insights into regional variations in sustainability governance and its impact on carbon emissions management.

The paper is organised as follows: Section 2 describes a review of the literature and formulates the research hypotheses. Section 3 presents the sample and methodology, including a description of the sample, a definition of the variables and the analytical methods used. Section 4 presents the main empirical findings. Finally, Section 5 addresses the robustness tests, and Section 6 concludes with final remarks.

2. Literature Review and Hypotheses Development

2.1 CSR, carbon Emissions and CSO: A Mediation Analysis

The relationship between CSR and carbon emissions has been widely studied (Kim et al., 2022; Liu et al., 2021; Serafeim & Grewal, 2017; Toukabri & Jilani, 2023), with a significant body of literature suggesting that CSR initiatives, particularly those focusing on sustainability, can lead to a negative impact on carbon emissions. Many scholars argue that CSR activities related to environmental management and green innovations contribute to reducing carbon footprints and promoting sustainable practices. This research explains the relationship between CSR and carbon emission through Legitimacy Theory and stakeholder Theory. According to Suchman (1995), Legitimacy Theory suggests that firms disclose environmental information, including carbon emissions, to respond to external pressures and maintain societal approval (Deegan, 2002; Patten, 2002). Firms use carbon disclosure to uphold their implicit social contract and avoid regulatory scrutiny (Hrasky, 2012). Large polluting companies, being more visible, face higher legitimacy pressures (Choi et al., 2013; Freedman & Jaggi, 2011). Stakeholder Theory (Freeman, 1984) suggests that firms must manage relationships with various stakeholders who demand greater corporate accountability for environmental impact. Companies with weaker carbon performance use disclosure as a strategic tool to justify sustainability efforts and align with societal expectations (Hummel & Schlick, 2016; Toukabri & Jilani, 2023). In this context, Lee and Klassen (2016) find that firms that actively engage in CSR initiatives focused on environmental sustainability tend to report lower carbon emissions due to their investments in energy efficiency and clean technologies. Similarly, Eccles et al. (2014) discuss how companies with strong SP are more likely to adopt green strategies, which directly contribute to reducing their carbon emissions. Their research shows that CSR and sustainability go hand in hand in fostering carbon management practices and, therefore, reducing a firm's environmental footprint.

Additionally, Bebbington and Larrinaga (2014) highlight that companies with robust CSR strategies, especially in terms of energy efficiency and resource optimisation are able to effectively reduce carbon emissions over time. They emphasise the importance of sustainability governance, where firms integrate environmental goals into their corporate strategies, thus aligning their CSR efforts with carbon reduction objectives.

Moreover, Serafeim and Grewal (2017) provide evidence that CSR initiatives related to environmental sustainability can significantly lower carbon emissions in firms, particularly when these efforts are tied to long-term strategic goals and company-wide commitment to reducing environmental impact.

Recently, Liu et al. (2021) examined the role of CSR in reducing carbon emissions within the context of China's corporate sector. Their study found that CSR initiatives focused on environmental sustainability were significantly associated with lower carbon emissions, especially when firms adopted green innovation practices. They emphasised the importance of CSR in achieving effective emissions reductions.

In the same area, Kim et al. (2022) explored the relationship between CSR and environmental sustainability in the European Union. They concluded that firms with higher CSR engagement, particularly in environmental governance, demonstrated a negative effect on carbon emissions, highlighting the importance of sustainability committees in managing environmental performance. Jain and Kaur (2022) focused on Indian firms and how their CSR practices influenced carbon emissions. Their research showed that CSR programmes, particularly those targeting energy efficiency and waste reduction, were associated with a significant reduction in carbon emissions in manufacturing industries. Li et al. (2023) investigated the moderating effect of CSR on carbon emissions in global corporations. In the same context, Zhang et al. (2022) provided insights into the relationship between CSR and carbon emissions in the tech sector in Asia. Their study emphasised how green CSR initiatives, such as sustainable product development, had a negative effect on carbon emissions, especially in firms that integrated sustainability into their core business model.

In contrast, Jain and Kaur (2022) argue that in the context of Indian firms, CSR practices have a direct influence on carbon emissions through initiatives targeting energy efficiency and waste management. Jain and Kaur (2022) assert that firms adopting these CSR-driven measures have been able to significantly reduce their environmental impact, especially in energy-intensive sectors. In a recent study, Li et al. (2023) propose that CSR not only influences corporate behaviour in terms of emissions reduction but can also be further enhanced when executive compensation is linked to environmental performance targets. Their research indicates that this alignment ensures that companies prioritise carbon reduction goals alongside financial performance (Wang et al., 2023). The review highlights the growing body of research examining the relationship between CSR and carbon emissions. Studies suggest that CSR initiatives, particularly those focused on environmental sustainability, lead to reduced carbon **emissions**. Based on the above findings, we formulate our hypothesis as follows:

H1a. CSR has a negative effect on carbon emissions.

The role of corporate governance in sustainability practices has gained increasing attention in recent years. One key figure in this domain is the CSO, whose function is to integrate sustainability into corporate strategies and oversee the implementation of environmental initiatives, including carbon emission reduction. According to the Upper Echelons Theory (Hambrick & Mason, 1984) posits that executives' values, experiences and backgrounds shape corporate decisions. A CSO, as a key member of the top management team (TMT), brings expertise in sustainability, ensuring that CSR policies translate into tangible carbon reduction measures (Cheng et al., 2014). Studies indicate that firms with a CSO are more likely to implement ambitious sustainability programmes and achieve lower carbon emissions (Eccles et al., 2012; Flammer et al., 2019). Previous research grounded in Upper Echelons Theory has explored the role of chief officers in various domains, including finance, strategy, and marketing, with a growing focus on sustainability (Menz & Scheef, 2014; Nath & Mahajan, 2008; Velte & Stawinoga, 2020). These studies highlight that senior executives contribute to financial performance (Wiengarten et al., 2017), innovation and competitive advantage (Angwin et al., 2009; Breene et al., 2007; Nath & Mahajan, 2008), as well as strategic change (Menz & Scheef, 2014), social performance (Fu et al., 2020; Mazutis, 2013) and environmental performance. In this context, research suggests that CSOs contribute to reducing corporate irresponsibility by implementing transparent governance structures and regulatory compliance mechanisms (Flammer et al., 2019). CSOs, in particular, act as environmental leaders who embody values of ecological interdependence and inclusiveness, inspiring others to embrace their vision (Egri & Herman, 2000).

Recently, Fu et al. (2020) argue that CSOs may struggle with balancing financial objectives and sustainability goals. In some cases, firms may engage in 'greenwashing' superficial CSR activities that mask underlying irresponsible practices. García-Sánchez et al. (2022) found that while CSOs improve sustainability reporting, their effectiveness in reducing corporate irresponsibility depends on board independence and executive support. CSOs must challenge existing procedures and embed sustainability practices into the organisation's institutional framework (Battilana, 2006; Garud & Karnøe, 2001). Their role requires them to consistently question established norms and processes. Effective environmental leadership involves not only advocating for sustainability but also empowering organisational members to view environmental challenges as opportunities for innovation (Anderson & Bateman, 2000). Although CSOs play a crucial role in CSR, their impact on preventing corporate irresponsibility remains debated.

The role of the CSO has emerged as a strategic response to growing environmental concerns, regulatory pressures and stakeholder expectations regarding corporate sustainability (Fu et al., 2020; Velte & Stawinoga, 2020). Unlike traditional executives such as CEOs and CFOs, who focus on financial performance and risk management (Peters et al., 2019), CSOs specialise in sustainable development, CSR and environmental performance (Miller & Serafeim, 2014). Organisations increasingly appoint CSOs to address climate change issues, reduce greenhouse gas (GHG) emissions and enhance corporate transparency regarding carbon footprint (Toukabri & Jilani, 2023). The appointment of a CSO signals a company's commitment to climate action and serves as a legitimacy-enhancing mechanism (Patten, 2020). In fact, Peters and Romi (2015) find that firms with CSOs are more likely to disclose climate-related risks and carbon emissions, enhancing transparency. Kanashiro and Rivera (2019) provide that CSOs with prior sustainability experience effectively implement carbon reduction strategies. Recently, Velte (2023) suggests that CSOs act as enablers within the TMT, ensuring that carbon reduction remains a strategic priority. Fu et al. (2020) find that while CSOs enhance carbon disclosure, their impact on actual emission reduction varies depending on firm size, industry, and governance structures. In summary, the CSO plays a critical mediating role between carbon emissions and CSR. By integrating carbon reduction efforts within broader CSR strategies, the CSO helps companies navigate environmental challenges while enhancing their social performance and legitimacy. This mediation process ensures that carbon emissions management is not an isolated task but rather an integral part of a company's broader commitment to sustainability and social responsibility. CSO's role in overseeing sustainability efforts enhances the relationship between carbon emissions and CSR, ensuring that companies not only reduce their environmental impact but also demonstrate responsible corporate citizenship. Based on the above findings, we formulate a research hypothesis as follows:

H1b. Chief Sustainability Officer mediates the relationship between corporate social responsibility (CSR) and carbon emissions.

2.2 CSR, SP and Carbon Emissions: A Mediated Moderation Analysis

The relationship between SP, CSO, CSR and carbon emissions is grounded in the premise that an organisation's SP is critical for ensuring effective environmental management. This includes reducing carbon emissions while achieving positive CSR outcomes. The CSO, being the key executive responsible for overseeing sustainability strategies, plays a vital role in influencing both the reduction of carbon emissions and the enhancement of CSR initiatives. In this context, SP acts as a critical variable that strengthens the CSO's role in mediating the relationship between CSR and carbon emissions. In fact, SP refers to the ability of a firm to implement practices that meet the needs of the present without compromising the ability of future generations to meet their own needs. These practices typically include reducing carbon emissions, improving energy efficiency, and ensuring responsible environmental stewardship. SP is seen as a key factor for a company's long-term viability and its ability to meet social, environmental and economic expectations from various stakeholders (Schaltegger & Csutora, 2012).

In the same area, CSO is tasked with spearheading sustainability initiatives within the company. According to Fu et al. (2020), the CSO plays a crucial role in driving SP by implementing strategies that reduce environmental impact, such as carbon emission reduction, waste management and sustainable resource utilisation. By leading sustainability programmes, the CSO ensures that the company meets its CSR obligations while also aligning with environmental sustainability goals (Weng & Lin, 2014).

In a study by Eccles et al. (2012), it was found that companies with a dedicated CSO have more effective sustainability practices, which directly influence their CSR outcomes. Therefore, the SP of a company is closely linked to the competence and leadership of the CSO, which, in turn, accentuates the mediation between CSR and carbon emissions.

For the same idea, the relationship between SP and carbon emissions is particularly important in the context of environmental sustainability. SP includes the implementation of carbon management strategies, which focus on reducing carbon footprints and improving environmental performance (Sullivan & Mackenzie, 2017). Companies with high SP are more likely to invest in clean technologies, renewable energy, and carbon offset programmes, which contribute to reducing carbon emissions. According to Kanashiro and Rivera (2019), companies with robust sustainability practices are typically better at reducing carbon emissions because they actively incorporate environmental management systems into their operations. These practices not only help mitigate climate change but also improve the firm's CSR performance by enhancing its environmental stewardship, an important aspect of CSR (Clarkson et al., 2011). Therefore, SP can significantly influence carbon emissions reduction, making it a crucial link in CSR strategies.

By the way, CSO plays a significant role in mediating the relationship between carbon emissions and CSR. As a top management executive, the CSO is responsible for setting sustainability strategies that guide the company's carbon reduction efforts and ensure alignment with CSR objectives (Flammer et al., 2019). The CSO leads the integration of sustainability into the core business strategy, ensuring that carbon emission reductions are consistent with the company's CSR commitments (Velte, 2023). Based on Upper Echelons Theory (Hambrick & Mason, 1984), the experience and values of the CSO significantly affect organisational outcomes. A well-experienced CSO can leverage their knowledge to implement effective sustainability strategies that reduce carbon emissions while simultaneously fulfilling CSR commitments (Cheng et al., 2014). The CSO's leadership in these areas accentuates the mediation between CSR and carbon emissions, ensuring that CSR strategies are not only socially responsible but also environmentally sustainable.

Therefore, SP is more than just a company's environmental impact; it also signals to stakeholders that the firm is committed to long-term social and environmental goals (Kramer & Porter, 2011). According to Peters et al. (2019), SP can act as a mediator itself by creating synergies between CSR and environmental management efforts, such as carbon emissions reductions. In firms with strong SP, the CSO's role becomes even more critical as they lead the company to enhance both its carbon emissions reduction strategies and CSR initiatives. A study by Toukabri and Jilani (2023) suggests that companies with high SP are more likely to align their CSR strategies with environmental goals, such as reducing carbon emissions. The CSO facilitates this alignment by overseeing the integration of sustainability into the firm's core values and operational decisions. Furthermore, SP strengthens the CSO's ability to mediate the relationship between CSR and carbon emissions by providing a structured framework for environmental reporting and accountability (Sullivan & Mackenzie, 2017). This ensures that CSR actions are supported by measurable and verifiable environmental impact, which enhances the company's reputation and legitimacy (Suchman, 1995). Overall, the CSO plays a vital role in mediating the relationship between CSR and carbon emissions, with SP accentuating this mediation role. SP not only enhances a company's ability to reduce its carbon emissions but also strengthens its CSR initiatives by integrating environmental goals into the company's broader social objectives. The CSO, leveraging their expertise and experience, leads the implementation of sustainability strategies that ensure carbon emissions reductions are aligned with CSR goals, contributing to improved environmental and social performance. The findings from studies by Eccles et al. (2012), Weng and Lin (2014), and Fu et al. (2020) underline the critical role of the CSO in enhancing SP and its impact on CSR and carbon emissions. Based on the above findings, we formulate research hypothesis as follows:

H2. Sustainability performance accentuates the mediation role of a chief sustainability officer on the relationship between corporate social responsibility (CSR) and carbon emissions.

As illustrated in Fig. 14.1, the conceptual framework integrates stakeholder theory, legitimacy theory and upper echelon theory to explain the relationships among CSR, CSOs and carbon emissions.

3. Research Design

3.1 Data and Sample Selection

The study sample consists of sample of Chinese listed companies' data from 2010 to 2024 in the CSI 300 index, which comprises the 300 firms traded on the Shanghai and Shenzhen Stock Exchanges. Firms operating in high-carbon industries are more exposed to climate change risks than others. As a result, they are more likely to disclose carbon-related information early to mitigate

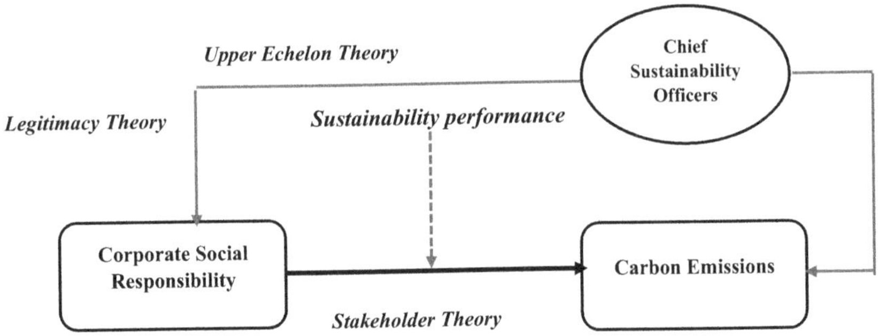

Fig. 14.1. Conceptual Framework. *Source:* Authors' own creation.

compliance costs. Numerous studies suggest that companies in high-carbon industries report more carbon information than those in low-carbon industries. The choice of Chine context is motivated by the reason that CSR in China has shifted from a philanthropy-based approach to a more strategic and regulatory-driven framework, particularly in carbon emission management. This transformation makes China an ideal case for analysing CSR's impact on carbon performance.

The study period extends from the beginning of 2010 to the end of 2024. This choice is justified by the availability of the database and by the choice of study variables. The sample data from the finance industry, which is not considered a high-carbon industry, was also excluded, along with samples that had significant gaps in essential information.[1] Finally, our sample consists of 4290 firm-year observations, providing a robust dataset for analysing the relationship between CSR, CSOs and carbon emissions.

3.2 Variables Measures

3.2.1 Carbon Emission: Dependent Variable

This study focuses on Scope 1 and Scope 2 GHG emissions as key dependent variables. Scope 1 emissions originate directly from a company's own operations or sources under its control, while Scope 2 emissions are associated with the indirect impact of energy purchased and consumed by the company. As defined by the GHG Protocol Standard (2001), GHG emissions are divided into three categories: Scope 1, Scope 2 and Scope 3. In China, publicly listed companies are required to report their Scope 1 and Scope 2 emissions. In contrast, information on Scope 3 emissions remains limited, as its disclosure is not mandatory and relies on voluntary reporting.

[1]Fourteen financial firms were excluded from the sample to ensure comparability, as their regulatory environment and financial reporting practices differ significantly from those of non-financial firms.

CO_2 to assets: GHG emissions measured by tonnes of CO_2 during year *t*/ Total assets at year *t*.

3.2.2 Corporate Social Responsibility: Independent Variable

The independent variable in this research is the CSR score assigned by Thomson Reuters through the ASSET4 database. CSR performance is assessed based on a composite score encompassing three main dimensions ESG as compiled by Thomson Reuters Eikon Asset4 for each firm. Thomson Reuters Eikon Asset4 assigns an annual CSR score to each company on a scale from 0 to 100. This score reflects a comprehensive assessment of the firm's performance across three key areas: ESG, based on publicly available data (Bacha et al., 2021; Zeng, 2021). Since the Kinder, Lydenberg and Domini score does not provide a unified metric that integrates all CSR dimensions, many researchers (Kachouri et al., 2020; Salhi et al., 2020) have opted to use the ESG scores from the Thomson Reuters ASSET4 database. In this study, the models incorporate the three distinct components evaluated by Thomson Reuters: the environmental score, the social score and the corporate governance score. Each of these indicators is rated on a scale from 0 to 100, with higher values indicating stronger CSR performance (Zeng, 2021).

3.2.3 Chief Sustainability Officer: Mediating Variable

We define CSOs as members of the TMT and executives who hold primary responsibility for CSR-related matters within an organisation (Fu et al., 2020; Strand, 2013, 2014). Therefore, companies are increasingly appointing CSOs to oversee the implementation of CSR strategies or to expand the roles of CEOs and CFOs. We acknowledge that this position may be referred to by other titles, such as Chief Ethics Officer, Chief Environmental Officer, Chief Social Officer or Chief CSR Officer, and that their responsibilities can vary in practice. The variable CSO was coded as 1 if there was an executive officer exclusively dedicated to overseeing the firm's SP and as 0 otherwise.

3.2.4 Sustainability Performance: Moderating Variable

In this study, we developed a composite SP index based on the annual environmental, social, and economic scores provided by Thomson Reuters-ASSET 4. SP was assessed across three dimensions – economic, social and environmental – using data from sustainability reports. Companies receive scores ranging from 0 to 100 for their economic, environmental, and social performance, with higher scores reflecting stronger performance. In this study, we consider three dimensions of SP economic, social and environmental, along with an overall SP score derived from these factors. The scores are measured on a scale from 0 to 100, where higher values indicate greater levels of SP (Zeng, 2021).

3.2.5 Control Variables

- *Economic growth:* Dong et al. (2020) explored the relationship between CO_2 emissions, international trade, GDP and the use of both renewable and non-renewable energy sources in China over the period 1980–2014. Employing ARDL and VECM models, their findings suggest that renewable energy consumption and foreign trade play a role in lowering CO_2 emissions, whereas economic growth and reliance on non-renewable energy contribute to higher emission levels. Within this framework, Sheng et al. (2020) investigated how economic growth influences CO_2 emissions across various provinces in China. Their analysis considered both short- and long-term dynamics, showing that in the early and advanced stages of development, economic growth has a positive effect on emissions, while a negative relationship emerges at the intermediate development stage. As noted by Dehdar et al. (2023), economic growth is quantified using real state-level GDP in dollars.
- *Energy consumption:* Muhammad and Long (2021) analysed Belt and Road Initiative (BRI) countries over the 2000–2016 period and demonstrated that energy consumption leads to environmental pollution and increases CO2 emissions across all income groups. Also, Acheampong et al. (2021) found that energy consumption increases carbon dioxide emissions in MENA. Energy consumption by state EC: total energy average energy consumption (Dehdar et al., 2023).
- *Board gender diversity:* Stakeholder theory posits that the presence of women on corporate boards enhances engagement with stakeholders, thereby promoting greater attention to environmental and social matters (Hussain et al., 2018). Similarly, Konadu (2017) argues that female directors tend to be more conscious of environmental challenges, including climate change, and their active involvement can significantly aid in lowering GHG emissions. Board gender diversity (BGD) is quantified by the proportion of women serving on the board of directors.
- *Firm size:* Another control variable is firm size (SIZE), as it is argued that this may influence carbon performance, measured as the natural logarithm of total assets (Haque, 2017).
- *Leverage:* We also incorporate leverage (LEV), which is measured by dividing total debt (including short-term debt, the current portion of long-term debt and long-term debt) by total assets (Luo et al., 2018).

Table 14.1 presents the definitions and measurement approaches for all variables used in this study, including carbon emissions, CSR, SP, CSP and control variables.

3.3 Model Building

We begin our multivariate analysis with the following equation model to estimate CSR and carbon emission (H1a). In other words, we employ the following baseline regression model to analyse the relationship between CSR and carbon emission.

Table 14.1. Variables Measures.

Variables	Symbols	Definition	Authors
Carbon emissions	CO2	CO2 to assets: GHG emissions measured by tons of CO2 during year *t*/Total assets at year *t*.	Dan et al. (2023), Rehman et al. (2023), and Toukabri (2025)
Corporate social responsibility	CSR	The CSR performance is measured by using score across three dimensions (social, environmental and governance).	Zeng (2021), Salhi et al. (2020), and Kachouri et al. (2020)
Chief sustainability performance	CSO	CSO was coded as 1 if there was an executive officer exclusively dedicated to oversee the firm's SP and as 0 otherwise.	Fu et al. (2020) and Strand (2013, 2014)
Sustainability performance	SP	The total score of the SP index has been computed based on environmental, social and economic items.	Zeng (2021)
Economic growth	GDP	GDP is measured by state GDP Real GDP by state dollars.	Chen et al. (2020) Sheng et al. (2020) Dehdar et al. (2023)
Energy consumption	EC	Energy consumption by state EC total energy average energy consumption	Muhammad and Long (2021), Acheampong et al. (2021), and Dehdar et al. (2023)
Energy prices	EAP	Energy prices by state EAP total energy average price by State	Li et al. (2021) and Dehdar et al. (2023)
Board gender diversity	BGD	BGD is measured by percentage of female directors on the board.	Hussain et al. (2018)
Firm size	SIZE	Natural logarithm of total assets	Haque (2017)
Leverage	LEV	Total debt/total assets	Luo et al. (2018)

Source: Table by authors.

$$\begin{aligned}CO2_{it} = {} & \beta_0 + \beta_1 CSR_{it} + \beta_2 GDP_{it} + \beta_3 EC_{it} + \beta_4 BGD_{it} + \beta_5 SIZE_{it} \\ & + \beta_6 LEV_{it} + \text{year fixed effect}_i + \text{industry fixed effect}_i + \epsilon_{it}\end{aligned}$$

(Model 14.1)

where CO2: Carbon emissions; CSR: corporate social responsibility index; GDP: the economic growth; EC: the energy consumption; BGD: board gender diversity; Size: the natural logarithm of total assets; LEV: the ratio of total debt to total assets.

To examine H1b, whether a CSO mediates the relationship between CSR and carbon emission, we adopt the methodology outlined by Baron and Kenny (1986) and Kenny et al. (1998) to test the mediation hypothesis. Specifically, we apply path analysis to analyse the data. Path analysis is selected because it allows for the simultaneous examination of variables and helps identify both direct and indirect effects. Specifically, our primary regression model is as follows:

$$\begin{aligned}CSO_{it} = {} & \beta_0 + \beta_1 CSR_{it} + \beta_2 BGD_{it} + \beta_3 SIZE_{it} + \beta_4 LEV_{it} \\ & + \text{year fixed effect}_i + \text{industry fixed effect}_i + \epsilon_{it}\end{aligned}$$

(Model 14.2)

where CO2: Carbon emissions; CSR: corporate social responsibility index; CSO: chief sustainability officer presence; GDP: the economic growth; EC: the energy consumption; BGD: board gender diversity; Size: the natural logarithm of total assets; LEV: the ratio of total debt to total assets.

$$\begin{aligned}CO2_{it} = {} & \beta_0 + \beta_1 CSR_{it} + \beta_2 CSO_{it} + \beta_3 GDP_{it} + \beta_4 EC_{it} \\ & + \beta_5 BGD_{it} + \beta_6 SIZE_{it} + \beta_7 LEV_{it} + \text{year fixed effect}_i \\ & + \text{industry fixed effect}_i + \epsilon_{it}\end{aligned}$$

(Model 14.3)

The second hypothesis (H2) was examined following the mediated moderation framework proposed by Baron and Kenny (1986), as well as the methodological refinements suggested by Muller et al. (2005). In the first stage, a regression model is estimated where CO2 is the dependent variable, and CSR, SP, and their interaction term (CSR × SP) are included as explanatory variables. Model 4 show that the initial variable (CO2) is correlated with the outcome (CSR*SP) (Model CO2 = CSR*SP). The second stage involves estimating a regression model where the mediating variable (CSO) is explained by CSR, SP, and their interaction term (CSR × SP). Model 5 shows that the variable (CSR*SP) is correlated with the mediator (CSO) (Model CSO = CSR*SP). The final regression model includes CO2 as the dependent variable, with CSR, SP, the interaction term (CSR × SP), and the mediator (CSO) as predictors. Model 6 shows that the mediator affects the outcome variable (Model CO2 = CSR*SP; CSO; CSO*SP). Accordingly, to examine our third hypothesis, we developed the conceptual framework through the following three models:

$$\begin{aligned}CO2_{it} = {} & \beta_0 + \beta_1 CSR_{it} + \beta_2 SP_{it} + \beta_3 CSR * SP_{it} + \beta_4 GDP_{it} \\ & + \beta_5 EC_{it} + \beta_6 BGD_{it} + \beta_7 SIZE_{it} + \beta_8 LEV_{it} \\ & + \text{year fixed effect}_i + \text{industry fixed effect}_i + \epsilon_{it}\end{aligned}$$

(Model 14.4)

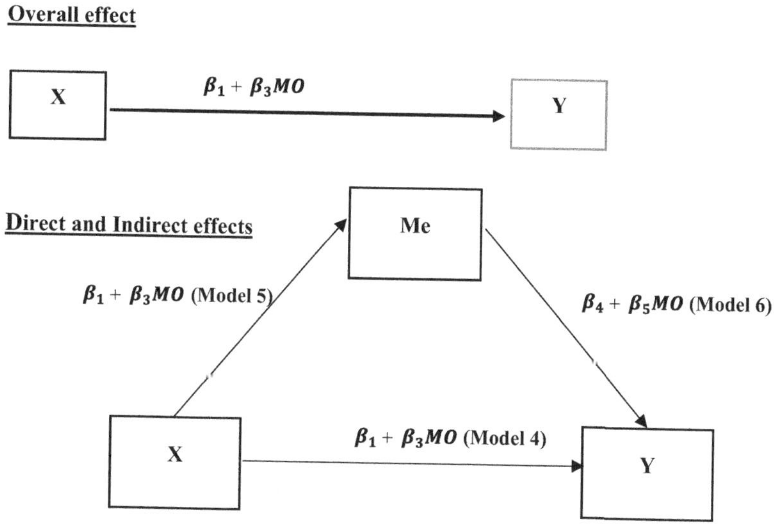

Fig. 14.2. Models Illustrating Mediated Moderation.
Source: Authors' own creation.

$$\begin{aligned} CSO_{it} = {} & \beta_0 + \beta_1 CSR_{it} + \beta_2 SP_{it} + \beta_3 CSR * SP_{it} + \beta_4 BGD_{it} \\ & + \beta_5 SIZE_{it} + \beta_6 LEV_{it} + \text{year fixed effect}_i \\ & + \text{industry fixed effect}_i + \epsilon_{it} \end{aligned}$$

(Model 14.5)

$$\begin{aligned} CO2_{it} = {} & \beta_0 + \beta_1 CSR_{it} + \beta_2 SP_{it} + \beta_3 CSR * SP_{it} + \beta_4 CSO_{it} + \beta_5 CSO * SP_{it} \\ & + \beta_6 GDP_{it} + \beta_7 EC_{it} + \beta_8 BGD_{it} + \beta_9 SIZE_{it} + \beta_{10} LEV_{it} \\ & + \text{year fixed effect}_i + \text{industry fixed effect}_i + \epsilon_{it} \end{aligned}$$

(Model 14.6)

With: (X: CSR; Y: CO2; Me: CSO; MO:SP).where CO2: Carbon emissions; CSR: corporate social responsibility index; CSO: chief sustainability officer presence; SP: sustainability performance index; GDP: the economic growth; EC: the energy consumption; BGD: board gender diversity; Size: the natural logarithm of total assets; LEV; the ratio of total debt to total assets.

4. Results

4.1 Descriptive Statistics

The descriptive statistics for our key variables are presented in Table 14.2. Table 14.2 presents the descriptive statistics for our key variables. In the Chinese context, the mean CSR index is 73.95, with a minimum of 57.26 and a maximum of 84.96. This range suggests a moderate variation in CSR practices across firms, potentially influenced by factors such as industry type, firm size, regulatory pressures or corporate governance structures. The average GHG emissions

Table 14.2. Summary Statistics of the Sample.

Variables	Mean	Min	Median	Max	SD
CO2	0.55	0.42	0.53	0.64	0.48
CSR	73.95	57.26	74.32	84.96	5.29
SP	56.21	38.98	58.66	71.54	6.24
CSO	0.65	0	0.64	1	0.63
BGD	25.16	7.23	28.17	65.42	8.21
GDP	6.35	2.20	6.98	9.67	2.65
EC	0.59	−1.86	0.48	0.75	1.38
SIZE	22.13	19.80	21.95	26.09	1.26
LEV	0.41	0.05	0.39	0.92	0.20

Source: Table by authors.

Notes: CO2: carbon emissions measured by tons of CO2 during year *t*/Total assets at year *t*; CSR: corporate social responsibility index; SP: The total score of the SP index; CSO: chief sustainability officer presence; BGD: board gender diversity: the percentage of female directors on the board; GDP: Economics growth; EC: Energy consumption; SIZE: is the natural logarithm of total assets; LEV: is the ratio total debt to total assets.

intensity, measured as the sum of Scope 1 and Scope 2 emissions divided by total assets, is 0.55. This means that, on average, firms in the sample emit 0.55 tonnes of CO_2 per unit of total **assets**. This measure provides insight into the carbon efficiency of firms, indicating how much CO_2 is emitted relative to their asset base. A lower value suggests that a company is more carbon-efficient, while a higher value may indicate higher emissions intensity. Variations in this ratio could be influenced by industry type, energy sources, production processes and firms' sustainability initiatives.

The presence of CSO in the board of directors is 0.65, sustainable performance is 56.21, which indicates that more than half of the companies in our sample use the sustainable performance strategy for better disclosure of information on climate change. The average firm size (SIZE) is 22.13, which suggests that our sample is characterised by large firms, with a financial leverage (LEV) of 41%. The average percentage of women on the board (BGD) is 25.16. The GDP (Mean: 6.35, SD: 2.65) reflects the economic growth rate during the study period, consistent with China's steady but slightly decelerating economic expansion. The wide range −1.86 to 0.75 indicates fluctuations in energy efficiency across firms, possibly linked to differences in industry type and energy policies.

Table 14.3 presents the Spearman and Pearson correlation coefficients for the variables in our study. The results indicate a negative relationship between the variable measuring carbon emissions (CO2) and CSR indicators. Additionally, CSO and SP exhibit negative correlations with both CO2 and CSR. Overall, these findings align with our three hypotheses. Notably, the correlation coefficients among the explanatory variables remain relatively low, suggesting that multicollinearity is not a major concern.

Table 14.3. Correlation Analysis.

	CO2	CSR	SP	CSO	BGD	GDP	EC	LEV	SIZE	VIF
CO2	1.000									1.25
CSR	−0.352***	1.000								1.86
SP	−0.137***	0.155**	1.000							1.33
CSO	−0.166**	0.245***	0.453***	1.000						1.54
BGD	−0.412**	0.162**	0.324**	0.145**	1.000					1.87
GDP	0.651**	0.210**	0.159*	0.155	0.122**	1.000				1.69
EC	−0.147	0.158*	0.781*	0.162**	0.148***	0.136**	1.000			1.55
LEV	0.155**	0.125**	0.133*	0.210**	0.189	0.252*	0.168**	1.000		1.66
SIZE	0.254**	0.321**	0.142**	0.158*	0.141	0.148	0.241*	0.251**	1.000	1.85

Source: Table by authors.

Notes: CO2: carbon emissions measured by tons of CO2 during year *t*/Total assets at year *t*; CSR: corporate social responsibility index; SP: The total score of the SP index; CSO: chief sustainability officer presence; BGD: board gender diversity: the percentage of female directors on the board; GDP: Economics growth; EC: Energy consumption; SIZE: is the natural logarithm of total assets; LEV: is the ratio total debt to total assets; *, ** and *** indicate significance at the 0.10, 0.05 and 0.01 levels, respectively.

4.2 Effect of CSR on Carbon Emissions

The results of our ordinal regression analysis for CSR in carbon emissions are presented in Table 14.4. As Table 14.4 shows, Model (1) includes only the main explanatory variable of CSR, Model (2) includes the CSO measured by presence in firms (CSO), while Model (3) tests the direct and indirect effect of CSR on carbon emissions through CSO and Models (4, 5, 6) test the moderating effect of SP on the mediation relationship.

Our findings reveal that a 1% reduction in carbon emissions leads to an increase of at least 3 points in CSR, allowing companies to improve their classification within the CSR. These results support H1.a, which suggests that enhancements in CSR correspond to negative changes in carbon emissions. Furthermore, the statistical coefficients indicate that carbon emissions are significantly affected by variations in total CSR ($\beta 2 = -0.125$; $Z = 3.05$), confirming H1.a. Recent studies have explored the relationship between CSR and carbon emissions within the Chinese context, providing insights into our findings of a negative correlation between these variables. A study published in 2023 analysed data from Chinese listed companies between 2011 and 2019 and found that CSR initiatives can effectively reduce corporate carbon intensity. Chen (2023) suggests that CSR activities alleviate financing constraints, enabling companies to invest more in carbon reduction technologies and practices. Another study (Zhang et al., 2022) examined data from 30 Chinese provinces between 2010 and 2016 and identified a significant negative correlation between CSR and carbon emission intensity. Contrarily, Li et al. (2021) analysed CSR disclosures and their impact on regional carbon emissions in China. The results indicated that, at that time, CSR practices did not have a clear impact on carbon emission reduction, suggesting that CSR development was in its early stages and internal incentives for firms to adopt CSR projects were low. In this context, firms with stronger CSR tend to have a better reputation, which facilitates the attainment of environmental legitimacy and further strengthens their commitment to environmental management (Liu et al., 2025). This result is consistent with the theoretical foundations of legitimacy theory and stakeholder theory, both of which highlight the importance of firms responding to external pressures and stakeholders' expectations regarding environmental performance. From a legitimacy theory perspective, companies aiming to enhance their SP may actively work to reduce their carbon footprint in order to align with societal demands for greater environmental responsibility.

For control variables, BGD exhibits a marginally significant effect, with a coefficient of -0.147 and a Z of -3.66. While this suggests that gender diversity on the board may negatively impact carbon emissions, the result reaches the conventional 1% significance threshold. Fan et al. (2023) found that firms with female outside directors are more likely to have lower carbon emissions. The results also indicate that economic growth (GDP) has a statistically significant negative impact on CO_2 emissions, consistent with the findings of Baek and Pride (2014), Dogan and Aslan (2017), and Mirziyoyeva and Salahodjaev (2022). In contrast, energy consumption has a positive and significant effect on carbon emissions. This finding is in line with the results reported by Sharif et al. (2019), Chontanawat (2020) and Salari et al. (2021). The significant impact of energy consumption on CO_2 emissions is mainly due to the heavy dependence on non-renewable energy sources within China's energy sector. The estimated coefficient for SIZE shows a significant negative association with carbon emissions, aligning with previous research (e.g., Luo & Tang, 2020; Moussa et al., 2020). This suggests that firms actively reduce carbon emissions and enhance their corporate green image by prioritising carbon-related initiatives (Ganda, 2018). However, leverage (LEV) exhibits a positive and significant association with carbon emissions, suggesting that highly leveraged firms tend to have higher carbon footprints.

4.3 The Mediation Effect of a CSO on the Relationship Between CSR and Carbon Emissions

To evaluate the mediating effect, Sobel (1982) proposed a method for testing the statistical significance of the indirect impact of the mediator variable. This

Table 14.4. Results of Regression Analysis for Mediated Analysis.

	CO2 Model 1	**CSO Model 2**	**CO2 Model 3**
Constant	0.314(11.21)***	0.411(5.12)***	0.511(3.20)***
CSR	−0.125(−3.05)**	0.246(6.22)***	−0.128
CSO	-	-	−0.158(−9.12)***
GDP	−0.259(−3.12)***	-	−0.254(−6.65)***
EC	0.223(2.65)***	-	0.123(9.62)***
BGD	−0.147(-3.66)***	0.221(2.06)**	−0.037(−2.59)***
SIZE	−0.312 (−2.69)**	0.188(8.12)***	0.145
LEV	0.145(3.51)***	0.241(4.12)***	0.528(−2.02)**
Industry fixed effects	Yes	Yes	Yes
Year fixed effects	Yes	Yes	Yes
R^2	0.512	0.483	0.651
N-obs	4290	4290	4290

Source: Table by authors.

Notes: CO2: carbon emissions measured by tons of CO2 during year *t*/Total assets at year *t*; CSR: corporate social responsibility index; CSO: chief sustainability officer presence; BGD: board gender diversity: the percentage of female directors on the board; GDP: Economics growth; EC: Energy consumption; SIZE: the natural logarithm of total assets; LEV: the ratio total debt to total assets; *, ** and *** indicate significance at the 0.10, 0.05 and 0.01 levels, respectively.

method tests the null hypothesis, which posits that the mediating variable has no indirect influence on the relationship between the independent and dependent variables.

Table 14.4 displays the results from the estimation of Eq. (14.2) used to test hypothesis H2a. According to the table, CSR has a positive and significant effect on the presence of a CSO (β = 0.246, Z = 6.22). This finding suggests that firms with a CSO are more likely to demonstrate greater engagement in CSR activities. The positive and significant coefficient indicates that firms actively engaged in CSR are more likely to appoint a CSO to oversee sustainability initiatives. This finding is consistent with Ioannou and Serafeim (2019), who highlight that firms with strong CSR commitments tend to establish dedicated leadership roles to integrate sustainability into corporate strategy. According to Eccles et al. (2014), firms face external pressures from investors, policymakers and consumers to strengthen sustainability governance, which explains why CSR engagement correlates with CSO appointments. In this context, Fu et al. (2020) found that companies with CSOs demonstrate higher environmental performance and stronger sustainability disclosures, reinforcing the idea that CSR-oriented firms institutionalise sustainability governance.

For model 3, we test the relationship between CSR and CO2 by adding the mediator variable, namely, CSO. Step 3 in testing for the mediating effect needs to evaluate the original direct effect (c) and indirect effect (c'), as illustrated in Fig. 14.2. When the CSO is incorporated into the full model, the coefficient of CSR becomes insignificant in Model 3, while the CSO coefficient is significant at the 1% level (Z = 9.12). CSO, as a strategic motive, acts to negate the impact of CSR on the corporate carbon emissions (CO2). These results collectively indicate that CSO fully mediates the relation between CSR and CO_2. These findings can be explicated by recent studies. Companies with significant carbon emissions may face increased stakeholder pressure (e.g., customers, investors, regulators) to reduce their environmental footprint. This pressure often leads companies to engage in more CSR activities to maintain legitimacy and meet expectations (Suchman, 1995). However, without a dedicated executive role like the CSO, such efforts may be fragmented or insufficient. The CSO mediates this by orchestrating the firm's strategic response, ensuring that carbon reduction initiatives are framed within the larger context of CSR objectives. In addition, the CSO develops and implements a corporate strategy for carbon emission reductions that aligns with the company's CSR goals. The CSO ensures that carbon disclosure and emission reductions are part of the company's CSR reporting, making these actions a visible part of the company's social responsibility efforts (Miller & Serafeim, 2014). The CSO helps the company navigate internal and external pressures related to carbon emissions, creating synergy between environmental management and CSR goals. Through their expertise, the CSO encourages the company to adopt more sustainable practices, ensuring that CSR and carbon emissions reduction are not siloed initiatives but rather mutually reinforcing (Fu et al., 2020).

4.4 The Mediated Moderation Effect of SP

Table 14.5 displays the regression models estimating Eqs. (14.4) to (14.6) using these variables. The table shows the unstandardised coefficients (b) along with their corresponding *t* statistics. These equations include product terms to capture the interaction effects (CSR*SP; CSO*SP). The results from Eq. (14.4) find evidence for the predicted interaction between CSR and SP on the outcome variable, CO2. As predicted, CSR firms are associated with a lower probability of carbon emissions, and this difference increases as sustainability s' strategies are more developed in Chinese firms. The treatment variable's (CSR) effect on the outcome (CO2) is moderated by SP. This negative relationship ($\beta = -0.123$; $Z = -5.66$) is strengthened when firms implement strong sustainability strategies, suggesting that CSR alone is not enough; its effectiveness depends on how well sustainability practices are integrated. These findings are consistent with Huang and Watson (2015) and Luo and Tang (2020), who argue that CSR initiatives are most effective in reducing emissions when firms actively develop and integrate sustainability-driven policies.

The results from Eq. (14.5) show an effect of the CSR on the mediator, that is, expectations about the CSO. This effect is moderated by CSR*SP interaction (the CSR*SP coefficient is significant $\beta = 0.145$; $Z = 7.88$). In fact, Eq. (14.5) reveals that CSR positively influences the expectations placed on CSOs, meaning firms engaged in CSR are more likely to appoint and empower sustainability officers to oversee environmental strategies. The significant interaction term (CSR*SP) suggests that the effectiveness of the CSO in driving sustainability goals is stronger in firms with higher SP. Fu et al. (2020) argue that CSOs play a pivotal role in translating CSR policies into measurable carbon reduction outcomes, particularly when sustainability strategies are embedded within corporate governance.

Consistent with this, Eq. (14.6) also reveals that the residual direct effect of the CSR on the CO2 is more accentuated by SP once the mediator (CSO) and its interaction with SP are controlled. Indeed, the coefficient associated with the CSR * SP interaction has been increased from ($Z = -2.66$) (in Eq. 14.4) to ($Z = -5.66$) (in Eq. 14.6). The increase in the coefficient of CSR * SP interaction suggests that the effect of CSR on CO_2 reduction is more pronounced when sustainability strategies are well-developed. This finding aligns with Cheng et al. (2014) and Luo and Tang (2020), who argue that firms with high sustainability commitments tend to have a stronger and more direct impact on carbon reduction efforts. Once CSO and its interaction with SP are controlled for in Eq. (14.6), the direct effect of CSR on CO_2 reduction becomes more pronounced. This suggests that while CSOs play a role in mediating CSR's impact, the broader sustainability strategy of the firm is the dominant force driving carbon reductions. Eccles et al. (2014) and Fu et al. (2020) support this by showing that CSOs are more effective in reducing emissions when firms already have strong sustainability practices in place. This finding aligns with upper echelons theory (Hambrick & Mason, 1984). In fact, according to upper echelons theory, a firm's

Table 14.5. Results of Regression Analysis for Mediated Moderation Analysis.

	CO2 Model 4	CSO Model 5	CO2 Model 6
Constant	0.158(9.12)***	0.233(9.62)***	0.354(11.96)***
CSR	−0.214(−9.17)***	0.243(6.03)***	−0.147(−1.06)**
SP	−0.147(−7.05)***	0.137(2.59)***	−0.188(−8.12)***
CSR*SP	−0.123(−2.66)**	0.145(7.88)***	−0.241(−5.66)***
CSO	-	-	−0.155(−6.33)***
CSO*SP	-	-	−0.151(−7.12)***
Industry fixed effect	Yes	Yes	Yes
Year fixed effect	Yes	Yes	Yes
R^2	0.5236	0.4563	0.5893
N-obs	4290	4290	4290

Source: Table by author.

Notes: CO2: carbon emissions measured by tons of CO2 during year *t*/Total assets at year *t*; CSR: corporate social responsibility index; SP: The total score of the SP index; CSO: chief sustainability officer presence; BGD: board gender diversity: the percentage of female directors on the board; GDP: Economics growth; EC: Energy consumption; SIZE: the natural logarithm of total assets; LEV: the ratio total debt to total assets; *, ** and *** indicate significance at the 0.10, 0.05 and 0.01 levels, respectively.

strategic decisions and performance outcomes are shaped by the characteristics, experiences, and expertise of its top executives.

5. Robustness Test

To ensure the validity and reliability of our findings on the relationship between CSR, the CSO, SP and carbon emissions (CO_2), we can conduct the following robustness tests. There is a potential endogeneity issue in our study because firms with lower carbon emissions may be more likely to engage in CSR initiatives rather than CSR directly causing lower emissions. To address this, we will use the instrumental variable (IV) approach. Specifically, we use lagged CSR scores (CSR at t-1) and industry-average CSR levels as instruments, following prior studies such as Luo and Tang (2020) and Cheng et al. (2014). The first-stage regression confirms the relevance of our instruments, as indicated by a high *F*-statistic (>10), ensuring strong predictive power. In the second stage, we replace the actual CSR variable with its predicted values from the first stage and re-estimate the main regression. The results remain consistent with our primary findings, indicating that firms with stronger CSR commitments are associated with lower carbon emissions, even after controlling for endogeneity. According

Table 14.6. Results of Robustness Test.

Variable	Coefficient	Std. Error	*t*-Statistic	*p*-Value
CSR	−0.215	0.072	−2.99	0.003
CSO	0.187	0.060	3.12	0.002
SP	−0.142	0.050	−2.84	0.005
CSR*SP	0.098	0.034	2.88	0.004
CSO*SP	−0.120	0.037	−3.24	0.001
Test	**Statistic**	***p*-Value**		
Hansen J-test (Overidentification)	8.45	0.322		
AR(1) test (First-order autocorrelation)	−2.14	0.032		
AR(2) test (Second-order autocorrelation)	−1.37	0.171		

to Table 14.6, the Hansen J-test confirms that our instruments satisfy the exogeneity condition, reinforcing the validity of our approach. These findings suggest that the observed relationship between CSR and carbon emissions is not merely correlational but likely reflects a causal impact.

6. Conclusion

This study examines the mediated moderation framework, where SP influences the relationship between CSR, the CSO and carbon emissions. The results suggest that firms engaged in higher CSR activities are more likely to appoint a CSO, reflecting a strategic shift towards institutionalising sustainability leadership. This supports the argument that CSR is not just a symbolic practice but a driver of organisational change, reinforcing sustainability governance and corporate environmental responsibility. The results confirm that CSR-driven firms reduce carbon emissions more effectively when SP is high, reinforcing the strategic importance of SP as a moderator. Our research contributes to several theoretical, managerial and policy implications. From a theoretical perspective, our findings contribute to the upper echelons theory by highlighting the role of CSOs as strategic assets in translating CSR initiatives into measurable environmental outcomes. In terms of managerial implications, this study emphasises the strategic importance of appointing a CSO and fostering a corporate culture centred on sustainability. Companies should not only engage in CSR initiatives but also ensure that sustainability governance structures, such as CSO expertise and sustainability committees, are in place to enhance the effectiveness of environmental policies. Among the key policy implications of this study, we recommend that future climate change disclosure policies actively involve the TMT members, particularly the CSO. Integrating TMT members into the design and execution of sustainable development strategies focused on managing climate risks enhances their expertise in carbon accounting. This, in turn, strengthens the firm's capacity to effectively monitor, report and reduce carbon emissions, ensuring the achievement of long-term sustainability goals.

Future research should explore additional factors influencing carbon performance across different countries, particularly considering how institutional and cultural contexts shape variations in carbon emissions. Future studies could also examine the impact of diverse climate change disclosure regulations, assessing how different regulatory frameworks influence mandatory climate disclosure practices and corporate environmental transparency.

References

Acheampong, A. O., Dzator, J., & Savage, D. A. (2021). The role of economic institutions in electricity consumption, economic growth, and CO2 emissions linkages: Evidence from sub-Saharan Africa. In *Environmental sustainability and economy* (pp. 61–83). Elsevier.

Anderson, L. M., & Bateman, T. S. (2000). Individual environmental initiative: Championing natural environmental issues in US business organizations. *Academy of Management Journal*, *43*(4), 548–570.

Angwin, D., Paroutis, S., & Mitson, S. (2009). Connecting up strategy: Are senior strategy directors a missing link? *California Management Review*, *51*(3), 74–94.

Bacha, S., Ajina, A., & Ben Saad, S. (2021). CSR performance and the cost of debt: Does audit quality matter? *Corporate Governance: International Journal of Business in Society*, *21*(1), 137–158.

Baek, J., & Pride, D. (2014). On the income–nuclear energy–CO2 emissions nexus revisited. *Energy Economics*, *43*, 6–10.

Baron, R. M., & Kenny, D. A. (1986). The moderator–mediator variable distinction in social psychological research: Conceptual, strategic, and statistical considerations. *Journal of Personality and Social Psychology*, *51*(6), 1173.

Battilana, J. (2006). Agency and institutions: The enabling role of individuals' social position. *Organization*, *13*(5), 653–676.

Bebbington, J., & Larrinaga, C. (2014). Accounting and sustainable development: An exploration. *Accounting, Organizations and Society*, *39*(6), 395–413.

Breene, R. T. S., Nunes, P. F., & Shill, W. E. (2007). The chief strategy officer. *Harvard Business Review*, *85*(10), 84.

Chen, P. (2023). Corporate social responsibility, financing constraints, and corporate carbon intensity: New evidence from listed Chinese companies. *Environmental Science and Pollution Research*, *30*(14), 40107–40115.

Chen, X., Cheng, Q., Hao, Y., & Liu, Q. (2020). GDP growth incentives and earnings management: Evidence from China. *Review of Accounting Studies*, *25*(3), 1002.

Cheng, B., Ioannou, I., & Serafeim, G. (2014). Corporate social responsibility and access to finance. *Strategic Management Journal*, *35*(1), 1–23.

Choi, B. B., Lee, D., & Psaros, J. (2013). An analysis of Australian company carbon emission disclosures. *Pacific Accounting Review*, *25*(1), 58–79.

Chontanawat, J. (2020). Relationship between energy consumption, CO2 emission and economic growth in ASEAN: Cointegration and causality model. *Energy Reports*, *6*, 660–665.

Clark, G. L., Feiner, A., & Viehs, M. (2015). From the stockholder to the stakeholder: How sustainability can drive financial outperformance. https://ssrn.com/abstract=2508281

Clarkson, P. M., Overell, M. B., & Chapple, L. (2011). Environmental reporting and its relation to corporate environmental performance. *Abacus*, *47*(1), 27–60.

Dan, E., Shen, J., Zheng, X., Liu, P., Zhang, L., & Chen, F. (2023). Asset structure, asset utilization efficiency, and carbon emission performance: Evidence from panel data of China's low-carbon industry. *Sustainability*, *15*(7), 6264.

Deegan, C. (2002). Introduction: The legitimising effect of social and environmental disclosures – A theoretical foundation. *Accounting, Auditing & Accountability Journal*, *15*(3), 282–311.

Dehdar, F., Fuinhas, J. A., Karimi Alavijeh, N., Nazeer, N., & Zangoei, S. (2023). Investigating the determinants of carbon emissions in the USA: A state-level analysis. *Environmental Science and Pollution Research*, *30*(9), 23023–23034.

Dogan, E., & Aslan, A. (2017). Exploring the relationship among CO2 emissions, real GDP, energy consumption and tourism in the EU and candidate countries: Evidence from panel models robust to heterogeneity and cross-sectional dependence. *Renewable and Sustainable Energy Reviews*, *77*, 239–245.

Dong, B., Ma, X., Zhang, Z., Zhang, H., Chen, R., Song, Y., Shen, M., & Xiang, R. (2020). Carbon emissions, the industrial structure and economic growth: Evidence from heterogeneous industries in China. *Environmental Pollution*, *262*, 114322.

Eccles, R. G., Ioannou, I., & Serafeim, G. (2012). *The impact of a corporate culture of sustainability on corporate behavior and performance*. (Vol. 17950, No. 1, pp. 2835–2857). National Bureau of Economic Research.

Eccles, R. G., Ioannou, I., & Serafeim, G. (2014). The impact of corporate sustainability on organizational processes and performance. *Management Science*, *60*(11), 2835–2857.

Egri, C. P., & Herman, S. (2000). Leadership in the North American environmental sector: Values, leadership styles, and contexts of environmental leaders and their organizations. *Academy of Management Journal*, *43*(4), 571–604.

Fan, P., Qian, X., & Wang, J. (2023). Does gender diversity matter? Female directors and firm carbon emissions in Japan. *Pacific-Basin Finance Journal*, *77*, 101931.

Flammer, C., Hong, B., & Minor, D. (2019). Corporate governance and the rise of integrating corporate social responsibility criteria in executive compensation: Effectiveness and implications for firm outcomes. *Strategic Management Journal*, *40*(7), 1097–1122.

Freedman, M., & Jaggi, B. (2011). Global warming disclosures: Impact of Kyoto protocol across countries. *Journal of International Financial Management & Accounting*, *22*(1), 46–90.

Freeman, R. E. (1984). *Strategic management: A stakeholder approach*. Pitman.

Fu, R., Tang, Y., & Chen, G. (2020). Chief sustainability officers and corporate social (IR) responsibility. *Strategic Management Journal*, *41*(4), 656–680.

Ganda, F. (2018). The effect of carbon performance on corporate financial performance in a growing economy. *Social Responsibility Journal*, *14*(4), 895–916.

García-Sánchez, I. M., Hussain, N., Khan, S. A., & Martínez-Ferrero, J. (2022). Assurance of corporate social responsibility reports: Examining the role of internal and external corporate governance mechanisms. *Corporate Social Responsibility and Environmental Management*, *29*(1), 89–106.

Garud, R., & Karnøe, P. (2001). Path creation as a process of mindful deviation. *Path Dependence and Creation*, *138*, 1–44.

Haque, F. (2017). The effects of board characteristics and sustainable compensation policy on carbon performance of UK firms. *The British Accounting Review*, *49*(3), 347–364.

Hrasky, S. (2012, September). Visual disclosure strategies adopted by more and less sustainability-driven companies. In *Accounting forum* (Vol. 36, No. 3, pp. 154–165). Elsevier.

Huang, X. B., & Watson, L. (2015). Corporate social responsibility research in accounting. *Journal of Accounting Literature*, *34*(1), 1–16.

Hummel, K., & Schlick, C. (2016). The relationship between sustainability performance and sustainability disclosure – Reconciling voluntary disclosure theory and legitimacy theory. *Journal of Accounting and Public Policy*, *35*(5), 455–476.

Hussain, N., Rigoni, U., & Orij, R. P. (2018). Corporate governance and sustainability performance: Analysis of triple bottom line performance. *Journal of Business Ethics*, *149*, 411–432.

Ioannou, I., & Serafeim, G. (2019). Corporate sustainability: A strategy? *Harvard Business School Accounting & Management Unit Working Paper*, 19–065.

Jain, M., & Kaur, S. (2022). Carbon emissions, inequalities and economic freedom: An empirical investigation in selected South Asian economies. *International Journal of Social Economics*, *49*(6), 882–913.

Kachouri, M., Salhi, B., & Jarboui, A. (2020). The impact of gender diversity on the relationship between managerial entrenchment and corporate social responsibility: Evidence from UK companies. *Journal of Global Responsibility*, *11*(3), 197–217.

Kanashiro, P., & Rivera, J. (2019). Do chief sustainability officers make companies greener? The moderating role of regulatory pressures. *Journal of Business Ethics*, *155*, 687–701.

Kenny, D. A., Kashy, D., & Bolger, N. (1998). Data analysis in social psychology. In D. Gilbert, S. T. Fiske, & G. Lindzey (Eds.), *Handbook of social psychology* (4th ed., Vol. 1, pp. 233–265). McGraw-Hill.

Kim, H. S., Kim, M., & Koo, D. (2022). From teamwork to psychological well-being and job performance: The role of CSR in the workplace. *International Journal of Contemporary Hospitality Management*, *34*(10), 3764–3789.

Kolk, A. (2008). Sustainability, accountability and corporate governance: Exploring multinationals' reporting practices. *Business Strategy and the Environment*, *17*(1), 1–15.

Konadu, R. (2017). Gender diversity impact on corporate social responsibility (CSR) and greenhouse gas emissions in the UK. *Economics and Business Review*, *3*(1), 127–148.

Kramer, M. R., & Porter, M. (2011). *Creating shared value* (Vol. 17, pp. 114–134). Boston, MA: FSG.

Lee, S. Y., & Klassen, R. D. (2016). Firms' response to climate change: The interplay of business uncertainty and organizational capabilities. *Business Strategy and the Environment*, *25*(8), 577–592.

Li, S., Cheng, W., Li, J., & Shen, H. (2021). Corporate social responsibility development and climate change: Regional evidence of China. *Sustainability*, *13*(21), 11859.

Li, T., Meng, X., Jia, F., Chen, L., & Wang, L. (2023). Do carbon neutrality initiatives affect the shareholder value of firms? Evidence from China. *Journal of Cleaner Production*, *418*, 138115.

Liu, D., Xiong, Y., Wang, L., & Yao, S. (2025). Corporate carbon risk and green M&As. *Research in International Business and Finance*, *75*, 102714.

Liu, Y., Jia, X., Jia, X., & Koufteros, X. (2021). CSR orientation incongruence and supply chain relationship performance—A network perspective. *Journal of Operations Management*, *67*(2), 237–260.

Luo, L., & Tang, Q. (2014). Does voluntary carbon disclosure reflect underlying carbon performance? *Journal of Contemporary Accounting and Economics*, *10*(3), 191–205.

Luo, L., & Tang, Q. (2020). Corporate governance and carbon performance: Role of carbon strategy and awareness of climate risk. *Accounting and Finance*, *61*(2), 2891–2934.

Luo, L., Tang, Q., & Peng, J. (2018). The direct and moderating effects of power distance on carbon transparency: An international investigation of cultural value and corporate social responsibility. *Business Strategy and the Environment*, *27*(8), 1546–1557.

Luo, X. R., Wang, D., & Zhang, J. (2017). Whose call to answer: Institutional complexity and firms' CSR reporting. *Academy of Management Journal*, *60*(1), 321–344.

Mazutis, D. D. (2013). The CEO effect: A longitudinal, multilevel analysis of the relationship between executive orientation and corporate social strategy. *Business & Society*, *52*(4), 631–648.

Menz, K. M. (2010). Corporate social responsibility: Is it rewarded by the corporate bond market? A critical note. *Journal of Business Ethics*, *96*(1), 117–134.

Menz, M., & Scheef, C. (2014). Chief strategy officers: Contingency analysis of their presence in top management teams. *Strategic Management Journal*, *35*(3), 461–471.

Miller, K., & Serafeim, G. (2014). *Chief sustainability officers: Who are they and what do they do?* Harvard Business School working paper series# 15-011. https://ssrn.com/abstract=2411976

Mirziyoyeva, Z., & Salahodjaev, R. (2022). Renewable energy and CO2 emissions intensity in the top carbon intense countries. *Renewable Energy*, *192*, 507–512.

Moussa, T., Allam, A., Elbanna, S., & Bani-Mustafa, A. (2020). Can board environmental orientation improve US firms' carbon performance? The mediating role of carbon strategy. *Business Strategy and the Environment*, *29*(1), 72–86.

Muhammad, S., & Long, X. (2021). Rule of law and CO2 emissions: A comparative analysis across 65 belt and road initiative (BRI) countries. *Journal of Cleaner Production*, *279*, 123539.

Muller, D., Judd, C. M., & Yzerbyt, V. Y. (2005). When moderation is mediated and mediation is moderated. *Journal of Personality and Social Psychology*, *89*(6), 852.

Nath, P., & Mahajan, V. (2008). Chief marketing officers: A study of their presence in firms' top management teams. *Journal of Marketing*, *72*(1), 65–81.

Patten, D. M. (2002). The relation between environmental performance and environmental disclosure: A research note. *Accounting, Organizations and Society*, *27*(8), 763–773.

Patten, D. M. (2020). Seeking legitimacy. *Sustainability Accounting, Management and Policy Journal*, *11*(6), 1009–1021.

Peters, G. F., & Romi, A. M. (2015). The association between sustainability governance characteristics and the assurance of corporate sustainability reports. *Auditing: A Journal of Practice & Theory*, *34*(1), 163–198.

Peters, G. F., Romi, A. M., & Sanchez, J. M. (2019). The influence of corporate sustainability officers on performance. *Journal of Business Ethics*, *159*, 1065–1087.

Rehman, A., Gonenc, H., & Hermes, N. (2023). Carbon disclosure policy, external financing needs and the cost of capital: Does financial market quality matter? *Business Strategy and the Environment*, *32*(8), 5854–5872.

Salari, M., Javid, R. J., & Noghanibehambari, H. (2021). The nexus between CO2 emissions, energy consumption, and economic growth in the US. *Economic Analysis and Policy*, *69*, 182–194.

Salhi, B., Riguen, R., Kachouri, M., & Jarboui, A. (2020). The mediating role of corporate social responsibility on the relationship between governance and tax avoidance: UK common law versus French civil law. *Social Responsibility Journal*, *16*(8), 1149–1168.

Schaltegger, S., & Csutora, M. (2012). Carbon accounting for sustainability and management. Status quo and challenges. *Journal of Cleaner Production*, *36*, 1–16.

Serafeim, G., & Grewal, J. (2017). The value relevance of corporate sustainability disclosures: An analysis of a dataset from one large asset owner. https://ssrn.com/abstract=2966767

Sharif, A., Raza, S. A., Ozturk, I., & Afshan, S. (2019). The dynamic relationship of renewable and nonrenewable energy consumption with carbon emission: A global study with the application of heterogeneous panel estimations. *Renewable Energy*, *133*, 685–691.

Sheng, P., Li, J., Zhai, M., & Huang, S. (2020). Coupling of economic growth and reduction in carbon emissions at the efficiency level: Evidence from China. *Energy*, *213*, 118747.

Sobel, M. E. (1982). Asymptotic confidence intervals for indirect effects in structural equation models. *Sociological Methodology*, *13*, 290–312.

Strand, R. (2013). The chief officer of corporate social responsibility: A study of its presence in top management teams. *Journal of Business Ethics*, *112*, 721–734.

Strand, R. (2014). Strategic leadership of corporate sustainability. *Journal of Business Ethics*, *123*, 687–706.

Suchman, M. C. (1995). Managing legitimacy: Strategic and institutional approaches. *Academy of Management Review*, *20*(3), 571–610.

Sullivan, R., & Mackenzie, C. (2017). The practice of responsible investment. In *Responsible investment* (pp. 332–346). Routledge.

Toukabri, M. (2025). Chief Sustainability Officer (CSO) power and sustainability-based compensation for climate change disclosure and carbon performance: Is it different for developed and developing nations? *Society and Business Review*, *20*(1), 52–102.

Toukabri, M., & Jilani, F. (2023). The power of critical mass to make a difference: How gender diversity in board affect US corporate carbon performance. *Society and Business Review*, *18*(4), 592–617.

Velte, P. (2023). Chief sustainability officer expertise, sustainability-related executive compensation and corporate biodiversity disclosure: Empirical evidence for the European capital market. *Journal of Global Responsibility*, *14*(2), 241–253.

Velte, P., & Stawinoga, M. (2020). Do chief sustainability officers and CSR committees influence CSR-related outcomes? A structured literature review based on empirical-quantitative research findings. *Journal of Management Control*, *31*(4), 333–377.

Wang, Q., Li, L., & Li, R. (2023). Uncovering the impact of income inequality and population aging on carbon emission efficiency: An empirical analysis of 139 countries. *Science of the Total Environment*, *857*, 159508.

Wang, W., & Zhang, Y. J. (2022). Does China's carbon emissions trading scheme affect the market power of high-carbon enterprises? *Energy Economics*, *108*, 105906.

Weng, D. H., & Lin, Z. (2014). Beyond CEO tenure: The effect of CEO newness on strategic changes. *Journal of Management*, *40*(7), 2009–2032.

Wiengarten, F., Lo, C. K., & Lam, J. Y. (2017). How does sustainability leadership affect firm performance? The choices associated with appointing a chief officer of corporate social responsibility. *Journal of Business Ethics*, *140*(3), 477–493.

World Bank. (2022). *World development indicators*. World Bank.

Zeng, T. (2021). Corporate social responsibility (CSR) in Canadian family firms. *Social Responsibility Journal*, *17*(5), 703–718.

Zhang, J., Wang, K., Zhao, W., Han, Y., & Miao, X. (2022). Corporate social responsibility and carbon emission intensity: Is there a marketization threshold effect? *Emerging Markets Finance and Trade*, *58*(4), 952–964.

Chapter 15

Geopolitical Tensions and the Strategic Deployment of ESG: A Conceptual Framework for Norm Diffusion and Corporate Resilience

Atar Derj[a,*], *Slimane Ed-Dafali*[b,†], *Adil Bami*[a,‡] *and Zahra Adardour*[b,§]

[a]Higher Institute of Business and Administration Studies (ISCAE), Morocco
[b]Chouaib Doukkali University, Morocco

Abstract

The paper investigates the increasing confluence of environmental, social and governance (ESG) frameworks with geopolitical dynamics. ESG, previously a voluntary construct for corporates with multiple forms of sustainability, has become a strategic mechanism of global governance, institutional legitimacy and risk management. Using case studies from Eastern Europe, South Korea, Ukraine and environmental multinational corporations, the paper demonstrates how firms and states are leveraging ESG as a way to mitigate geopolitical risk, parcel to global norms and gain access to investment capital and market opportunities. The paper introduces a conceptual framework that brings together geopolitical risk, ESG strategy and regulatory institutionalisation and argues that ESG is functioning simultaneously as a buffer against uncertainty, a device of reputational signalling and a normative mechanism of global power. For policymakers from governments, multinational enterprises and international organisations to emphasise the point that ESG should be seen not as

[*]https://orcid.org/[0009-0001-3568-9763]
[†]https://orcid.org/[0000-0003-3412-1559]
[‡]https://orcid.org/[0009-0008-9214-1105]
[§]https://orcid.org/[0009-0009-7187-3558]

Sustainability in Accounting and Finance Education, 277–291

doi:10.1108/978-1-80686-393-820261015

a marginal sustainability issue, but as a central pillar of economic diplomacy, post-conflict development and global standard-setting.

Keywords: ESG; geopolitical risk; corporate governance; regulation; conflict; sustainability policy; norms

1. Introduction

In recent years, the role of environmental, social and governance (ESG) frameworks has shifted considerably – from being an ethical add-on to being a strategic tier of governance for corporations and states. As rising geopolitical instability continues to weigh on the world, ESG frameworks have become more than compliance mechanisms – they are now a means to navigate political uncertainty, secure investment and exercise soft power. Conflicts such as the Russia–Ukraine war, tensions between China and the West and a global energy crisis highlight how deeply geopolitical shocks influence markets, institutions and value systems. ESG frameworks are now political. They are politically charged instruments, not only for sustainability but for meaningful strategic position in international relations (Gossain, 2023; Reyad et al., 2024).

In the original frame of reference, ESG was based on corporate social responsibility (CSR), in which firms themselves were voluntarily providing non-financial performance measures. But the paradigmatic nature of using ESG has shifted. ESG is now being mobilised as a nonmarket strategy in the current geopolitical environment. Multinational corporations (MNCs) are mobilising ESG to mitigate regulatory retaliation, reputational risk and stakeholder confidence in region of political sensitivity (Kim et al., 2024). This is especially evident in markets where the historical conflict or undue media coverage has elevated the institutional pressure on firms to be socially responsible.

Contemporaneously, global institutions are expanding the framework of ESG into legal and regulatory contexts, solidifying them from 'soft' norms into hard governance tools. The European Union's (EU's) Sustainable Finance Disclosure Regulation (SFDR), International Sustainability Standards Board (ISSB)'s International Financial Reporting Standards S1 (IFRS S1) and India's recent directives on ESG disclosures are rapid and contemporaneous examples of how ESG is juridified (Gossain, 2023; Li, 2024). In this context, ESG standards both have an economic function, while additionally being an exercise of norm diffusion; in other words, to catalyse the extent to which states and corporations conform to the ideals of global governance.

Geopolitical instability has also re-examined the material performance and prioritisation of ESG strategies. In instances of conflict or in high-risk markets, ESG performance typically wanes, unless companies engage with ESG as a strategic buffer (Abdullah et al., 2024). For example, in post-conflict or fragile states, an ESG focus has become necessary if businesses want access to international aid or investment as shown in Ukraine's post-war focus on ESG (Livoshko, 2022).

Likewise, ESG is also being addressed increasingly through a biopolitical lens, where power is enacted not through control but through conduct, risk and ethics regulation. Luke (2022) notes that ESG standards are types of biopower, where corporation and individual behaviour is governed through a moralised form of market participation (Luke, 2022). Therefore, ESG may be viewed not as just an ethical legitimation, but as a geopolitical mechanism; and powerful actors are able to leverage ESG to structure access to markets, dictate investor flows and leverage to disadvantage some actors over others.

In totality, these shifts indicate ESG is not just a proactive tool for sustainability, rather it is a currency of geopolitical power, outlawed, coerced and resisted across all forms of global power. This chapter develops a conceptual framework for exploring where and how ESG norms, geopolitical risk and strategic behaviour then shape corporate action, regulatory trends and international economic governance.

2. Literature Review

In light of the recent literature pertaining to corporate and public policy domains, the evolving role of ESG has been heavily researched, especially in the context of geopolitical uncertainty. There is increasing evidence that ESG strategies are not always motivated by only ethics but are being applied as risk management strategies, and corporate resilience strategies and in some cases, geopolitical signalling. This situates ESG agendas with core strategic objectives of firms and governments in an unstable global order.

Many have demonstrated the role of ESG in mitigating effects of geopolitical risk on performance. For example, research on firms in Eastern Europe during the Russia–Ukraine conflict showed that firms with a stronger ESG performance saw less of a decline in profitability compared to firms without an ESG framework, thus demonstrating that ESG engagement increases adaptive capacity in a volatile environment (Reyad et al., 2024). Similarly, global panel data indicates that while geopolitical risk has a negative impact on ESG performance overall, firms in politically stable environments often raised their ESG commitments, indicating that stability creates incentives for increased sustainability engagement (Abdullah et al., 2024). In the South Korean firms studied, the authors found that firms increased ESG activities during episodes of geopolitical tension, largely as a means to protect their moral capital and stakeholder trust in uncertain time periods (Chun & Moon, 2024).

While some of the responses to geopolitical risk have been strategic decisions made in response to crisis, the use of ESG is evolving to be used as a nonmarket strategy in geopolitically sensitive markets. MNCs frequently elevate their ESG efforts when working in host countries with strained political relations to home countries, or particularly when media narratives are negative or historical war exists. In these circumstances, ESG acts as a sort of insurance policy, which serves and bolsters the ability to justify and legitimise itself to the public and external stakeholders over time (Kim et al., 2024). These scenarios are not isolated from one another; they are further magnified by investor preferences. Socially conscientious investors are more likely to allocate their capital to a firm that communicates its ESG efforts externally to the public, and socially conscientious investors are even more likely to allocate capital to firms with communicated ESG measures when conditions of higher risk (Pokou et al., 2024; Zhang, 2024).

Cyber risk is increasingly recognised as a distinct type of geopolitical risk, especially when cyberattacks are politically motivated. It has been shown that firms leverage ESG frameworks, particularly the governance dimension, to mitigate these interrelated risks (Abdelraouf & Hussainey, 2025). Through standardised cyber risk disclosures and alignment with regulatory requirements, organisations enhance transparency and accountability, which are essential for managing complex geopolitical threats (Bamiatzi et al., 2023; Khan et al., 2025). Furthermore, by integrating emerging themes such as artificial intelligence (AI) ethics and data morality into ESG practices, companies are building resilience not only against technical cyber threats, but also against broader sociopolitical risks associated with global instability (Abdelraouf & Hussainey, 2025). Indeed, the unethical use of technology and AI is becoming an important geopolitical risk. AI can be used for harmful purposes such as spreading false information, spying, launching cyberattacks and disrupting critical infrastructure (Méndez-Suárez et al., 2023). This demonstrates that ESG-focused governance is becoming a vital strategy for navigating and mitigating the multifaceted challenges posed by geopolitical tensions.

In parallel to the strategy of corporations improving their ESG to re-engage a new nation-state, ESG is being increasingly institutionalised. Specifically, it is being institutionalised via the law and regulatory agencies. Examples of how ESG reporting has been institutionalised into both national and international regulatory agencies, include the EU's SFDR, India's Business Responsibility and Sustainability Reporting (BRSR) framework, and IFRS S1 introduced by the ISSB (Gossain, 2023; Li, 2024). The enactment of these rules is not merely mere make-believe, but they establish regulation – laws that tie ESG compliance to financial access, markets and reputation. In the emerging market, however, there exists barriers to the fulfilling the social responsibility of ESG purchase and use. In Indonesia, ESG practices are frequently used as a means for external legitimacy – aimed at appeasing international observers or investors – as opposed to real commitments to transforming sustainability. This could lead to 'greenwashing' where ESG becomes more performative than substantive (Wahyuni & Syamsuddin, 2024).

The importance of ESG grows in economies that are impacted by conflict and even post-conflict economies. ESG is becoming a requirement to garner foreign capital and international aid in Ukraine. ESG is now a function of governance as a filter for reconstruction and investment post-conflict (Livoshko, 2022). The other global efforts to deploy ESG that relate to efforts of re-envisioning United Nations (UN) Sustainable Development Goals (SDGs) – have also positioned ESG practices in a manner that works to reduce systemic risks in vulnerable settings. In these situations, ESG practices are being used in relation to human security and positive peace, and as metrics of assessing the societal impact of business in vulnerable settings (Van Dorp & Smits, 2020).

Theoretical lenses also can look at ESG as a biopolitical technology of governance. Utilising Michel Foucault's theory of biopolitics, ESG can be examined as a means through which ethical behaviour, corporate discipline and risk consciousness are governed not by coercive actions but by normalised practices (Luke, 2022). ESG frameworks provide expectations of what behaviour is 'responsible' or 'sustainable' at the corporate level that influence decision-making ranging from employee working standards to emissions reports. This form of soft power is far-reaching, not only has influence over access or forms of capital, it also has reputational limits of participating in the market and is contributing to the global reordering of corporate sovereignty.

Additionally, ESG is being utilised increasingly as a form of geopolitical currency in and of itself. Governments and regional blocs – like that of the EU – are using regulations on the basis of ESG to shape the behaviour of foreign firms and assert itself along the global supply chains (Gossain, 2023; Li, 2024). This signals that ESG is becoming an artefact of economic statecraft – located somewhere between considerations of national security and international normative leadership. In the fragile or post-war rebuild state, ESG is becoming if not already positioned as a gatekeeper of whether reconstruction funding will be granted, or a contractor is allowed an investment. In highly industrialised countries, ESG may be leveraged by leadership in the area of sustainability while also determining the conditions in which global trade occurs (Lagodiyenko, 2024; Thompson & Colquhoun, 2023).

Put together, the literature suggests that ESG has emerged not only as an effective governance instrument that engages with corporate strategy, but as an instrument of governance in relation to international law, development policy and geopolitical power. ESG is no longer only an artefact of reputation management or risk avoidance. It is a platform for conducting business through a complex and consequential global environment. The next section proposes a conceptual model that brings together these findings and consideration regarding the interplay of geopolitical risk and ESG norms to inform firm behaviour and regulatory response.

3. Conceptual Framework

In this paper, we offer a conceptual framework that connects geopolitical risk, ESG norms and corporate strategic action through three distinct axes: ESG as a risk management strategy; ESG as a geopolitical signalling mechanism; and ESG as a normative governance regime. Together, these axes intersect to form a dynamic system where ESG practices not only respond to external threats but alter the global diffusion of power, legitimacy and investment. This relationship is illustrated in Fig. 15.1, which shows how ESG practices emerge as a corporate and institutional response to geopolitical pressures, leading to outcomes that reinforce global governance systems.

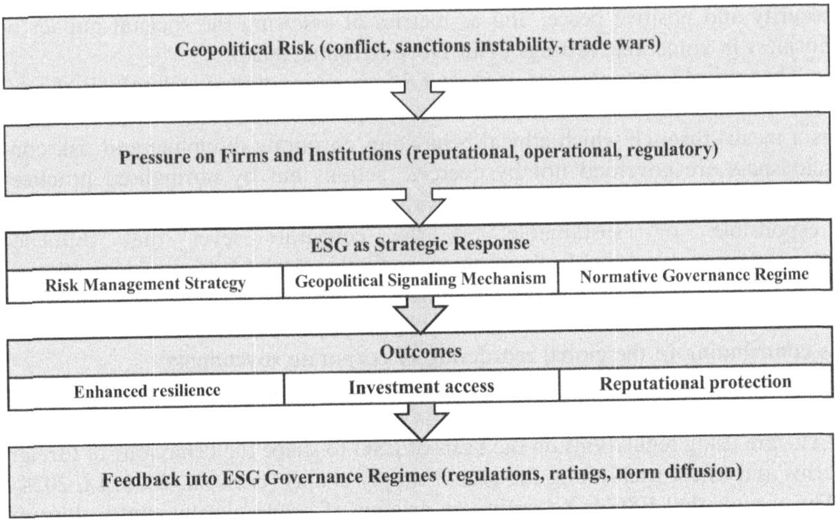

Fig. 15.1. Conceptual Framework: ESG as a Strategic Response to Geopolitical Risk. *Source:* Authors' elaboration.

At the centre of the framework is the premise that geopolitical instability (in the form of war, sanctions, trade conflict or political repression) fundamentally jeopardises firm performance, regulatory prerogative and stakeholder trust. In these circumstances, ESG strategies appear to be stabilising mechanisms. Evidence suggests that for firms operating in Eastern Europe, ESG involvement significantly mitigated the negative effects of geopolitical uncertainty on profitability – suggesting that ESG can enhance a firm's adaptive capacity when operating in a high-risk context (Reyad et al., 2024). This accords with findings from firms in South Korea, where ESG activities increased amid periods of elevated inter-Korean tension, offering a reputational buffer against political and financial backlash from stakeholders (Chun & Moon, 2024).

Therefore, the first axis of the concept, understands ESG to function as a defensive strategy – a type of intangible capital utilised to hedge against geopolitical shock. In terms of sectors directly exposed to long-term global risk (oil, mineral extraction and international real estate), ESG performance has been shown to be correlated with investor confidence and availability of sustainable finance (Newell et al., 2023; Pokou et al., 2024).

The second axis assesses ESG through the lens of geopolitics and as a mechanism for signalling legitimacy. This aspect emphasises the use of ESG to pivot from a defence against risk to a legitimacy signal, in terms of one's alignment with values, positionality or neutrality, or corporate citizenship ethos, in situations of geopolitical hostility or polarisation. For instance, Kim et al. (2024) document that multinational enterprises (MNEs) increase investment in

ESG in host countries when they are experiencing bilateral political tensions with their home country, especially when tensions are highlighted through media or historical contexts. This suggests that ESG operates as a nonmarket strategy to legitimise the behaviour of the multinational firms and avoid backlash from institutions.

This signalling function is reinforced through investor behaviour. More specifically, asset managers and other investors in ESG-exclusive funds are increasingly using sustainability metrics to identify companies that deliver long-term returns while adhering to normative compliance with global governance (Zhang, 2024). This dynamic generates a feedback loop in which investor access to capital is increasingly tied to adherence to ESG practices, while divesting or penalising firms that fall short of the perceived compliance thresholds. The strength of the feedback loop increases in places where disclosure of – or compliance to – ESG is mandated or sanctioned (Gossain, 2023; Li, 2024).

The third, and final, axis of the framework situates ESG within the wider normative governance regime of the global economy. According to this perspective, ESG represents a regulatory and ideological instrument employed by international organisations and powerful states to homogenise corporate behaviour across sovereign states. For example, the advent of IFRS S1 and the EU's SFDR indicates a trend towards not just addressing ESG as a form of normative law but integrating ESG norms within formalised economic governance systems (Li, 2024). These systems are not only regulatory tools, but also slippery forms of soft power – tools that dominant actors use to shape the global business environment in accordance with their own sustainability and political ideals (Luke, 2022).

This logic is present in fragile or post-conflict scenarios such as Ukraine, where ESG-related standards are increasingly used as a requisite for viable investment, the award of reconstruction contracts and access to donor funding (Livoshko, 2022). In these cases, ESG acts as a gatekeeping mechanism that adjudicates which parties are legitimate or credible during the reconstruction process. In these scenarios, ESG is also used to ensure foreign direct investment is aligned with development objectives, human security priorities and peace-building agendas (Van Dorp & Smits, 2020).

The conceptual framework informs us about the coupling of three forces – geopolitical instability, ESG institutionalisation and firm strategy – within a cyclical system:

- Geopolitical Risk raises costs of reputational risk through operational exposure.
- The firm adopts ESG as a strategy to manage risk and in signal of alignment with global imaginaries.
- Institutions reinforce ESG through regulatory standards of investment and global imaginaries that reinforce the strategic value of ESG compliance.

It is also recognised as a recursive relationship, as the more geopolitically unstable the global world becomes, the more strategically valuable ESG is becomes. Thus, in this way, ESG moves from soft corporate tool to a literal mechanism of economic governance, and purposeful geopolitical manoeuvring.

The framework also implicates variations across regions and sectors. Within stable democracies with high levels of institutional trust, CSR is likely to be adopted as a values-based strategy. In fragile or authoritarian states, ESG is more likely to be adopted semi-tactically – to appease foreign investors or to comply with conditions attached to donor financing (Wahyuni & Syamsuddin, 2024). In contrast, ESG itself becomes site of ideological conflict within contexts of politicised economies such as the United States (US), representing culture wars over climate, labour and governance (Hilson, 2024).

In summary, the conceptual framework gives us a way to engage in a comprehensive analysis of how ESG is a response to geopolitical disorder, a tool organisation use to manage their legitimacy institutional legitimacy, while also multi-functionalising the enforcement of global imaginaries. The framework lays the groundwork for empirical and case study analysis of how specific firms, sectors or regions take up ESG and respond to geopolitical instability.

4. Case Studies and Empirical Application

To demonstrate the interplay of ESG in geopolitically challenging contexts, this section presents applied examples in three distinct contexts – conflict zones, politically sensitive host countries and regulated investment markets. Each example illustrates how businesses and governments strategically mobilise ESG as a strategy for resilience, legitimacy or positioning.

One particularly striking empirical example is the case of the Russia–Ukraine conflict, where public firms in Ukraine, Poland and Russia, witnessed acute declines in profitability, amid heightened geopolitical risk. A quantitative analysis of over 1,300 firm-year observations from 2014 to 2023 has been conducted and concluded that firms with strong ESG ratings experienced less financial loss than their counterparts without ESG investments (Reyad et al., 2024). Specifically, ESG acted as a moderating factor, cancelling some of the negative financial impact that geopolitical volatility has on return on assets (ROA). This example thus robustly establishes that ESG strategies are not only symbolic, but they also support a firm's capacity for resilience under severe duress (Reyad et al., 2024).

A similar dynamic was noted in South Korea, where firms throughout the course of business have had recourse to military tensions with North Korea. Chun and Moon (2024) completed an analysis of companies in Korea in periods of heightened North Korea threats, noting that at such points South Korean firms have found strategic ways to enhance their ESG disclosures, and make associated investments. This alteration was not attributable to recent changes in domestic regulation or changes in consumer demand, but rather a deliberate attempt to improve (or rebuild) reputational capital, particularly among international investors. Their study suggests that ESG engagement is not always data driven or simply reactionary but is used by firms as a proactive engagement tool to influence stakeholder perceptions during geopolitical crises (Chun & Moon, 2024).

A compelling case comes from how MNEs adjust their ESG strategies to operate in politically antagonistic host countries. The impact of MNEs' home country relationships (especially those with tension with the host country) has been conducted on ESG practices of firms headquartered in either South Korea or the United States (Kim et al., 2024). In their case study, compared to home country practices, MNEs were using higher levels of ESG engagement to mitigate reputational risk when there was political hostility; specifically, when there was either public awareness of tension or media scrutiny of the firm's relationships. For example, in a period of high tension between South Korea and China, Korean firms operating in China modified their ESG communications to cope with the risk posed by the political antagonism. ESG engagement is thus seen as a purposeful reaction to geopolitical diplomacy, with firms viewing it as a form of reputational armour used in uncertain political environments (Kim et al., 2024).

A fourth context centres around post-conflict recovery, such as we see emerging in Ukraine. It has been pointed out that compliance with ESG metrics is becoming a formalised best practice, particularly for any private company developing access to international investment and reconstruction financing (Livoshko, 2022). Both bilateral and multilateral funding agencies are requiring ESG disclosure from private firms, particularly in labour practices, emissions and community engagement. This discussion illustrates the ways in which ESG has a geopolitical dimension. ESG is embedded in national recovery plans and is used as a gatekeeping mechanism to determine participation in reconstruction efforts to support Ukraine. For example, its government has begun providing ESG training to Ukrainian companies to improve their prospects of attracting foreign capital (Livoshko, 2022).

Financial institutions are another way in which ESG captures the geopolitical dimension. Being said, ESG metrics are not used solely for risk-adjusted return purposes, but also to avoid being exposed to sensitive political sectors or jurisdictions when investing in institutional investors in the United States (Harper, 2020). Examples include pension and sovereign wealth fund ESG investment filters that take into account whether the invested firms operate in authoritarian states or operate in contested sectors relating to geopolitical hot buttons, such as surveillance and fossil fuels. Such filters indicate a more indirect use of ESG as a form of geopolitical alignment, or, in the case of those excluded from the investment, a realignment of capital flows that reflect political and normative preferences (Harper, 2020).

Finally, the EU offers another example of ESG as a mechanism for global norm setting. It has been argued that EU regulatory instruments, including the SFDR and the Corporate Sustainability Reporting Directive (CSRD) function as extraterritorial governance mechanisms (Gossain, 2023). Companies who operate in the EU or export to the EU must comply with the EU ESG disclosures, regardless of their domestic laws. In this context, ESG standards serve as leverage in a geopolitical sense, where profitable market access is contingent on adhering to the EU's sustainability norms (Gossain, 2023).

Taken together, these cases further support the claim that ESG has a substantive and consequential intersection with global politics. ESG is not only a tool for business in pursuit of ethical practice, but a pragmatic mechanism for risk management, signalling geopolitical compatibility, and access to global capital. ESG is valued to corporations navigating tensions, states courting reconstruction funds and institutional investors avoiding political exposure, and has therefore become a variable to the geopolitics of commercial exchange at the global level.

5. Policy Implications and Strategic Recommendations

The escalating intertwining of ESG norms with geopolitical risk indicates a need for a more considered, strategic approach in policymaking. ESG is no longer a voluntary ethical practice but a significant instrument of international legitimacy, economic security and access to international markets, leading public and private actors to formulate adaptable policies in this context.

One of the primary implications is that governments must formally incorporate ESG into national security and economic strategy. As illustrated by the case studies from Ukraine and South Korea, ESG is no longer ancillary to state interests; ESG is foundational to how states seek to attract investment, rebuild after conflict and shape foreign corporate conduct (Livoshko, 2022; Reyad et al., 2024). National governments, particularly in fragile or high-risk environments, should examine how they might develop policies that integrate ESG into industrial strategies, while encouraging firms to adopt an ESG framework as a type of geopolitical and reputational risk insurance, including possible tax incentives or procurement preferences related to ESG, and/or investment guarantees that link capital to ESG.

At the same time, governments in donor or investor countries – such as in the EU and northern states in North America – should recognise the frequently extraterritorial ramifications of the ESG regulations. EU sustainability regulations are producing de facto global standards, which effectively force firms nationally and internationally to align their own values with those of their European counterparts in order to access EU markets (Gossain, 2023). While this increases the EU normative power, it may also lead to the potential alienation of developing countries that may not have the institutional capacity to adjust to the EU's values expectations. Hence, the international body must provide support for capacity-building programmes to assist firms in emerging economies enhance ESG compliance without succumbing to greenwashing (Wahyuni & Syamsuddin, 2024).

At the international level, there is an immediate need to harmonise ESG disclosure and rating systems. ESG frameworks are proliferating, including the Global Reporting Initiative (GRI), the Task Force on Climate-related Financial Disclosures (TCFD) and ISSB's IFRS S1, leading to confusion and inefficiencies for companies which operate across jurisdictions (Li, 2024). Policymakers and standards organisations need to expedite convergence movements, especially around definitions of materiality and universal metrics, for various sectors of the economy. The result of greater harmonisation will have benefits of greater transparency of ESG, reduction in compliance costs for firms and the geopolitical utility of ESG will be enhanced through norms that are clearer and more enforceable.

Corporate actors, particularly multinationals, will then have to evolve their own strategies. Firms should advance beyond only thinking about ESG as a compliance or branding exercise and now consider treating ESG as risk management and a navigation tool for geopolitical issues. As well, firms that proactively modify their ESG processes based on geopolitical signals – public opinion, bilateral tensions, regulatory changes, are more likely to maintain stakeholder trust, investor confidence and corporate legitimacy in times of crisis (Chun & Moon, 2024; Kim et al., 2024). Firms should further institutionalise ESG foresight and scenario planning into their risk departments in order to make ESG modifications quicker and strategic given the changing political contexts facing firms.

Institutional investors can also support these dynamics. Institutional investors should, as much as possible, use investment filters that consider ESG factors not only on environmental and social measurement, but also on exposure to political risks, involvement in conflict and compliance to worldwide norms. Some studies demonstrate how ESG aligned funds already consider these issues into portfolio risk calculations (Harper, 2020). Policymakers should develop mandatory ESG impact disclosures that allow for large institutional investors to consider in their portfolio makeup, particularly in cases where political risks like evasion of sanctions and human rights violations may occur as a byproduct of capital movements.

Finally, ESG should be reconceptualised in policy discussions, not only as a tool for sustaining sustainability, but as a tool for global order making. The norms associated with ESG now decide access to capital, who is deemed legitimate, and what development is acceptable practice. In fragile states, ESG standards dictate the flow of donor capital and investment capital into those states. In advanced economic states, ESG can dictate access to any market and reputational capital on firms. Policymakers need to remove the notion that ESG is only for green growth, and intentionally start to develop ESG frameworks to not only develop green growth but to fortify systems of global governance that are peaceful, inclusive and just (Luke, 2022; Van Dorp & Smits, 2020).

Overall, this combination of policy recommendations demonstrates the need to approach ESG not as compliance burden, or marketing fad, but rather as a governance tool that has some strategic value to a firm to be aligned with ESG, and as a governance process that is utilised to gain market access, mitigate risk and/or project geopolitical power. In a disaggregated, fragmented and conflict driven global economy, the strategic value of ESG and what it means to be involved with ESG will only increase. This is music to the ears of governments, firms and global institutions seeking to leverage ESG as a source of political, economic and/or social capital.

6. Conclusion

This paper has illustrated that ESG frameworks are no longer an outlier to global governance or the ethics of business; they are now central to how firms manage and mitigate risk, how governments are able to project soft power and how institutions are able to shape global norms. Further, the combination of ESG and geopolitics is not a coincidence; rather it is rooted in deeper structural change in how legitimacy, investment and strategic behaviour is administrated in a world of increasing volatility.

In high-risk contexts, ESG has been shown empirically to serve a stabilising effect. For instance, firms engaged in geopolitical risk contexts such as Ukraine, Poland and Russia which are highlighted with the Russia–Ukraine conflict, showed less financial decline when remaining aligned with ESG norms and performance (Reyad et al., 2024). Similarly, companies in South Korea engaged in heightened ESG activity and performance during evacuations of geopolitical tensions. In these cases, firms were engaging ESG to build reputational capital and moral capital (Chun & Moon, 2024). In general, these examples highlight that ESG is not simply reactive but intentionally anticipatory to manage uncertainty and trust of institutional structures.

Multinational firms even utilise ESG as a nonmarket strategy in hostile political climates. During geopolitical escalation between home and host countries, firms engaged in action changes in their ESG behaviour to mitigate any backlash and stay consistent with the regulatory environment, while also being cognisant of public perception and sentiment from the media (Kim et al., 2024). Investor pressure bolsters this activity; investors who prioritise ESG want to limit financial as well as reputational/political risks, opting for firms that appear responsive to social and environmental problems (Pokou et al., 2023; Zhang, 2024).

In a systems-level sense, ESG is becoming institutionalised through legal settings; such regulatory structures are increasingly binding and are transnational, meaning that both domestic and foreign firms must comply with detailed, audited ESG reporting requirements and performance standards (Gossain, 2023; Li, 2024). However, expanding regulation can create asymmetries. In developing economies such as Indonesia, ESG can at times be used more for external legitimacy than for meaningful organisational change, which raises questions of performativity and greenwashing (Wahyuni & Syamsuddin, 2024).

The chapter also incorporated the role of ESG within fragile and post-conflict contexts. Ukraine has recognised ESG criteria as a precondition for reconstruction investment, where ESG criteria become envelopes for credibility and capital (Livoshko, 2022). On a more global scale, ESG is a mechanism to align firms with the SDGs, especially in contexts affected by conflict where human security and positive peace are primary issues (Van Dorp & Smits, 2020).

Within a theoretical framework, ESG can be understood as a biopolitical instrument that shapes behaviour through the form of governance that is normatively-produced rather than coercively produced. It has been suggested that ESG regulation has become to shape what is ethically acceptable and economically viable, which consequently shapes corporations' engagement in patterns of sovereignty/investors' legitimacy on a global scale (Luke, 2022) suggests. The softness of this regulation extends jurisdictionally, thus shaping the relationships among the cavalcade of stakeholders, thus shape from supply chains to finance and political relationships.

The conceptual framework displayed in this chapter relies upon the interplay of these forces: geopolitical risk, the adoption of ESG and normative governance processes are in recursivity. Specifically, as geopolitical risk increases, ESG affords greater value. As ESG is more widely adopted, it shapes legitimacy, investment and influence in global markets. Even further, this dynamic is most felt in sectors such as oil, gas, real estate and international finance, where firms' access to global capital is contingent on ESG performance (Arboleda, 2023; Harper, 2020; Newell et al., 2023).

The implications for policy is clear. Governments should implement ESG in national economic and security strategies. International and transnational institutions must consolidate ESG frameworks in order to lessen regulatory fragmentation and ensure equitable access to capital. As well, multinational companies should institutionalise ESG into their geopolitical risk analysis. Moreover, managers are called to embed comprehensive cyber risk management, including addressing the risks of unethical AI use, within ESG strategies to safeguard organisational resilience and stakeholder trust in an increasingly volatile geopolitical environment. To address this, governments, companies and international organisations need to work together to create ethical guidelines, increase transparency in how AI is used and include these risks in their ESG strategies. This will help improve their ability to manage and prepare for these complex geopolitical challenges. Investors should expand ESG frameworks to incorporate potential exposure to conflict and are at political risk. These efforts can, together, elevate ESG from reactive measures of reporting, assessing vulnerability or risk management to a proactive strategy for governance, development and peace-building.

As the world becomes more fragmented and unstable, with the climate crisis, economic inequality, rising authoritarianism and war, the strategic value of ESG will continue to rise. ESG not only serves as a mirror for global values but a mechanism to enforce them. ESG represents a new scalar infrastructure for a global order, determining who thrives and trades, and governs in the decades ahead.

References

Abdelraouf, M., & Hussainey, K. (2025). Systematic review of cyberrisk disclosure practices: Insights and implications. *The Journal of Risk Finance*. https://doi.org/10.1108/JRF-07-2024-0210

Abdullah, M., Tiwari, A. K., Hossain, M. R., & Abakah, E. J. A. (2024). Geopolitical risk and firm-level environmental, social and governance (ESG) performance. *Journal of Environmental Management*, *363*, 121245. https://doi.org/10.1016/j.jenvman.2024.121245

Arboleda, J. M. (2023). ESG. A challenge for the oil & gas industry? In *ADIPEC, D031S080R001*. https://doi.org/10.2118/216583-MS

Bamiatzi, V., Dowling, M., Gogolin, F., Kearney, F., & Vigne, S. (2023). Are the good spared? Corporate social responsibility as insurance against cyber security incidents. *Risk Analysis*, *43*(12), 2503–2518. https://doi.org/10.1111/risa.14122

Chun, H., & Moon, B. (2024). Do firms increase ESG activities during periods of geopolitical risk? Evidence from Korean business groups. *Borsa Istanbul Review*, *24*(6), 1393–1401. https://doi.org/10.1016/j.bir.2024.11.002

Gossain, R. (2023). Legal underpinnings drive ESG amidst global flux. *Paradigm: A Management Research Journal*, *27*(1), 27–46. https://doi.org/10.1177/09718907231173333

Harper, H. (2020). One institutional investor's approach to integrating ESG in the investment process. *Journal of Portfolio Management*, *46*(4), 110–123. https://doi.org/10.3905/jpm.2020.1.131

Hilson, C. (2024). Climate change and the politicization of ESG in the US. *Frontiers in Political Science*, *6*, 1332399. https://doi.org/10.3389/fpos.2024.1332399

Khan, W. N., Lee, J. K., & Liu, S. (2025). Is cybersecurity a social responsibility? *Information Systems Frontiers*. https://doi.org/10.1007/s10796-024-10565-z

Kim, J. H., Kwak, J., & Park, H. (2024). ESG as a nonmarket strategy to cope with geopolitical tension: Empirical evidence from multinationals' ESG performance. *Strategic Management Journal*, *46*(3), 693–722. https://doi.org/10.1002/smj.3671

Lagodiyenko, O., Lagodiienko, V., Ivanchenkova, L., Romanashenko, I., & Laskaiev, O. (2023). Prospects for the development of the ESG concept in the face of new challenges. *Collection of Papers New Economy*, *1*(1), 179–195. https://doi.org/10.61432/CPNE0101179l

Li, Z. (2024). The impact of IFRS S1 on corporate ESG disclosure: A comparative analysis of SMIC and MTR corporation. *Finance and Economics*, *1*(10). https://doi.org/10.61173/5a4tgb09

Livoshko, T. (2022). Monitoring according to ESG principles and its impact on the competitiveness of business entities. *Herald of Khmelnytskyi National University. Economic sciences*, *310*(5(1)), 158–164. https://doi.org/10.31891/2307-5740-2022-310-5(1)-26

Luke, T. W. (2022). Investment and rapid climate change as biopolitics: Foucault and governance of the self and others through ESG. *Sustainability*, *14*(22), 14974. https://doi.org/10.3390/su142214974

Méndez-Suárez, M., Simón-Moya, V., & Muñoz-de Prat, J. (2023). Do current regulations prevent unethical AI practices? *Journal of Competitiveness*, *15*(3). https://doi.org/10.7441/joc.2023.03.11

Newell, G., Nanda, A., & Moss, A. (2023). Improving the benchmarking of ESG in real estate investment. *Journal of Property Investment & Finance*, *41*(4), 380–405. https://doi.org/10.1108/JPIF-10-2021-0084

Pokou, F., Kamdem, J. S., & Benhmad, F. (2023). Empirical Performance of an ESG assets portfolio from US market. *Computational Economics*, *64*(3), 1569–1638. https://doi.org/10.1007/s10614-023-10491-3

Pokou, F., Sadefo Kamdem, J., & Benhmad, F. (2024). Empirical performance of an ESG assets portfolio from US market. *Computational Economics, 64*(3), 1569–1638. https://doi.org/10.1007/s10614-023-10491-3

Reyad, H. M., Ayesha, M., Iqbal, M. M., & Zariyawati, M. A. (2024). The role of ESG in enhancing firm resilience to geopolitical risks: An eastern European perspective. *Business Strategy & Development*, *7*(4), e70027. https://doi.org/10.1002/bsd2.70027

Thompson, J., & Colquhoun, M. (2023). The 12 Pillars model of ESG: Bringing practical clarity to ESG across the Australian gas industry. *The APPEA Journal, 63*(2), S105–S108. https://doi.org/10.1007/s10614-023-10491-3

Van Dorp, M., & Smits, M. (2020). *The social impact of business in fragile and conflict-affected settings: Contributing to the SDGs and reducing local ESG risks by using human security and positive peace* (Knowledge Platform Security & Rule of Law) [Policy Brief]. LSE. https://kpsrl.org/sites/default/files/2021-01/UN-Policy-Brief-December-2020-van-Dorp-and-Smits.pdf

Wahyuni, P. D., & Syamsuddin, M. M. (2024). Epistemological foundation of ESG-based investment in Indonesia's economic policy. *International Journal of Economics and Management Sciences*, *1*(4), 388–400. https://doi.org/10.61132/ijems.v1i4.371

Zhang, Y. (2024). ESG perceptions: Investigating investor motivations and characteristics. *Financial Services Review*, *32*(2), 29–52. https://doi.org/10.61190/fsr.v32i2.3591

Section 4

Policy, Responsibility and Inclusive Development

Chapter 16

Accounting Responsibility: Higher Education, Tax Innovation and Sustainable Development

Nizar Baklouti

University of Sfax, Tunisia

Abstract

The significance of incorporating the concepts of accountability, sustainability and innovation into university instruction and accounting practice is examined in this study, which also examines higher education, tax innovation and sustainable development. Investigating the ways in which environmental and social issues interact and contribute to a more sustainable and equitable future is crucial in a world that is becoming more interconnected and conscious of these issues. Social justice, environmental preservation and sustainable economic growth can all be supported by the efficient use of ethical accounting principles as well as the encouragement of tax and budgetary innovation.

Keywords: Accounting responsibility; higher education; tax innovation; sustainable development; equity

1. Introduction

Learning environments have been altered by the incorporation of digitalisation into higher education, especially in reaction to worldwide disruptions like the COVID-19 pandemic. 'It is good that this is possible thanks to digital tools,' one pupil said. We utilise our resources as efficiently as possible. We must contribute ideas and engage in change processes, making use of whatever resources are available at the moment. It refers to the virtual realm during a pandemic. The move towards sustainable development and the growing significance of digital

Sustainability in Accounting and Finance Education, 295–304

Published under exclusive licence by Emerald Publishing Limited
doi:10.1108/978-1-80686-393-820261016

transformation in education are two major themes influencing universities today, as this statement highlights.

Sustainability, tax innovation and accounting responsibility are all directly impacted by these changes. By encouraging openness and responsible decision-making, digitalisation offers new resources for incorporating sustainability into accounting and financial management (Stoltenberg & Michelsen, 2020). At the same time, universities are essential in giving students the tools they need to deal with these changing environments, especially when it comes to sustainable taxation and finance.

The relationship between sustainability, tax innovation and accounting accountability in digitalised higher education is examined in this chapter. It investigates how cutting-edge teaching strategies, such as project-based learning and digital learning, might help colleges incorporate sustainability into accounting curricula. In order to promote transdisciplinary, participative and responsible accounting practices that are in line with the Sustainable Development Goals (SDGs), the main question is whether digitalisation strengthens or undermines the concepts of education for sustainable development (ESD).

2. Theoretical and Conceptual Framework

Theoretical foundations for improvement in university accounting lie in the transition from static financial practices to dynamic, performance-oriented models, as emphasised by Gray (2010).

2.1 Current Situation and Challenges of Accounting in Universities

The basic framework of university accounting primarily involves the accurate recording of revenues and expenditures, as well as the reasonable preparation of financial statements. First, through the daily recording and analysis of economic activities, universities can gain a clear understanding of their sources of income and expenditure destinations. Second, the preparation of financial statements aims to accurately reflect the financial position of the university during a given period and provide an important reference for financial management and decision-making.

Traditional accounting methods used in colleges and universities have shown certain limitations in the face of the rapidly changing educational environment and complex financial activities. These methods lack the flexibility to adapt to the dynamic changes in financial needs, which restricts the agility of financial management and the speed of decision-making.

Currently, many colleges and universities exhibit weaknesses in financial information disclosure. Some important financial information is not presented to stakeholders in a timely and comprehensive manner, which affects the credibility and social recognition of financial management in higher education institutions.

Johanson et al. (2019) observe that financial management in universities faces increasing operating costs, an uncertain economic environment and sector-specific management challenges. These difficulties expose institutions to more complex situations in fund management, financial planning and investment in educational projects, requiring more refined and scientifically grounded financial management methods to address them effectively.

2.2 Tax Innovation as a Driver of Sustainable Development

The Value-added tax (VAT) refund policy can promote green innovation among enterprises, both in terms of innovation motivation and innovation capacity. First, the VAT refund strengthens enterprises' motivation to innovate. As rational economic agents, enterprises weigh costs and benefits when making decisions. If the external costs of green innovation cannot be internalised, the private marginal cost of green innovation will exceed the social marginal cost, increasing the burden on enterprises and harming their motivation for green innovation.

The refund of retained tax credits can be seen as an interest-free loan provided by the government to ease internal cash flow pressure on enterprises, thereby partially alleviating the additional burden imposed by the external costs of green innovation. Moreover, the 'signalling effect' of the tax refund policy can guide green innovation by reducing the risk burden on covered industries and enterprises, and by decreasing the uncertainty associated with green innovation (Czarnitzki et al., 2011). Therefore, the retained tax refund policy helps to internalise the benefits of green innovation to some extent, thus stimulating enterprises' endogenous motivation for green innovation.

Secondly, the retained tax refund policy can enhance the green innovation capacity of enterprises. VAT is neutral and transferable, with limited distortion on production, sales and investment behaviours of enterprises.

However, before the actual deduction, the input VAT to be deducted may compress the enterprise's current cash flow and influence its production and investment decisions. This affects the intended neutrality of the tax system, exacerbates financial pressure and increases financing constraints, placing enterprises in a 'willing but under-resourced' dilemma. The VAT refund policy can alleviate financial pressure and financing constraints by reducing the tax burden and increasing liquidity. This helps to ease the pressure of higher taxes on enterprises, supports them in expanding investment, promotes technological upgrading and ultimately equips enterprises with stronger green innovation capabilities.

3. Higher Education as a Catalyst for Sustainable Development

3.1 ESD in Higher Education

Developing a 'global environmental awareness' and 'future education' is a fundamental mission of scientific and educational systems. Training individuals as actors of digital change represents the core approach of contemporary higher education, which integrates knowledge and digital culture in line with the 'quality education for all' goal of the 2030 Agenda (UN, 2015).

ESD, politically legitimised since 1992 in Agenda 21 (UN, 1992) and reinforced by successive United Nations Educational, Scientific and Cultural Organisation (UNESCO) programmes (UNESCO, 2014a, 2014b, 2017, 2020), aims to empower individuals to shape a sustainable world. The current ESD for 2030 programme (UNESCO, 2020) seeks to structurally embed this education within institutions and link it to the 17 SDGs. In an emancipatory approach (Vare & Scott, 2007; Wals, 2011), ESD constitutes a social learning process opening transformative perspectives for self-reflection and developing judgement and action capacities.

Universities are called upon to integrate ESD holistically (HRK & DUK, 2010; van Hauff & Nguyen, 2014) to contribute significantly to the SDGs (Ahel & Lingau, 2021). Higher education must enable students, as future decision-makers, to develop their awareness of (non-)sustainability and acquire key competencies such as critical, interdisciplinary and forward-thinking skills, problem-solving and active participation (Rieckmann, 2018; Wiek et al., 2011).

3.2 Digital Integration in Sustainable Pedagogical Approaches

Digitisation in education refers to the technical process of transferring non-digital resources into digital ones (Zhao et al., 2020), while digitalisation focuses on digital culture and changes in individual action options, social practices and economics (Stalder, 2019).

According to Mayrberger (2020), the current debate on higher education is still 'primarily characterized by a focus on technology regarding infrastructure processes and organizational strategy development.' Digitisation must 'serve as a lever and support for the major transformation toward sustainability' (WBGU, 2019), leveraging its potential to design educational processes emphasising social responsibility, action and participation opportunities.

The educational concepts of ESD and digital education share many parallels: future orientation and skill development promoting an active and reflective approach to challenges in a complex world (Lexa, 2021; Schrüfer & Brendel, 2018).

3.3 Improving Accounting in Universities

To improve the openness and transparency of university financial management, the first task is to establish and refine information disclosure standards. By clarifying the content, format and frequency of financial information disclosure, colleges and universities can ensure that all aspects of their financial activities are fully presented, which helps various stakeholders accurately understand the financial situation of the institutions.

Building on this foundation, improving transparency is not only a regulatory requirement but also a key step in building trust and enhancing the image of universities.

4. Practical Applications and Innovations

4.1 The Link Between Planning, Performance and Budgeting in Universities

The implementation of economic and patrimonial accounting in universities has required an organisational effort to shift budgetary culture towards planning (Marlina et al., 2019). Analytical accounting allows for linking resources to performance objectives by tracking indicators and analysing variances to assess efficiency and effectiveness (Klychova et al., 2014). However, assigning measurable objectives presents difficulties, particularly for research and education, which rely on intangible assets and unpredictable factors (Johanson et al., 2019).

University decision-making follows a circular logic where ministerial directives define strategy, performance and budget, leading to a structured system of objective setting and ex-post evaluation (Marlina et al., 2019). Analytical accounting thus serves as a tool for planning and management control, enabling resource allocation according to objectives and evaluating discrepancies between forecasts and actual outcomes (Klychova et al., 2014).

However, the rigidity of university structures complicates the application of performance objectives to individual units, as achieving results does not necessarily guarantee an improvement perceived by stakeholders (Johanson et al., 2019).

The economic evaluation of research activities is more feasible through project-based objectives and specific budgets. Finally, for analytical accounting to be relevant, it must rely on strategic governance that integrates economic forecasts, territorial requirements and quality standards in the university sector (Johanson et al., 2019).

4.2 Integrating Environmental Accounting Into Organisational Practices

The integration of environmental accounting into business practices represents a critical evolution in the sustainable development paradigm. Accounting serves not only to record and communicate financial information but also to cover environmental and social aspects that affect the long-term viability of businesses and society (Gray, 2010).

Environmental accounting emerges as a response to the need for transparency regarding the environmental impacts of business activities. According to Burritt and Schaltegger (2010), this branch of accounting provides the means to measure, manage and communicate the environmental effects of a company's actions, enabling more informed decision-making. The use of environmental performance indicators helps organisations comply with stricter regulations and enhance corporate reputation (Schaltegger & Csutora, 2012).

4.3 The Impact of Environmental Taxes on Corporate Performance

Research on the impact of environmental taxes on corporate performance presents contrasting perspectives, structured around Porter's hypothesis (1991), which posits that strict regulations stimulate innovation and productivity. Liao and Zhu (2023) highlight that such innovations, being difficult to imitate, enhance performance, while Peng et al. (2021) identify three mechanisms: cost optimisation through market reforms, increased competitiveness and sector-specific effects.

Empirical studies show divergent results: in Canada, the carbon tax reduced overall productivity by 1% (Yamazaki, 2020), whereas in China, the 2018 reform increased profitability (+2.11%) and green investments (+5%), validating Porter's hypothesis through a combination of taxes and subsidies (He & Jing, 2022; Wang et al., 2022).

A synthesis by Li et al. (2022) confirms a positive impact on competitiveness, particularly in polluting industries, regardless of national development levels. The success of environmental taxes depends on their integration with incentive and sectoral policies, offering the potential for a dual ecological and economic dividend.

5. Empirical Analysis: The Eurydice Report on Learning for Sustainability in Europe

The report *Learning for Sustainability in Europe: Building Competences and Supporting Teachers and Schools*, published in 2024 by the European Commission, provides an in-depth analysis of progress in integrating ESD into European educational systems. This study aligns perfectly with our chapter's objectives by examining how educational institutions can serve as catalysts for sustainable development.

5.1 Methodology and Objectives of the Report

The report is based on qualitative data from 39 European educational systems, primarily covering primary and secondary education levels. Its main goal is to support the implementation of the European Union (EU) Council's (2022) recommendations on the green transition and sustainable development by identifying best practices and persistent gaps.

5.2 Key Findings on Curricular Integration

All European countries now incorporate sustainability into their curricula, mainly through cross-disciplinary approaches in subjects such as science, geography and civic education. The *GreenComp* framework identifies seven key competences for sustainable development:

- valuing sustainability;
- promoting nature;
- systems thinking;
- future literacy (ability to envision sustainable scenarios);
- adaptability (circular economy, sustainable lifestyles);
- political agency (understanding responsibilities);
- individual and collective action.

The study reveals that *future literacy* remains the least developed competence in curricula, whereas *promoting nature* is the most widespread. This observation echoes our discussions on the importance of a forward-looking vision in accounting education and tax innovation.

5.3 Teacher Training and Educational Resources

Initial teacher education (ITE) includes sustainability objectives in only 17 educational systems, with notable gaps in systems thinking and collective action. Continuous professional development (CPD), although available in most countries, is often optional and rarely tailored to school leaders.

Regarding resources, 75% of systems provide educational materials, but only 12 countries have dedicated sustainability centres. This situation reflects challenges identified in our analysis of higher education, where structural integration of the SDGs remains insufficient.

5.4 Holistic Approaches and Community Engagement

The report highlights that 17 countries offer environmental certification programmes (e.g., Eco-Schools), but their pedagogical impact remains limited. Sustainable infrastructures (school gardens, recycling) and educational projects (nature outings) receive funding in only 12 to 13 countries.

Community engagement, through partnerships with Non-governmental Organisations (NGOs) or municipalities, is encouraged but varies across regions. This observation aligns with our analysis of responsible accounting practices, which also require a holistic approach involving all stakeholders.

5.5 Monitoring and Evaluating Progress

Less than one-third of countries incorporate sustainability criteria into school evaluations. The lack of systematic monitoring hinders the measurement of progress and transnational comparisons. This finding parallels challenges in implementing environmental performance indicators in organisational accounting practices.

6. Implications and Recommendations for the Future

The findings of the Eurydice report, combined with our analysis of innovative accounting and tax practices, allow us to formulate integrated recommendations for the future:

(1) *Strengthen Professional Training:* Integrate sustainability into the skills of accountants, tax professionals and educators by developing modules on transformative approaches.
(2) *Support Institutions Financially and Pedagogically:* Increase funding for green infrastructures and provide tools for interdisciplinary approaches linking accounting, taxation and sustainability.
(3) *Improve Monitoring and Evaluation:* Develop standardised indicators to measure the integration of sustainability in accounting and tax practices, as well as in educational curricula.
(4) *Encourage Holistic Approaches:* Engage all stakeholders in concrete projects that demonstrate the positive impact of accounting and tax innovation on sustainable development.
(5) *Promote Synergies Between Disciplines:* Create learning spaces where accounting, tax innovation and ESD reinforce each other.

For these recommendations to be effective, they must be embedded in a holistic perspective that recognises the interdependence of educational, economic and environmental systems. Higher education, in particular, has a crucial role to play as a catalyst for these transformations.

7. Conclusion

This study highlights the importance of accounting responsibility, green taxes and higher education in the sustainable transition, demonstrating that environmental accounting enhances transparency, incentive-based taxes stimulate innovation (partially confirming Porter's hypothesis) and active pedagogies (such as design thinking) develop actors capable of systemic thinking. However, the findings, primarily focused on Europe and based on qualitative data, limit their applicability to developing countries and long-term impact assessments.

Moving forward, it is crucial to develop interdisciplinary educational tools, experiment with incentive-based fiscal policies for small and medium enterprises (SMEs) and strengthen transnational collaborations to harmonise sustainability standards. These pathways, combined with the adoption of hybrid indicators by practitioners, offer a framework to transform economic and educational systems into drivers of a just transition, meeting the needs of researchers and policy-makers committed to climate and social action.

References

Ahel, O., & Lingau, K. (2021). Education for sustainable development and the SDGs. *Sustainability Science*, *16*(1), 43–56.

Burritt, R. L., & Schaltegger, S. (2010). Sustainability accounting and reporting: Fad or trend? *Accounting, Auditing & Accountability Journal*, *23*(7), 829–846.

Czarnitzki, D., Hand, P., & Rosa, J. (2011). Evaluating the impact of R&D tax credits on innovation: A micro-econometric study on Canadian firms. *Research Policy*, *40*(2), 217–229.

Gray, R. (2010). Is accounting for sustainability actually accounting for sustainability…and how would we know? An exploration of narratives of organisations and the planet. *Accounting, Organizations and Society*, *35*(1), 47–62.

He, L., & Jing, S. (2022). Environmental tax reform, energy efficiency, and corporate carbon reduction. *Energy Policy*, *169*, 113158.

HRK & DUK (Hochschulrektorenkonferenz & Deutsche UNESCO-Kommission). (2010). *Hochschulen für nachhaltige Entwicklung*. https://www.hrk.de/fileadmin/redaktion/A4/Hochschulen_und_Nachhaltigkeit_HRK_DUK.pdf

Johanson, U., Almqvist, R., & Skoog, M. (2019). A conceptual framework for integrated performance management systems. *Journal of Public Budgeting, Accounting and Financial Management*, *31*(3), 309–324. https://doi.org/10.1108/jpbafm-01-2019-0007

Klychova, G. S., Faskhutdinova, M. S., & Sadrieva, E. R. (2014). Budget efficiency for cost control purposes in management accounting system. *Mediterranean Journal of Social Sciences*, *5*(24), 79–84. https://doi.org/10.5901/mjss.2014.v5n24p79

Learning for Sustainability in Europe. (2024). *Building competences and supporting teachers and schools: Eurydice Report*. https://data.europa.eu/doi/10.2797/81397. Accessed on May 10, 2024.

Lexa, C. (2021). Digital transformations in higher education for sustainability. *International Journal of Sustainability in Higher Education*, *22*(5), 1176–1193.

Li, Y., Wang, Z., & Zhao, T. (2022). Environmental regulation and corporate performance: A meta-analysis. *Journal of Cleaner Production*, *334*, 130229.

Liao, Z., & Zhu, X. (2023). The role of different fiscal policies in inducing environmental innovation and enhancing firm competitiveness. *Emerging Markets Finance and Trade*, *59*, 688–697. https://doi.org/10.1080/1540496X.2022.2119845

Marlina, E., Ardi, H. A., Samsiah, S., Ritonga, K., & Tanjung, A. R. (2019). Strategic costing models as strategic management accounting techniques at private universities in Riau, Indonesia. *International Journal of Financial Research*, *11*(1), 274–282. https://doi.org/10.5430/ijfr.v11n1p274

Mayrberger, K. (2020). Digitalisierung im Kontext von Nachhaltigkeit - eine komplexe Beziehung mit Gestaltungsspielräumen. *Erziehungswissenschaft*, *31*(2), 35–50.

Peng, H., Tan, X., Li, Y., & Hu, L. (2021). Economic growth, industrial structure and carbon dioxide emissions: Evidence from 36 countries. *Economic Analysis and Policy*, *69*, 275–288.

Porter, M. E. (1991). America's green strategy. *Scientific American*, *264*(4), 168.

Rieckmann, M. (2018). Learning to transform the world: Key competencies in education for sustainable development. In A. Leicht, J. Heiss, & W. J. Byun (Eds.), *Issues and trends in education for sustainable development* (pp. 39–59). UNESCO.

Schaltegger, S., & Csutora, M. (2012). Carbon accounting for sustainability and management. Status quo and challenges. *Journal of Cleaner Production*, *36*, 1–16.

Schrüfer, G., & Brendel, N. (2018). Global education for sustainable development. *The German Journal of Economic Geography*, *62*(1), 49–64.

Stalder, F. (2019). *Kultur der Digitalität*. Suhrkamp.

Stoltenberg, U., & Michelsen, G. (2020). Digitalisierung im Kontext von Bildung für NE. In M. Hauff & A. Reller (Eds.), *Nachhaltige Digitalisierung – eine noch zu bewältigende Zukunftsaufgabe* (pp. 49–64). Hessische Landeszentrale für politische Bildung.

UNESCO. (2014a). *Shaping the future we want: UN decade of education for sustainable development (2005-2014): Final report*. https://sustainabledevelopment.un.org/content/documents/1682Shaping%20the%20future%20we%20want.pdf

UNESCO. (2014b). *UNESCO roadmap for implementing the global action programme on education for sustainable development*. UNESCO.

UNESCO. (2017). *Education for sustainable development goals: Learning objectives*. UNESCO.

UNESCO. (2020). *ESD for 2030: Education for sustainable development: A roadmap*. https://unesdoc.unesco.org/ark:/48223/pf0000374802.locale=en

UN (United Nations). (1992). *Agenda 21: Programme of action for sustainable development*. United Nations Department of Public Information.

UN (United Nations). (2015). *Transforming our world: The 2030 agenda for sustainable development*. Resolution adopted by the General Assembly on 25 September 2015. A/RES/70/1.

van Hauff, M., & Nguyen, T. (2014). Universities as potential actors for sustainable development. *Sustainability*, *6*(5), 3043–3063.

Vare, P., & Scott, W. (2007). Learning for a change: Exploring the relationship between education and sustainable development. *Journal of Education for Sustainable Development*, *1*(2), 191–198.

Wals, A. E. J. (2011). Learning our way to sustainability. *Journal of Education for Sustainable Development*, *5*(2), 177–186.

Wang, C., Wang, Z., Zhu, N., & Geng, Y. (2022). The impact of environmental taxes on economic benefits and technology innovation input of heavily polluting industries in China. *Frontiers in Environmental Science*, *10*, 959939. https://doi.org/10.3389/fenvs.2022.959939

WBGU (Wissenschaftlicher Beirat der Bundesregierung Globale Umweltveränderungen). (2019). *Unsere gemeinsame digitale Zukunft*. WBGU.

Wiek, A., Withycombe, L., & Redman, C. L. (2011). Key competencies in sustainability: A reference framework for academic program development. *Sustainability Science*, *6*(2), 203–218. https://doi.org/10.1007/s11625-011-0132-6

Yamazaki, A. (2020). Jobs and climate policy: Evidence from British Columbia's revenue-neutral carbon tax. *Journal of Environmental Economics and Management*, *83*, 197–216.

Zhao, Y., Pinto Llorente, A. M., & Sánchez, M. C. (2020). Digital competence in higher education research: A systematic literature review. *Computers & Education*, *168*, 104212.

Chapter 17

The Complementary Relationship Between Innovation and Sustainable Development: Towards a More Inclusive and Resilient Economy

Mohammad Kamal Abuamsha[*]

Palestine Technical University, Palestine

Abstract

Sustainable production and consumption are needed worldwide for environmental and economic reasons. This trend threatens environmental balance and long-term economic stability by depleting natural resources faster than they can be regenerated. Sustainable innovation can rebalance the economic, environmental and social elements by improving resource efficiency, reducing emissions and addressing intergenerational equity in an integrated sustainable development framework.

Digital financial services design green bonds, environmental and social impact finance and environmental, social and governance (ESG)-based financial evaluation models to support sustainable models. They boost energy efficiency and transparency with blockchain and artificial intelligence (AI). They increase financial inclusion by giving excluded groups, especially distant ones, new opportunities.

Although progress has been made, substantial challenges prevent widespread, sustainable adoption. Digitalisation of sectors and professions brings social risks, including automation-related job losses. The growing carbon neutrality funding gap and poor digital infrastructure in underdeveloped nations are hindering development.

Next, implement more inclusive and flexible models that promote sustainable innovation through international cooperation and regulatory

[*]https://orcid.org/0000-0002-9085-3132

Sustainability in Accounting and Finance Education, 305–328

Published under exclusive licence by Emerald Publishing Limited
doi:10.1108/978-1-80686-393-820261017

reforms while balancing immediate and long-term profits. An equitable transition to a green economy and sustainable society requires public–private partnerships and comprehensive finance.

Keywords: ESG; innovation; sustainability; environmental; economic; social; corporate governance

1. Introduction

It has become increasingly clear over the past five decades that current consumption patterns exceed ecosystems' regenerative capacity, accelerating natural resource depletion and threatening ecological balance, economic and social sustainability (Pastoors, 2020). This necessitates the adoption of sustainability, which aims to balance present needs with future rights through environmentally and economically responsible activities (Abuamsha & Hattab, 2024).

Unsustainable consumption in one place can have worldwide environmental and economic effects; therefore, sustainability applies to society. Restructuring production and consumption is crucial for resource conservation and ecological and economic justice. Einstein stated, 'We cannot solve problems with the same thinking we used to create them.'

Sustainable innovation develops technologies and products that support environmental, economic and social development (Pastoors, 2020). This improves social balance, environmental impact and institutional competitiveness.

- One of the main features of sustainable innovation is improving existing products to boost economic efficiency and performance.
- Using creative technology to create new items that meet market needs.
- In computers and healthcare, cheap solutions have increased technological access (Pastoors, 2020) (see Fig. 17.1).

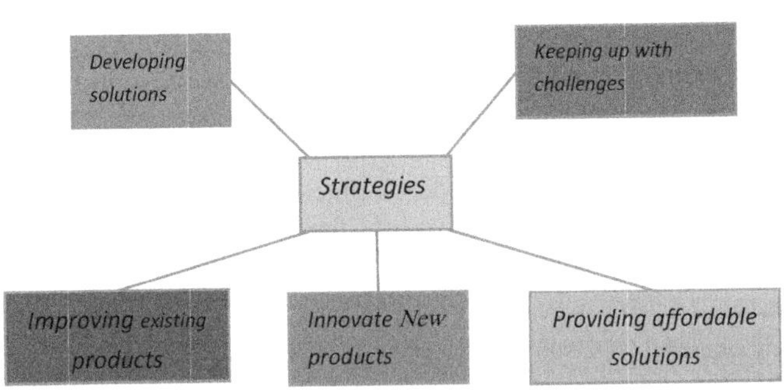

Fig. 17.1. Modern Marketing Trends and Corporate Strategies.
Source: Prepared by the author.

The market-technology dilemma is a significant concern nowadays. When client expectations clash with technological capabilities or ethical considerations, innovation and adaptability are essential to fulfil market demands or create new opportunities (Pastoors, 2020). No more than 6% of innovative products attain market sustainability (Pastoors, 2020).

Sustainability is a complex subject that impacts environmental, economic and social domains. Globalisation has become an unsustainable practice, a global concern, necessitating international collaboration (Pastoors, 2020).

Sustainable development is characterised as 'meeting the needs of the present without compromising the ability of future generations to meet their own needs' (World Commission on Environment and Development, 1987), a pivotal definition in the debate on global sustainability.

Despite humanity's longstanding recognition of the imperative for sustainable resource utilisation, genuine interest in its implementation is recent (Busse, 2012; Ozili, 2018). In the 18th century, 'sustainability' referred to forest management; nevertheless, it currently incorporates all environmental and socioeconomic concerns (Busse, 2012; Ozili, 2018). The economic crisis of the 1970s highlighted worries over resource overexploitation, hence augmenting global interest in the subject (Pastoors, 2020). Environmental, economic and social concerns must be concurrently addressed to attain sustainability (Pastoors, 2020).

2. Sustainable Innovation: Theory and Practice

2.1 Sustainability Includes Four Main Dimensions (Rogall, 2012)

Sustainability encompasses three main, interconnected dimensions:

(1) Environmental sustainability reduces damage and replenishes resources by rationally using natural resources throughout a product's life cycle.
(2) Social/ethical sustainability emphasises social fairness and stakeholder equity within corporate social responsibility.
(3) Economic sustainability demands balanced resource use to maintain growth without jeopardising future rights.
(4) Empowerment is needed through business policies and initiatives, education, capacity building and innovation (see Fig. 17.2).

Sustainability integrates environmental, social and economic factors to balance current demands with future rights. The Aral Lake disaster in Uzbekistan showed how industrial, agricultural and transportation operations have made the air, water and soil unfit for natural life, environmental degradation and biodiversity loss (Pastoors, 2020). With 1.5 million species expected to go extinct in the next decade, ecosystems suffer from agricultural losses and disease outbreaks (Pastoors, 2020).

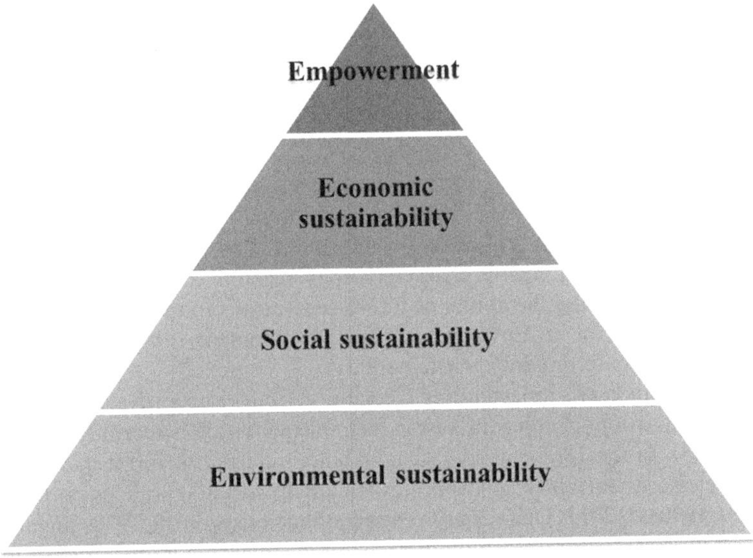

Fig. 17.2. Dimensions of Sustainability. *Source:* Prepared by the author.

The 2015 Paris Agreement to reduce carbon emissions and limit global warming to far below 2°C relative to pre-industrial levels while helping underdeveloped nations adapt (Pastoors, 2020). Despite this progress, natural resource depletion and population growth require global action (Pastoors, 2020).

2.2 The Interaction and Balance Between Innovation and Sustainable Development

Innovation fosters sustainable growth and solves environmental and social challenges. Researchers have examined this link from many viewpoints. Kwilinski (2023) analyses innovation and sustainable development utilising systems analysis, institutional sociology and network analysis using both conventional and modern methods. Quantitative studies emphasise the significance of scientific research and innovation in tackling environmental concerns (Aricò, 2014; Voegtlin & Scherer, 2017).

Small and Medium-sized Enterprises (SMEs) innovative entrepreneurship enhances local and global competitiveness and sustainable development (Kardos, 2012). To promote technology innovation for climate change, food safety and biodiversity, Ashford and Hall (2011) advocate regulating environmental, health and labour markets. Islam (2024) and Shumali and Abuamsha (2021) says innovation boosts governance and social stability. Many firms prioritise short-term profits over sustainability, but governments and international organisations can foster responsible innovation.

Wu et al. (2024) say an innovative technology like robotics enhances production and creates jobs. This emphasises the need for educational and training programmes that balance technical advancement and societal stability. Islam (2024) says sustainable development involves environmental, economic and social balance. Pastoors (2020) provides a five-stage sustainable innovation model that dynamically integrates technical, institutional and organisational components within a strategic vision to address these issues:

(1) Awareness of the problem: recognising current and future environmental and social problems.
(2) Problem definition: definition of the problem to be resolved as precisely as possible to shape further innovative activity.
(3) Idea generation: creation of innovative solutions using tools, i.e., design thinking.
(4) Testing the solution: testing the proposed solution against sustainability criteria, i.e., life cycle assessment and social responsibility.
(5) Implementation and marketing: using green marketing to make the market believe that the proposed solutions are worth implementing.

This model allows the effective management of sustainable innovation within a company while combining environmental, social and economic objectives (see Fig. 17.3).

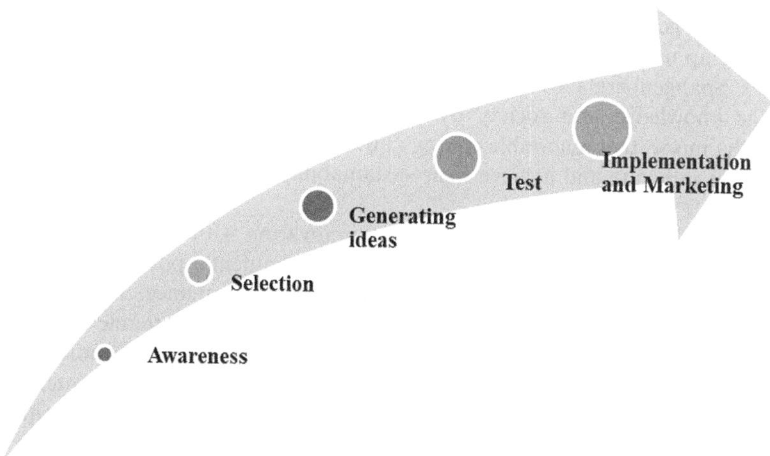

Fig. 17.3. Stages of Sustainable Innovation. *Source:* Prepared by the author.

Innovative and sustainable financial services institutions (FSIs) survive in increasingly competitive markets (Sendjaja et al., 2022). The S&P Global Index reported around 2,900 bank branch closures worldwide by 2021, including US and Indonesian institutions (Laucereno, 2022). Environmental, social and governance (ESG) aspects in Corporate Strategy have enabled sustainable financial gains, investor interest and stakeholder trust. Ottosson et al. (2017) define sustainable innovation as environmentally friendly and economically profitable ideas that enable firms to achieve ESG requirements for long-term competitive advantage.

A recent study suggests that green bonds and sustainable financial technology (FinTech) can significantly contribute to the development of a low-carbon economy by enhancing transparency and directing financial resources toward environmentally sustainable projects (Zairis et al., 2024). Sustainable financial services are a systemic move towards Sustainable Development Goal (SDG) 2030 (Miroshnychenko & De Massis, 2022). Sustainable banking, created in the 1990s, needs improvement and is underutilised (Gassmann et al., 2020; Weber, 2012). Weber (2012) noted dramatic changes in ethics, social responsibility and sustainable innovation (Abuamsha, 2022a).

Financial industry ethics and transparency were exposed by the 2007–2009 global financial crisis. The techniques above promoted and solidified ethical finance services (Climent, 2018; Magazzino et al., 2021). This technique established sustained innovation in this industry and earned consumer and investor support (Ascher, 2020; Climent, 2018).

2.3 The Role of Sustainable Development in Promoting Innovation

Innovation generates new answers to unmet social and environmental demands, opening up new markets and making enterprises more competitive (Walz et al., 2017). Spangenberg (2011) further suggests that sustainability science should bridge knowledge and society by rethinking sustainability challenges. Additionally, innovative renewable energy and resource efficiency solutions can help countries innovate and achieve their sustainability goals (Walz et al., 2017) (see Fig. 17.4).

Sustainable growth requires long-term innovation with future ramifications. Albino et al. (2009) say contextual factors, environmental policy, sector nature and municipal legislation affect green innovation performance. The company's internal and external environments must cooperate for sustainable innovation. Innovation can help prolong sustainability, but it can also replace human labour with technology, especially with the increasing expansion of artificial intelligence (AI). According to Mavlutova et al. (2021), these shifts could raise unemployment in technologically advanced countries, necessitating proper education and training measures to help workers adapt.

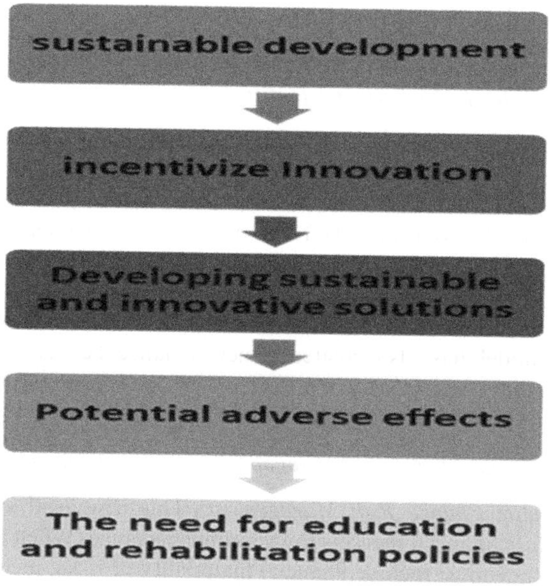

Fig. 17.4. The Role of Sustainable Development in Promoting Innovation. *Source:* Prepared by the author.

2.4 Sustainable Innovation as a Lever for Comprehensive Development

Innovation boosts productivity, pricing and quality, making organisations more competitive. This helps companies access new markets and grow sustainably (Porter, 2011). Social advancement is driven by innovation in strategically crucial industries, transport, education, health and social security (Mulder, 2007), job creation, and complete economic and social development.

Sustainable development benefits from innovation's rational resource usage and long-term financial gain (Voegtlin & Scherer, 2017). Organisations must now commit to environmental and social sustainability through cross-cutting plans (Albino et al., 2009; Takalo & Tooranloo, 2021).

Numerous studies suggest that technological innovation boosts firm sustainability. Wang et al. (2023) linked digital transformation to Chinese environmental performance. Lv et al. (2024) and Li et al. (2019) found that exploratory and exploitative innovation improves corporate sustainability by creating organisational learning and institutional flexibility for dynamic situations. Mulder (2007) found that the technology revolution can maximise sustainability through efficient and sustainable solutions.

Given this, all forms of innovation are vital for corporate resilience and sustainability, allowing organisations to integrate environmental responsibility into their operational and strategic activities.

3. Finance and Innovation (ESG, FinTech)

3.1 Sustainable Innovation and the Financial Sector: A Comprehensive Analysis of Financial Markets and Institutions

Climate change, a major threat to the economy and society, is linked to the Paris Agreement's SDGs (UNFCCC, 2015). This risk is gaining attention from governments, financial markets and academia (Alonso & Marqués, 2019). Establish a solid foundation for coordinated efforts to prevent its detrimental effects. Since adapting to environmental and social needs is now part of public policy design, this transformation has been one of the biggest drivers of change in the financial sector's markets and banks (Alonso & Marqués, 2019). A more inclusive development model has also created a new balance between economic and environmental aims (see Table 17.1).

3.1.1 First: Financial Markets – Sustainable Transformations and New Services

3.1.1.1 Climate Change Risk Management. This new legal and investment framework forces financial markets to face climate change. When analysing asset performance, they must include financial materiality of risks, including physical risks from natural disasters and transition risks from new policies and technology. The materiality of the company's operations, environmental and social repercussions, and climate change's financial impact are relevant (TEG, 2019).

3.1.1.2 Growth of Sustainable Financial Services and Initiatives. Innovative services and initiatives have improved financial market, environmental and social transparency. An external auditor is required for European Union (EU) green bond ratings (CBI, 2018). ESG ratings have enhanced corporate sustainability performance evaluation (ICMA, 2018), despite methodological flaws and diverse information sources (CBI, 2018). Sustainability indexes like the Morgan Stanley Capital International All Country World Index (MSCI ACWI) Sustainable Impact Index and FTSE4GOOD let investors passively manage low-carbon companies according to environmental and social standards (Alonso & Marqués, 2019; CBI, 2018).

3.1.2 Second: Financial Institutions – Sustainable Innovation and Risk Management

3.1.2.1 Addressing Climate Change in Enterprise Risk Management. Incorporating climate change into enterprise risk management.

Financial institutions face a dual dilemma. They must integrate climate change concerns with their traditional risk management frameworks. Conversely, they must ascertain the 'carbon footprint' of their operations to comply with the norms of the green economy. Approximately 30 financial institutions have undertaken the initiative to incorporate these principles into their investment funds (UNFCCC, 2015).

3.1.2.2 FinTech and Sustainable Innovation. Technological advances like big data analytics and AI improve financial organisations' operations. Natural

Table 17.1. Summary of the Main Elements of Sustainable Innovation in Markets, Financial Institutions and Developing Economies.

Main Theme	Key Elements	Challenges	Examples/Initiatives
Financial markets	• Climate change risk management • Sustainable services and initiatives	• Complexity of risk assessment • Differing classification methodologies	• Green Bonds • ESG Ratings • MSCI and FTSE4GOOD Indices
Financial institutions	• Integrating climate change into risk management • Leveraging financial technology	• High carbon footprint of technologies • Challenges of integrating risks into traditional systems	• Using Artificial Intelligence and NLP • The World Bank Project in Guatemala
International policies and coordination	• Reforming regulatory frameworks • International initiatives to support sustainability	• Limitations of the role of central banks • Weak international coordination	• The Alliance of Finance Ministers for Climate Action – The Helsinki Principles
Sustainable banking	*Concepts:* Ethical, social, responsible and values-based banks	• Lack of a unified definition • Weak practical application	• Sustainable Finance Exceeds $2.3 Trillion • WWF Study on ASEAN Banks
Sustainable innovation and the economy	• Reshaping markets • External collaboration with partners	• High short-term costs – Challenges of open innovation	• Massive Environmental Investments • Post-2008 Crisis Policies
Financial innovation in developing countries	• Microfinance • Financial technologies (FinTech)	• Weak legislation • Risks of excessive debt	• The Grameen Bank Experience in Bangladesh • E-Wallets and Crowdfunding

Source: Prepared by the author.

language processing (NLP) is used to evaluate sustainability reporting and ESG compliance (Hawley, 2017). The World Bank's Guatemala effort reduced assessment costs by 70% using satellite and drone image recognition to assess climate threats in distant areas (Allen et al., 2017).

The above inventions have many benefits, but their implementation harms the environment, especially due to the carbon footprint of data analytics needed to train AI systems. Energy-efficient and sustainable technology is the solution (Hawley, 2017).

3.1.3 Third: Public Policy and International Coordination for Financial Sustainability

Public policies and international laws promote the development of sustainable technologies in the financial sector. The Alliance of Finance Ministers for Climate Action (AFMA), established in 2019 in Helsinki, is one of the current efforts designed to provide support for this cause. A coalition of 20 nations aims to incorporate environmental issues into financial and economic policies through the adoption of the Helsinki Principles (CAPE, 2019). Supplementary regulatory agencies are seeking modifications to existing legislation to improve financial institutions' ability to manage climate risks (Molina Romo & Godino Pons, 2018). However, these initiatives are limited by the central banks' institutional mandate, which prioritises price stability and inflation control, rather than actively addressing climate policies (Villeroy, 2019).

3.1.4 Fourth: Sustainable Banks – Concepts and Practices

Sustainable banking research often lacks a coherent idea, making evaluation difficult (Abuamsha & Shumali, 2022; Jasmine & Rohim, 2024). Many researchers must compare values-based, social and responsible banks, which share goals but use different methods (Da Silva Inácio & Delai, 2021). Ethical banks prioritise honesty, openness and accountability in operations and funding. In contrast, responsible banks promote microfinance instruments for financial welfare and social inclusion (Green, 2012). Social banks consider societal needs and integrate sustainability into their operations (Győri et al., 2021). Sustainable banks lead in environmental governance, Abuamsha (2021) carbon footprint reduction, community investment and financial inclusion (Bouma et al., 2017, 2021). Green finance, social finance and impact investing are also used interchangeably (Jasmine & Rohim, 2024). Statistics show that over 90% of these institutions have sustainability policies and goals, but have allocated less than \$2.3 trillion to sustainable financing. This cost is small compared to the \$100 trillion needed to transition to a low-carbon economy by 2050 (UNEP FI, 2021). WWF research on Southeast Asian banks found that only 2% have adopted and implemented banking practices (Jasmine & Rohim, 2024). Sustainable banking needs more promotion.

3.1.5 Fifth: Sustainable Innovation and Economic Dynamics

Sustainable innovation is increasingly seen as a solution to complex concerns, including climate change, an ageing population, resource limitations and pollution (Montalvo, 2006). Sustainable innovation may boost the economy and reshape emerging economies (Montalvo et al., 2011). After the 2008 global financial crisis, many countries have passed policies to foster sustainable innovation rather than short-term profit (Boons et al., 2013). Porter and Kramer (2011) argue that governments and organisations will be competitive if they can innovate and create new markets, not only compete in existing ones. From 2007 to 2011, eco-innovation investment totalled USD 2.4 trillion, and by 2020, it is expected to reach USD 10 trillion (Ethical Markets Media, 2011). Sustainability is seen as a commercial opportunity, not a moral requirement.

According to Porter and Kramer (2011), 'the nations and corporations poised for future competitiveness are those that will create new markets, rather than contend for existing ones.' New business models are spreading quickly. Global eco-innovation investments were $2.4 trillion from 2007 to 2011 and $10 trillion in 2020 (Ethical Markets Media, 2011). Sustainability is an economic opportunity, not a moral responsibility (Sustainable Brands). Supplier, university, non-profit and customer collaboration offer an alternative road to success. Superior regulatory and social integration increases societal and market acceptance (Arnold, 2011; Carrillo-Hermosilla et al., 2010; Lozano, 2007). Open innovation uses external information sources (Chesbrough, 2003). Cognitive decline, higher costs and administrative complexity are the challenges (Dahlander & Gann, 2010; Stefan & Bengtsson, 2017; Vezzoli & Manzini, 2017).

3.1.6 Sixth: Financial Innovation in Developing Countries – Between Empowerment and Challenges

Financial innovation boosts financial inclusion and economic prosperity in low- and middle-income nations. Access to banking services is limited since many people cannot use them. Access to banking provides more flexible and affordable financial solutions to poor, women and rural people who have been excluded from mainstream finance (Bangura, 2021).

3.2 Microfinance and FinTech as a Tool for Development

Bangladesh is the country with the most effective microfinance trial for community development. Those receiving Grameen Bank funding can benefit from this effort. It aims to improve livelihoods, boost economic growth and empower people to make decisions. It empowers women to make important financial decisions and boosts their income (Malik et al., 2019).

Developing nations have adopted FinTech-driven financial innovations, including e-wallets, mobile payments and crowdfunding. They provide fast, secure financial services to underserved populations (Bangura, 2021). Recent studies show that FinTech improvements can boost savings, facilitate small company loans and streamline remittances, which affect many countries' budgets.

3.2.1 Challenges and Recommendations

3.2.1.1 Institutional and Regulatory Challenges. However, many developing nations face barriers to sustainable financial advances. The causes include a weak legal system, a lack of skills and low financial literacy (Malik et al., 2019). Fast microloans can cause over-indebtedness and inadequate consumer protection, which could have long-term financial and societal consequences.

In these conditions, comprehensive financial and regulatory policies must consider the complexities of these markets, encourage innovation, protect consumers, increase transparency and align financial services with national development goals (Bangura, 2021).

3.2.1.2 Sustainable Financial Services: Digital Innovations and Crisis Adaptation. Sustainable digital financial services (DFS) are among the primary instruments that have undergone significant transformation in recent years due to digitalisation and several global crises (Jasmine & Rohim, 2024). The COVID-19 pandemic revealed the inadequacies of traditional financial services, prompting the development of other financial products, distribution systems and marketing tactics (see Fig. 17.5).

3.2.1.2.1 First: Innovations in Financial Products

(1) Financial Inclusion
Despite increased access to financial institutions for individuals in remote regions, many remain excluded from the system due to the limited banking infrastructure in rural areas. Digital technologies can enhance the understanding of financial inclusion for the local populace. For instance, financial services may be provided online (Tay et al., 2022).

(2) Rural Finance
Small and micro enterprises in remote regions are frequently impacted by the inadequate financial infrastructure in rural locales. Consequently, digital technology can assist smaller enterprises through financial solutions offered by specialist online services tailored for small firms (Brickell et al., 2020).

(3) Entrepreneurship Financing
Startups and small to medium firms are pertinent in both emerging and developed markets. Their access to money during the initial phase is the most critical factor. Consequently, digital methodologies such as digital venture capital and private equity may assist. Consequently, novel methodologies are implemented to improve corporate finance (Gompers et al., 2022).

(4) Wealth Management
Changes in wealth management are linked to the trend of digitalisation. An increasing number of individuals utilise digital methods, including digital financial planning and intelligent advice services. Consequently, an increased population has access to wealth management (Archuleta et al.,

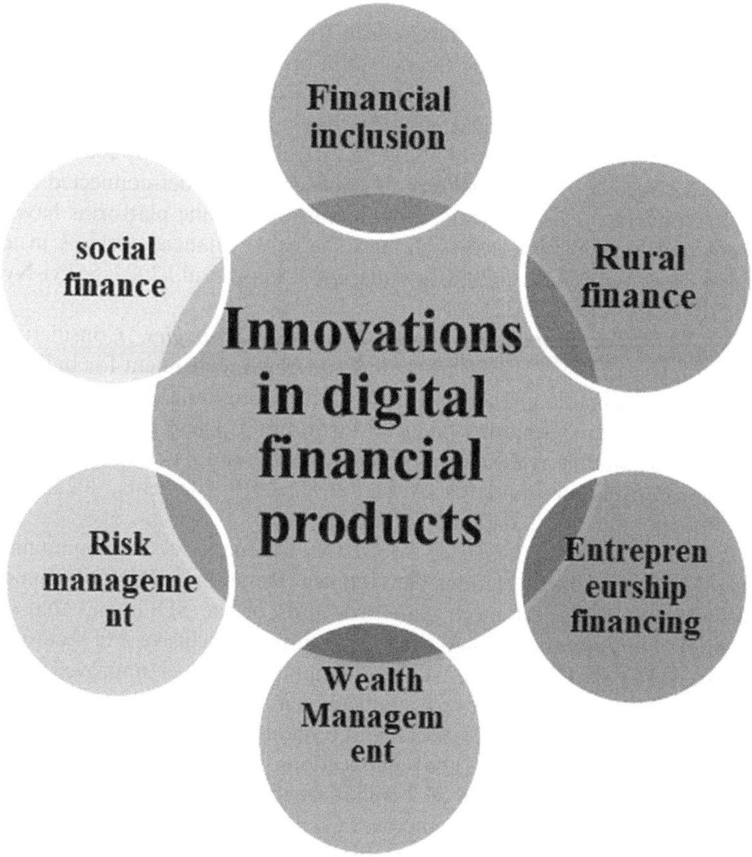

Fig. 17.5. Innovations in Financial Products. *Source:* Prepared by the author.

2021; Atif et al., 2021; Dziawgo, 2021; Fox & Bartholomae, 2020; Gan et al., 2021; Phoon & Koh, 2017; Sanguino et al., 2020).

(5) Risk Management

Several structural gaps were identified in the provision of insurance for pandemic risks within the contemporary insurance industry. The coronavirus crisis demonstrated that this circumstance impacted numerous individuals' livelihoods, necessitating the activation of the State Aid system and supplementary financial assistance. The government's and community's capacity to provide social support during future crises may stem from innovative digital insurance products (Haas et al., 2021).

(6) Social Finance
Social finance is a crucial mechanism for facilitating social and economic development. While social finance solutions are currently unavailable, the concept of social finance is gaining traction. This presents an opportunity to create innovative financial services that integrate financial returns with social objectives (Hassan et al., 2022; Kuchler & Stroebel, 2021).

3.2.1.2.2 Second: Service Delivery Mechanisms. In under-connected and less digitally connected environments, mobile apps and online platforms have been instrumental in delivering accessible and shareable financial services in a sustainable way (Agur et al., 2020; Clements, 2022; Feng et al., 2022; Sakyi-Nyarko et al., 2025; Tay et al., 2022).

3.2.1.2.3 Third: Sustainable Digital Marketing Strategies. Considering the sustainability paradigm, digital marketing can be an instrument for building the notion of a sustainable financial service and attracting other segments interested in working with green-minded financial institutions. These tools can become a base for a sustainable relationship between a bank and its customers according to the current market standards (Aitken et al., 2019; Clements, 2022; Lozano, 2008; Rosenbaum et al., 2022; Sheth, 2021).

3.2.1.3 Innovation in Service of the SDGs. International Telecommunication Union (ITU) and United Nations Development Programme (UNDP) found that digital technologies affect more than two-thirds of the SDGs and that digital innovation will drive the 2030 Agenda through more inclusive and secure digital solutions (ITU & UNDP, 2023). Digital innovation has improved financial inclusion, education, health, poverty eradication and essential services for the most vulnerable (World Bank, 2022). Social and economic growth are driven by digital innovation. United Nations (UN) publications suggest massive digital infrastructure spending to close the $3.7 trillion deficit, increase connection through public-private collaboration and empower young people digitally (ITU & UNDP, 2023). Digital public infrastructure (DPI) should provide government services, education, e-governance (Abuamsha, 2022b) and health to sustain growth.

FinTech must develop in DFS for financial inclusion and economic prosperity. It has helped women and small businesses get finance and overcome geographical and economic constraints (GSMA, 2020; World Bank, 2022). DFS aids vulnerable communities during the COVID-19 pandemic and reduces financial services gender gaps (Gates Foundation, 2019). Public and private sector solutions are needed for DFS's infrastructure, regulations and cybersecurity (World Bank, 2022). Public policy should address economic (profitability and financial stability), social (equity and inclusion) and environmental (reduced carbon footprint) issues (UNDP, 2020).

Blockchain, AI, Internet of Things (IoT) and cloud computing increased institutional performance, sustainability, transparency and operational costs (Thanasi-Boçe & Hoxha, 2024; Yoon et al., 2018). Financial institutions are reconsidering how to balance technological innovation and environmental sustainability in the Fourth Industrial Revolution (Schwab, 2016). Because of this, FinTech – activity based on modern technologies like AI, blockchain and others – must be paired with sustainable finance – investments in ESG-compliant initiatives. Modern finance must promote innovation, efficiency, sustainability and longevity.

3.2.2 FinTech: Promoting Environmental and Economic Sustainability

FinTech addresses climate change, social inequality and economic prosperity through environmentally, economically and socially sustainable financial solutions. Blockchain-based green finance platforms reduce corruption, increase transparency and direct investments to greener projects (Song et al., 2022). Accounting for environmental impacts with big data and AI algorithms helps financial institutions make green choices.

Financial innovations have helped SMEs access the market and find flexible financing through low-cost electronic payment instruments, digital banking services, operational efficiency and decreased banking expenses (Chen et al., 2020). FinTech crowdfunding, digital loans and smart transfers have assisted remote disenfranchised populations in overcoming the social welfare and income gap (Anand et al., 2021; Li & Li, 2022). FinTech offers flexible financial solutions to women and youth.

A recent study found that FinTech is driving financial system change through new models. Climate-friendly cryptoassets include digital green bonds (Ghosh, 2022). Blockchain reduces carbon footprints and increases supply chain transparency (Kim et al., 2019). Rethinking public policies to enable responsible financial innovation and enough infrastructure to balance profitability, environmental protection and social justice.

To make the digital economy greener, more inclusive and fairer, new FinTech trends could direct funds to low-carbon and high-social-impact projects (Kong et al., 2022; Migliorelli & Dessertine, 2019).

3.2.2.1 How Can ESG Ratings Promote Innovation in the Field of DFS?. Big data, cloud computing and AI use have exploded. These technologies assist companies in improving their business model. They provide real-time data analysis, dynamic decision-making and market responsiveness (Antenozio & Di Berardino, 2023). Speed and cost savings from intelligent automation boost productivity (De Cianni et al., 2023). They support digital economy-friendly business models (Guo et al., 2024).

ESG criteria in strategic sustainable digital transformation's third pillar instil environmental and social responsibility in the organisation (Foley et al., 2024). AI for energy efficiency, big data and analytics for supply chain transparency and efficiency (Xu & Xu, 2023). Safe, accurate and reliable blockchain databases strengthen corporate governance (Abuamsha & Razia, 2022; Appio et al., 2021).

Digital transformation, sustainable innovation, better environmental and social reaction, and fast business response (Hao et al., 2024). Recent research shows that ESG ratings boost digital innovation. High-ESG companies have better market capitalisation and receive more funding for innovative technology (Hao et al., 2024). The following ESG rating techniques could enhance digital innovation:

First, Fund R&D: Companies with high 'ESG' ratings have additional funding choices, the survey revealed. Companies can get more R&D funding (Wang & Dong, 2021). R&D can stimulate technical innovation and sustain regional industry and technology (Wang & Dong, 2021). They may spend more on 'innovative technology' to improve their environmental, social and economic performance. This gives them a regional and global edge (Hao et al., 2024).

Second, access to funds has been enhanced. Companies with high 'ESG' rankings have greater access because they lower investment risk. He et al. (2025) found that companies with strong 'ESG' scores can acquire better terms to invest in innovative technologies and promote sustainable innovation.

Third, they lower 'ESG' risk uncertainty. High ratings encourage long-term innovation investment by boosting a company's stability and investor confidence. High-rated companies can manage environmental and social uncertainties, improve sustainability and create innovative technologies (Wang et al., 2023).

Fourth, it can improve the company's image. Higher evaluations mean greater market reputation, more customers buying it and more innovative employees (Hao et al., 2024). Better corporate reputations make it easier to invest in performance and make more money, increasing long-term sustainable technological innovation (Hao et al., 2024). This positive feedback will encourage innovation and ensure its long-term competitive edge (Mo et al., 2024).

ESG ratings spur digital innovation. In heavily regulated eastern and central China, a better ESG score helps high-tech enterprises raise funds and innovate (Hao et al., 2024). R&D investment in less-regulated industries benefits less from ESG ratings. Companies' reputation, capital flow and sustainable growth benefit from an ESG rating. Digital FinTech sustains growth. Blockchain, AI and cloud computing can foster financial inclusion, meet the SDGs and close the economic divide (Alexander, 2014; Beck et al., 2010; UN, 2015; Yip & Bocken, 2018).

Digital technologies are revolutionising finance, promoting good governance, social equity and economic and environmental innovation, a study shows. Digital finance improves financial institutions' ESG, transparency, carbon footprint and inclusivity. Environmental challenges like energy-intensive data centres make digital transformation unsustainable. So, coordinated initiatives to improve banking ESG ratings are essential. Flexible regulatory reforms, financial institutions' social and environmental responsibility, and ethical leadership and staff training are needed to stimulate innovation (Hao et al., 2024).

4. Conclusion

Business sustainability is innovation. In the face of climate change and environmental degradation, the study shows that environmental, economic and societal challenges must be balanced. Innovation is now used to alter the production and consumption system by reducing carbon emissions and increasing transparency using green technologies like AI and blockchain (Song et al., 2022). ESG-based sustainable finance promotes investment and innovation, which benefits sustainability (Hao et al., 2024). Sustainable finance requires finance, hence sustainability causes financial issues. Financial managers oversee $2.3 trillion in sustainable funding. This is 2% of the $100 trillion needed to establish carbon neutrality by 2050 (UNEP, 2021). Despite better theory, just 2% of ASEAN banks practise sustainability (Jasmine & Rohim, 2024).

Data centre energy utilisation and algorithmic efficiency are examples of sustainability challenges (Xu & Xu, 2023). Automation removes millions of jobs, yet reskilling initiatives create renewable energy and digital jobs (Islam, 2024; Magazzino et al., 2021). Successful, sustainable transformation requires rigorous governance, sustainability criteria, large digital infrastructure expenditures and international cooperation to transfer technology to developing nations (CAPE, 2019; ITU-UNDP, 2023). Research emphasises open innovation and government-private-civil society interaction for a circular economy (Pastoors, 2020). Finally, a sustainable economy is a humanitarian imperative that requires an integrated vision that balances short-term profitability with ecosystem resilience, technology and social justice (Islam, 2024; Voegtlin & Scherer, 2017).

Acknowledgements

Many deep thanks to Palestine Technical University – Kadoorie – in Tulkarm, Palestine, for their support work.

References

Abuamsha, M. K. (2021). The impact of corporate governance mechanism on financial performance in the Palestinian firms listed in the stock exchange. *Academy of Accounting and Financial Studies Journal*, *25*, 1–13.

Abuamsha, M. K. (2022a). The fact of corporate governance in the Palestinian territories. In *Future of organizations and work after the 4th industrial revolution: The role of artificial intelligence, big data, automation, and robotics* (pp. 463–496). Springer International Publishing.

Abuamsha, M. K. (2022b). The role of the banking sector in financing the real estate and contracting sector in the Palestinian territories. *International Journal of Housing Markets and Analysis*, *15*(2), 357–374. https://doi.org/10.1108/IJHMA-11-2020-0135

Abuamsha, M. K., & Hattab, L. M. (2024). Shadow economy–financial sustainability nexus: The case of Palestine. *Journal of Economic Studies*, *51*(2), 375–393. https://doi.org/10.1108/JES-01-2023-0026

Abuamsha, M. K., & Razia, B. (2022, March). The role of corporate governance in managing risks: An applied case on companies listed on the Palestine stock exchange. In *International conference on business and technology* (pp. 415–427). Springer International Publishing.

Abuamsha, M., & Shumali, S. (2022). Debt structure and its impact on financial performance: An empirical study on the Palestinian stock exchange. *Journal of International Studies (2071-8330)*, *15*(1).

Agur, I., Peria, S. M., & Rochon, C. (2020). *Digital financial services and the pandemic: Opportunities and risks for emerging and developing economies*. https://www.imf.org/-/media/files/publications/covid19-special-notes/en-special-series-on-covid-19-digital-financial-services-and-the-pandemic.pdf?la=en&utm_source=chatgpt.com

Aitken, R., Watkins, L., & Kemp, S. (2019). Envisioning a sustainable consumption future. *Young Consumers*, *20*(4), 299–313.

Albino, V., Balice, A., & Dangelico, R. M. (2009). Environmental strategies and green product development: An overview on sustainability-driven companies. *Journal of Cleaner Production*, *18*(2), 83–96.

Alexander, K. (2014). *Stability and sustainability in banking reform: Are environmental risks missing in Basel III?* CISI & UNEPFI.

Allen, E., Lyons, K., & Tavares, R. (2017). The application of machine learning to sustainable finance. *Journal of Environmental Investing*, *8*(1).

Alonso, A., & Marqués, J. M. (2019). *Financial innovation for a sustainable economy*. Banco de España Occasional Paper, (1916). https://ideas.repec.org/p/bde/opaper/1916e.html?utm_source=chatgpt.com

Anand, J., McDermott, G., Mudambi, R., & Narula, R. (2021). Innovation in and from emerging economies: New insights and lessons for international business research. *Journal of International Business Studies*, *52*(4), 545–559.

Antenozio, L., & Di Berardino, D. (2023). Exploring the interplay between digital implementation and SMEs' performance: An empirical study. In Sinergie-SIMA 2023 management conference. https://doi.org/10.7433/SRECP.EA.2023.01

Appio, F. P., Frattini, F., Petruzzelli, A. M., & Neirotti, P. (2021). Digital transformation and innovation management: A synthesis of existing research and an agenda for future studies. *Journal of Product Innovation Management*, *38*(1), 4–20.

Archuleta, K. L., Glenn, C., Lawson, D. R., Clady, J. P., & Solomon, S. (2021). I know I should, but do I do it? Connecting covert and overt financial behaviors. *Journal of Financial Counseling and Planning*, *32*(3), 550–563.

Aricò, S. (2014). The contribution of the sciences, technology and innovation to sustainable development: The application of sustainability science from the perspective of UNESCO's experience. *Sustainability Science*, *9*(4), 453–462.

Arnold, G. (2011). *The financial times handbook of corporate finance: A business companion to financial markets and decisions*. Pearson.

Ascher, W. (2020). *The psychology of poverty alleviation: Challenges in developing countries*. Cambridge University Press.

Ashford, N. A., & Hall, R. P. (2011). *Technology, globalization, and sustainable development: Transforming the industrial state*. Yale University Press.

Atif, M., Hassan, M. K., Rabbani, M. R., & Khan, S. (2021). Islamic FinTech: The digital transformation bringing sustainability to Islamic finance. In *COVID-19 and Islamic social finance* (pp. 91–103). Routledge.

Bangura, A. K. (2021). Ŝankhu: A meta-analysis of research on financing sustainability in Africa from a Diopian perspective. *African Development Finance Journal*, *6*(1), 45–65.

Beck, T., Demirgüç-Kunt, A., & Levine, R. (2010). Financial institutions and markets across countries and over time: The updated financial development and structure database. *The World Bank Economic Review*, *24*(1), 77–92.

Boons, F., Montalvo, C., Quist, J., & Wagner, M. (2013). Sustainable innovation, business models and economic performance: An overview. *Journal of Cleaner Production*, *45*, 1–8.

Bouma, J. J., Jeucken, M., & Klinkers, L. (Eds.). (2017). *Sustainable banking: The greening of finance*. Routledge.

Bouma, J., Pinto-Correia, T., & Veerman, C. (2021). Assessing the role of soils when developing sustainable agricultural production systems focused on achieving the UN-SDGs and the EU Green Deal. *Soil Systems*, *5*(3), 56.

Brickell, K., Picchioni, F., Natarajan, N., Guermond, V., Parsons, L., Zanello, G., & Bateman, M. (2020). Compounding crises of social reproduction: Microfinance, over-indebtedness and the COVID-19 pandemic. *World Development*, *136*, 105087.

Busse, D. (2012). *Nachhaltigkeitsaspekte in Theorie und Praxis der Entscheidungsfindung: Perspektiven institutioneller Steuerung in der Immobilienwirtschaft*. Springer-Verlag.

CAPE. (2019, June). *The coalition of finance ministers for climate action*. Santiago de Chile.

Carrillo-Hermosilla, J., del Río, P., & Könnölä, T. (2010). Diversity of eco-innovations: Reflections from selected case studies. *Journal of Cleaner Production*, *18*(10–11), 1073–1083.

CBI. (2018, March). *Post-issuance reporting in the green bond market*. The Climate Bonds Initiative.

Chen, X., Zhang, Y., & Liu, H. (2020). Open innovation in financial services: Evidence from China. *Asian Financial Review*, *18*(2), 105–120.

Chesbrough, H. (2003). *Open innovation: The new imperative for creating and profiting from technology*. Harvard Business Press.

Clements, R. (2022). Misaligned incentives in markets: Envisioning finance that benefits all of society. *DePaul Business and Commercial Law*, *19*(1), 11–64.

Climent, F. (2018). Ethical versus conventional banking: A case study. *Sustainability*, *10*(7), 2152.

Dahlander, L., & Gann, D. M. (2010). How open is innovation? *Research Policy*, *39*(6), 699–709.

Da Silva Inácio, L., & Delai, I. (2021). Sustainable banking: A systematic review of concepts and measurements. *Environment, Development and Sustainability*, 1–39.

De Cianni, R., Varese, G. C., & Mancuso, T. (2023). A further step toward sustainable development: The case of the edible mushroom supply chain. *Foods*, *12* (18), 3433.

Dziawgo, T. (2021). Wealth tech impact on wealth management sector. *European Research Studies*, *24*(3B), 141–151.

Ethical Markets Media. (2011). *Green Transition Scoreboard August 2011 Update*. Ethical Markets Media, St. Augustine.

Feng, J., Goodell, J. W., & Shen, D. (2022). ESG rating and stock price crash risk: Evidence from China. *Finance Research Letters*, *46*, 102476.

Foley, A. M., Heffron, R. J., Al Kez, D., Furszyfer Del Rio, D. D., McInerney, C., & Welfle, A. (2024). Restoring trust in ESG investing through the adoption of just transition ethics. *Renewable and Sustainable Energy Reviews*, *199*, 114557.

Fox, J., & Bartholomae, S. (2020). Household finances, financial planning, and COVID-19. *Financial Planning Review*, *3*(4), e1103.

Gan, Q., Yang, L., Liu, J., Cheng, X., Qin, H., Su, J., & Xia, W. (2021). The level of regional economic development, green image, and enterprise environmental protection investment: Empirical evidence from China. *Mathematical Problems in Engineering*, *2021*(1), 5522351.

Gassmann, O., Frankenberger, K., Choudury, M., & Csik, M. (2020). *The business model navigator: The strategies behind the most successful companies*. Pearson.

Ghosh, S. (2022). Gender and financial inclusion: Does technology make a difference? *Gender, Technology and Development*, *26*(2), 195–213.

Gompers, P. A., Kaplan, S. N., & Mukharlyamov, V. (2022). Private equity and COVID-19. *Journal of Financial Intermediation*, *3*(2), 100968.

Green, D. (2012, January). The ESGI (née SRI) challenge. In *Investment management: Meeting the noble challenges of funding pensions, deficits, and growth* (pp. 201–212). John Wiley & Sons, Inc.

GSMA. (2020). *Mobile money and gender equality: Financial inclusion through mobile technology*. GSMA.

Guo, B., Hu, P., & Lin, J. (2024). The effect of digital infrastructure development on enterprise green transformation. *International Review of Financial Analysis*, *92*, 103085.

Győri, Z., Khan, Y., & Szegedi, K. (2021). Business model and principles of a values-based bank—Case study of MagNet Hungarian community bank. *Sustainability*, *13*(16), 9239.

Haas, R., Ajanovic, A., Ramsebner, J., Perger, T., Knápek, J., & Bleyl, J. W. (2021). Financing the future infrastructure of sustainable energy systems. *Green Finance*, *3*(1), 90–118. https://doi.org/10.3934/GF.2021006

Hao, P., Alharbi, S. S., Hunjra, A. I., & Zhao, S. (2024). How do ESG ratings promote digital technology innovation? *International Review of Financial Analysis*, *97*, 103886.

Hassan, I., Paltrinieri, A., Floreani, J., & Dreassi, A. (2022). Corporate social responsibility and financial stability: Evidence from the global financial sector. *Journal of Financial Stability*, *58*, 100960.

Hawley, J. P. (2017). Responsible investing and the value of the long term. *Journal of Applied Corporate Finance*, *29*(2), 35–40.

He, H., Zhang, B., & Huang, X. (2025). *Can China's fintech ecosystem function as a shock absorber for corporate bankruptcy risk?* https://doi.org/10.2139/ssrn.5178756

ICMA. (2018). *Green bond principles: Voluntary process guidelines for issuing green bonds*. ICMA.

Islam, M. Z. (2024). Can China's rural revitalisation policies be an example for other countries aligning with sustainable development goals (SDGs)-1, 2 and 12? *China Agricultural Economic Review*, *16*(4), 763–786.

ITU, UNDP & Partners. (2023). *The role of digital technologies in accelerating progress towards the sustainable development goals*. https://www.itu.int/itu-d/reports/statistics/idi2023/

Jasmine, J., & Rohim, A. N. (2024). Sharia green crowdfunding as a sustainable financing solution for halal MSMEs empowerment. *SERAMBI: Jurnal Ekonomi Manajemen dan Bisnis Islam*, *6*(3), 271–288.

Kardos, M. (2012). The relationship between entrepreneurship, innovation and sustainable development. Research on European Union countries. *Procedia Economics and Finance*, *3*, 1030–1035.

Kim, Y., Lee, J., & Ahn, J. (2019). Innovation towards sustainable technologies: A socio-technical perspective on accelerating transition to aviation biofuel. *Technological Forecasting and Social Change*, *145*, 317–329.

Kong, T., Sun, R., Sun, G., & Song, Y. (2022). Effects of digital finance on green innovation considering information asymmetry: An empirical study based on Chinese listed firms. *Emerging Markets Finance and Trade*, *58*(15), 4399–4411.

Kuchler, T., & Stroebel, J. (2021). Social dynamics of ESG investing. *Review of Financial Studies*, *34*(2), 622–668.

Kwilinski, A. (2023). The relationship between sustainable development and digital transformation: Bibliometric analysis. *Virtual Economics*, *6*(3), 56–69.

Laucereno, S. F. (2022). The role of green fintech in promoting financial inclusion and sustainability. *Journal of Sustainable Finance & Investment*, *12*(2), 459–474.

Li, L., Hong, X., & Peng, K. (2019). A spatial panel analysis of carbon emissions, economic growth and high-technology industry in China. *Structural Change and Economic Dynamics*, *49*, 83–92.

Li, J., & Li, B. (2022). Digital inclusive finance and urban innovation: Evidence from China. *Review of Development Economics*, *26*(2), 1010–1034.

Lozano, R. (2007). Collaboration as a pathway for sustainability. *Sustainable Development*, *15*(6), 370–381.

Lozano, R. (2008). Envisioning sustainability three-dimensionally. *Journal of Cleaner Production*, *16*(17), 1838–1846.

Lv, X., Wang, Y., Liu, L., & Yin, S. (2024). Digital green innovation economy for Industry 5.0. *Sustainable Economies*, *2*(1), 8.

Magazzino, C., Mutascu, M., Mele, M., & Sarkodie, S. A. (2021). Energy consumption and economic growth in Italy: A wavelet analysis. *Energy Reports*, *7*, 1520–1528.

Malik, S., Fatima, F., Imran, A., Chuah, L. F., Klemeš, J. J., Khaliq, I. H., Asif, S., Aslam, M., Jamil, F., Durrani, A. K., Akbar, M. M., Shahbaz, M., Usman, M., Atabani, A. E., Naqvi, S. R., Yusup, S., & Bokhari, A. (2019). Improved project control for sustainable development of construction sector to reduce environment risks. *Journal of Cleaner Production*, *240*, 118214.

Mavlutova, I., Volkova, T., Natrins, A., Spilbergs, A., Arefjevs, I., & Miahkykh, I. (2021). Financial sector transformation in the era of digitalization. *Estudios de Economia Aplicada*, *38*(4). https://doi.org/10.25115/eea.v38i4.4055

Migliorelli, M., & Dessertine, P. (2019). *The rise of green finance in Europe. Opportunities and challenges for issuers, investors and marketplaces* (Vol. 2, p. 2019). Palgrave Macmillan.

Miroshnychenko, I., & De Massis, A. (2022). Sustainability practices of family and nonfamily firms: A worldwide study. *Technological Forecasting and Social Change*, *174*, 121079.

Mo, R., Peng, X. H., Wang, S. B., & Zhang, J. Z. (2024). Knowledge mapping of green economy research: A bibliometric analysis. *SAGE Open*, *14*(4). https://doi.org/10.1177/21582440241293581

Molina Romo, Ó., & Godino Pons, A. (2018). *Bargaining for social rights in the public sector: Spain*. https://ddd.uab.cat/record/196435

Montalvo, C. (2006). What triggers change and innovation? *Technovation*, *26*(3), 312–323.

Montalvo, C., Diaz-Lopez, F., & Brandes, F. (2011). *Eco-innovation opportunities in nine sectors of the European economy*. European Sector Innovation Watch. European Commission, Directorate General Enterprise and Industry.

Mulder, K. F. (2007). Innovation for sustainable development: From environmental design to transition management. *Sustainability Science*, *2*(2), 253–263.

Ottosson, S., Moldavska, A., Ogorodnyk, O., & Skogsrød, T. (2017). What is and how to develop sustainable innovation? In *Leadership, innovation and entrepreneurship as driving forces of the global economy* (pp. 191–209). Springer International Publishing.

Ozili, P. K. (2018). Impact of digital finance on financial inclusion and stability. *Borsa Istanbul Review*, *18*(4), 329–340.

Pastoors, S. (2020). *Towards sustainable innovation*. Tectum Wissenschaftsverlag.

Phoon, K., & Koh, F. (2017). Robo-advisors and wealth management. *Journal of Alternative Investments*, *20*(3), 79–94.

Porter, M., & Kramer, M. (2011, January–February). Creating shared value. *Harvard Business Review*, *17*.

Porter, M. E. (2011). *Competitive advantage of nations: Creating and sustaining superior performance*. Simon & Schuster.

Rogall, H. (2012). Wirtschaftliches Wachstum in einer nachhaltigen Ökonomie–Ein Widerspruch? *Gesellschaftsreform und ökologisches Wirtschaften*, *46*.

Rosenbaum, M. S., Russell-Bennett, R., & Contreras-Ramírez, G. (2022). Research priorities in the new service marketplace. *Journal of Services Marketing*, *36*(8), 1009–1014.

Sakyi-Nyarko, C., Ahmad, A. H., Akolgo, P. M., & Murinde, V. (2025). Digital financial inclusion–trade nexus in Africa: Evidence, constraints, and future directions. In *Trade and investment in Africa* (pp. 453–478). Routledge.

Sanguino, R., Barroso, A., Fernández-Rodríguez, S., & Sánchez-Hernández, M. I. (2020). Current trends in economy, sustainable development, and energy: A circular economy view. *Environmental Science and Pollution Research*, *27*(1), 1–7.

Schwab, K. (2016). The fourth industrial revolution. *World Economic Forum*, *12*.

Sendjaja, T., Zainal, V. R., Imaningsih, E. S., Nawangsari, L. C., & Lo, S. J. (2022). Digital bank transformation: Sustainable innovation in financial institutions. *Journal of World Science*, *1*(12), 1118–1131.

Sheth, J. (2021). New areas of research in marketing strategy, consumer behavior, and marketing analytics: The future is bright. *Journal of Marketing Theory and Practice*, *29*(1), 3–12.

Shumali, S. I., & Abuamsha, M. K. (2021, November). The impact of ownership concentration on stock performance in the Palestinian firms listed in the stock exchange. In *International conference on business and technology* (pp. 385–402). Springer International Publishing.

Song, M., Zheng, C., & Wang, J. (2022). The role of digital economy in China's sustainable development in a post-pandemic environment. *Journal of Enterprise Information Management*, *35*(1), 58–77.

Spangenberg, J. H. (2011). Sustainability science: A review, an analysis and empirical lessons. *Environmental Conservation*, *38*(3), 275–287.

Stefan, I., & Bengtsson, L. (2017). Unravelling appropriability mechanisms and openness depth effects on firm performance across stages in the innovation process. *Technological Forecasting and Social Change*, *120*, 252–260.

Takalo, S. K., & Tooranloo, H. S. (2021). Green innovation: A systematic literature review. *Journal of Cleaner Production*, *279*, 122474.

Tay, L. Y., Tai, H. T., & Tan, G. S. (2022). Digital financial inclusion: A gateway to sustainable development. *Heliyon*. https://doi.org/10.1016/j.heliyon.2022.e09766

TEG. (2019, January). *Consultation document on the update of the non-binding guidelines on non-financial reporting*. European Commission.

Thanasi-Boçe, M., & Hoxha, J. (2024). Blockchain technology as a catalyst for sustainable development: Exploring economic, social, and environmental synergies. *Academic Journal of Interdisciplinary Studies*, *13*(2), 151–170. https://doi.org/10.36941/ajis-2024-0041

The Bill and Melinda Gates Foundation. (2019). *Digital financial services for women: Empowering women through mobile technology*. Bill & Melinda Gates Foundation.

UN. (2015). *Transforming our world: The 2030 agenda for sustainable development*. United Nations.

UNDP. (2020). *Sustainable development goals and innovation*. United Nations Development Programme. https://www.undp.org:contentReference[oaicite:14]{index=14}

UNEP. (2021). *Global environment outlook*. UNEP.

UNEP FI. (2021). *Principles for responsible banking*. UNEP FI.

UNFCCC. (2015). *The Paris Agreement*. United Nations Framework Convention on Climate Change.

Vezzoli, C., & Manzini, E. (2017). Design for sustainable consumption and production systems. In *System innovation for sustainability* (Vol. 1, pp. 148–168). Routledge.

Villeroy, F. V. (2019, July 14). Climate change: A financial risk for banks. *The Wall Street Journal*. https://www.wsj.com/articles/climate-change-a-financial-risk-for-banks-11563125833?eafs_enabled=false&utm_source=chatgpt.com

Voegtlin, C., & Scherer, A. G. (2017). Responsible innovation and the innovation of responsibility: Governing sustainable development in a globalized world. *Journal of Business Ethics*, *143*, 227–243.

Walz, R., Pfaff, M., Marscheider Weidemann, F., & Glöser-Chahoud, S. (2017). Innovations for reaching the green sustainable development goals – Where will they come from? *International Economics and Economic Policy*, *14*, 449–480.

Wang, Q., & Dong, Z. (2021). Does financial development promote renewable energy? Evidence of G20 economies. *Environmental Science and Pollution Research*, *28*(45), 64461–64474.

Wang, J., Ma, M., Dong, T., & Zhang, Z. (2023). Do ESG ratings promote corporate green innovation? *International Review of Financial Analysis*, *87*, 102623.

Weber, O. (2012). Environmental credit risk management in banks and financial service institutions. *Business Strategy and the Environment*, *21*(4), 248–263.

World Bank. (2022). *World development report*. World Bank.
World Commission on Environment and Development. (1987). *Our common future*. United Nations.
Wu, R., Li, J., Dai, Y., Shen, X., & Hossain, M. A. (2024). Impact of environmental, social, and governance on innovation in Chinese listed firms. *Sustainability*, *16* (17), 7482.
Xu, X., & Xu, R. (2023). Role of green financing and stability in the development of green resources in China. *Resources Policy*, *85*, 103954.
Yip, A. W., & Bocken, N. M. (2018). Sustainable business model archetypes for the banking industry. *Journal of Cleaner Production*, *174*, 150–169.
Yoon, B., Lee, J. H., & Byun, R. (2018). Does ESG performance enhance firm value? Evidence from Korea. *Sustainability*, *10*(10), 3635.
Zairis, G., Liargovas, P., & Apostolopoulos, N. (2024). Sustainable finance and ESG importance: A systematic literature review and research agenda. *Sustainability*, *16* (7), 2878.

Section 5

Finance, FinTech and Sustainability

Chapter 18

Does FinTech Adoption Matter for Bank Performance? Evidence From Tunisian Conventional Banks

Eya Belaid[a] *and Issal Haj-Salem*[b]

[a]University of Monastir, Tunisia
[b]University of Monastir, Tunisia and Université de la Manouba, Tunisia

Abstract

The purpose of this chapter is to investigate whether the financial technologies (FinTech) adoption by Tunisian conventional banks affects bank performance. As a measure of FinTech adoption, the authors used a dichotomous variable following the implementation of a collaboration with FinTech. The authors relied on a final sample of 154 bank-year observations for the period of 2009–2022. The authors find that the adoption of FinTech has a negative impact on bank financial performance. The authors' chapter adds to the existing literature by being the first empirical evidence in the Tunisian context for the impact of FinTech adoption on bank performance. It offers some implications relevant to the debate about the consequences of FinTech adoption. Indeed, given that the effective collaboration of banks with FinTechs in the Tunisian context remains in its infancy and is constantly evolving, this could explain this negative impact. Accordingly, it is necessary to have a clear legal framework to avoid operational risks for banks collaborating with FinTechs and to take advantage of such collaboration.

Keywords: FinTech; technologies; bank performance; conventional banks; Tunisia

Sustainability in Accounting and Finance Education, 331–345

Published under exclusive licence by Emerald Publishing Limited
doi:10.1108/978-1-80686-393-820261018

1. Introduction

The Tunisian banks play a central role in the architecture of the national financial system. As pillars of economic stability and drivers of the country's competitiveness, they occupy a strategic position in financing the economy and supporting various economic actors. Their essential mission is based on collecting deposits, managing payment methods and distributing credit, thus contributing to the fluidity and efficiency of financial transactions. At the same time, the rise of digital technologies has profoundly transformed many sectors, including finance. Indeed, the emergence of financial technologies (FinTech) constitutes one of the most significant developments of recent decades. Emerging in the aftermath of the 2008 global financial crisis, FinTech are the result of the reorientation of many financial professionals, particularly bankers, who sought to redefine financial services by exploiting the opportunities offered by technological innovation. Their goal is to make financial services more accessible, faster and less expensive, leveraging advanced technological solutions. The term 'FinTech' is a contraction of the words 'finance' and 'technology' referring to innovative companies that are reinventing financial and banking services through the use of emerging technologies. These include the internet, artificial intelligence (AI), data mining, big data processing, cloud computing and blockchain technology. The rapid evolution of digital technologies has transformed the global financial landscape, giving rise to FinTech, a sector that combines finance and technological innovation to improve financial services. In Tunisia, the adoption of FinTech is part of a dynamic digital transformation aimed at modernising the financial system and promoting financial inclusion. According to data from the Tunisian Monetics Company (SMT, Société Monétique Tunisie), the volume of electronic transactions reached 27,891 billion dinars in 2024, recording a growth of 10.6% compared to the previous year. The total number of transactions increased from 149 million to 163 million, an increase of 9.4% in one year (We Are Tech Africa, 2024). This increase reflects the rise of digital payments and the growing interest of Tunisians in these solutions. Furthermore, mobile payments via electronic wallets have seen strong growth, with 5.1 million transactions in 2024, representing a volume of 1,394 million dinars. This growing adoption is explained by the simplicity and speed of the transactions carried out, which are mainly divided between payments at merchants (49.4%) and money transfers between users (36.6%) (We Are Tech Africa, 2024).

However, despite this momentum, the FinTech sector in Tunisia faces several challenges, particularly regulatory ones. A study conducted by Tunisian Startups in 2023 revealed that 52.6% of FinTech startups find the regulatory framework daunting, while 57.9% consider administrative procedures to be a hindrance. Furthermore, 90% of FinTech players believe that collaboration with financial system regulators is insufficient (Agence Ecofin, 2023). Faced with these challenges, the Tunisian authorities are multiplying initiatives to support this transformation. The Central Bank of Tunisia (BCT) has implemented projects such as the TuniCheck platform, aimed at digitising checks, and the adoption of the Society for Worldwide Interbank Financial Telecommunication – International Organization for Standardization 20022 standard, facilitating international financial exchanges. Furthermore, Tunisia's integration into the Pan-African Payment and Settlement System (PAPSS) is expected to simplify cross-border payments across the African continent (We Are Tech Africa, 2024). There is a notable lack of literature investigating the impact of FinTech on banking performance in the Tunisian context.

Indeed, recent research has investigated the consequences of FinTech. Some studies have been interested in the impact of FinTech on financial stability (e.g., Cheng & Qu, 2020; Haj-Salem, 2025; Liem et al., 2022; Phan et al., 2020; Safiullah & Paramati, 2022), on stock returns (e.g., Missaoui et al., 2025), on the societal sustainability effects (e.g., Hiew et al., 2025) and bank performance (e.g. Baker et al., 2023; Kayed et al., 2025; Phan et al., 2020). Even though the impact of FinTech on bank performance has been recently investigated in some studies, we consider that it still needs further investigation, mainly in emerging markets and particularly in the Tunisian one, which, to the best of our knowledge, has not been investigated until today. Our research, therefore, aims to examine the impact of FinTech adoption on banking performance for Tunisian conventional banks. As banking performance is a major strategic issue, financial institutions are currently striving to improve their measurement and analysis tools to more accurately assess their profitability, optimise their processes and refine their strategies. The integration of FinTech, therefore, represents an essential lever for strengthening banking competitiveness in the face of changes in the global financial landscape (Acar & Çıtak, 2019). Our study aims to provide an understanding of the relationship between FinTech and banking financial performance. Researchers have recently begun to study the impact of FinTech on banking performance (Kharrat et al., 2024). However, to our knowledge, this is the first study on conventional Tunisian banks to examine the impact of FinTech on banking performance.

To do this, our study was based on a final sample of 154 bank-year observations over the period from 2009 to 2022. The empirical findings show that the FinTech adoption has a negative impact on bank performance. Consequently, we conclude that FinTech adoption decreases the bank performance, which could mainly be explained through the agency theory and resource-based view theory.

We believe that our study has several contributions. Indeed, investigating FinTech consequences adds to the growing stream of FinTech research. Moreover, to the best of our knowledge, no study, to date, has investigated the impact of FinTech adoption on bank performance in the Tunisian context.

The remainder of this chapter will be organised as follows. Section 2 is dedicated to the literature review and hypothesis development. Section 3 is concerned with the research methodology. Section 4 is about the presentation and results discussion. And finally, Section 5 concludes.

2. Literature Review and Hypothesis Development

A literature review showed us that some authors have studied the impact of FinTech on banking financial performance. The contexts and results of these studies differ. For example, Aduda and Kingoo (2012) (Kenya), Akhisar et al. (2015) (Developed and developing countries), Shelar and Kumar (2019) (India), Lee et al. (2021) (China) and Kharrat et al. (2024) working on the banking sector in the Middle East and North Africa (MENA) region. For instance, Akhisar et al. (2015) analysed the impact of technological innovations on banking performance in developed and developing countries over the period 2005 to 2013 using a dynamic panel model. They concluded that electronic banking services, whether in developing or developed countries, have a significantly positive effect on the overall performance of banks, particularly in terms of profitability (ROE, ROA), when the results are assessed globally.

Furthermore, Shelar and Kumar (2019) highlighted that digitalisation has become a necessity within the banking sector in India. This necessity stems from the fierce competition within the sector and changes in the expectations of the next generation of customers. Their findings showed that the impact of digitalisation on banks' profitability is negative, which can lead to a reduction in profitability even with increased lending. This trend could be explained by an increase in operational costs, including fixed costs and personnel expenses, which is consistent with the findings of other reviewed studies. However, it is noted that digitalisation had a positive impact on liquidity by improving the cash position of banks through the release of working capital. Moreover, Lee et al. (2021) studied the impact of FinTech development on the profitability of the Chinese banking sector from 2003 to 2017. For this analysis, banks' accounting data were collected from Bureau van Dijk – from the international banking database Bank scope BVD-IBCA Bank Focus database for a sample of 590 observations. FinTech industry development indices were constructed. The study results show that state-owned commercial banks use less advanced technologies but still display the best cost-effectiveness. Furthermore, the authors found that FinTech innovations improve both the technology adopted by banks and their profitability.

Delgado and Nieto (2004) analysed the development of online banking services in Spain and their impact on bank profitability. This research is based on a 2002 survey conducted by the Bank of Spain, in which banking institutions participated voluntarily. The authors emphasised that Spanish banks are investing heavily in information technology, particularly the Internet. However, their situation differs from that of financial institutions in other major industrialised economies such as France, Germany, Italy and the United States. Indeed, Northern European countries have significantly higher adoption rates of online banking. Despite this, Spanish banks make more intensive use of online banking services than the country's population as a whole. The survey reveals that, although the market share of Spanish banks' deposits remains relatively low compared to that observed in other European countries, it remains comparable. However, their overall profitability is negative, due to a decline in revenues from banking fees and an increase in financial costs. This situation reflects increased competition, not only between online banks and traditional banks, but also among online banks themselves, despite the cost savings that the internet is expected to generate in transactions. Finally, this study highlights the challenges facing Spanish authorities in adopting new technologies, particularly in terms of regulation and stability of the banking system. The authors emphasise the need for regulators to preserve the balance of the financial sector while respecting the principle of neutrality with respect to the various banking distribution channels.

Another study of Frederica et al. (2021) analysed the impact of FinTech cooperation and bank performance, while incorporating regulatory implementation as a moderating variable. To conduct this research, the authors collected primary data by distributing questionnaires to bank employees holding senior positions and with at least three years of professional experience. A total of 170 responses were obtained. In this study, bank performance is the dependent variable. It is assessed along four dimensions: customer satisfaction, learning and growth, financial results and internal process efficiency. The independent variable is collaboration between FinTech and banks, measured across three dimensions: processes, costs and services. Finally, the moderating variable chosen by the authors is regulatory implementation, assessed across five dimensions: attitudes, communication, external environment, problem characteristics and resources. The results obtained do not demonstrate a significant link between cooperation between banks and FinTech and banking performance. Furthermore, regulatory implementation does not appear to strengthen the influence of this collaboration. From a policy perspective, the study highlights the need to establish a specific regulatory framework for FinTech services, as well as regulations adapted to cooperation between banks and FinTech. Furthermore, it highlights the importance of financial and digital education for the general public to limit the risks associated with illegal FinTech. Finally, the protection of customer data appears to be a major issue, requiring the implementation of appropriate policies to ensure its security.

This literature review showed that several studies have examined the impact of FinTech on banking performance, with mixed results. Some studies, such as those by Lee et al. (2021) and Campanella et al. (2020), highlight a positive effect of financial innovation on bank performance. However, other studies, such as those by Delgado and Nieto (2004) and Frederica et al. (2021), highlight negative effects linked to this transformation of the banking sector.

Furthermore, the impact of FinTech adoption on bank performance could be explained according to the agency theory (Jensen & Meckling, 1976). Indeed, the collaboration between banks (principal) and FinTech (agent) may generate conflicts of interest, given that the former is likely to seek financial profitability and financial stability, while the latter is more interested in technological development. In addition, the delegation of some operations to FinTech (agent) may cause operational risks that we believe will have negative consequences on banking performance.

Moreover, according to the resource-based view theory (Barney, 1991), adopting FinTech requires skills and technological resources within the bank that can generate considerable costs. However, such expensive technological installations may harm performance, especially if there is no real value creation.

In our study, following the agency theory and the resource-based view theory, and following prior research (e.g., Delgado & Nieto, 2004; Frederica et al., 2021), we formulate the following hypothesis:

H1. The FinTech adoption has a negative impact on bank performance.

3. Methodology

3.1 Sample Selection

The aim of this study is to examine the impact of FinTech on the financial performance of Tunisian banks. The study was conducted on a sample of 11 conventional Tunisian banks listed on the Tunisian Stock Exchange (BVMT) over a 14-year period from 2009 to 2022. This represents 154 bank-year observations.

Data collection was carried out manually from annual reports available on banks' websites, the BVMT website and the Financial Market Council (CMF) website. Only listed banks were considered due to data availability. Table 18.1 presents the complete list of banks selected for our analysis.

Table 18.1. List of Sample Banks.

Bank Name	Abbreviation	Web Site
La Banque de Tunisie	BT	http://www.bt.com.tn/
Société Tunisienne de banque	STB	http://www.stb.com.tn/
Banque Nationale Agricole	BNA	http://www.bna.com.tn/
Amen Bank	AB	http://www.amenbank.com.tn/
Banque Attijari de Tunisie	ATTJ	http://www.attijaribank.com.tn
Banque internationale arabe de Tunisie	BIAT	http://www.biat.com.tn/
Banque de l'Habitat BH	BH	http://www.bh.com.tn/
Banque de Tunisie et des émirats	BTE	http://www.bte.com.tn/
L'Arab Tunisian Bank	ATB	http://www.atb.com.tn/
Union International Bank	UIB	http://www.uib.com.tn/
Union Bancaire pour le Commerce et l'Industrie	UBCI	http://www.ubci.com.tn/

Source: Author's own creation.

Note: This table provides a list of the conventional Tunisian banks in the study sample.

3.2 Variable Definitions

3.2.1 Dependent Variable

We used the ROA ratio to measure the bank's performance. This measure was widely used in previous studies to examine the relationship between FinTech and bank performance (e.g., Aduda & Kingoo, 2012). The ROA is calculated by dividing net income by the bank's total assets: ROA = Net income/Total assets.

3.2.2 Independent Variable

In our study, the independent variable is the FinTech adoption, which we measured through a dichotomous measure that takes the value of 1 for the period following the establishment of a collaboration with a FinTech, otherwise 0 (Zhang et al., 2022). This approach allows us to clearly distinguish the two phases and assess the impact of FinTech on bank performance.

3.2.3 Control Variables

For this study, several control variables were used, which are the following:

Age is measured as the difference between the year at time t and the year at time $t-1$ when the bank was established (Kharrat et al., 2024; Talavera et al., 2018).

Size: Firm size is measured by the natural logarithm of the bank's total assets (Talavera et al., 2018).

Solvency ratio (SOLV) is an effective tool for assessing a banking institution's ability to meet its financial commitments using all of its assets, while also providing insight into the bank's overall profitability. It is calculated by the total net equity divided by the total risk-weighted assets.

Liquidity Coverage Ratio (LCR) is used to assess a bank's liquidity by comparing a bank's total credits to its total deposits for the same period (Kharrat et al., 2024).

Market Capitalisation Ratio (MCR) is the valuation of all the shares outstanding calculated as calculated by multiplying the current market price per share by the total number of outstanding shares.

Debt-to-Equity Ratio (DER) is calculated as the ratio of total debt to total equity.

Net Banking Income: The bank's net banking income is calculated as the difference between the operating income and the operating expenses.

3.3 Regression Model

$$\begin{aligned} \text{ROA}_{it} = {} & \alpha_0 + \beta_1 \text{ FINTECH}_{it} + \beta_2 \text{ AGE}_{it} + \beta_3 \text{ SIZE}_{it} + \beta_4 \text{ SOLV}_{it} + \beta_5 \text{ LCR}_{it} \\ & + \beta_6 \text{ DER}_{it} + \beta_7 \text{ MCR}_{it} + \beta_8 \text{ NBI}_{it} + \epsilon \end{aligned}$$

Where:

α = The intercept.
$\beta_1, \ldots, \beta_8$ = Regression coefficients.
ϵ = Error term.

Table 18.2 presents the variables' definition of the model.

4. Results

In our study, we adopt a rigorous methodology to examine the impact of FinTech on bank performance. Our methodological approach includes stationarity tests, cointegration assessments and panel data specification tests using Eviews 10 software. Before estimating our model, we check the stationarity of our variables using both graphical representations and descriptive statistics. This preliminary step will allow us to better understand the nature of the time series under study and ensure the robustness of our subsequent analyses.

Table 18.2. Variables' Definition.

Variable	Symbol	Description
Bank performance	ROA	ROA = Net income/Total assets
FinTech adoption	FINTECH	Takes 1 for the period following the establishment of a collaboration with a FinTech, otherwise 0
Bank age	AGE	The year at time t − The year at time $t-1$ when the bank was established
Bank size	SIZE	Ln (total assets)
Solvency ratio	SOLV	Total equity/Total risk-weighted assets
Liquidity coverage ratio	LCR	Total credits/Total deposits
Debt-to-Equity ratio	DER	Total debt/Total equity
Market capitalisation ratio	MCR	Market price per share × The total number of outstanding shares
Net banking income	NBI	The operating income − The operating expenses

Source: Author's own creation.
Note: This table defines the variables of the study.

First, in this model, we perform a series of tests to assess the stationarity and cointegration of the variables. We begin by using the Levin, Lin & Chu *t* linear stationarity test to examine the stability of the variables. Then, we apply the 'Auto Regressive Distributed Lag' ('ARDL') approach of Pesaran and Shin (1999) to determine if there is a cointegration relationship, considering the 0th and 1st order integration of the variables. Subsequently, we note the presence of stationarity between the variables except for the market capitalisation.

4.1 Descriptive Statistics and Graphical Presentation

To increase the clarity and depth of our analysis of the variables, we chose to use a graphical representation to examine the evolution of bank branches as a function of these variables. The Fig. 18.1 demonstrates the non-stationarity of all variables, as they represent peaks and jumps.

The descriptive statistics for our study are presented in Table 18.3.

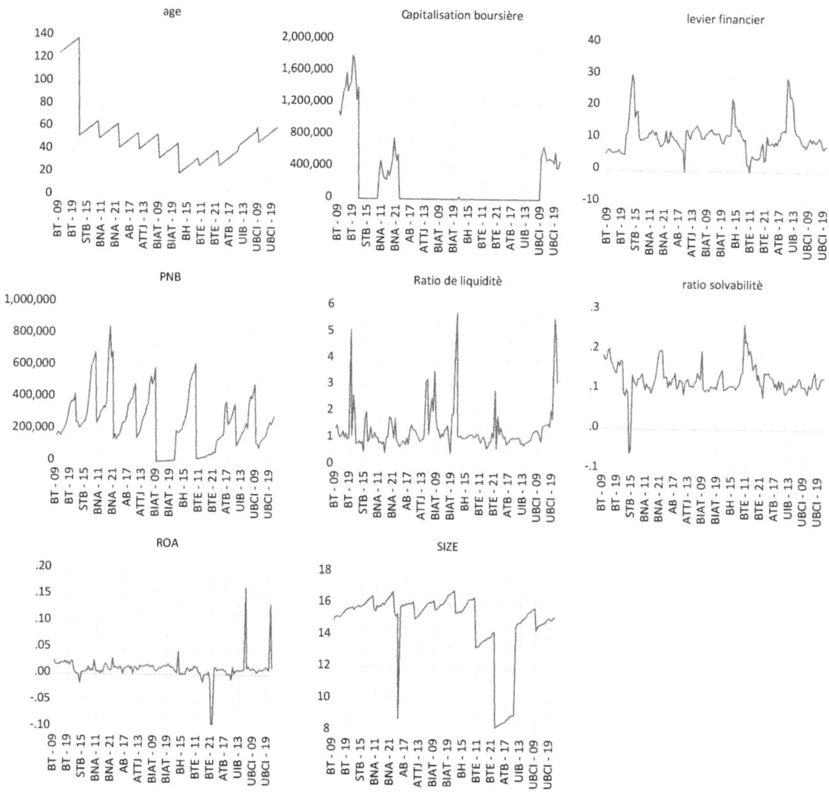

Fig. 18.1. Graphic Presentation. *Source:* Author's own creation.

Table 18.3. Descriptive Statistics.

	ROA	AGE	SIZE	SOLV	LCR	DER	MCR	NBI
Mean	0.011081	52.88312	14.84100	0.125131	1.357140	10.61232	213029.4	253334.0
Median	0.010800	49.00000	15.55679	0.118200	1.084950	10.14141	662.2500	239018.5
Maximum	0.165200	138.0000	16.86550	0.265000	5.760000	30.01217	1797750.	849997.0
Minimum	−0.092500	20.00000	8.258681	−0.062100	0.462000	−0.250507	7.980000	2629.000
Std. Dev.	0.021320	27.20125	2.168126	0.037738	0.856355	5.082403	425105.4	177383.2
Obs.	154	154	154	154	154	154	154	154

Source: Author's own creation.
Note: This table provides descriptive statistics. ROA is the Return on Assets. SIZE is the Bank Size. AGE is the Bank. SOLV is the Solvency of the Bank. LCR is the Liquidity Coverage Ratio. DER is the Debt-to-Equity Ratio. MCR is the Market Capitalisation Ratio. NBI is the Net Banking Income All variable measures are presented in Table 18.1.

4.2 Regression Results

To successfully examine the stationarity of variables, we have chosen two specific methods: a unit root method to perform a Philipe Person linear stationarity test, and another, the Pesaran and Shin ARDL method, to study a cointegration relationship by taking into account the I(0) and I(1) order integration of the variables. To verify the stationarity of variables, we will select a test specifically adapted to panel regression data. This choice is essential given its ability to account for potential irregularities that may arise during the processing of these data, particularly when the panels are not balanced.

To assess the stationarity of the variables, we used a unit root test as shown in Table 18.4. The results highlight the importance of considering the stability of variables when analysing the financial sector. In summary, when the probabilities associated with these results exceed the *p*-value of 5%, this suggests that these variables are not stationary, thus confirming this trend. On the other hand, for variables with a *p*-value less than 5%, they are considered stationary. Thus, we accept the null hypothesis of non-stationarity for variables with a *p*-value greater than 5%, which means that a unit root is present. Therefore, we reject the alternative hypothesis that there is no stationarity. In other words, this indicates the absence of a unit root and confirms that our series is stationary, and vice versa. From our results, it is evident that our variables do not present the same integration, some being of order 0 and others of order 1. To correct the non-stationarity, it is therefore necessary to resort to an ARDL estimation method. This test will help us to evaluate and correct the co-integration relationships between the variables, thus allowing a more precise analysis of their interactions.

Table 18.4. Unit Root Test.

Variables	Probability	Coefficient
NBI	0.09978	2.84341
MCR	0.0001	−3.87172
DER	0.1494	−1.039920
LCR	0.919	1.39948
SOLV	0.5066	0.01646
ROA	0.5199	0.04991
SIZE	0.53	0.09515
FINTECH	0.000	−7.00550

Source: Author's own creation.

Note: This table provides the Unit Root Test. FINTECH is the FinTech adoption for the bank. ROA is the Return On Assets. SIZE is the Bank Size. AGE is the Bank. SOLV is the Solvency of the Bank. LCR is the Liquidity Coverage Ratio. DER is the Debt-to-Equity Ratio. MCR is the Market Capitalisation Ratio. NBI is the Net Banking Income. All variable measures are presented in Table 18.1.

Table 18.5. Results ARDL.

Variables	Probability	Coefficient	Integration Degree
FINTECH	**0.0000*** **	−0.002636	I (0)
Age	**0.0000*** **	−0.00093	I (0)
MCR	0.4938	−2.20	I (1)
NBI	**0.0000*** **	−0.0000	I (0)
DER	**0.0000*** **	−0.000259	I (0)
LCR	**0.0408** **	0.001280	I (0)
SOLV	**0.0000*** **	0.017563	I (0)
SIZE	**0.0000*** **	0.003482	I (0)

Source: Author's own creation.
Note: This table provides the findings. FINTECH is the FinTech adoption for the bank. SIZE is the Bank Size. AGE is the Bank. SOLV is the Solvency of the Bank. LCR is the Liquidity Coverage Ratio. DER is the Debt-to-Equity Ratio. MCR is the Market Capitalisation Ratio. NBI is the Net Banking Income. All variable measures are presented in Table 18.1. *** and ** indicate statistical significance at 1 and 5 levels of statistical significance.

In our study, we use the ARDL cointegration method. A key feature of the ARDL procedure is that it does not require variables to have the same order of integration. Therefore, this technique is relevant even when the variables have different orders of integration, whether type I (0) or I (1).

The ARDL test, as presented in Table 18.5, shows the relationship between the dependent variable (D(ROA)) and a set of explanatory variables such as FinTech, age, leverage, net banking income, liquidity ratio, SOLV and size. Thus, using the ARDL (1,1,1,1) method, with a lag order of 1, it was found that the market capitalisation variable is not stationary, indicated by a probability greater than 5%. With a negative, insignificant coefficient. However, for the other variables, stationarity is observed, but with different coefficients.

First, we note that the FinTech, net banking income and debt have significant effects that negatively affect ROA. Second, we note that the liquidity ratio, SOLV and size variables have significant effects that positively affect ROA.

The FinTech variable has a significant negative impact at the 5% threshold. Accordingly, the hypothesis is confirmed. This means that banks' collaboration with FinTech will lead to a decrease in ROA. This result could be explained in light of the agency theory, since agency conflicts may arise from the adoption of FinTech. Moreover, banks may be subject to operational risks due to the loss of control over some operations delegated to FinTech. In addition, the FinTech adoption is likely to generate considerable costs, which may have a negative impact on bank performance.

5. Conclusion

This study aims to understand the influence of FinTech adoption on bank performance. We adopted a dichotomous measure to measure FinTech adoption, and ROA to measure bank performance. Our sample included 11 conventional listed banks for the period from 2009 to 2022.

Our empirical findings highlighted the negative impact of FinTech on ROA for Tunisian banks. Therefore, our hypothesis was confirmed. Our results are consistent with Delgado (2021) and Frederica et al. (2021), showing that the adoption of FinTech can lead to increased pressure on banks' operational costs and increase risks related to cybersecurity and regulation. This was explained in the light of agency theory and resource-based view theory.

Furthermore, our study has practical implications. Indeed, it highlights the need for banks to adopt a cautious approach to integrating new technologies to better manage the associated risks and optimise their long-term performance.

However, we acknowledge that our study is not without limitations. These limitations are primarily inherent to the sample size. However, we were limited to studying conventional banks listed on the stock exchange. Furthermore, we did not take into account the impact of the health crisis that occurred in 2019.

Finally, given that the effective collaboration of banks with FinTech in the Tunisian context remains in its infancy and is constantly evolving, this leads us to call on financial analysts and researchers to conduct further research on the impact of FinTech on banking performance by focusing on both conventional and Islamic banks. Furthermore, a study on the impact of the health crisis on the association between FinTech and banking performance would be interesting.

References

Acar, O., & Çıtak, Y. E. (2019). Fintech integration process suggestion for banks. *Procedia Computer Science*, *158*, 971–978.

Aduda, J., & Kingoo, N. (2012). The relationship between electronic banking and financial performance among commercial banks in Kenya. *Journal of Finance and Investment Analysis*, *1*(3), 99–118.

Agence Ecofin. (2023). *Étude sur les startups FinTech en Tunisie : défis réglementaires et administratifs*. https://www.agenceecofin.com

Akhisar, I., Tunay, K. B., & Tunay, N. (2015). The effects of innovations on bank performance: The case of electronic banking services. *Procedia-Social and Behavioral Sciences*, *195*, 369–375.

Baker, H., Kaddumi, T. A., Nassar, M. D., & Muqattash, R. S. (2023). Impact of financial technology on improvement of banks' financial performance. *Journal of Risk and Financial Management*, *16*(4), 230.

Barney, J. (1991). Firm resources and sustained competitive advantage. *Journal of Management*, *17*(1), 99–120.

Campanella, F., Serino, L., Battisti, E., Christofi, M., & Giakoumelou, A. (2020, November). Financial technology: Evidence in the European banking system. In *2020 IEEE international conference on technology management, operations and decisions (ICTMOD)* (pp. 1–6). IEEE.

Cheng, M., & Qu, Y. (2020). Does bank FinTech reduce credit risk? Evidence from China. *Pacific-Basin Finance Journal, 63*, 101398.

Delgado, M. (2021). *Digital transition in the banking business. Lessons after COVID-19.* Bank for International Settlements.

Delgado, J., & Nieto, M. J. (2004). Internet banking in Spain: Some stylized facts. *Monetary Integration, Markets and Regulation, Research in Banking and Finance, 4*, 187–209.

Frederica, D., Augustine, Y., Murwaningsari, E., & Mayangsari, S. (2021). The effect of fintech and bank collaboration on banking performance in Indonesia moderated by the implementation of regulations. *International Journal of Business, Economics and Law, 24*(1), 1.

Haj-Salem, I. (2025). Does FinTech disclosure disrupt financial stability? Evidence from Tunisian conventional banks. *Journal of Financial Reporting & Accounting*. https://doi.org/10.1108/JFRA-12-2024-0944

Hiew, L.-C., Lam, M.-T., & Ho, S.-J. (2025). Unveiling the nexus: Unravelling the dynamics of financial inclusion, FinTech adoption and societal sustainability in Malaysia. *Journal of Financial Reporting & Accounting, 23*(2), 575–593. https://doi.org/10.1108/JFRA-12-2023-0791

Jensen, M. C., & Meckling, W. H. (1976). Theory of the firm: Managerial behavior, agency costs and ownership structure. *Journal of Financial Economics, 3*(4), 305–360.

Kayed, S., Alta'any, M., Meqbel, R., Khatatbeh, I. N., & Mahafzah, A. (2025). Bank FinTech and bank performance: Evidence from an emerging market. *Journal of Financial Reporting & Accounting, 23*(2), 518–535.

Kharrat, H., Trichilli, Y., & Abbes, B. (2024). Relationship between FinTech index and bank's performance: A comparative study between Islamic and conventional banks in the MENA region. *Journal of Islamic Accounting and Business Research, 15*(1), 172–195.

Lee, C. C., Li, X., Yu, C. H., & Zhao, J. (2021). Does fintech innovation improve bank efficiency? Evidence from China's banking industry. *International Review of Economics & Finance, 74*, 468–483.

Liem, N. T., Son, T. H., Tin, H. H., & Canh, N. T. (2022). FinTech credit, credit information sharing and bank stability: Some international evidence. *Cogent Business & Management, 9*(1), 2112527.

Missaoui, I., Shah, W. U., & Ben Rejeb, A. (2025). Impact of FinTech and technological innovation on African stock returns: Fresh insights from crisis. *Journal of Financial Reporting & Accounting*. https://doi.org/10.1108/JFRA-10-2024-0716

Pesaran, M. H., & Shin, Y. (1999). An autoregressive distributed lag modelling approach to cointegration analysis. In S. Strom (Ed.), *Econometrics and economic theory in the 20th century* (pp. 371–413). Cambridge University Press.

Phan, D. H. B., Narayan, P. K., Rahman, R. E., & Hutabarat, A. R. (2020). Do financial technology firms influence bank performance? *Pacific-Basin Finance Journal, 62*, 101210.

Safiullah, M., & Paramati, S. R. (2022). The impact of FinTech firms on bank financial stability. *Electronic Commerce Research*, 1–23.

Shelar, S., & Kumar, S. (2019). *Impact of digitisation on efficiency of the working capital finance process & financial Performance-A study of Kotak Mahindra Bank Limited*. SSRN Network.

Talavera, O., Yin, S., & Zhang, M. (2018). Age diversity and bank performance. *Journal of Banking and Finance*, *98*, 181–202.

We Are Tech Africa. (2024). *Tunisian Monetics: Electronic transactions reach 27,891 billion dinars in 2024*. https://www.wearetechafrica.com

Zhang, A., Wang, S., Liu, B., & Liu, P. (2022). How fintech impacts pre-and post-loan risk in Chinese commercial banks. *International Journal of Finance & Economics*, *27*(2), 2514–2529.

Section 6

Digital and Data Capabilities in Sustainability-Aware Assurance

Chapter 19

Vital Skills for Future Auditors in the Digital Age: A Literature Review

Vusani Moyo[a], *Ayodeji Michael Obadire*[b] *and Modimowabarwa Kanyane*[a]

[a]University of Venda, South Africa
[b]Botswana Accountancy College, Botswana

Abstract

The transformation of business models and environments, driven by rapid digitalisation, the globalisation of business and the auditing profession, alongside the growing demand from businesses, investors and stakeholders for enhanced governance, is significantly impacting the auditing profession. Current and future auditors must acquire new skills to remain relevant and competent in delivering high-quality, technology-enabled, real-time audits and assurance services effectively and efficiently. Based on a comprehensive literature review, this study identifies highly developed technical professional skills and business ethics as foundational competencies for auditors. The public expects auditors to safeguard the public interest, make informed professional judgements and uphold the highest standards of professionalism, ethics, integrity, independence and professional scepticism. To ensure relevance, audit quality, efficiency and effectiveness, auditors' technical and professional ethics must be complemented by advanced digital literacy, data analytics, data ethics, professional scepticism, assurance, critical thinking and both soft and business skills. Furthermore, auditors must be proficient in providing assurance services on their clients' digital tools and evaluating reported non-financial information, including environmental, social and governance (ESG) sustainability reports. The capability to conduct forward-looking, continuous and real-time auditing and financial reporting is increasingly essential for auditors. Higher Education Institutions (HEIs) and professional bodies must revise their curricula and competency frameworks to include auditing digital skills, both basic and

Sustainability in Accounting and Finance Education, 349–377

Published under exclusive licence by Emerald Publishing Limited
doi:10.1108/978-1-80686-393-820261019

advanced data analytics, critical thinking, essential soft skills, sustainability and ESG assurance skills, as well as forward-looking, continuous, real-time auditing and financial reporting skills.

Keywords: Digital skills; current and future auditors; vital skills for auditors; ESG; sustainability; auditing technologies

1. Introduction

The auditing profession is changing in response to the rapidly changing business models and environments. According to the surveys done by the Association of Chartered Certified Accountants (ACCA) (2016) and ACCA and Chartered Accountants in Australia and New Zealand (CA ANZ) (2019), the changes in the accountancy and auditing professions are driven by increased regulation and the business stakeholders' demand for stronger governance, the rapid evolution and adoption of the Fourth Industrial Revolution (4IR) digital technologies by business and auditing firms; the globalisation of business and the accountancy and auditing professions; and business, investors and the public's expectations about auditing.

ACCA (2016) asserts that businesses face increased regulation and governance as governments widen their tax nets due to declining tax revenues. On the other hand, investors and other business stakeholders' increased demand for stronger governance and business sustainability is forcing businesses to disclose an increased volume of non-financial information, such as sustainability reports and other environmental, social and governance (ESG) information (Farrell & Paquette, 2023). These changes expand auditor attestation roles as stakeholders expect auditors to assure their clients comply with all regulations and that the disclosed non-financial information is accurately and truthfully reported.

In response to the global transition to the 4IR, businesses are increasingly adopting and using 4IR digital tools, which include artificial intelligence (AI), virtual reality (VR), augmented reality (AR), robotic process automation (RPA), autonomous guided vehicles, cloud technology, Internet of things (IoT), Fintech, blockchain and distributed ledger technologies (BDLT), drone technology and sensors, nanoparticles and additive engineering such as 3-D printing, in their systems and processes (McKinsey & Company, 2022). These 4IR digital tools have accelerated business efficiency, competitiveness and globalisation, enabling them to work seamlessly across jurisdictions (Moyo & Kanyane, 2024). Digitalisation and globalisation of business have also resulted in the exponential growth of Big Data produced by businesses. Businesses and their stakeholders expect their auditors to deliver technology-enabled audits and understand their 4IR digital tools and associated risks for assurance (BDO, 2022).

The auditing profession, especially the Big 4 and mid-tier firms, has responded positively to these demands and expectations by developing and using its own 4IR digital tools. The 4IR auditing digital tools that are shaping the audit profession include AI, RPA, machine learning (ML), natural language processing (NLP), deep learning (DL), drone technology, IoE, sensor technologies, BDLT, smart contracts, cloud technologies and data analytics (ACCA & CA ANZ, 2019; Almufadda & Almezeini, 2022). These technologies enable auditors to reduce costs while effectively and efficiently delivering high-quality, forward-looking, continuous, real-time auditing.

According to Vitali and Giuliani (2024), automating some audit functions also gives auditors time to focus on value-adding activities. The globalisation of business has also resulted in the globalisation of the auditing profession. Consequently, current and future auditors must be able to work across jurisdictions with diverse teams using cloud computing technology and other advanced 4IR auditing digital technologies (Jackson et al., 2022). Cloud computing enables auditors from different jurisdictions to share client information from the same database.

Finally, in the face of increased accounting scandals, businesses, investors and the public expect auditors to safeguard the public interest, make professional judgements, prevent and uncover fraud and exercise the highest standards of professionalism, integrity, independence and professional scepticism. There is a heightened focus on risk, professional scepticism and high-quality audits by the business stakeholders (ACCA & Grant Thornton, 2016).

Despite all these changes, the auditing profession remains at the core of organisations' reporting frameworks. Elliott and Duan (2022) predict that the audit function will remain in demand as long as the principal-agent relationship continues to exist. The auditing profession has always played a critical role in assuring organisation stakeholders, including present and future investors, capital markets, the government (tax authorities and regulators), employees, suppliers, customers and the public, of the truthfulness and fairness of the organisation's reported annual financial statements. Investors and the public rely on the auditors' reports to make investment decisions based on the published financial statements. Regulatory authorities also rely on audited financial statements to determine taxes and levies payable by companies. For these reasons, organisational stakeholders expect auditors to efficiently and effectively deliver quality audits, exercise the highest standards of professionalism, integrity, independence and scepticism and always act in the public interest (ACCA, 2016).

These changes in the business models and environments and the auditing profession demand that current and future auditors develop new skill sets to complement and enhance their traditional technical and professional ethics skills. These new skill sets will enable current and future auditors to deliver high-quality, technology-enabled, real-time audits and assurance services competently and efficiently.

Several studies, including those of ACCA (2016), ACCA and CA ANZ (2019), Kroon et al. (2021), Moyo and Kanyane (2024) and Tsiligiris and Bowyer (2021), have attempted to identify the skill sets of future professional accountants in response to these changes in business models and environments and the accountancy profession. Professional accountants include those working in business, the public sector and public practice (auditors and consultants). On the contrary, limited studies, such as those of BDO (2022), Barac et al. (2016),

Barac et al. (2021), Elliott and Duan (2022) and Farrell and Paquette (2023), have focused on identifying skill sets for current and future auditors. However, these studies tend to be limited in skills and geographical focus and fail to discuss the implications of these changes to the auditing ecosystem. Brydon (2019) recommended the establishment of a corporate auditing profession based on a core set of principles. The focus of corporate auditors will include, but not be limited to the statutory audit of financial statements and assurance of reported non-financial information and regulatory compliance. It is, therefore, important to identify the complete skillsets for current and future auditors and explore how the auditor training ecosystem can support the profession in developing these skills in current and trainee auditors.

Through a structured and comprehensive literature review of 62 journal articles, 9 surveys conducted by professional accounting bodies, the International Federation of Accountants® (IFAC®) current handbook, and 14 published auditing expert opinions, this study aimed to identify the complete skillset for current and future auditors and discuss how the auditor training ecosystem can support current and trainee auditors in developing this complete skillset. Such a skillset will ensure that the audit profession remains relevant and that current and future auditors continue to effectively, efficiently and competently deliver high-quality, technology-enabled, real-time audits and assurance services.

The main findings of the study are as follows. The auditing profession will remain in demand if the principal-agent relationship exists. The technical and professional skills of auditors will remain core to the profession. Auditors must be highly competent in financial accounting and corporate reporting, auditing and assurance, governance and risk management, taxation, financial management, management accounting, business management and strategy and professional and business ethics. To adapt to the changing business models and environment and the globalisation of the auditing profession, current and future auditors must complement these traditional skills with well-developed 4IR auditing skills to enhance their relevance and audit quality, efficiency and effectiveness. These 4IR auditing skills include digital literacy, data analytics, data ethics, professional scepticism, assurance, critical thinking and soft and business skills. Current and future auditors must be skilled in providing assurance services on digital tools their clients use and the reported non-financial information, including ESG (sustainability) reports. Forward-looking, continuous, real-time auditing and financial reporting are increasingly important skills for current and future auditors.

The rest of the paper is structured as follows. Section 2 of the paper identifies the drivers of change in business models and the auditing profession. This is followed by Section 3, which discusses the impact of digital technologies on the auditing profession. Section 4 identifies and discusses the vital skills of current and future auditors. The roles of Higher Education Institutions (HEIs) and Professional Bodies in Shaping the Future Auditors are discussed in Section 5. Section 6 concludes the paper.

2. Drivers of Change in the Auditing Profession

Forbes and KPMG (2017) concede that the accountancy profession, which includes the auditing profession, is changing rapidly. A comprehensive study by ACCA (2019) identified globalisation, geopolitics, resource scarcity and climate change (sustainability), increased business regulation and governance and the changing business and societal expectations of professional accountants, 4IR auditing digital technologies and Big Data and data analytics as the key drivers of change in the accountancy profession. Another survey study by the ACCA and CA ANZ (2019) conclude that the changes in auditing are driven by the volume of data, changes in business models, the shift towards automation and the demand for a proactive and forward-looking approach to audit.

The impact of globalisation on the auditing profession is twofold. The globalisation of business means that auditors must collaborate with their international peers in auditing a multinational business client. This collaboration involves sharing company data, usually through a cloud-based computing platform. The globalisation of business has, in turn, resulted in the globalisation of the auditing profession, as auditors working across jurisdictions must at least have almost the same technical expertise for successful collaboration.

According to Farrell and Paquette (2023), financial statement users want organisations to disclose more information about their activities because of the increased business regulation and governance and focus by businesses, investors and other business stakeholders on resource scarcity, climate change and sustainability. These users want organisations to disclose detailed forward-looking financial and non-financial information, including ESG (sustainability) reports. In turn, the financial statement users expect auditors to assure them that non-financial information reported by the organisations is fairly and accurately disclosed (ACCA & Grant Thornton, 2016; PwC, 2019).

Organisations also increasingly use innovative, sustainable finance funding models to address climate change. Auditors are expected to assure investors that these funding models are effectively used to enhance shareholder value. BDO (2022) and Elliott and Duan (2022) argue that the traditional historical financial statements audit is insufficient to meet these increased business assurance needs. Auditors must, therefore, broaden their audit and assurance scopes and develop specialist attestation skills in these new areas of business reporting to meet these needs.

The rapidly changing business environment and increased financial scandals have also triggered changes in business and societal expectations of auditors. The public also expects auditors to exercise the highest standards of professionalism, integrity, independence and professional scepticism (ACCA, 2016; ACCA & CA ANZ, 2019; Farrell & Paquette, 2023). Professional scepticism involves a critical assessment of evidence and thus supports effective decision-making (ICAEW, 2022). Furthermore, the public expects auditors to protect the public interest, make sound professional judgements and prevent and uncover fraud. These changes in business models, environments and the societal expectations of auditors have huge implications for the skill sets of current and future auditors.

3. The Impact of Digitalisation on the Auditing Profession

Digital technological advancements are the key drivers of change in business models and processes in the 4IR era. Most businesses have responded positively and adopted these 4IR digital technologies and automated manufacturing and management processes (including the finance function). The digitalisation of business has increased business globalisation and accelerated the growth of Big Data. These 4IR digital technologies have significantly changed how organisations and individuals function and make decisions (Arnaboldi et al., 2017).

Because of the client-auditor relationship and the public expectation of the audit function, it is unsurprising that the rapid 4IR technological advancements, changes in the business environment and models and the accelerated growth in Big Data have also impacted the audit profession. The audit profession is thus also undergoing rapid changes driven by Big Data, changes in business models, increased audit and attestation scope, the shift towards digitalisation and automation and the demand for a proactive, forward-looking, continuous and real-time approach to auditing (ACCA & CA ANZ, 2019).

The top audit firms have fully embraced data analytics and digital tools, automating most of the audit process. The 4IR technologies changing the auditing profession include cloud computing, IoE, drone technology, sensors, AI, RPA, Big Data analytics, smart contracts and BDLT (Davern et al., 2019; Jackson et al., 2022; Kroon et al., 2021). Almufadda and Almezeini (2022) asserted that AI and its subcomponents, which include ML (artificial neural network [ANN] and DL) and NLP, are the key components of auditing RPA systems. Auditing firms' use of these 4IR digital technologies has increased audit efficiency, effectiveness and quality (Sun & Vasarhelyi, 2017). Some audit firms have started using predictive analytics, BDLT and continuous financial reporting apps to deliver high-quality, forward-looking, continuous and real-time auditing effectively and efficiently.

According to Singhvi et al. (2021), these auditing 4IR digital technologies improve audits' efficiency, productivity and accuracy as they enable auditors to gain a deeper understanding of their client's organisations. Auditing firms are now intelligently using AI and RPA technologies to automate their auditing and assurance, and financial accounting structured, simple, rule-based and repetitive processes (Bakarich & O'Brien, 2021; ICAEW, 2018; Kokina & Davenport, 2017; Moffitt et al., 2018).

The Big Four and mid-tier audit firms have embraced data analytics and digital technologies, automating most of their manual and repetitive tasks. Below are some of the digital technologies being used by the Big Four audit forms:

(1) Deloitte

- *Optix*: Used for data analytics (Kokina & Davenport, 2017).
- *Argus*: AI NLP application for analysing documents such as leases or contracts (Almufadda & Almezeini, 2022; Dickney et al., 2019; Kokina & Davenport, 2017).

- *GRAPA*: Strategic planning and benchmarking AI tool (Almufadda & Almezeini, 2022).
- *IDO*: AI tool for quick strategic decision-making while reducing costs (Zhang et al., 2020).
- *Icount*: AI tool used to collect and consolidate inventory counts (Raphael, 2017).
- *Omnia DNAV*: AI tool used for investment valuations and related procedures (Almufadda & Almezeini, 2022).
- *BEAT*: AI tool used to analyse voice interactions and behaviours (Zhang et al., 2020).

(2) PWC

- *Halo analytics platform*: This platform tests all journal entries and identifies outliers with the highest risks (Almufadda & Almezeini, 2022; Dickney et al., 2019; M2 Presswire, 2016).
- *GL.ai*: This detects anomalies within the GL and recognises unusual transactions as possible errors or fraud (Almufadda & Almezeini, 2022).
- *Cash.ai.*: This conducts cash audits (Almufadda & Almezeini, 2022).
- *AI in Inventory Controls*: This evaluates inventory controls (Almufadda & Almezeini, 2022).

(3) KPMG

- *Watson*: Analytics tool for analysing huge volumes of financial data to spot anomalies (Almufadda & Almezeini, 2022; Issa et al., 2016; Melendez, 2016).
- *KPMG Ignite*: Used to enhance business decisions and processes (Almufadda & Almezeini, 2022).
- *AI Inventory controls*: Used to evaluate inventory controls (Almufadda & Almezeini, 2022).
- *Strategic Profitability insights*: Recognises key financial data and provides insights regarding the value of a deal (Almufadda & Almezeini, 2022).
- Developed advanced predictive analytics tools to examine financial statement risk (Sinclair, 2020).

(4) EY

- *EY NLP System*: Analyses documents such as contracts and leases to extract key information (Almufadda & Almezeini, 2022).
- *EY Canvass*: Online audit platform (EY, 2016; Persico & Sidhu, 2017).
- *EY Helix GL Anomaly Dictator*: A data analytics programme used for fraud detection with journal entries (Almufadda & Almezeini, 2022; Fotoh & Lorentzon, 2021).
- *Deep Learning*: This AI tool extracts key information from unstructured data (Almufadda & Almezeini, 2022).
- *EY Atlas*: Updates auditors and clients on the newest accounting and auditing developments (Persico & Sidhu, 2017).
- *AI Inventory controls*: Used to evaluate inventory controls (Almufadda & Almezeini, 2022).

These auditing digital tools and data analytics procedures demonstrate the extent of the digitalisation of the auditing profession. According to ACCA and Grant Thornton (2016), stakeholders expect auditors to be innovative and optimise auditing digital tools and data analytics to reduce auditing reporting timetables, risk and costs while enhancing audit quality and efficiencies. Auditing digitalisation demands that current and future auditors be digitally literate and have well-developed data analytics skills.

4. The Vital Skills for Future Auditors

This section explores the essential skills auditors must possess to remain relevant and effective in meeting client and public expectations. The rapidly changing business environment and the increasing complexity of financial and non-financial information require auditors to develop a transformative skillset to stay effective and relevant. These changes impacting the auditing profession have enormous implications for the current and future auditors' skills. The audit industry must embrace and adapt to these changes to remain relevant. The industry must continue to meet stakeholder expectations and use the 4IR digital technologies to reduce costs while enhancing audit quality, effectiveness and efficiency (Elliott & Duan, 2022). Current and future auditors must be highly technically and professionally competent, highly digitally literate and able to collaborate competently with teams from other jurisdictions and professions.

Scholars such as Ham et al. (2024), Vitali and Giuliani (2024), Abu Huson et al. (2024), Jackson et al. (2023), Barac et al. (2021) and Tsiligiris and Bowyer (2021) have identified several crucial skills for future auditors. These include advanced digital literacy skills, particularly proficiency in cloud computing, IoE, drone technology, sensors, AI, RPA, Big Data analytics, smart contracts and BDLT, which are vital for streamlining audit processes and detecting anomalies. Furthermore, auditors must possess ESG and sustainability reporting expertise to assure non-financial disclosures. In addition to technical capabilities, a strong understanding of business operations and industry-specific nuances, enhanced professional scepticism and ethical awareness are paramount. Soft skills, including communication, collaboration, teamwork, leadership, critical thinking, problem-solving and a commitment to lifelong learning, will enable auditors to navigate technological advancements and maintain relevance in an increasingly digital world. These skills are reinforced by leading professional accountancy bodies such as ACCA (2016, 2018), AICPA and CIMA (2019), ICAEW (2018) and CA ANZ (2019) and are diagrammatically represented in Fig. 19.1:

Fig. 19.1 visually represents the relationships between 'The Vital Skills for Future Auditors', 'Traditional Technical and Professional Ethics Skills', and 'Emergent Skills for Future Auditors'. The Emergent Skills for Future Auditor's branch expands into specialised skills such as Business Skills, Soft Skills, Critical Thinking and Problem-Solving, Digital Literacy Skills, Data Analytics Skills, Digital Ethics Proficiency and Assurance of ESG and Sustainability Reports. The figure illustrates the flow and interconnectedness of these categories,

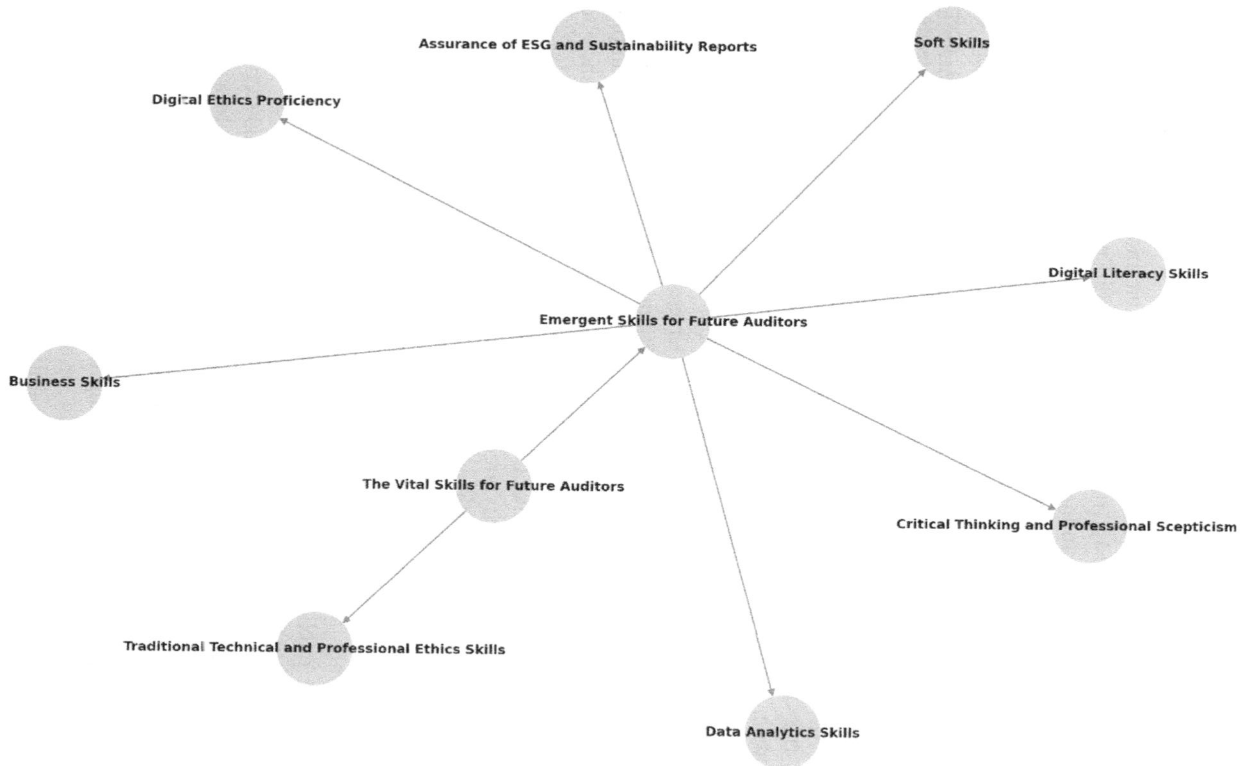

Fig. 19.1. Diagrammatic Representation of the Vital Skills for Future Auditors.

providing an intuitive way to understand how each skill area contributes to preparing future-ready auditors.

4.1 Traditional Technical and Professional Ethics Skills

According to Tiberius and Hirth (2019), Barrainkua and Espinosa-Pike (2018) and Siriwardane et al. (2014), traditional auditing and professional ethics skills remain the bedrock of the auditing profession, even as it evolves in response to changing business landscapes and technological advancements. Current and future auditors must be highly technically and professionally competent, as the auditing 4IR digital tools will not replace this skillset but only complement it. Technical expertise is foundational, as auditors must demonstrate a deep understanding of core auditing and accounting standards such as the International Standards on Auditing (ISA) and International Financial Reporting Standards (IFRS). These skills extend to a solid grasp of management accounting, finance and financial management, business strategy and governance, risk management and internal control, taxation laws and regulatory compliance, enabling auditors to understand business, navigate complex financial structures and ensure accurate reporting (ACCA, 2016; ACCA & CA ANZ, 2019; IFAC®, 2019; Tsiligiris & Bowyer, 2021). The ability to apply these frameworks rigorously in diverse contexts underpins the credibility of the audit process and safeguards stakeholders' trust in financial information (Barrainkua & Espinosa-Pike, 2018). Messier et al. (2017) note that mastery of accounting and auditing standards is essential for auditors to provide credible assurances to stakeholders and uphold trust in financial reporting.

Barrainkua and Espinosa-Pike (2018) and Small et al. (2017) emphasize that professional ethics and integrity are fundamental and non-negotiable for auditors, as they underpin the profession's commitment to safeguarding the public interest. Similarly, Sambo and Kanyane (2024), in their study 'Who Audits the Auditor', highlighted the auditing profession's critical role in promoting good governance. They argued that auditors' unethical behaviour can result in significant corporate failures. Businesses, investors and the public rely on auditors to protect the public interest by making sound professional judgements, preventing and detecting fraud and upholding the highest standards of professionalism, integrity, confidentiality, independence and professional scepticism. This ensures that their work is free from bias or undue influence. In a rapidly changing profession, these ethical principles are challenged by the integration of digital tools and the vast amounts of data they process (West, 2017). Auditors must navigate ethical dilemmas related to data privacy, algorithmic transparency and AI-driven analytics while maintaining unwavering adherence to their professional code of conduct. As the audit profession adopts advanced methodologies, the enduring importance of traditional skills lies in their role as a foundation for integrating new competencies while preserving the integrity and reliability of the audit function (Howieson, 2005). However, future auditors must complement their technical and professional ethics skills with well-developed IT,

4IR digital technological skills, advanced data analytics, business and soft skills to efficiently and effectively deliver quality audits and attestation services. The expanded skillsets will also enable auditors to add value to their clients.

4.2 Emergent Skills for Future Auditors

Emergent skills represent the 'skills of the future', which are increasingly essential in today's dynamic audit environment. Beyond traditional technical expertise, auditors must develop business and soft skills, like effective communication, collaboration and adaptability, to manage complex stakeholder relationships and diverse team dynamics. Additionally, the digitalisation of audit processes demands proficiency in digital tools, AI and RPA, enabling auditors to analyse large datasets and enhance audit quality efficiently (Tsiligiris & Bowyer, 2021). Data analysis has also emerged as a critical skill, allowing auditors to extract actionable insights from structured and unstructured data while upholding accuracy and integrity in decision-making processes (Jackson et al., 2023). The following critical skills are discussed below.

4.2.1 Business Skills

Using 4IR digital technologies and data analytics reduces audit time, allowing the auditor to add value to the client's business's future development (BDO, 2022). This requires business acumen on the part of the auditor. A thorough understanding of the context of business and industry is vital for future auditors. Beyond technical accounting and auditing expertise, auditors must grasp the operational, regulatory and economic landscapes in which their clients operate (Barac et al., 2021). This includes recognising industry-specific risks, compliance requirements and key performance drivers that shape financial and operational results. Siriwardane et al. (2014) argued that future auditors must be able to interpret emerging trends such as technological advancements, globalisation and societal shifts and assess their impacts on business strategies and reporting practices. Such an understanding enables auditors to identify potential risks, provide meaningful insights, add value to their clients' business and enhance audit quality beyond the traditional focus on compliance (Jackson et al., 2023). Additionally, auditors must integrate knowledge of business strategy with risk management to evaluate how strategic decisions affect financial and non-financial outcomes. For instance, with the increasing emphasis on non-financial measures embedded in sustainability and environmental issues, auditors must assess various non-financial measures to improve audit quality and reporting (Brazel et al., 2014). Thus, foundational competencies in business laws and regulations, economics, business and organisational environment, strategic thinking and planning will be key for future auditors (Elliott & Duan, 2022; IFAC, 2019).

4.2.2 Soft Skills

The International Education Standards (IES) defined soft skills as a critical set of competencies essential for individuals aiming to excel as professional accountants and auditors. These skills encompass abilities beyond technical expertise, equipping professionals with the tools needed to thrive in dynamic and collaborative environments (IAESB, 2010). Scholars such as Abu Asabeh et al. (2023), Malan and Dyk (2021), Barac et al. (2021) and Douglas and Gammie (2019) have highlighted the significance of soft skills, often describing them as essential yet non-technical competencies. These are generic, transferable, employability, pervasive, or emotional intelligence skills. They encompass interpersonal and communication abilities, collaborative and team management capabilities, adaptability and other critical proficiencies supporting effective professional practice and career development. Future auditors must possess strong interpersonal and communication abilities to navigate the complexities of modern audit engagements effectively (Malan & Dyk, 2021). Barac et al. (2021) allude to the fact that soft skills enable auditors to bridge technical findings with business insights, fostering trust and collaboration with clients and stakeholders. These skills are essential for effective interaction and enhancing the profession's credibility and relevance in an era of rapid change. According to Malan and Dyk (2021), effective communication is a cornerstone of auditing, encompassing the ability to translate complex technical insights into language easily understood by diverse stakeholders. Additionally, advanced business writing and presentation skills are critical for preparing reports and delivering compelling presentations that convey technical accuracy while addressing business implications (Douglas & Gammie, 2019).

The globalisation of business and the auditing profession, coupled with advancements in auditing 4IR digital technologies, especially cloud computing, means that future auditors can collaborate with their peers from different jurisdictions on a particular client. Future auditors will also be expected to work with multidisciplinary teams comprising professionals like data scientists, computer experts, lawyers and digital technologists in their intricate audit and assurance work. Auditors will coordinate such collaborations. Future auditors must be adept at navigating diverse perspectives and fostering a collaborative environment to resolve challenges efficiently. Effective leadership within audit teams ensures that tasks are distributed appropriately, resources are utilised optimally and timelines are adhered to (Barac et al., 2021). The ability to manage and motivate teams while focusing on quality underscores the growing importance of leadership as a soft skill in the audit profession. Well-developed teamwork, collaboration, leadership, communication (written and oral), relationship-building, conflict resolution, emotional intelligence and time management skills will be vital for the career success of future auditors (Abu Asabeh et al., 2023).

Adaptability is indispensable for auditors in responding to the dynamic nature of their profession. Changes in technology, regulations and client expectations require auditors to embrace continuous learning and swiftly adjust to new tools, methods and environments (McGuire et al., 2023; Pan & Zhu, 2024). Adaptability also includes the capacity to manage ambiguity, a skill increasingly critical as auditors face novel challenges such as assessing non-financial information, integrating sustainability metrics and leveraging digital tools (Lansdell et al., 2020). Together, these soft skills ensure that future auditors remain resilient and effective in a world of constant transformation.

4.2.3 Critical Thinking and Professional Scepticism Skills

Professional scepticism has become increasingly vital in the contemporary audit landscape as fraud risks grow more sophisticated and financial instruments become more complex (Agrawal et al., 2021). This skill requires auditors to approach their work with a questioning mindset, maintaining an objective stance to detect potential misstatements or irregularities. The increased usage of 4IR digital technologies and Big Data analytics, coupled with complex business models, demands critical thinking from auditors. Auditors must question the data, analytics results and client information used in the audit, as the increased use of AI poses a serious risk of generating non-existent information.

Critical thinking forms the foundation of professional scepticism, enabling auditors to evaluate evidence comprehensively and challenge assumptions, even when supported by advanced digital tools and automated processes. Alnafisah (2019) adds that with the integration of technologies such as AI and RPA into audit procedures, auditors must not only trust the outputs of these tools but also critically examine their inputs, algorithms and assumptions to ensure their reliability and relevance.

The heightened focus on critical thinking and professional scepticism also necessitates fraud detection expertise (Kwock et al., 2016). Future auditors are expected to leverage advanced techniques, such as forensic data analysis and anomaly detection algorithms, to uncover irregularities in complex financial datasets. Fraud risks are increasingly embedded within sophisticated schemes involving digital transactions, blockchain technology, or cross-border operations. Auditors must combine their technical knowledge with a sceptical and critical mindset to identify red flags and inconsistencies that might signal fraud. Additionally, this skill extends to evaluating management's representations and estimates, particularly in areas of judgement such as asset valuations, provisions and going concern assessments (Chiang, 2016; Hurtt et al., 2013). By rigorously applying critical thinking and scepticism throughout the audit process, auditors enhance the quality and credibility of their work, reinforcing their role as protectors of public trust. Critical thinking and professional scepticism skills will be important for future auditors.

4.2.4 Digital Literacy Skills

The increasing automation and digitisation of the auditing profession have made digital literacy a fundamental skill for future auditors. Well-developed 4IR digital technology skills will be key to the career success of future auditors (ACCA & CA ANZ, 2019; ICAEW, 2018). According to BDO (2022), the 4IR digital technologies are taking auditors to the 22nd century, and they will offer new opportunities arising from the changed expectations of investors and regulators. Proficiency in automated tools is no longer optional; auditors must now leverage platforms that streamline risk assessment, sampling and reporting processes. These tools, powered by AI and RPA, enable auditors to handle large datasets, automate repetitive tasks and enhance accuracy (Zhang et al., 2020). For instance, RPA can extract and analyse financial transactions, freeing auditors to focus on judgement-intensive areas like evaluating complex estimates and addressing compliance issues. This shift demands that auditors understand the functionality of digital systems and ensure their effective integration into the audit workflow (Barac et al., 2021; Zhang et al., 2020). Byrnes et al. (2018) state that big data, ML and DL technologies have revolutionised auditors' financial and operational data analysis. These technologies enable auditors to assess entire populations of transactions instead of relying on traditional sampling, providing a more comprehensive view of risks and anomalies.

Also, ML algorithms can detect patterns and outliers in financial data, helping auditors identify potential fraud or inefficiencies. However, to effectively use these tools, auditors must possess technical expertise and the ability to interpret outputs critically, ensuring that the insights generated align with audit objectives. Such capabilities underscore the need for future auditors to adopt a data-driven mindset while maintaining professional scepticism to validate algorithmic findings (Alnafisah, 2019; Pan & Zhu, 2024). Zhang et al. (2020) express that the rise of blockchain technology has transformed financial reporting, requiring auditors to understand how decentralised ledgers operate and their implications for assurance services. Blockchain's transparency and immutability offer opportunities for real-time auditing and verification, but they also introduce complexities, such as ensuring the integrity of smart contracts and addressing cybersecurity risks. Future auditors must also evaluate how various technologies interconnect across financial reporting, taxation and business analysis, ensuring that digital solutions are accurate and compliant with regulatory standards (McGuire et al., 2023).

Goh et al. (2019) recommend that future auditors develop basic programming skills in core programming languages like Python and R. Auditors are also expected to provide assurance on 4IR digital technologies used by their clients and advise on cybersecurity risks arising from these digital technologies. These digital literacy skills position auditors to deliver audits that meet the evolving demands of the profession while maintaining stakeholder confidence in a digital-first environment.

4.2.5 Data Analytics Skills

Data analytics has rapidly emerged as a fundamental skill for future auditors, transforming how audits are conducted. Current and future auditors must also develop basic and advanced data analytics, as BDO (2022) predicts that data analytics will become a prerequisite for auditors. Identifying patterns and anomalies within vast datasets allows auditors to detect trends, outliers and potential instances of fraud that might not be apparent through traditional methods (Richins et al., 2017). Earley (2015) writes that by analysing large volumes of data, auditors can more accurately assess financial statements, uncover hidden risks and evaluate the validity of transactions, providing higher levels of assurance. With the power of analytics, auditors can move beyond simple compliance checks, offering a deeper, more thorough analysis of financial records, thus ensuring that businesses operate transparently and are trustworthy. Basic and advanced data analytics skills include Big Data, data extraction, data preparation and application, visualisation, communication and storytelling, predictive analytics and audit analytics. Current and future auditors can use predictive analytics, BDLT and continuous financial reporting apps to effectively and efficiently deliver high-quality, forward-looking, continuous, real-time auditing. This shift in approach requires auditors to be proficient in using data analytics tools and techniques, including statistical analysis and inference, regression modelling and anomaly detection algorithms, which are now indispensable in modern audit processes (Elliott & Duan, 2022; Omitogun & Al-Adeem, 2019).

Moreover, Zin et al. (2022) argue that enhanced decision-making is a key outcome of integrating data analytics into the audit function. Auditors can leverage data-driven insights not only to improve the accuracy of their audit findings but also to guide clients in refining their strategic direction and governance practices. By harnessing data analytics, auditors provide invaluable advice on identifying inefficiencies, improving risk management and enhancing operational performance. Additionally, developing predictive models using data analytics enables auditors to forecast potential risks and opportunities, allowing clients to proactively manage business challenges before they become significant (Richins et al., 2017). These advanced data analytics and digital capabilities skills enhance the auditors' technical skills, making them indispensable partners in helping organisations navigate the complexities of modern business environments (Kend & Nguyen, 2020).

4.2.6 Digital Ethics Proficiency Skills

This is a necessary skill set encompassing the ability to navigate the ethical implications of using several digital tools, such as the integration of AI and automation into the audit profession, which brings unparalleled efficiency and precision but also introduces complex ethical challenges (ACCA, 2017; Munoko et al., 2020). Future auditors must understand the ethical implications of using these technologies, particularly concerning data privacy and stakeholder trust. For instance, AI-powered tools often rely on vast amounts of sensitive client data, raising concerns about confidentiality, compliance with data protection laws and potential misuse of information (Cobey et al., 2018). Auditors need to assess whether AI tools align with professional and societal expectations of transparency and accountability. Additionally, they must address algorithmic bias, which can inadvertently reinforce inequalities or lead to flawed audit outcomes, potentially undermining audit reports' reliability and stakeholders' trust (Kokina & Davenport, 2017).

Promoting the responsible use of AI and automation requires auditors to ensure that these tools adhere to ethical and legal standards. This includes thoroughly evaluating AI systems for vulnerabilities, such as their susceptibility to manipulation or unintended errors. Auditors must also demand decision-making transparency, where the processes and logic behind AI-driven conclusions are comprehensible and auditable (Wakunuma & Stahl, 2014). By understanding and mitigating these risks, auditors can ensure that digital tools enhance audit quality without compromising ethical integrity. Furthermore, future auditors must advocate for continuous monitoring and updating of AI systems to adapt to evolving regulatory environments and emerging threats, reinforcing their role as guardians of public interest in a digital era (HLEG, 2018).

4.2.7 Assurance of ESG and Sustainability Reports

As businesses increasingly adopt integrated reporting, the demand for auditors to assure ESG metrics and sustainability disclosures has grown substantially. Future auditors must be proficient in assessing the credibility of ESG metrics, such as carbon emissions, social impact initiatives and governance practices, which are critical in evaluating the sustainability performance of companies (Lee et al., 2022). With stakeholders, including investors and regulatory bodies, demanding greater transparency on a company's environmental and social responsibilities, auditors must ensure the accuracy and reliability of these non-financial disclosures (Hwara et al., 2024). This requires auditors to go beyond traditional financial auditing methods, applying a more holistic and integrated approach to assess the tangible and intangible factors influencing a company's performance. Auditors must validate ESG claims by scrutinising data sources, measurement methodologies and reporting frameworks, ensuring that businesses are genuinely committed to their sustainability objectives and adhering to established global standards.

To effectively conduct ESG and sustainability audits, future auditors must also have a solid understanding of global sustainability standards such as the Global Reporting Initiative (GRI), Sustainability Accounting Standards Board (SASB) (IFRS S1 and IFRS S2) and the Task Force on Climate-related Financial Disclosures (TCFD) (Hwara et al., 2024). These frameworks guide businesses in reporting non-financial information and are critical for auditors when evaluating sustainability disclosures. With the growing importance of climate-related risks and social factors in financial reporting, auditors must be well-versed in these global standards to provide accurate assessments of a company's sustainability practices (Asante-Appiah & Lambert, 2023). Moreover, as regulatory requirements surrounding ESG disclosures continue to evolve, auditors will play an increasingly important role in helping businesses navigate and comply with both local and international reporting obligations (Gipper et al., 2024). This expansion of services beyond traditional financial auditing highlights the evolving role of auditors in ensuring businesses' long-term sustainability and ethical practices.

5. The Roles of HEIs and Professional Bodies in Shaping the Future Auditors

HEIs and professional bodies have played a crucial role in shaping technically proficient auditors and accountants. HEIs provide comprehensive curricula covering financial management, corporate governance and ethical principles, ensuring foundational knowledge is imparted effectively (Fotoh & Lorentzon, 2021; Jackson et al., 2022). Professional bodies such as ACCA, ICAEW and AICPA complement these efforts through globally recognised qualifications that emphasise technical expertise and practical application (ACCA, 2016; CA ANZ, 2019). Collaborative initiatives between HEIs and professional bodies, including internships and case-based learning, have further enriched auditor training by bridging academic learning with real-world scenarios (ACCA, 2018).

However, the historical focus of HEIs and professional bodies on technical expertise and ethical competencies has often come at the expense of fostering creativity, emotional intelligence and adaptability (Fotoh & Lorentzon, 2021). While effective in instilling foundational accounting and auditing skills, traditional curricula frequently neglect the development of forward-looking competencies such as predictive analytics and interdisciplinary collaboration. This oversight is increasingly problematic as stakeholders demand transparency and assurance in ESG reporting (Hwara et al., 2024).

Moreover, adopting cutting-edge technologies such as AI and blockchain into educational frameworks has been inconsistent and slower than the rapid pace of technological advancements. As a result, many auditors remain underprepared for the demands of automated processes and AI-driven systems, which are reshaping the profession (Tavares et al., 2023). Additionally, the traditional emphasis on historical financial reporting limits auditors' ability to provide proactive, value-added insights. Training programmes often fail to integrate real-time auditing techniques or address auditors' strategic role in guiding organisations through complex decision-making. Another critical gap lies in the insufficient emphasis on soft skills, such as creative problem-solving, ethical judgement and effective communication, which are vital in navigating the complexities of modern business environments (Tsiligiris & Bowyer, 2021).

HEIs and professional bodies must adopt an agile, future-focused approach that balances technical, digital and interpersonal skill development to bridge these gaps. Such a holistic framework would ensure that future auditors are technically competent and equipped to address the dynamic and interdisciplinary challenges of a globalised and digitised world. The following practical solutions are advanced to address these shortcomings and fill these gaps.

5.1 Revamping Curriculum to Incorporate Advanced Technological Skills

A curriculum overhaul to integrate advanced technologies is crucial for preparing future auditors to navigate an increasingly digital and data-driven landscape (Novak et al., 2021). HEIs and professional bodies must ensure that their educational programmes reflect the latest technological trends, such as AI, ML, blockchain and predictive analytics (Byrnes et al., 2018; McGuire et al., 2023). By introducing specialised courses or modules on these emerging technologies, students can develop the technical expertise to effectively leverage these tools in audit practices. For example, integrating AI into auditing curricula can teach students how to use ML algorithms to detect patterns in financial data or identify potential risks. Similarly, blockchain technology could be explored for its potential to enhance transparency and security in financial reporting. By focusing on the practical application of these technologies, HEIs can better equip students to address the demands of modern audit practices (Chaffer & Webb, 2017).

In addition to integrating advanced technologies into academic curricula, collaboration between professional bodies and technology providers is essential to create a learning ecosystem that keeps pace with technological advancements (Zin et al., 2022). Professional bodies like ACCA and ICAEW can play a pivotal role by partnering with technology companies to offer certification programmes, workshops, or webinars focusing on the practical application of emerging tools. These programmes could help professionals stay current with industry changes and gain hands-on experience with cutting-edge technology. For instance, offering certifications in data analytics or blockchain could help auditors develop specialised knowledge that adds value to their practice (Barac et al., 2021; Zhang et al., 2020). By bridging the gap between academia and industry through such collaborations, HEIs and professional bodies can create a more agile and relevant learning environment that ensures students and professionals are fully prepared to face the challenges of a technology-driven audit world.

5.2 Emphasis on Non-Financial Reporting and ESG Assurance

As stakeholder interest in ESG issues continues to rise, HEIs and professional bodies must prioritise non-financial reporting in their training programmes. Auditors must be equipped with the skills to assess ESG metrics effectively, ensuring that companies report on sustainability and corporate social responsibility transparently and accountably. This requires integrating ESG criteria into existing auditing standards and providing auditors with specialised training on evaluating non-financial disclosures (Lee et al., 2022). By incorporating ESG considerations into audit practices, auditors can help organisations demonstrate their commitment to sustainability while meeting growing investor and regulatory expectations for accurate and comprehensive ESG reporting (Gipper et al., 2024).

More so, collaboration with sustainability-focused organisations and regulators could further enrich training programmes and enhance the credibility of

ESG auditing. Professional bodies and HEIs can partner with regulatory authorities, environmental agencies and CSR organisations to develop industry-relevant materials that reflect the latest standards in non-financial reporting (Hwara et al., 2024). Additionally, offering specialised certifications in ESG auditing and incorporating real-world case studies of sustainability practices can provide auditors with practical insights into assessing ESG factors. These collaborations will ensure that auditors are familiar with ESG frameworks and skilled in evaluating complex non-financial data and providing actionable insights to businesses. In doing so, HEIs and professional bodies can play a crucial role in shaping a new generation of well-equipped auditors to address the growing demand for comprehensive and accurate ESG disclosures.

5.3 Incorporation of Forward-Looking, Continuous and Real-Time Audit Techniques

As the audit landscape evolves, there is a growing need to shift from traditional, historical audits to a more forward-looking and continuous approach. According to Almufadda and Almezeini (2022) and Alles et al. (2022), advancements in predictive analytics, AI, BDLT, App-based financial reporting systems and cloud computing technologies make forward-looking, continuous, real-time auditing and financial reporting possible. Financial statement users increasingly demand organisations disclose forward-looking and non-financial information, including ESG and sustainability reports about their activities, to aid decision-making. Auditors must attest to this additional information to assure users that it is fairly and accurately disclosed (ACCA & Grant Thornton, 2016; PwC, 2019). Real-time auditing and attestation skills of forward-looking and non-financial information will be important for future auditors.

Future audits will require auditors to incorporate predictive analytics and real-time auditing into their practices to provide proactive insights and add greater client value. HEIs should adapt their curricula to teach students to analyse trends and use data-driven techniques to predict future outcomes. This enables them to go beyond verifying past financial data (Carayannis & Morawska-Jancelewicz, 2022). This can include introducing specialised courses in data analytics, risk management and advanced technologies like AI to enhance forecasting capabilities (Richins et al., 2017). By equipping students with the tools and methodologies to perform forward-looking audits, HEIs can ensure that future auditors are prepared to meet the demands of a rapidly changing business environment.

Professional bodies also have a critical role in emphasising the importance of forward-looking audit techniques in their certification programmes. As these techniques become essential for providing value-added services, certification programmes should include modules that teach predictive analytics, real-time monitoring and other forward-thinking audit methodologies (ACCA, 2016). By integrating these skills into the professional development journey, bodies like ACCA and ICAEW can ensure that auditors can handle current audit requirements and are prepared for future challenges. Furthermore, by promoting continuous learning and professional development in these areas, professional bodies can encourage auditors to stay ahead of trends and contribute more strategically to clients, helping them make better-informed decisions.

5.4 Enhanced Focus on Soft Skills Development

While technical and digital skills are undoubtedly vital for auditors in the digital age, the human element of auditing remains just as crucial. As the auditing profession becomes more complex and integrated with advanced technologies, auditors must be able to navigate interpersonal dynamics, effectively communicate findings and understand clients' needs (Abu Asabeh et al., 2023). Therefore, HEIs and professional bodies should focus on developing soft skills such as emotional intelligence, adaptability, communication and creative thinking (Jackson & Meek, 2021). These competencies will enable auditors to build strong relationships with clients, collaborate effectively within multidisciplinary teams, and manage the increasing complexity of audits. Through dedicated courses, seminars and workshops, future auditors can be trained to balance technical expertise with the ability to engage in critical thinking and demonstrate empathy, all while managing the challenges of a rapidly evolving business environment (Dolce et al., 2020).

To ensure the development of these soft skills, HEIs and professional bodies can incorporate interactive methods such as case studies, role-playing exercises and group projects into their training programmes (Wats & Wats, 2009). These methods allow students and professionals to experience real-world scenarios that challenge their problem-solving and communication abilities, simulating the situations auditors are likely to encounter in practice. Additionally, providing platforms for peer feedback and reflection can help future auditors develop self-awareness and emotional intelligence, which are key to managing stakeholder relationships and navigating the complexities of the audit process (Malan & Dyk, 2021). As auditors are expected to manage financial data and the increasing demands for transparency and ethical decision-making, integrating soft skills into curricula will be crucial in preparing well-rounded professionals who can effectively adapt to the profession's changing demands.

5.5 Stronger Collaboration Between Academia and Industry

Stronger collaboration between academia and industry is essential to keep curricula relevant and current with the fast-paced changes in the auditing profession (Jackson et al., 2022). HEIs should actively partner with industry leaders, regulators and professional bodies to co-develop course content that reflects the current and future demands of the profession. This collaboration will ensure that students are equipped with the latest knowledge and practical skills that directly align with the evolving needs of the profession (Wells et al., 2014). By involving industry professionals in developing learning materials, guest lectures and workshops, students can gain valuable insights into the practical applications of auditing principles, especially to emerging technologies like AI, blockchain and predictive analytics (Jones, 2014). This can also give students a clearer understanding of the challenges and opportunities they will encounter in their professional careers.

In addition to co-developing curricula, HEIs can strengthen industry connections by offering internships, mentorship programmes and industry-driven research projects. These initiatives will allow students to gain hands-on experience in real-world audit scenarios and work with emerging technologies under the guidance of experienced professionals (Tavares et al., 2023). Internships and mentorship programmes, in particular, provide a platform for students to apply their academic knowledge to practical challenges, enhancing their understanding of the audit process and industry trends. By engaging in these real-world experiences, students will be better prepared to transition smoothly from academia to industry, ensuring they are well-equipped to meet the expectations of employers and regulatory bodies. This collaboration will also help to bridge the gap between theoretical learning and the practical realities of the auditing profession, fostering a more agile and adaptable workforce.

5.6 Lifelong Learning and Continuing Professional Development (CPD)

In the face of rapid technological advancements and changing business practices, lifelong learning through CPD courses is critical for auditors to remain competitive and effective in their roles (Wilkinson et al., 2018). HEIs and professional bodies must instil the importance of CPD early in auditors' careers, ensuring they understand the need to constantly update their skills and knowledge. As such, auditors must be equipped to handle new tools and methodologies that shape the profession (Asante-Appiah & Lambert, 2023). HEIs can integrate lifelong learning into their curricula by highlighting the need for ongoing education and encouraging students to engage in post-graduation CPD. This proactive approach can help bridge the gap between academic training and the evolving demands of the profession.

Professional bodies are central to the CPD process, offering programmes and certifications that help auditors stay current in emerging areas (ACCA, 2018). For example, professional organisations can provide specialised CPD courses in AI auditing, blockchain applications and ESG auditing to ensure auditors are ready to tackle the complexities of modern audits (Gipper et al., 2024; ICAEW, 2018). These programmes can be designed to allow flexibility, enabling auditors to learn at their own pace while balancing work commitments. By promoting CPD through structured learning paths, professional bodies can help auditors adapt to new technologies, regulatory changes and industry shifts (ICAEW, 2018). This commitment to lifelong learning ensures that auditors remain competent, competitive and capable of meeting the dynamic needs of clients and stakeholders in an increasingly digital and complex business environment.

As such, HEIs and professional bodies are crucial in shaping the future of auditing by equipping professionals with the skills needed to navigate an increasingly complex and technology-driven landscape. By revising curricula to include advanced digital tools, focusing on forward-looking audit techniques, emphasising soft skills and promoting continuous professional development, these institutions can better prepare auditors for future challenges. Through collaboration with industry leaders and a commitment to innovation, HEIs and professional bodies can ensure that auditors are technically proficient, adaptable and forward-thinking, enabling them to provide value in a rapidly changing business environment.

6. Conclusion

The auditing profession is rapidly changing in response to changes in business models and the environment. These changes are mainly driven by the rapid digitalisation of business and the auditing profession, the globalisation of business and the auditing profession, the business, investors and the public's expectations about auditing and increased regulation, and the business stakeholders' demand for stronger governance. In response to these changes, current and future auditors must develop new skills to remain relevant, meet the expectations of the businesses and their stakeholders, and competently, effectively and efficiently deliver high-quality, technology-enabled, forward-looking, continuous, real-time audits and assurance services.

This study reviewed journal articles, surveys conducted by selected professional accounting bodies, the IFAC® current Handbook and published auditing expert opinions to identify the vital skills for current and future auditors. The study also discussed how the auditor training ecosystem could support current and trainee auditors in developing these skills.

The study found that technical and professional ethics auditing skills will remain the profession's bedrock. Current and future auditors must be highly competent in all accountancy areas: auditing and assurance, governance and risk management, financial accounting and corporate reporting, financial management, management accounting, business management and strategy, taxation and professional and business ethics. The public expects current and future auditors to safeguard the public interest, make professional judgements, prevent and uncover fraud and exercise the highest standards of professionalism, integrity, independence and professional scepticism.

The auditors' technical and professional ethics auditing skills must be complemented with well-developed 4IR digital literacy, data analytics, data ethics, professional scepticism, assurance, critical thinking and soft and business skills to ensure the auditors' relevance, audit quality, efficiency and effectiveness. Current and future auditors must also be skilled in providing assurance services on digital tools their clients use and the reported non-financial information, including ESG (sustainability) reports. Forward-looking, continuous, real-time auditing and financial reporting are increasingly important skills for current and future auditors.

HEIs and professional bodies play a pivotal role in the training of auditors, and they deliver the auditing academic programme. To adapt to these changes in current and future auditors' skill sets, HEIs and professional accounting bodies must review their curricula and competency frameworks to include all these skills. In particular, the curricula and competency frameworks must include 4IR auditing digital skills, basic and advanced data analytics, critical thinking, business and key soft skills, sustainability and ESG assurance skills, forward-looking, continuous, real-time auditing and financial reporting skills. These skills are vital for future auditors. Collaboration between HEIs, professional accounting bodies and industry will be key to developing the 4IR digital, data analytics and soft skills.

Use of AI Declaration

ChatGPT Version 3.5 was used to concise the manuscript, paraphrase and communicate the findings in a clear and systematic way.

References

Abu Asabeh, S., Alzboon, R., Alkhalaileh, R., Alshurafat, H., & Al Amosh, H. (2023). Soft skills and knowledge required for a professional accountant: Evidence from Jordan. *Cogent Education*, *10*(2), 2254157.

Abu Huson, Y., Sierra-García, L., & Garcia-Benau, M. A. (2024). A bibliometric review of information technology, artificial intelligence, and blockchain on auditing. *Total Quality Management and Business Excellence*, *35*(1–2), 91–113.

Agrawal, P., Birt, J., Holub, M., & van Zyl, W. (2021). Professional scepticism and the accounting classroom. *Accounting Education*, *30*(3), 213–233.

AICPA and CIMA. (2019). *Future re-inventing finance for a digital world* (pp. 1–44). https://www.cgma.org/content/dam/cgma/resources/reports/downloadabledocuments/future-re-inventing-finance-for-a-digital-world.pdf

Alles, M., Palas, R., Vasarhelyi, M. A., & Xiong, F. (2022). The case for an app-based financial reporting system. *Journal of Emerging Technologies in Accounting*, *19*(2), 1–21. https://doi.org/10.2308/jeta-10827

Almufadda, G., & Almezeini, N. A. (2022). Artificial intelligence applications in the auditing profession: A literature review. *Journal of Emerging Technologies in Accounting*, *19*(2), 29–42.

Alnafisah, Y. A. (2019). *The practice of professional scepticism in auditing*. The University of Manchester.

Arnaboldi, M., Busco, C., & Cuganesan, S. (2017). Accounting, accountability, social media and big data: Revolution or hype? *Accounting, Auditing & Accountability Journal*, *30*(4), 762–776. https://doi.org/10.1108/AAAJ-03-2017-2880

Asante-Appiah, B., & Lambert, T. A. (2023). The role of the external auditor in managing environmental, social, and governance (ESG) reputation risk. *Review of Accounting Studies*, *28*(4), 2589–2641.

Association of Chartered Certified Accountants (ACCA). (2016). *Professional accountants – The future: Drivers of change and future skills* (p. 188). ACCA.

https://www.accaglobal.com/content/dam/members-beta/images/campaigns/pa-tf/pi-professional-accountants-the-future.pdf. Accessed on April 17, 2023.

Association of Chartered Certified Accountants. (2017). *Ethics and trust in a digital age*. https://www.accaglobal.com/content/dam/ACCA_Global/Technical/Future/pi-ethics-trust-digital-age.pdf. Accessed on December 9, 2024.

Association of Chartered Certified Accountants. (2018). *Learning for the future* (pp. 1–50). The Association of Chartered Certified Accountants. https://www.accaglobal.com/gb/en.html

Association of Chartered Certified Accountants (ACCA) and Chartered Accountants Australia and New Zealand. (2019). *Audit and technology* (pp. 1–22). ACCA and CA ANZ. https://www.accaglobal.com/content/dam/ACCA_Global/professional-insights/audit-and-tech/pi-audit-and-technology.pdf. Accessed on April 17, 2023.

Association of Chartered Certified Accountants and Grant Thornton. (2016). *The future of audit*. https://www.accaglobal.com/content/dam/ACCA_Global/Technical/audit/ea-future-of-audit.pdf. Accessed on December 18, 2024.

Bakarich, K. M., & O'Brien, P. E., (2021). The robots are coming... but aren't here yet: The use of artificial intelligence technologies in the public accounting profession. *Journal of Emerging Technologies in Accounting*, *18*(1), 27–43. https://doi.org/10.2308/JETA-19-11-20-47

Barac, K., Gammie, E., Howieson, B., & van Staden, M. (2016). *The capability and competency requirements of auditors in today's complex global environment* (pp. 1–142). Institute of Chartered Accountants Scotland and the Financial Reporting Council. https://www.icas.com/professional-resources/research/the-capability-and-competency-requirements-of-auditors-in-todays-complex-global-business-environment. Accessed on April 17, 2023.

Barac, K., Plant, K., Kunz, R., & Kirstein, M. (2021). Generic skill profiles of future accountants and auditors–moving beyond attributes. *Higher Education, Skills and Work-based Learning*, *11*(4), 908–928.

Barrainkua, I., & Espinosa-Pike, M. (2018). The influence of auditors' professionalism on ethical judgement: Differences among practitioners and postgraduate students. *Revista de Contabilidad*, *21*(2), 176–187.

BDO. (2022). *The future of auditing in five predictions*. www.bdo.com/getmedia/f7de81af-d3cd-40bf-bebd-1fbbe7cf0785/ASSR_5-Predictions-for-the-Future-of-the-Audit.pdf?ext=.pdf. Accessed on April 17, 2023.

Brazel, J. F., Jones, K. L., & Prawitt, D. F. (2014). Auditors' reactions to inconsistencies between financial and nonfinancial measures: The interactive effects of fraud risk assessment and a decision prompt. *Behavioral Research in Accounting*, *26*(1), 131–156.

Brydon, D. (2019). *Report of the independent review into the quality and effectiveness of the audit*. https://assets.publishing.service.gov.uk/media/5df8edfced915d0938597e1f/brydon-review-final-report.pdf. Accessed on December 18, 2024.

Byrnes, P. E., Al-Awadhi, A., Gullvist, B., Brown-Liburd, H., Teeter, R., Warren Jr, J. D., & Vasarhelyi, M. (2018). Evolution of auditing: From the traditional approach to the future audit. In *Continuous auditing: Theory and application* (pp. 285–297). Emerald Publishing Limited.

CA ANZ. (2019). *The future of trust: New technology meets old-fashioned values*. Chartered Accountants Australia and New Zealand. https://www.charteredaccountantsanz.com/newsand-analysis/insights/research-and-insights/the-future-of-trust

Carayannis, E. G., & Morawska-Jancelewicz, J. (2022). The futures of Europe: Society 5.0 and Industry 5.0 as driving forces of future universities. *Journal of the Knowledge Economy*, *13*(4), 1–27. https://doi.org/10.1007/s13132-021-00854-2

Chaffer, C., & Webb, J. (2017). An evaluation of competency development in accounting trainees. *Accounting Education*, *26*(5–6), 431–458.

Chiang, C. (2016). Conceptualising the linkage between professional scepticism and auditor independence. *Pacific Accounting Review*, *28*(2), 180–200.

Cobey, C., Strier, K., & Boillet, J. (2018). *How do you teach AI the value of trust?* https://www.ey.com/en_gl/digital/how-do-you-teach-ai-the-value-of-trust. Accessed on December 9, 2024.

Davern, M., Weisner, M., & Fraser, N. (2019). *Technology and the future of the profession.* https://www.cpaaustralia.com.au/-/media/project/cpa/corporate/documents/achivies/technology-and-the-future-research-report.pdf. Accessed on December 18, 2024.

Dickney, G., Blanke, S., & Seaton, L. (2019). Machine learning in auditing current and future applications. *The CPA Journal*, *89*(6), 16–21.

Dolce, V., Emanuel, F., Cisi, M., & Ghislieri, C. (2020). The soft skills of accounting graduates: Perceptions versus expectations. *Accounting Education*, *29*(1), 57–76.

Douglas, S., & Gammie, E. (2019). An investigation into the development of non-technical skills by undergraduate accounting programmes. *Accounting Education*, *28*(3), 304–332.

Earley, C. E. (2015). Data analytics in auditing: Opportunities and challenges. *Business Horizons*, *58*(5), 493–500.

Elliott, R., & Duan, H. K. (2022). The future of auditing: An interview with Robert Elliott. *Journal of Emerging Technologies in Accounting*, *19*(2), 23–27. https://doi.org/10.2308/jeta-10823

Ernst and Young (EY). (2016). *Leading-edge digital technology powering the EY audit.* https://cdn.ey.com/echannel/gl/technologypoweringtheEYaudit-v9/download/Leading-edge%20digital%20technology%20powering%20the%20EY%20audit.pdf

Farrell, J., & Paquette, H. (2023, January/February 6–7). Get ready for the future of auditing. *The CPA Journal.* https://www.cpajournal.com/2023/03/31/get-ready-for-the-future-of-auditing/#:~:text=To%20prepare%20for%20the%20future,managing%20risks%20through%20digital%20transformation. Accessed on April 17, 2023.

Forbes and KPMG. (2017). *The future is now.* https://assets.kpmg.com/content/dam/kpmg/us/pdf/2017/03/us-audit-2025-final-report.pdf. Accessed on December 18, 2024.

Fotoh, L. E., & Lorentzon, J. I. (2021). The impact of digitalization on future audits. *Journal of Emerging Technologies in Accounting*, *18*(2), 77–97.

Gipper, B., Ross, S., & Shi, S. X. (2024). ESG assurance in the United States. *Review of Accounting Studies*, 1–51.

Goh, C., Pan, G., Sun, S. P., Lee, B., & Yong, M. (2019). *Charting the future of accountancy with AI* (p. 74). CPA Australia and Singapore Management University School of Accountancy.

Ham, C., Hann, R. N., Rabier, M., & Wang, W. (2024). Auditor skill demands and audit quality: Evidence from job postings. *Management Science.* https://doi.org/10.1287/mnsc.2022.01640

HLEG, A. (2018). *Ethics guidelines for trustworthy AI*. https://www.euractiv.com/wp-content/uploads/sites/2/2018/12/AIHLEGDraftAIEthicsGuidelinespdf.pdf. Accessed on December 9, 2024.

Howieson, B. (2005). Can we teach auditors and accountants to be more ethically competent and publicly accountable. *Ethics and Auditing, 265*.

Hurtt, R. K., Brown-Liburd, H., Earley, C. E., & Krishnamoorthy, G. (2013). Research on auditor professional scepticism: Literature synthesis and opportunities for future research. *Auditing: A Journal of Practice & Theory, 32*(Suppl. 1), 45–97.

Hwara, T. D., Moyo, N. T., & Obadire, A. M. (2024). Exploring sustainability reporting and non-financial reporting in green finance: A literature review. In *The Palgrave handbook of green finance for sustainable development* (pp. 207–235). Palgrave Macmillan.

Institute of Chartered Accountants in England and Wales (ICAEW). (2018). *Understanding the impact of technology of technology in audit and finance* (pp. 1–16). ICAEW Middle East. https://www.icaew.com/-/media/corporate/files/middle-east-hub/understanding-the-impact-of-technology-in-audit-and-finance.ashx. Accessed on April 17, 2023.

Institute of Chartered Accountants in England and Wales (ICAEW). (2022). *ACA syllabus and technical knowledge grids. Professional level. For exams in 2023* (pp. 1–137). ICAEW. https://www.icaew.com/-/media/corporate/files/learning-and-development/aca-syllabus/2023/aca-syllabus-handbook-professional-2023.ashx?la=en. Accessed on April 17, 2023.

International Accounting Education Standards Board (IAESB). (2010). *Handbook of international education pronouncements* (2010 ed.). International Federation of Accountants.

International Federation of Accountants® (IFAC®). (2019). *Handbook of international education pronouncements* (pp. 1–214). International Accounting Education Standards Board™ (IES™). https://www.ifac.org/_flysystem/azure-private/publications/files/Handbook-of-International-Education-Standards-2019.pdf. Accessed on December 22, 2024.

Issa, H., Sun, T., & Vasarhelyi, M. A. (2016). Research ideas for artificial intelligence in auditing: The formalization of audit and workforce supplementation. *Journal of Emerging Technologies in Accounting, 13*(2), 1–20. https://doi.org/10.2308/jeta-10511

Jackson, D., & Meek, S. (2021). Embedding work-integrated learning into accounting education: The state of play and pathways to future implementation. *Accounting Education, 30*(1), 63–85.

Jackson, D., Michelson, G., & Munir, R. (2022). Developing accountants for the future: New technology, skills, and the role of stakeholders. *Accounting Education, 32*(2), 1–28. https://doi.org/10.1080/09639284.2022.2057195

Jackson, D., Michelson, G., & Munir, R. (2023). Developing accountants for the future: New technology, skills, and the role of stakeholders. *Accounting Education, 32*(2), 150–177.

Jones, R. (2014). Bridging the gap: Engaging in scholarship with accountancy employers to enhance understanding of skills development and employability. *Accounting Education, 23*(6), 527–541.

Kend, M., & Nguyen, L. A. (2020). Big data analytics and other emerging technologies: The impact on the Australian audit and assurance profession. *Australian Accounting Review*, *95*(30), 269–282. https://doi.org/10.1111/auar.12305

Kokina, J., & Davenport, T. H. (2017). The emergence of artificial intelligence: How automation is changing auditing. *Journal of Emerging Technologies in Accounting*, *14*(1), 115–122.

Kroon, N., do Céu Alves, M., & Martins, I. (2021). The impacts of emerging technologies on accountants' role and skills: Connecting to open innovation—A systematic literature review. *Journal of Open Innovation: Technology, Market, and Complexity*, *7*(3), 163. https://doi.org/10.3390/joitmc7030163

Kwock, B., Ho, R., & James, M. (2016). The effectiveness of professional scepticism training for auditors in China: Evidence from a university in China. *China Journal of Accounting Studies*, *4*(2), 205–224.

Lansdell, P. A., Marx, B., & Mohammadali-Haji, A. (2020). University accounting programmes and the development of Industry 4.0 soft skills. *Journal of Economic and Financial Sciences*, *13*(1), 1–17.

Lee, J., Kim, S., & Kim, E. (2022). Environmental responsibility, social responsibility, and governance from the perspective of auditors. *International Journal of Environmental Research and Public Health*, *19*(19), 12181.

M2 Presswire. (2016). *PwC wins "Audit Innovation of the Year" at the accountant and international accounting Bulletin Awards*. https://www.pwc.com/lv/en/news/pwc-wins-audit-innovation-of-the-year.html. Accessed on April 17, 2023.

Malan, M., & Dyk, V. V. (2021). Students' experience of pervasive skills acquired through sponsored projects in an undergraduate accounting degree. *South African Journal of Accounting Research*, *35*(2), 130–150.

McGuire, D., McVicar, O., & Tariq, U. E. H. (2023). Skills audits: An integrative literature review. *Industrial & Commercial Training*, *55*(1), 34–46.

McKinsey & Company. (2022). *What are Industry 4.0, the Fourth Industrial Revolution, and 4IR?* (pp. 1–7). McKinsey Global Publishing. https://www.mckinsey.com/featured-insights/mckinsey-explainers/what-are-industry-4-0-the-fourth-industrial-revolution-and-4ir. Accessed on April 17, 2023.

Melendez, C. (2016). Artificial intelligence gets into auditing, what's next? https://www.infoworld.com/article/3044468/artificial-intelligence-gets-into-auditing-whats-next.html. Accessed on April 17, 2023.

Messier Jr, W. F., Glover, S. M., & Prawitt, D. F. (2017). *Auditing & assurance services: A systematic approach*. McGraw-Hill.

Moffitt, K. C., Rozario, A. M., & Vasarhelyi, M. A. (2018). Robotic process automation for auditing. *Journal of Emerging Technologies in Accounting*, *15*(1), 1–10.

Moyo, V., & Kanyane, M. (2024). The future world of work for professional accountants: The top employability skills that industry expects from university graduates. In E. Loots & J. Oberholster (Eds.), *Rethinking commerce education in South Africa: The case for change to develop future-fit business leaders* (pp. 49–66). AOSIS Books. https://doi.org/10.4102/aosis.2024.BK454.04

Munoko, I., Brown-Liburd, H. L., & Vasarhelyi, M. (2020). The ethical implications of using artificial intelligence in auditing. *Journal of Business Ethics*, *167*(2), 209–234.

Novak, A., Žager, K., & Barišić, I. (2021, September). Innovation in accounting education: The impact of information technology on teaching methods. In *European conference on innovation and entrepreneurship* (pp. 660–XXV). Academic Conferences International Limited.

Omitogun, A., & Al-Adeem, K. (2019). Auditors' perceptions of and competencies in big data and data analytics: An empirical investigation. *International Journal of Computer Auditing*, *1*(1), 92–113.

Pan, X., & Zhu, L. (2024). *The digital transformation of auditing: Skill requirements and adaptation strategies within the Big 4 firms in Sweden*. https://hdl.handle.net/2077/82873

Persico, F., & Sidhu, H. (2017). How AI will turn auditors into analysts. *Accounting Today*. https://www.accountingtoday.com/opinion/how-ai-will-turn-auditors-into-analysts. Accessed on April 17, 2023.

PwC. (2019). *Harnessing AI to pioneer new approaches to the audit*. https://www.pwc.com/gx/en/about/stories-from-across-the-world/harnessing-ai-to-pioneer-new-approaches-to-the-audit.html. Accessed on April 17, 2023.

Raphael, J. (2017). Rethinking the audit. *Journal of Accountancy*, *223*(4), 29–32.

Richins, G., Stapleton, A., Stratopoulos, T. C., & Wong, C. (2017). Big data analytics: Opportunity or threat for the accounting profession? *Journal of Information Systems*, *31*(3), 63–79.

Sambo, V., & Kanyane, M. (2024). Who audits the auditors? In *Corruption, ethics, and governance in South Africa* (pp. 116–135). Routledge.

Sinclair, N. (2020). How KPMG is using Formula 1 to transform audit. *Accountancy Daily*. https://www.accountancydaily.co/kpmg-accelerates-audit-analytics-fast-lane-mclaren-deal. Accessed on April 17, 2023.

Singhvi, M., Hossain, A., & Brodmann, J. (2021). New auditors are coming: Disrupting the fixed mindset and exploring dynamic changes in auditing. *EDPACS*, *63*(2), 1–8. https://doi.org/10.1080/07366981.2020.1812813

Siriwardane, H. P., Kin Hoi Hu, B., & Low, K. Y. (2014). Skills, knowledge, and attitudes important for present-day auditors. *International Journal of Auditing*, *18* (3), 193–205.

Small, R., Smidt, L., & Moola-Yasseen, M. (2017). Ethics and integrity of a professional accountant. *Professional Accountant*, *2017*(30), 10–11.

Sun, T., & Vasarhelyi, M. A. (2017). Deep learning and the future of auditing: How an evolving technology could transform analysis and improve judgment. *CPA Journal*, *87*(6).

Tavares, M. C., Azevedo, G., Marques, R. P., & Bastos, M. A. (2023). Challenges of education in the accounting profession in the Era 5.0: A systematic review. *Cogent Business & Management*, *10*(2), 2220198.

Tiberius, V., & Hirth, S. (2019). Impacts of digitization on auditing: A Delphi study for Germany. *Journal of International Accounting, Auditing and Taxation*, *37*, 100288. https://doi.org/10.1016/j.intaccaudtax.2019.100288

Tsiligiris, V., & Bowyer, D. (2021). Exploring the impact of 4IR on skills and personal qualities for future accountants: A proposed conceptual framework for university accounting education. *Accounting Education*, *30*(6), 621–649.

Vitali, S., & Giuliani, M. (2024). Emerging digital technologies and auditing firms: Opportunities and challenges. *International Journal of Accounting Information Systems*, *53*, 100676.

Wakunuma, K. J., & Stahl, B. C. (2014). Tomorrow's ethics and today's response: An investigation into the ways information systems professionals perceive and address emerging ethical issues. *Information Systems Frontiers*, *16*, 383–397.

Wats, M., & Wats, R. K. (2009). Developing soft skills in students. *International Journal of Learning*, *15*(12).

Wells, P., Gerbic, P., Kranenburg, I., & Bygrave, J. (2014). Professional skills and capabilities of accounting graduates: The New Zealand expectation gap? In *The interface of accounting education and professional training* (pp. 81–98). Routledge.

West, A. (2017). The ethics of professional accountants: An Aristotelian perspective. *Accounting, Auditing & Accountability Journal*, *30*(2), 328–351.

Wilkinson, S., Halvitigala, D., & Antoniades, H. (2018). Educators, professional bodies and the future of the valuation profession. *Property Management*, *36*(4), 389–399.

Zhang, Y., Xiong, F., Xie, Y., Fan, X., & Gu, H. (2020). The impact of artificial intelligence and blockchain on the accounting profession. *IEEE Access*, *8*, 110461–110477.

Zin, N. M., Kasim, E. S., Kandasamy, I. D., Khairani, N. S., Noor, N. M., & Sufian, N. I. M. (2022). Big data analytics knowledge and skills: What you need as a 21st century accounting graduate. *Management & Accounting Review*, *21*(3), 159–179. https://doi.org/10.24191/MAR.V21i03-07

Printed and bound by CPI Group (UK) Ltd, Croydon, CR0 4YY

21/09/2026

14966039-0007